D0570857

ST. LOUIS UNION STATION

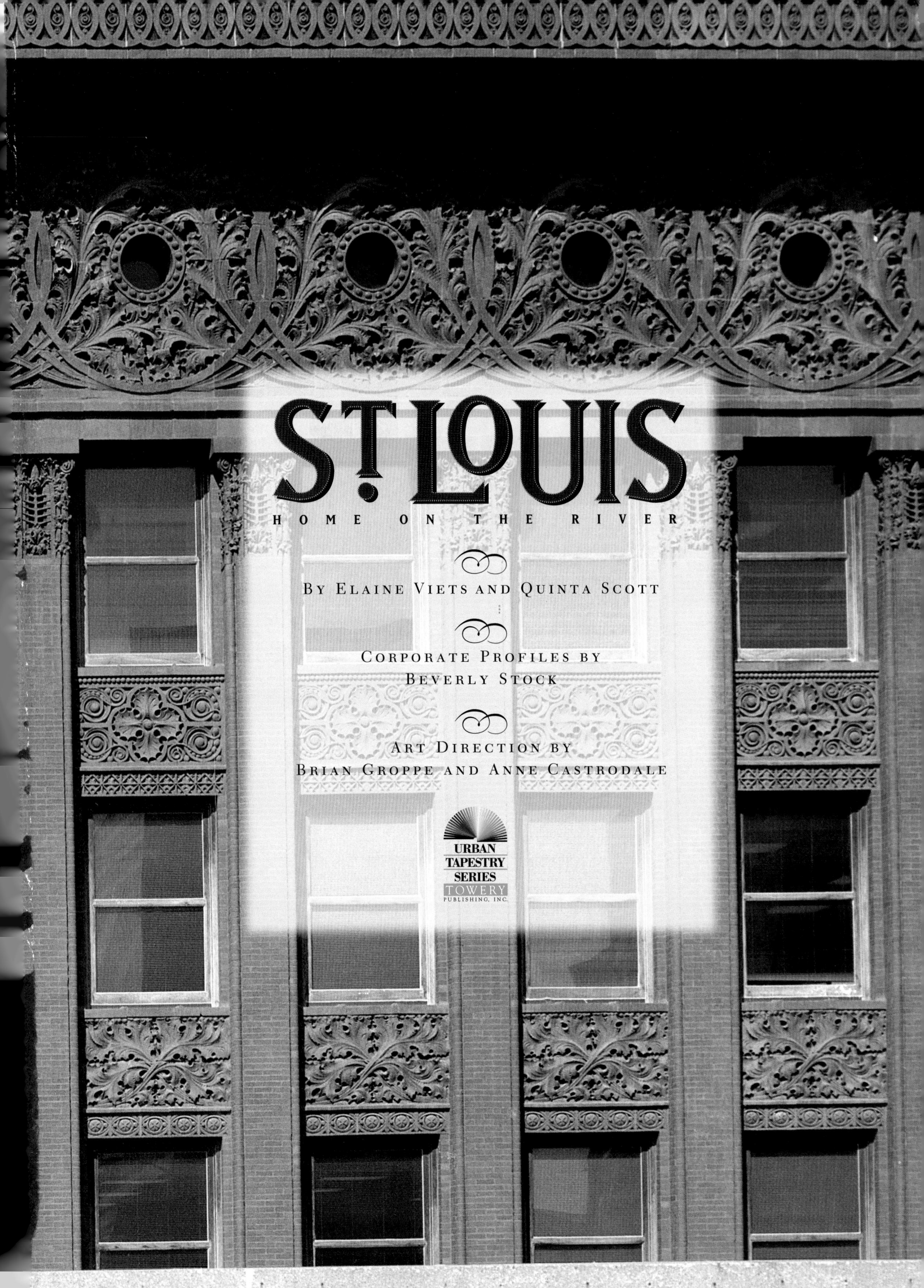

St. Louis

HOME ON THE RIVER

By Elaine Viets and Quinta Scott

Corporate Profiles by
Beverly Stock

Art Direction by
Brian Groppe and Anne Castrodale

URBAN TAPESTRY SERIES
TOWERY
PUBLISHING, INC.

EE
AT
pany
S, CAPS
and
OVES
7
6
CINDY
MFRS
5
Bee
4
KNIT HEAD
3
2
Bee
2
BE
LEAT

St. Louis is truly in the heart of the country. It is the closest major city to the nation's population center.

PRECEEDING PAGE PHOTO CREDITS:
PAGES 1, 2 & 3 BY QUINTA SCOTT
PAGES 2 & 3 INSETS BY WALTER DEPTULA

Library of Congress Cataloging-in-Publication Data

Viets, Elaine, 1950-
St. Louis: home on the river / by Elaine Viets and Quinta Scott.
p. cm. — (Urban tapestry series)
Includes index.
ISBN 1-881096-18-1
1. Saint Louis (Mo.) — Pictorial works. 2. Saint Louis (Mo.) — Description and travel. I. Scott, Quinta, 1941- . II. Title. III. Series.
F474.S243V54 1995 95-16038
977.8'65—dc20 CIP

Towery Publishing, Inc., 1835 Union Avenue, Memphis, TN 38104

Publisher: J. Robert Towery
Executive Publisher: Jenny McDowell
Vice President-National Sales Manager: Stephen Hung
Project Directors: Harry Nelson, Dawn Olson, Thom Singer
Executive Editor: David Dawson
Senior Editors: Michael C. James, Ken Woodmansee
Associate Editors: Lynn Conlee, Carlisle Hacker, Stinson Liles
Editorial Contributors: Patricia Bohn, Shirley Browne, Charlie DiLeo, Norman Lambert, Hillary Levin, Deborah Linder, Irv Litvag, John Miller, David Ressner, Mike Schmidt, Phyllis Wheeler
Profile Designer: Lawanda McClellan
Production Assistant: Brenda Pattat
Technical Director: William H. Towery

DAVID HINKSON

Contents

On the Fourth of July, St. Louisans celebrate at the V.P. Fair (pages 6 & 7). Here's what a lot of us look like at night under the Arch. So many, in fact, that you can almost consider this the city's group photo.
DON McLAUGHLIN PHOTO

REGAL

Adam
Mark
HOTEL

by Elaine Viets

▼ PAUL MARSHALL

ST. LOUIS IS A CITY OF PEOPLE WHO STAY.

In Miami, New York, or Los Angeles, everyone is from somewhere else.

St. Louisans never leave their hometown. We even have kindergarten reunions here.

That's why the Arch is the perfect city symbol. It celebrates our role as the Gateway to the West. Only St. Louis would build a monument to the people who left.

We're grateful to those who got out of town.

▲ BRIAN GROPPE

After all, some of our ancestors made a lot of money from the pioneers who couldn't stay put. They outfitted their wagons, then waved good-bye.

"So long," they said. "Sorry you can't stay. But there's more for us."

Their leaving helped make St. Louis a better place to live. The city is a manageable size. Our whole metro area has only 2.5 million people.

What we call a traffic jam makes someone from either coast smile—with delight. St. Louisans like to say that you can get anywhere in 20 minutes.

Yet we have the advantages of much larger cities. Our symphony ranks up there with the top five: Boston, Chicago, New York, Cleveland, and Philadelphia.

FIREWORKS LIGHT UP THE ARCH AND THE OLD COURTHOUSE (OPPOSITE). A GLORIOUS ART GLASS WINDOW LIGHTS UP THE GRAND HALL AT UNION STATION (ABOVE). THE ARTIST DEPICTED THE NATION'S THREE MAIN 1890S TRAIN STATIONS AS WISE AND BEAUTIFUL WOMEN—THAT'S ST. LOUIS IN THE CENTER, SAN FRANCISCO ON THE LEFT, AND NEW YORK ON THE RIGHT. THE ROMANTIC WINDOW TOPS A "WHISPERING" ARCH WHERE MANY ST. LOUISANS HAVE WHISPERED TO THEIR SWEETHEARTS.

RAY MARKLIN

When St. Louis throws a party, it's a real blowout. At the V.P. Fair, we shoot off fireworks from a barge in the Mississippi. The explosive colors shimmer and shine and slide down the Arch (opposite).

The *New York Times* praised our Opera Theatre. We have a first-class repertory theater and a good dance company.

You'll have to find these things out for yourself. St. Louisans don't brag. Boosterism is for bumptious western places. We are the last eastern city. We prefer understatement.

Because St. Louis has so many natives, newcomers have a tough time here. They don't understand our language and customs.

They can't even get the name straight. Only tourists and Judy Garland call it "St. Louie."

"St. Louie" makes you an instant mark. Bartenders tack another dollar to your drink price. Crafty cabbies take the scenic route to your hotel.

I'VE SPENT MUCH OF MY NEWSPAPER CAREER explaining St. Louis to outsiders. I can give you three hints on how to pass as one of us:

Introductions

Whenever two St. Louisans meet for the first time, they ask each other, "What high school did you go to?"

Outsiders never understand this greeting. My husband, Don, is from Marshalltown, Iowa. He said, "I went to Marshalltown senior high, and who cares?"

I explained we St. Louisans are very polite. We'd never ask:

◄ SPECTRA-ACTION, INC. / LEWIS PORTNOY

SOME 1,200 FLIGHTS TAKE OFF AND LAND DAILY AT LAMBERT ST. LOUIS INTERNATIONAL AIRPORT. MOST OF THE COUNTRY IS LESS THAN A TWO-HOUR FLIGHT FROM ST. LOUIS.

"Hi, is your family important?"

"Do you have any money?"

"What's your religion?"

Instead we ask, "What high school did you go to?"

It's all there. For the record, I went to St. Thomas Aquinas. That's blue collar, north county, and Catholic.

Language

St. Louisans speak a language similar to English. Many outsiders are startled when they hear St. Louisans say they're taking Highway "Farty."

They can't imagine any city would name a highway that.

They don't understand. In St. Louis, "farty" is the

number after 39. We also eat with "farks." Then we "waRsh" them—we need that R for traction.

Ice-cream "sun-dahs" are a treat you'll find only in St. Louis. They taste just like ice-cream sundaes. But linguists say we are the only city in the country that pronounces it "sun-dah."

Driving Habits

St. Louis stop signs look like the ones in any other city, but we treat them differently.

We don't sit at a St. Louis stop sign. We slide on through.

The cars approach the intersection, slow down to a cruising speed of 15, look around, and roll through. Meanwhile, all the other cars are doing the same thing.

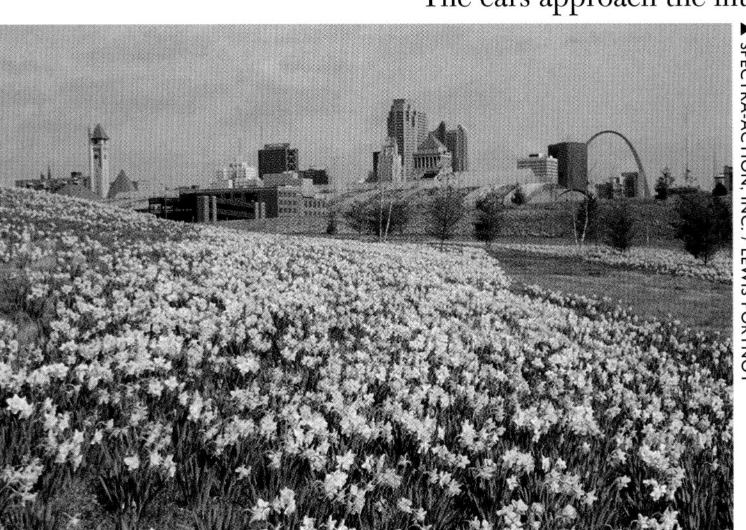

▲ SPECTRA-ACTION, INC. / LEWIS PORTNOY

St. Louis decorates its highways with spring flowers and puts up a warm welcome in many languages—we expect visitors from all over. Thirty percent of the nation lives within a one-day drive of St. Louis.

Nobody ever makes a full stop. We get through on a kind of natural radar.

The St. Louis stop is a native custom that takes skill and nerve, like the running of the bulls at Pamplona.

But making a full stop is even more dangerous. The last person I know who did it got hit in the rear.

By a cop.

St. Louisans are easy to spot, because we talk and drive the same way. But it will take some time to learn our differences.

WE ARE A CITY OF NEIGHBORHOODS. Each area thinks its own neighborhood is best.

Two west county suburbs, Kirkwood and Webster Groves, look about the same to outsiders.

Both have old, tree-lined streets with big "Father Knows Best" houses. Both have more than their share of antique shops, bookstores, and fern bars.

They're about the same size: Webster Groves has about 23,000 people; Kirkwood has some 5,000 more.

But talk to the people who live there, and you'd think these two places were as different as England and France.

ST. LOUIS CITY AND COUNTY SPLIT IN 1876. IT WAS ONE OF OUR FOREFATHERS' LESS ENLIGHTENED DECISIONS. ST. LOUIS COUNTY NOW HAS SOME 90 DIFFERENT MUNICIPALITIES.

▼ SPECTRA-ACTION, INC. / LEWIS PORTNOY

This rivalry goes deeper than the traditional Turkey Day football game between Kirkwood and Webster Groves high schools.

"Kirkwood's better," a Kirkwood woman told me quite seriously.

"Kirkwood is less snobbish than Webster Groves. Kirkwood taxes are cheaper and we get more for our money. For years, Webster had worse streets, and everyone knew it. Kirkwood is clearly superior."

Webster believes Kirkwood has more new money and more "corporate people." It sees itself as more artistic. Webster has the justly famed Repertory Theatre of St. Louis, the Opera Theatre, and Webster University.

Kirkwood, sniffs Webster, has a junior college.

▲ G. ROBERT BISHOP

Many of the houses on The Hill, the city's Italian section, were built with leftover materials from the 1904 World's Fair. These people created a neighborhood that lasted. Even today, it has a strong sense of identity.

The identities go so deep that when several women gardeners moved from Webster to Kirkwood, they didn't give the club a new name. They called it the Kirkwood chapter of the Webster Groves Garden Club.

Newcomers have a terrible time figuring out these fine distinctions. Here's a handy guide:

The city is divided into three areas—North St. Louis, South St. Louis, and the West End.

Not so long ago, the North Side was mostly African-American, the South Side was German, and the Central West End was rich.

Those divisions are starting to blur.

Each section is further divided into distinct neighborhoods with names like The Ville, Tower Grove Heights, and Grand-Oak Hill.

The Ville is the black historic district with Sumner High School, the school that turned out Tina Turner, Grace Bumbry, Chuck Berry, and Dick Gregory.

Tower Grove Heights and Grand-Oak Hill are two old German neighborhoods.

South St. Louis is known for its tidy lawns and neat brick houses. Inside, every inch of those houses is polished and shined. Outside, some lawns are literally manicured with scissors in between mowings.

The county has even more divisions. St. Louis County has 90 different municipalities. Some suburbs, like Florissant, are actually respectable cities of 50,000, while little Vinita Park has 2,001 people.

St. Louisans settle in an area, and stay there. If they move to a more expensive house, it's usually in the same North, South, or West corridor.

I live in South St. Louis, the city's old German section. I used to make fun of my German relatives. They'd move from Virginia to Ohio to Michigan.

Those are streets, not states, and they're all a block or two apart.

I couldn't understand why people would bother to move from one red brick house to another. To me, they all looked like.

Then I got married and moved to a red brick house on Utah Place. After 15 years I moved one block. To another red brick house. I didn't even change streets. I moved from 3800 to 3700 Utah.

I quit laughing.

2641

GARY TETLEY

But I couldn't live anywhere else in the city but South St. Louis. It's my neighborhood.

Everyone in St. Louis thinks their neighborhood is best. That is the city's charm.

That is also the city's tragedy. We don't visit other neighborhoods.

We don't know how they are changing, often for the better. We cling to ideas that are 20 or even 40 years old.

When I hear people say my South Side neighborhood is all white, I know they haven't been there in awhile. It's been integrated for over a decade.

Many white St. Louisans still think all of North St. Louis, the traditional African-American area, is rundown

ELIZABETH CROSBY

OLDER ST. LOUIS HOMES ARE SYMPHONIES IN BRICK AND STONE. DOORWAYS AND WINDOWS ARE BEAUTIFULLY ORNAMENTED. FIFTY YEARS AGO, THOSE STONE STEPS WERE FAITHFULLY SCRUBBED ONCE A WEEK TO REMOVE THE COATING OF COAL DUST.

and dangerous. They'll tell me St. Louis has no black middle class.

The North Side has some serious problems. But it's developing a thriving black middle class. Black mail carriers, doctors, and hospital workers are rehabbing the turn-of-the-century houses.

St. Louis is proud it finally elected its first African-American mayor, Freeman Bosley, Jr. But many whites can't name the neighborhood where the new mayor lives.

He lives in the O'Fallon Park neighborhood. He has a rehabbed house on Palm Place, right down the street from his parents' home.

That puts him squarely in the city tradition—a rehabber with roots.

Federhofer's
BAKERY
QUALITY - VARIETY
HOT CROSS
BUNS
PARKING

◀ SUE FORD

We miss so much of our own city, because we don't look at other neighborhoods. We have great excuses: The city is too dangerous; the suburbs are too far away.

One of my favorite art projects is on the North Side in O'Fallon Park. The park had some dead trees that had to be cut down. African-American artist Robert A. Powell turned the stumps into artwork. He carved sculptures out of the dead trunks, and left them rooted in the ground.

One sculpture is a massive throne called "Chair for the Common Man." The back is the strong face of an African-American woman. Kids like to climb up on the chair and sit in it, making themselves kings.

▶ DAVID HINKSON

This brains sign got a laugh on the David Letterman show. No one laughed when it was torn down. But the sign survives on postcards and T-shirts and in our hearts. Hot cross buns are one of the first signs of spring in St. Louis (opposite).

That's exactly what Powell wanted. He said everyone should sit on a throne at least once.

St. Louis is so divided, we even have separate city sandwiches.

South St. Louis has the brain sandwich, deep-fat-fried cows' brains on rye with ketchup.

North St. Louis has the pig snoot sandwich. That's deep-fat-fried pig noses, covered in barbecue sauce.

I have eaten both.

They contain equal amounts of cholesterol, fat, and fried grease. Snoots taste like pork rinds, if you can get past the nostrils.

The best snoot sandwiches are at the C&K Barbecue

QUINTA SCOTT

QUINTA SCOTT

QUINTA SCOTT

QUINTA SCOTT

St. Louis restaurants provide a rich stew of food from Africa, Asia, the Middle East, and the Americas.

Restaurant No. 3, 4390 Jennings Station Road. If you're not brave enough to bite a pig nose, the ribs are tasty, too.

Brains are like a liver souffle with a crispy coating. The best brains are at Bud Dieckmeyer's bar and restaurant, 6201 South Broadway in South St. Louis.

Bud gives free samples, but you can also chicken out. Literally. His chicken and dumplings are tops.

If you're not ready for either sandwich, you can get a taste of the city with our special coffee cake, the gooey butter cake, as rich and sugary as it sounds. No St. Louis bakery makes a bad one, but I like the coffee cake at Rozanek Bakery.

You may have noticed I mention food a lot. St. Louisans eat for recreation. We like to go out to dinner.

Most people think the Midwest is the land of white bread and WASPs. They don't know St. Louis. Consider my neighborhood.

The South Grand business district, a six-block stretch between Arsenal Street and Utah Place, has Thai,

PAT DONOVAN

Vietnamese, Chinese, Mexican, Italian, and Philippine restaurants.

The Mid-Eastern Market has falafel and feta cheese. There's a giant Asian grocery with 20 kinds of rice.

The cosmopolitan look isn't confined to one area. The University City Loop is another great people-watching place.

On any warm day, umbrella tables spring up on the Loop sidewalks like mushrooms. You can get fresh, frosty root beer, made on the spot at Fitz's Bottling Co. You can browse in the new and used bookstores.

Or stop by Blueberry Hill, a nightspot and restaurant run by Joe and Linda Edwards, two '60s hippies who've kept the faith. The Hill's vintage juke boxes glow like strange shrines.

The Loop is also where you can walk on the stars. The St. Louis Walk of Fame has some 56 famous St. Louis names on big brass stars in the sidewalk. It's your chance to step on Vincent Price, Josephine Baker, and Tennessee Williams.

St. Louis is indeed a tasteful city. We love to go out for the night, enjoy a wonderful meal, and talk things over with friends. This sidewalk cafe in the suburb of Clayton is a prime example.

◄ SPECTRA-ACTION, INC. / LEWIS PORTNOY

UNLIKE SOME MIDWESTERN CITIES, St. Louis is surprisingly broad-minded, if you're discreet.

You can drink free at one downtown gay bar on underwear night—provided you show up in your Skivvies.

Professional city boosters don't mention it, but we're also a major center for female impersonators. This May, St. Louis hosted the Miss Gay USA Pageant. Eighty-eight female impersonators from around the nation competed for the foot-high rhinestone crown.

Yet St. Louis is also a family city. Some of the best things here are free, or dirt cheap.

► LISA A. JOHNSTON

AT 100 YEARS OLD, UNION STATION IS AS BEAUTIFUL ON THE INSIDE AS IT IS ON THE OUTSIDE (LEFT). ONCE THE WORLD'S LARGEST TRAIN STATION, IT'S NOW PACKED WITH SHOPS, RESTAURANTS, AND ENTERTAINMENT. IT EVEN HAS A LAKE FOR BOATING AND A RESTORED CAROUSEL. EVEN A BEER FACTORY IN ST. LOUIS IS A HEADY ARCHITECTURAL EXPERIENCE (OPPOSITE). SOME 13 MILLION BARRELS A YEAR ARE MADE AT ANHEUSER-BUSCH.

I love to go to the zoo, watch the fat bears roll around, and see the lions and tigers lounging about like huge house cats in Big Cat Country.

It's one of the few free zoos in the country.

It doesn't cost anything to get into Union Station, although it may cost you to get out.

The castlelike former train station is a rehabbing success. It now has more than 100 shops and restaurants, plus the Hyatt Regency St. Louis Hotel.

One of the hotel's highlights is another freebie, the Whispering Arch, on the grand staircase.

The splendid marble arch has a jewellike stained-glass window. Step into a shallow recess in the wall and whisper. Someone at the other end, 40 feet away, can hear

▲ DAVID HINKSON

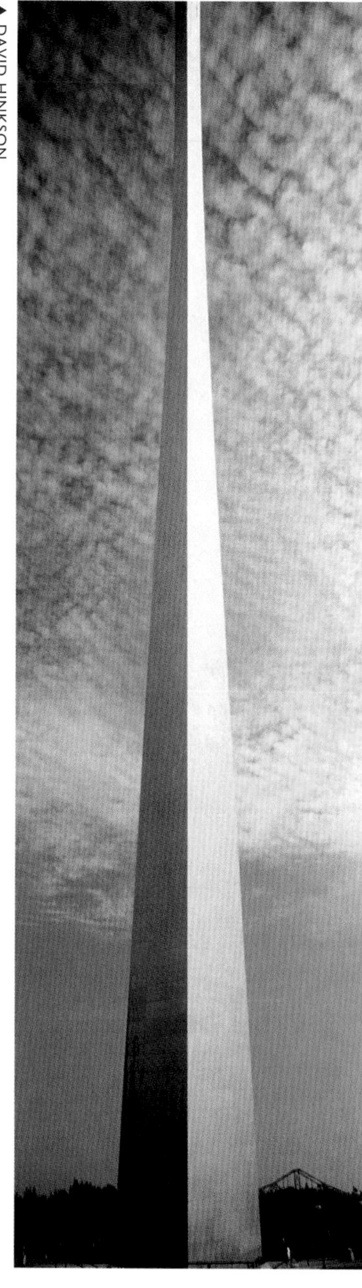

To truly appreciate the Gateway Arch, stand under its soaring 630 feet of stainless steel. It is graceful from every angle.

you. It's whispered that some people propose marriage there.

My favorite free tour is the Anheuser-Busch Brewery, more than 100 years old. This is truly the Sistine Chapel of beer. Even the brewery's Clydesdale horses live like 19th-century beer barons, in mahogany stables with stained-glass windows.

At the end of the tour, Anheuser-Busch serves the coldest free samples in town.

That's another surprise. St. Louis is beautiful. Even a beer factory is a knockout.

We add quirky details to the most prosaic places. The old Bee Hat Co. in downtown St. Louis has naked women holding up its roof.

But the most beautiful structure in St. Louis is the Arch. It is simple, slender, and sophisticated.

The sunlight shimmers on the sleek stainless steel. By moonlight, it is silvery and mysterious.

You can stand under it, and see its soaring curves, 630 feet high. Then you can ride inside.

That's an unforgettable experience.

Riding in the tiny Arch train cars is like being shoved into a clothes dryer with several strangers. The cramped cars tip and rumble all the way to the top.

This is one trip that will take your breath away.

Especially when you realize the train was built by the lowest bidder. ■

▲ WALTER DEPTULA

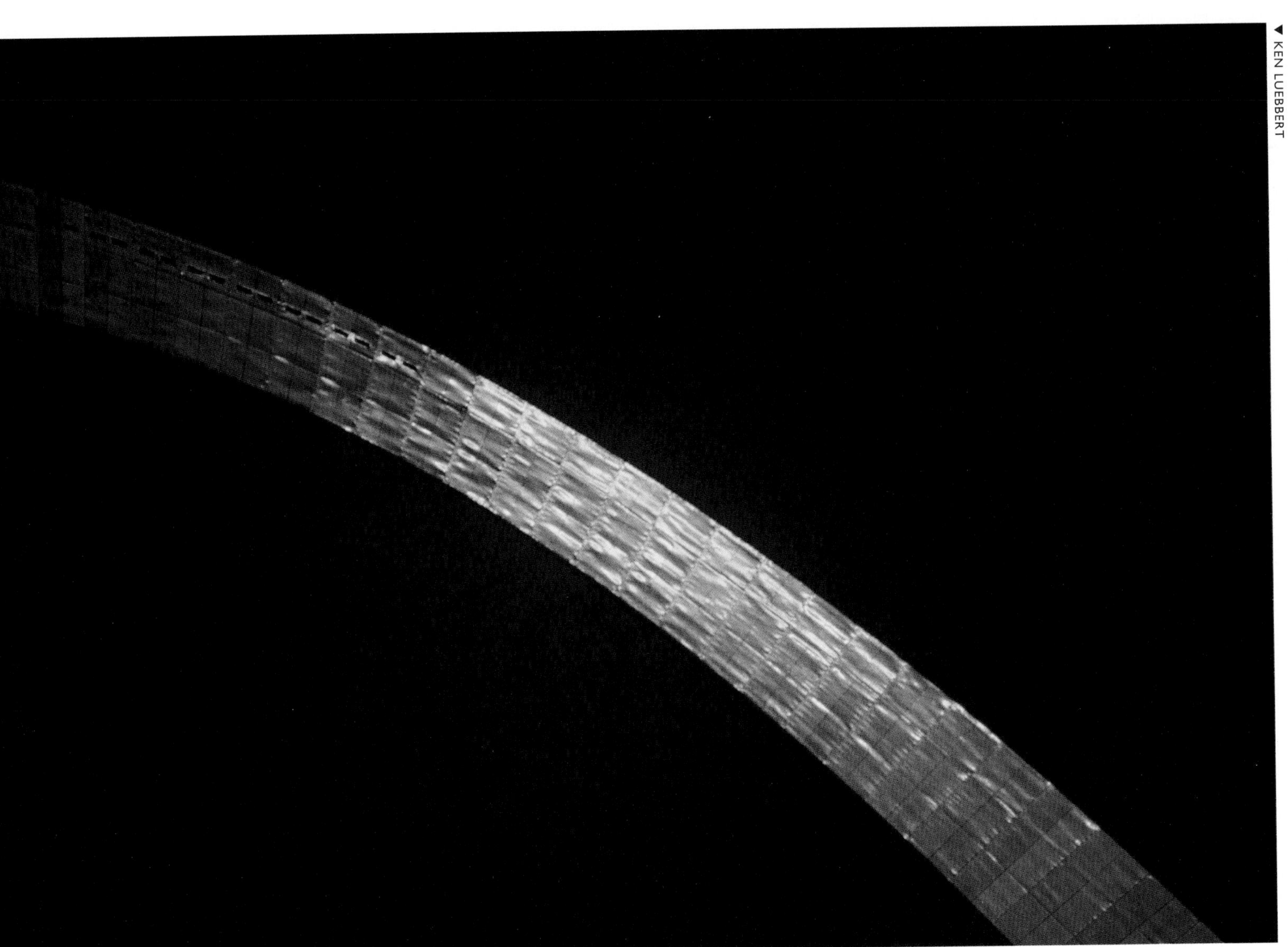

▼ KEN LUEBBERT

Ero Saarinen designed the celebrated Arch. The sleek symbol is a perfect reflection of St. Louis.

▲ KATHLEEN M. O'DONNELL

THE COOL CURVES OF THE planetarium at the St. Louis Science Center shelter a high-tech star show.

THE ARCH STEPS ARE MONUMENTAL, in more ways than one (OPPOSITE AND BOTTOM). The Civil War started under the dome of the Old Courthouse (TOP). In 1847, a slave named Dred Scott began legal actions for his freedom here. He lost, and his case helped spark the war.

▼ DOUGLAS ABEL

ST. LOUIS' NEWLY EXPANDED convention center is now one of the largest meeting places in the country. The $120 million America's Center won an award for its outstanding service and ambience.

▲ DOUGLAS ABEL

KIENER PLAZA IS A DOWNTOWN gathering place—the scene of concerts, sports rallies, and a host of other citywide events.

THE MILLES FOUNTAIN, ACROSS from Union Station, is a fantasy of river gods and water creatures. It symbolizes the confluence of the Mississippi and the Missouri rivers near St. Louis. The fountain was originally called "The Marriage of the Waters" until prudes protested. It was renamed "The Meeting of the Waters."

◆ WALTER DEPTULA

▼ PAUL MARSHALL

▼ DAVID ALTMAN

▼ BRIAN GROPPE

▼ SPECTRA-ACTION, INC. / LEWIS PORTNOY

ST. LOUIS UNION STATION WAS headed for bankruptcy and possible demolition when it was bought in 1979 and redeveloped. Six years and $140 million later, it's back on track as a hotel, shopping, and entertainment complex.

▲ SPECTRA-ACTION, INC. / LEWIS PORTNOY

THROUGH WORLD WAR II, UNION Station was one of the nation's busiest passenger hubs. As many as 100,000 people passed under its train shed each day. Now, the station is still crowded, but this time with shoppers and diners.

▶ QUINTA SCOTT
◀ DAVID HINKSON

◀ GARY TETLEY

THE MERCANTILE TOWER LOOKS like a 36-floor sculpture (OPPOSITE). St. Louis Centre, a four-story shopping mall in downtown, features airy barrel vaults and walkways (ABOVE).

THE ST. LOUIS CENTRE PROVIDES a greenhouselike environment for wandering shoppers (TOP). You never know what exotic visitors you'll see downtown. It could be anyone from suit-coated statesmen to ribboned and ruffled square dancers (BOTTOM).

St. Louisans like to complain about the sticky hot summers, but Rand McNally takes another view. It says St. Louis is one of the top seven most livable metro areas in the country, and they looked at 329 other places (OPPOSITE).

◆ SPECTRA-ACTION, INC. / LEWIS PORTNOY

◆ SPECTRA-ACTION, INC. / LEWIS PORTNOY

PARK

▼ WALTER DEPTULA

EVEN A PARKING GARAGE IS GOOD-looking in downtown St. Louis. Taking your car down those clean curves can be interesting.

▲ LORETTE BURKE

▲ GARY TETLEY

LET US NOT FORGET THE USEFUL folks who keep the city clean, comfortable, and on the go: the garages, the gas stations, and the fearless window washers.

THE OLD UNION ELECTRIC STEAM plant in Laclede's Landing is a study in shapes and shadows. Settlers once outfitted their wagons for the journey west on Laclede's Landing (PAGES 44-45).

SHERI SAUNIER PHOTOS

NOW MOST OF THE VICTORIAN warehouses and buildings on Laclede's Landing have been converted into bars and restaurants, shops and attractions for merrymakers. The Branson High School marching band adds to the festivities (BOTTOM).

SPECTRA-ACTION, INC. / LEWIS PORTNOY

QUINTA SCOTT

FROM A DISTANCE, THE OLD Union Electric steam plant looks like one of the riverboats. The view under the bridge is also quite riveting (BOTTOM).

▲ QUINTA SCOTT
▼ KEN LUEBBERT

THE STEEL AND STONE OF EADS Bridge melt in the Mississippi River fog. Mark Twain saw this marvelous bridge span the majestic river more than 100 years ago.

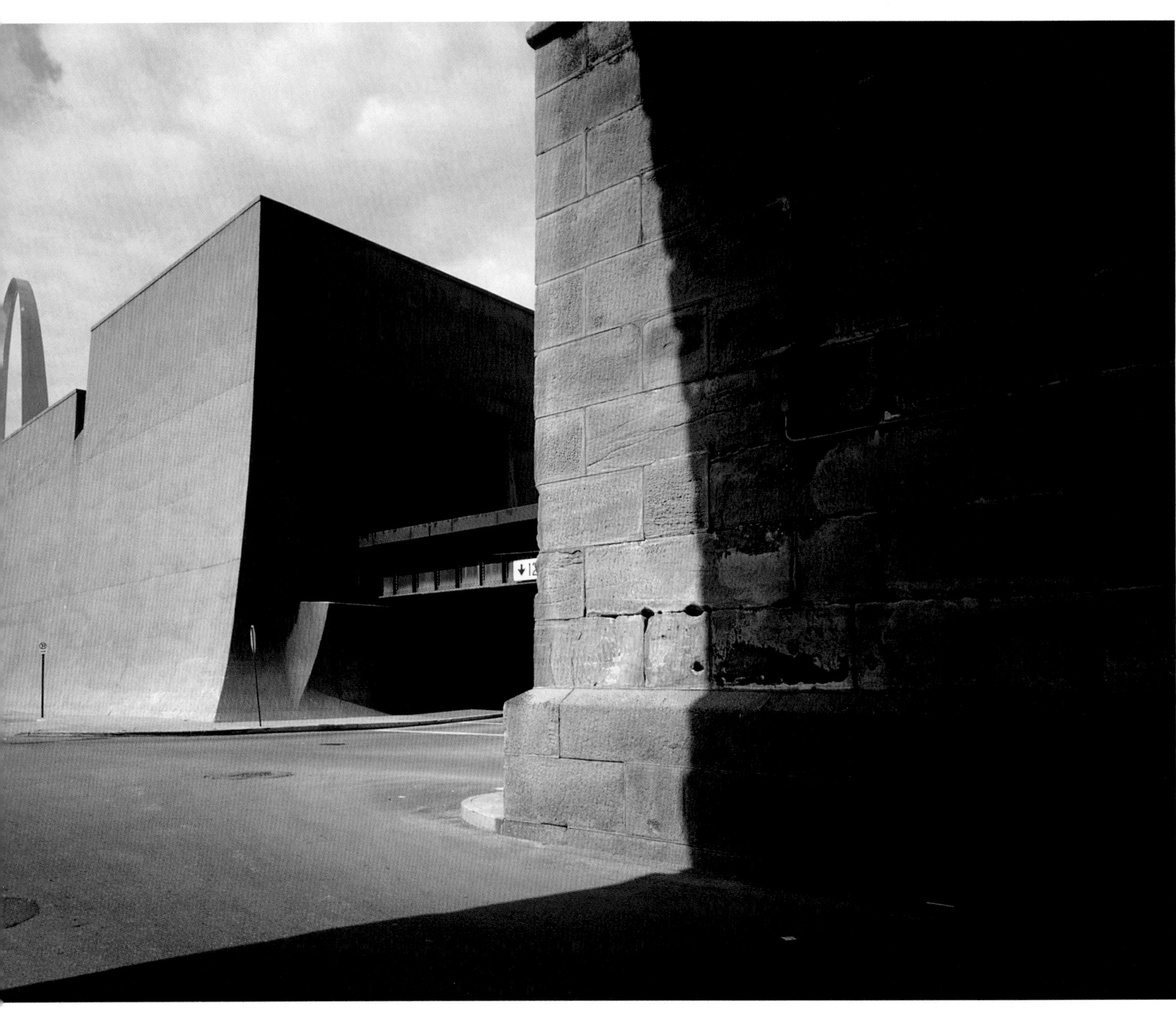

MASSIVE FLOODGATES AND bridge footings keep the mighty Mississippi River in check.

▲ QUINTA SCOTT

THE SERRA SCULPTURE AND THE Gateway Arch are two artful, yet diverse uses of steel.

FOLLOWING PAGES: THE ARCH pops up everywhere downtown, playing peekaboo as an arch within an arch on the Eads Bridge, and glowing through a many-paned window of the Old Cathedral.

PAGE 52: SPECTRA-ACTION, INC. / LEWIS PORTNOY

PAGE 53: DAVID HINKSON

ST. LOUIS IX

DOUGLAS ABEL

PAUL MARSHALL

THE BEAUTIFUL OLD CATHEDRAL was consecrated in 1834 (OPPOSITE). However, the New Cathedral isn't all that new either (LEFT). It was built in 1907. The Byzantine-Romanesque church glows with rare marble, stained glass, and the largest collection of mosaics in the world.

IT WAS A HISTORIC MOMENT AT the New Cathedral when Archbishop Justin F. Rigali was installed as the ninth head of the archdiocese of St. Louis.

KAY DAVIS

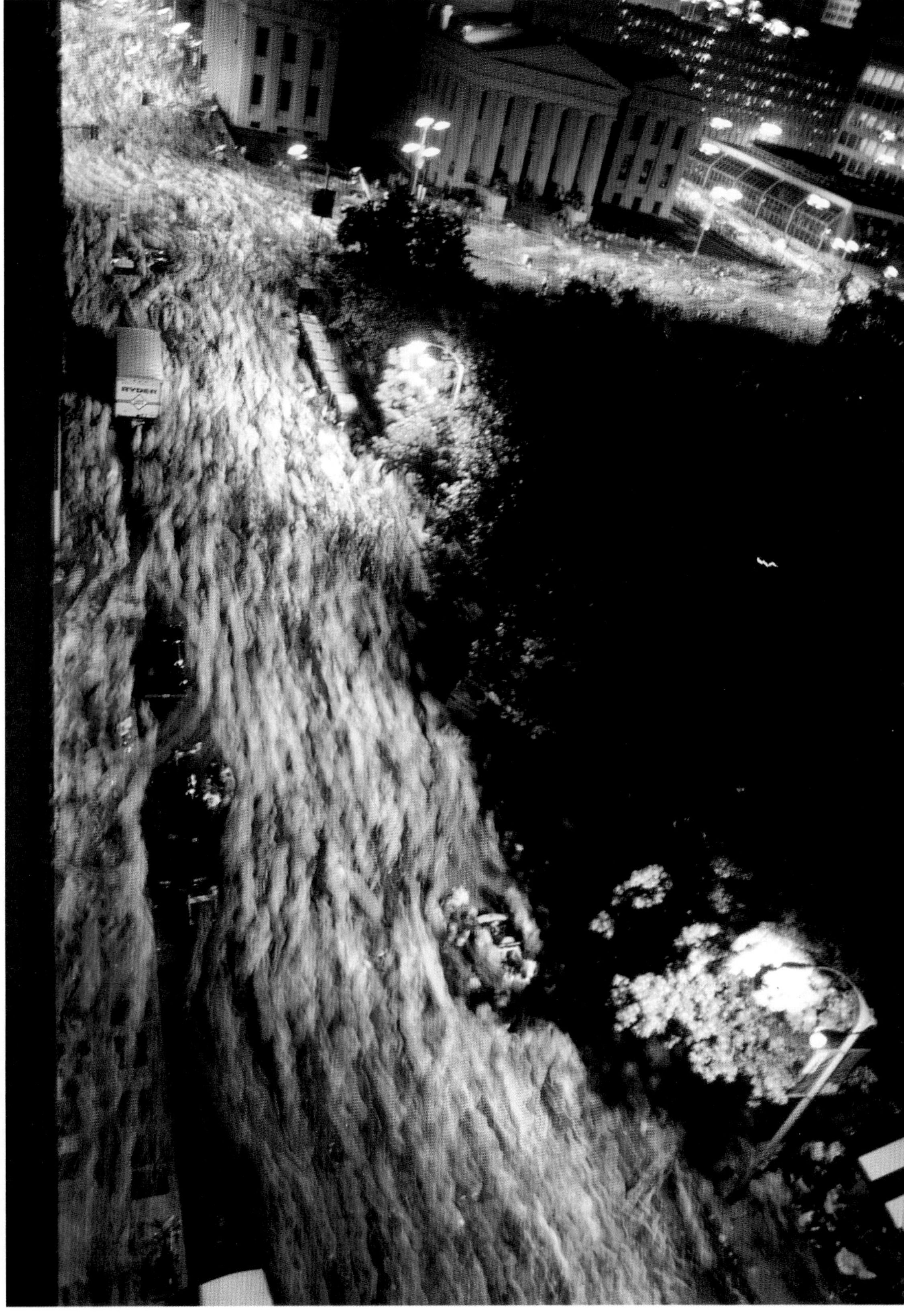

For the Fourth of July holiday, St. Louis throws one of the biggest parties in the country. The three-day V.P. Fair stands for Veiled Prophet, a St. Louis social organization. In 1995, the fair became known by a fairer name: Fair Saint Louis.

▼ DAVID HINKSON

▼ DAVID HINKSON

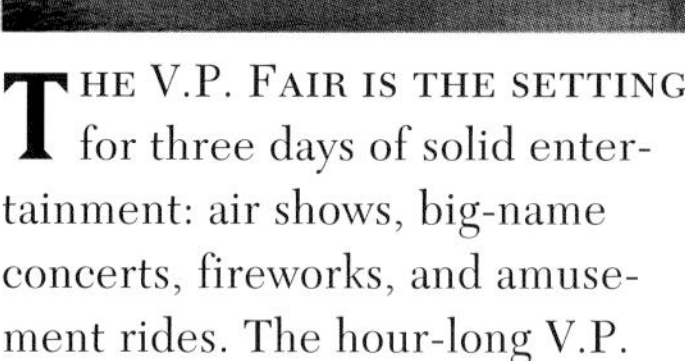

The V.P. Fair is the setting for three days of solid entertainment: air shows, big-name concerts, fireworks, and amusement rides. The hour-long V.P. Fair parade is the city's biggest and oldest, with blocks of floats, marching bands, inflatable characters, and dancers, and miles of parade watchers.

ST. LOUIS STILL SINGS THE BLUES at the annual Blues Heritage Festival, an event that attracts thousands of music lovers from around the world.

▲ SPECTRA-ACTION, INC. / LEWIS PORTNOY

ST. LOUISANS SHOW UP EARLY for their fairs and festivals and stake out their spot with blankets and beer coolers.

CATHY FERRIS

THIS CITY LINES UP FOR ANY excuse to have a parade or a festival. St. Louis honors its diversity with a variety of ethnic and cultural celebrations throughout the year.

▲ QUINTA SCOTT

▲ ERNST STADLER

St. Louisans love to celebrate the city's melting-pot culture, as evidenced by this kilt-clad bagpiper and folks wearing lederhosen.

▼ SUE FORD

SOME YOUNG SOLDIERS LIE in old graves at Jefferson Barracks National Cemetery. The burial ground is almost 170 years old. Robert E. Lee and John Pershing served at the barracks, which is now a historical park.

▲ PAT DONOVAN

A Civil War reenactment reminds us that the young fight wars, while an elderly veteran reminds us that only the lucky ones survive.

▼ QUINTA SCOTT

THE FLAGPOLES, PILLARS, AND posts adorning St. Louis buildings are decorated down to the smallest and most intricate detail.

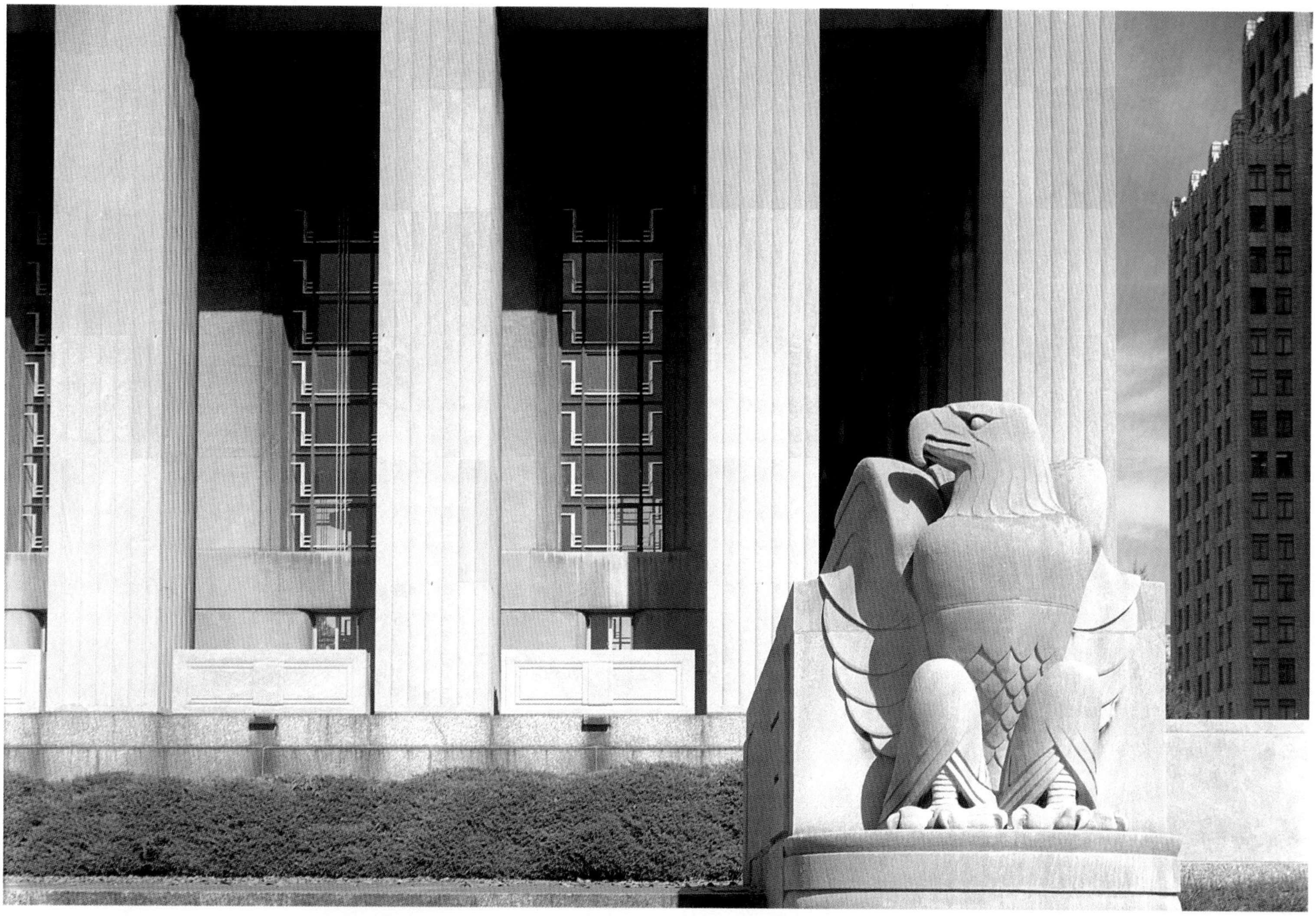

▲ GARY TETLEY

THE SOLDIERS' MEMORIAL Military Museum is dedicated to St. Louis warriors and war dead. It is guarded by a sentry of stern figures.

IT'S 190 FEET STRAIGHT UP from the limestone floor to the cupola of the Old Courthouse. Architect William Rumbold modeled the dome after St. Peter's Basilica in Rome. The 150-year-old courthouse has some delightful touches. According to some reports, the cast-iron fence has a turtle motif in honor of a janitor who once kept a turtle in the fountain.

▶ BRENT REED

CITY HALL

LOCAL BUREAUCRATS AND aldermen wheel and deal, work, and sometimes steal a nap in the St. Louis City Hall (OPPOSITE), modeled after the Hotel de Ville de Paris. Our Old Post Office is equally grand (ABOVE, FOREGROUND).

QUINTA SCOTT

DECORATIVE SHELLS ARE scattered all over the Shell Building, which was constructed for the giant oil corporation (OPPOSITE). Above, a trio of beautiful buildings—the St. Louis Library (LEFT), the Shell Building (CENTER), and Christ Church Cathedral—enhances the St. Louis landscape.

▼ ANNE CASTRODALE

The Gateway Arch is not the only arch in the city. St. Louis has some lesser-known but often more decorated arches spread throughout town.

GARY TETLEY

THE BEST OF ST. LOUIS IS easily overlooked. The city loads its buildings with details at the top.

▼ JIM SOKOLIK

Designed by Louis H. Sullivan more than 100 years ago, the Wainwright State Office Building is one of the city's first modern high-rises. It has teak-framed windows and terra-cotta garlands.

▲ JIM SOKOLIK

THE SHRINE OF ST. JOSEPH was the site of an actual miracle, later authenticated by the Catholic church.

park

▲ QUINTA SCOTT

▲ QUINTA SCOTT

WASHINGTON STREET, ONCE the center of St. Louis' rag trade, now has nightclubs, handsome offices, and fashionable apartments in many of those old lofts and warehouses (OPPOSITE). St. Louis public buildings were built to inspire the people they served. The Civil Courts building (TOP LEFT) has lofty columns. City Hall has marble staircases (BOTTOM LEFT). The St. Louis Library (TOP & BOTTOM RIGHT) is a temple of learning. Architect Cass Gilbert gave St. Louis a library with carved marble lamps, Tennessee marble floors, and massive oak furniture.

▼ QUINTA SCOTT

THE CHARMING FRIVOLITY OF the Campbell House survives amid the workaday downtown business buildings. The museum is the Victorian mansion of Robert Campbell, one-time commissioner of the Bureau of Indian Affairs.

▲ QUINTA SCOTT

THE SERRA SCULPTURE, possibly St. Louis' most controversial public art, stands beside the Civil Courts building, scene of the city's legal controversies.

▼ QUINTA SCOTT

True St. Louisans consider grease to be one of the basic food groups. We love coffee shops and late-night diners, so it's only right and natural that we are also home to the headquarters for Tums (opposite).

77
ET STRIP

St. Louis poet Donald Finkel drinks in the nostalgia of Blueberry Hill (opposite). *Cash Box* magazine declared its jukebox the best in America. Many St. Louisans grew up on a diet of White Castle burgers—better known as belly bombers (top). In the '50s and '60s, Steak 'n' Shake was a classic teen hangout, complete with carhops (bottom).

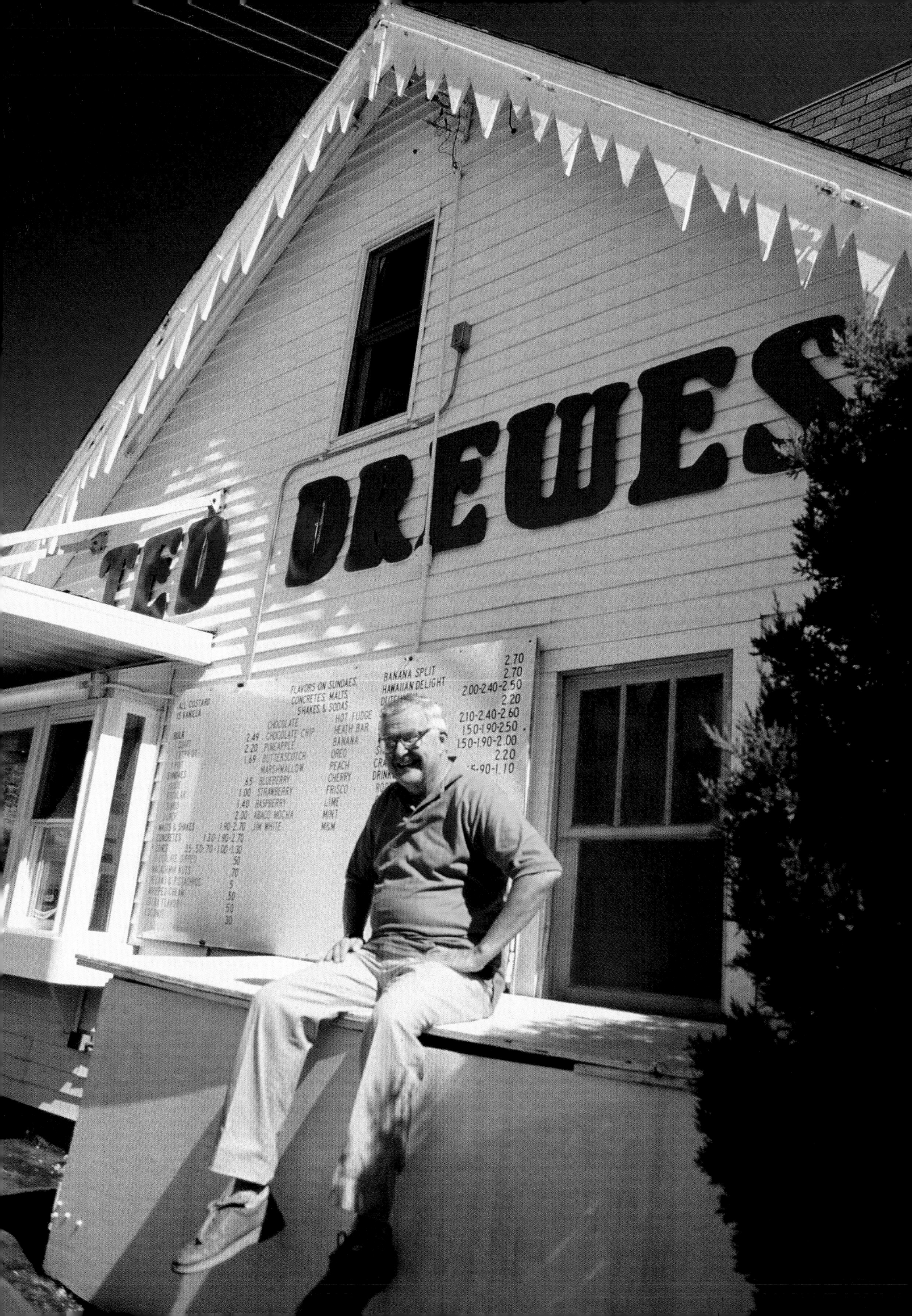

TED DREWES
BANANA SPLIT
HAWAIIAN DELIGHT
FLAVORS ON SUNDAES, CONCRETES, MALTS, SHAKES, & SODAS
CHOCOLATE
CHOCOLATE CHIP
PINEAPPLE
BUTTERSCOTCH
MARSHMALLOW
BLUEBERRY
STRAWBERRY
RASPBERRY
ABACO MOCHA
JIM WHITE
HOT FUDGE
HEATH BAR
BANANA
OREO
PEACH
CHERRY
FRISCO
LIME
MINT
M&M

▶ JIM SOKOLIK

▶ PHIL BRAMMER

▶ PHIL BRAMMER

▶ TED KIBURZ

TED DREWES IS THE CITY'S beloved frozen custard king (OPPOSITE). You haven't had a real visit until you've tried a "concrete" at his south-side stand decorated with wooden icicles. Of course, St. Louis has plenty of other food to enjoy as well.

▼ DAVID W. PRESTON

THE SOULARD FARMERS MARKET has been in operation for more than 200 years. You can buy anything from homegrown tomatoes to live chickens.

▲ JIM SOKOLIK

▲ JANICE BRODERICK

THE SOULARD NEIGHBORHOOD, with its jazz joints and hangouts, has the color and feel of New Orleans—especially during Mardi Gras.

DAVID SWIMMER

The Bosman twins are legendary local jazz artists who still perform regularly in some of the city's smoky clubs.

RAY MARKLIN

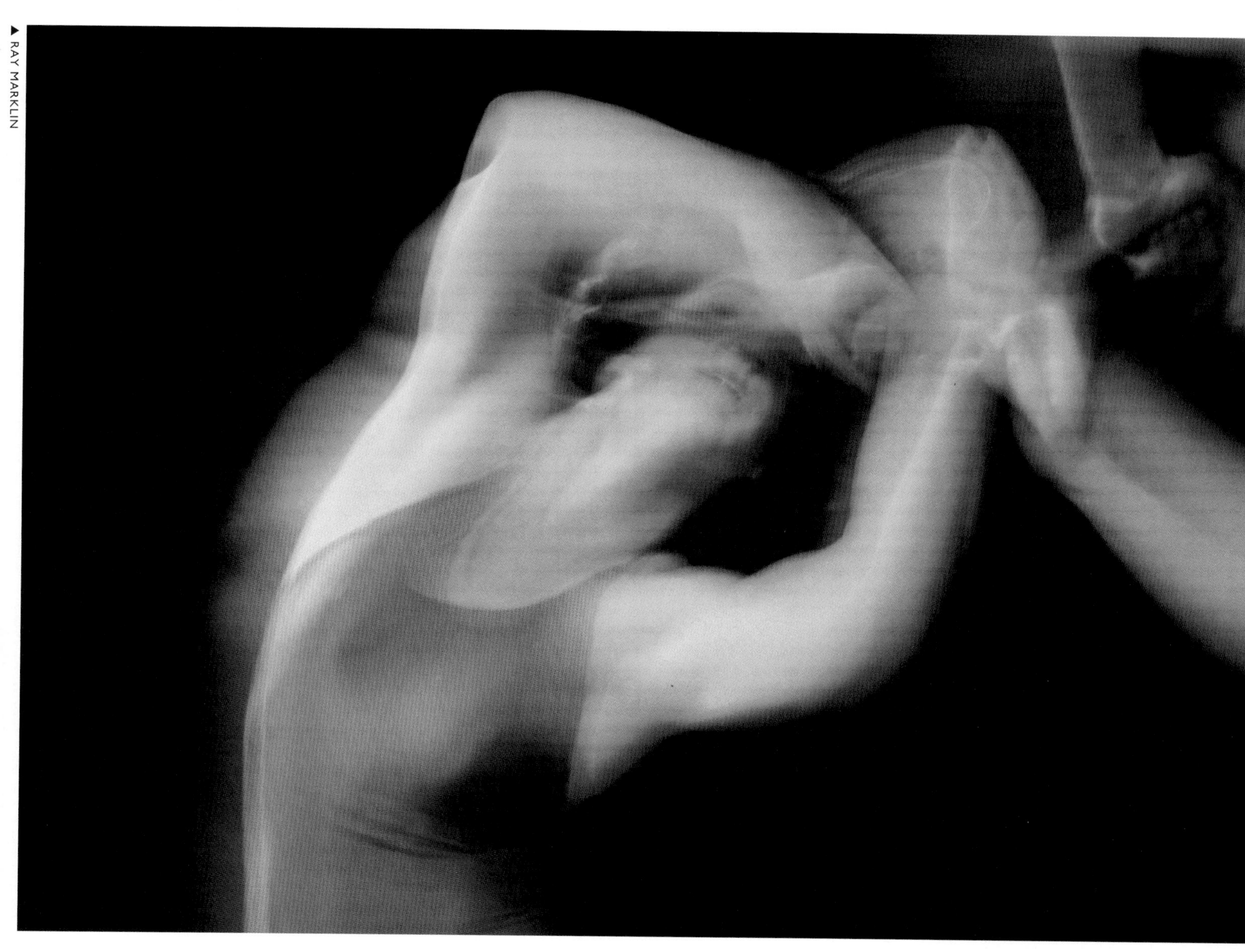

THE DARING MOVES OF THE Atrek Contemporary Dance Theatre are an integral part of the city's diverse cultural mix.

The 44-story Southwestern Bell Building was the tallest high-rise in Missouri when it was completed in the mid-1980s (opposite), adding to St. Louis' already impressive skyline.

302
302
302

▲ SPECTRA-ACTION, INC. / LEWIS PORTNOY

MORE THAN 54,000 BASEBALL fans have been known to roar together in Busch Stadium, home of the St. Louis Cardinals. Loyal fans—and there is no other kind in St. Louis—support their team by wearing red.

ST. LOUIS HAS PRODUCED SOME of the finest soccer players in the country. They start kicking young, often on a Catholic school team. If they're lucky enough and good enough, they may end up playing at the Kiel Center for the St. Louis Ambush (OPPOSITE).

The new Kiel Center is host to St. Louis Blues National Hockey League action, St. Louis University basketball, Ambush soccer, and a number of other sporting events.

▼ COURTESY ST. LOUIS BLUES

▼ COURTESY ST. LOUIS BLUES

St. Louis Blues hockey provides plenty of fast action on the ice—a hockey puck has been clocked at more than 100 miles per hour. Brett Hull—son of the legendary Bobby Hull—is the star of the city's favorite hockey team.

STANLEY CUP 1893-1993
ST. LOUIS
Heaton
Heaton

DAVID W. PRESTON

BASKETBALL LEGEND Charlie "Spoon" Spoonhour is the popular coach of the St. Louis University Billiken team (LEFT). College basketball is a hot city sport. For the NCAA finals, every office has its pool, and we eagerly await the outcome.

▲ DAVID W. PRESTON

COACH

Coach Derril Johnson has trained hundreds of young boxers at the Mathews-Dickey Boys Club (opposite). He's shown here with Cayce Evans (standing) and Jay C. Washington. Martin L. Mathews (left), the club cofounder, is surrounded by some of his young ballplayers. His favorite phrase is the club's motto, "respect, restraint, and responsibility."

3336

▲ LEE HARRIS

▲ LEE HARRIS

AFRICAN-AMERICANS ADDED their heritage to St. Louis, with color-splashed Caribbean-style houses (TOP LEFT), the Prince Hall Masons (TOP RIGHT), and most of all, music. St. Louis is the hometown of the late ragtime artist Scott Joplin. And local jazz and blues artists still entertain at clubs and festivals.

GALLONS
PER GALLON
Wayne

PART OF THE OLD ROUTE 66—the Mother Road—passes through St. Louis. The automobile is still the city's main form of transportation, and you can find gas station signs and pumps and garages that have served travelers for decades.

Cherokee Street, a long-time city shopping district, has become the city's antique row. Collectors can find anything from old neon signs to salt and pepper shakers.

CHEROKEE STATION
SHOPPING AREA

▼ CATHY FERRIS

PRECEDING PAGES: ST. LOUISANS decorate by the yard. A lawn isn't finished without concrete saints and animals. Live animals can also be for show—like this soulful pair at a pet show in Kirkwood (ABOVE).

PAGES 110 & 111: GARY TETLEY PHOTOS

WM. STAGE

DOGS GIVE DEVOTION FOR A lifetime, but their owners' love can last beyond the grave. This touching tombstone is in a pet cemetery in south St. Louis.

▶ QUINTA SCOTT

▶ QUINTA SCOTT

On the Hill, even the fireplugs are Italian (opposite). The Rudolph Torrini sculpture is dedicated to the Italian immigrants who first settled this neighborhood more than 100 years ago (top left). Torrini talked with the old people on the Hill in order to make sure his statue was authentic, right down to the straps on the suitcase. The statue stands in front of St. Ambrose Church, which feeds the neighborhood's soul. The many restaurants on the Hill provide a different kind of nourishment.

THE GATEHOUSES TO GRAND Westmoreland Place, a private street in the Central West End, are as rich as the residents.

THIS PILLARED PAVILION CAN be found in Tower Grove Park, a rare Victorian walking park (BOTTOM). Created by Henry Shaw in 1868, the park is dotted with 19th-century delights—fountains, statues, and ornate gazebos (TOP).

▲ KEN LUEBBERT

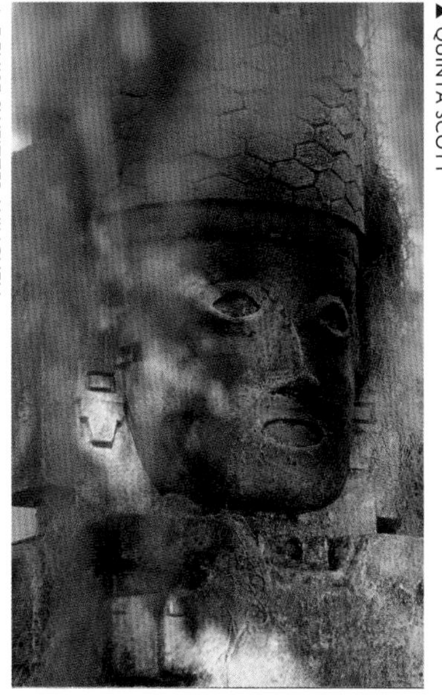

▲ DENISE SWEITZER-WINCHELL

▲ QUINTA SCOTT

THE MISSOURI BOTANICAL Garden is known as Shaw's Garden, because it, too, is the creation of Henry Shaw. Shaw is buried in his beloved garden, but it did not stop growing when he died. It's had many new additions, from the Ridgeway Center (TOP) to the well-fed carp (BOTTOM RIGHT).

SUE FORD

THE JAPANESE GARDEN IS 14 acres of peace and beauty found within the Missouri Botanical Garden. It is the largest traditional Japanese garden in North America.

▲ SPECTRA-ACTION, INC. / LEWIS PORTNOY

THE MISSOURI BOTANICAL Garden is a showcase for human and natural events, including these lily pads and the Japanese festival.

QUINTA SCOTT

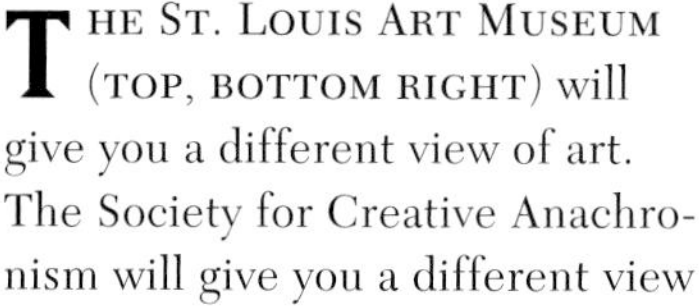

THE ST. LOUIS ART MUSEUM (TOP, BOTTOM RIGHT) will give you a different view of art. The Society for Creative Anachronism will give you a different view of another time (ABOVE). At far right is an equestrian statue of the city's namesake, the saintly French King Louis IX.

GENERATIONS OF BRIDES have been photographed among the flowers at the Jewel Box in Forest Park.

▲ SPECTRA-ACTION, INC. / LEWIS PORTNOY

THE MUNY IS ANOTHER CITY tradition (TOP). In the summer, Broadway shows are presented at this outdoor amphitheater in Forest Park. Before the show, many St. Louisans picnic in the park.

▼ SPECTRA-ACTION, INC. / LEWIS PORTNOY

Forest Park is almost 1,300 acres in the heart of the city. In 1904 it was the scene of the St. Louis World's Fair. Now, it is a good place for a family reunion, for a handball match, or simply to watch the ducks.

▲ SPECTRA-ACTION, INC. / LEWIS PORTNOY

FOREST PARK IS BIGGER THAN New York's Central Park. There's room for a golf course and a seven-mile path for jogging, cycling, and in-line skating.

DENISE SWEITZER-WINCHELL

THIS TRAIN TAKES YOU AROUND the 83-acre St. Louis Zoo in style (LEFT). Of course, if you're a kid who needs a rest, you can hop in this hippo.

WYN WINCHELL

RAY MARKLIN

The St. Louis Zoo lets you study its creatures from a distance, or get up close in the petting zoo. Rated one of the top zoos in the country, the price of admission is at the bottom. The zoo is free.

▼ LEON D. ALGEE, JR.

LIONS AND TIGERS AND BEARS, oh my! On a good day, they may even pose for a photograph.

▲ LEON D. ALGEE, JR.

Baby Raja is the first elephant ever born at the St. Louis Zoo.

Sinclair

THE GREAT FOREST PARK Balloon race is a monster event each September.

CARNIVAL RIDES, COLORFUL clowns, and smiling faces are all part of the many fairs and events held every summer in St. Louis.

RAY MARKLIN

THE BIG FOOT 4X4 IS MADE in St. Louis, as any truck-loving 10-year-old will tell you (TOP). Paul Pagano, who calls himself Father Time and promotes patriotism with his "God Bless America" campaign, is another city original (BOTTOM).

COURTESY CIRCUS FLORA

COURTESY CIRCUS FLORA

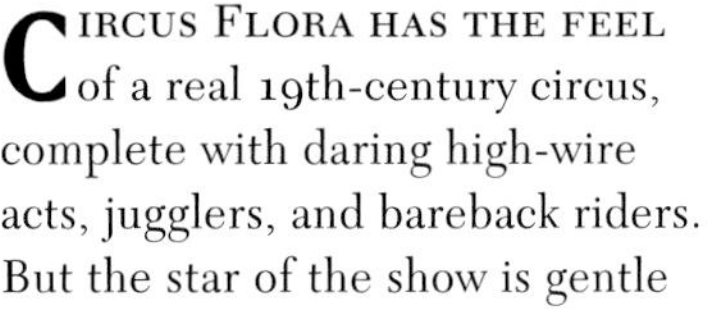

CIRCUS FLORA HAS THE FEEL of a real 19th-century circus, complete with daring high-wire acts, jugglers, and bareback riders. But the star of the show is gentle Flora, the elephant. Circus Flora is also a favorite attraction during the parade through University City (OPPOSITE).

Circus

UNIVERSITY CITY'S CITY HALL is splendid and cerebral (OPPOSITE). The shops and eateries in U. City, as it's known locally, have a smart, offbeat, eclectic style.

◂ COURTESY WASHINGTON UNIVERSITY

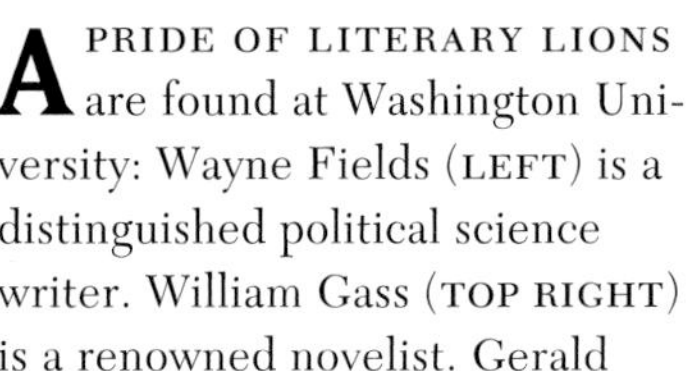

A PRIDE OF LITERARY LIONS are found at Washington University: Wayne Fields (LEFT) is a distinguished political science writer. William Gass (TOP RIGHT) is a renowned novelist. Gerald Early (BOTTOM RIGHT) is a recent winner of the National Book Award, and was interviewed extensively throughout the 1994 film documentary "Baseball" on PBS.

▲ COURTESY WASHINGTON UNIVERSITY

TWO OTHER NATIONALLY known authors who make their homes in St. Louis are novelist Stanley Elkin (TOP LEFT) and Mona Van Duyn (BOTTOM LEFT), the first female poet laureate. At right is Douglas C. North, who won the Nobel Prize for economics in 1993. North did the major portion of his prize-winning work at Washington University.

ALAN E. SCHLESINGER

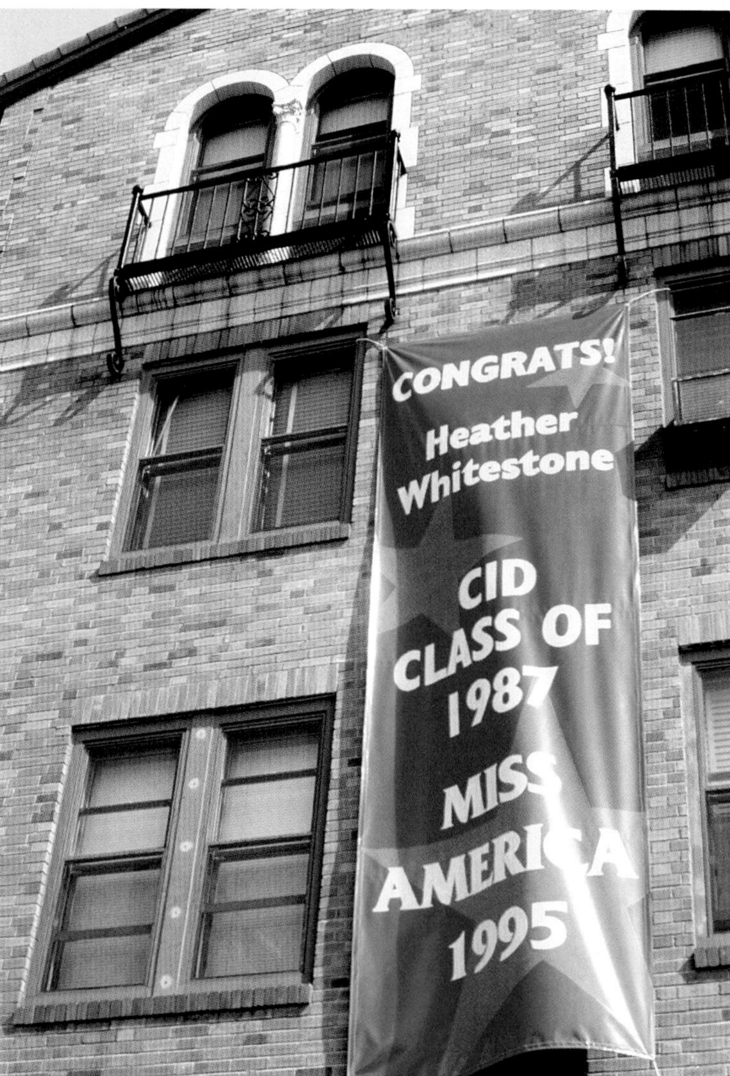

TRAVIS A. CURD III

EACH NEIGHBORHOOD IN St. Louis has its own sharply defined character. The Central West End has some of the city's finest medical treatment centers, including Barnes Hospital (TOP LEFT). Heather Whitestone, 1995 Miss America, was a student at the Central Institute for the Deaf (BOTTOM LEFT). The thriving University City Loop (TOP RIGHT) has a Walk of Fame honoring St. Louis celebrities, including baseball Hall of Famer Cool Papa Bell (BOTTOM RIGHT).

▲ CATHY FERRIS

▲ CATHY FERRIS

▲ KEN LUEBBERT

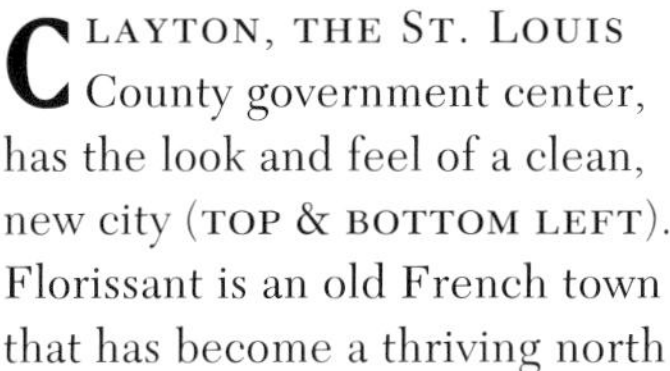

CLAYTON, THE ST. LOUIS County government center, has the look and feel of a clean, new city (TOP & BOTTOM LEFT). Florissant is an old French town that has become a thriving north county suburb with more than 55,000 people (TOP RIGHT). Some of the first settlers' houses survive. Florissant is proud of its Old St. Ferdinand Shrine (BOTTOM RIGHT). Father de Smet, the missionary who preached to the area's Native American population, was ordained here in 1827. St. Louis Saint Philippine Duchesne also lived in the facility.

CATHY FERRIS

THIS TRAIN STATION LINKED Kirkwood, the area's first true suburb, with the city. There were trains for "the works, the clerks, and the shirks," depending on what time they went into the city. The station is now the centerpiece of the old town's shopping area.

▲ CASEY GALVIN

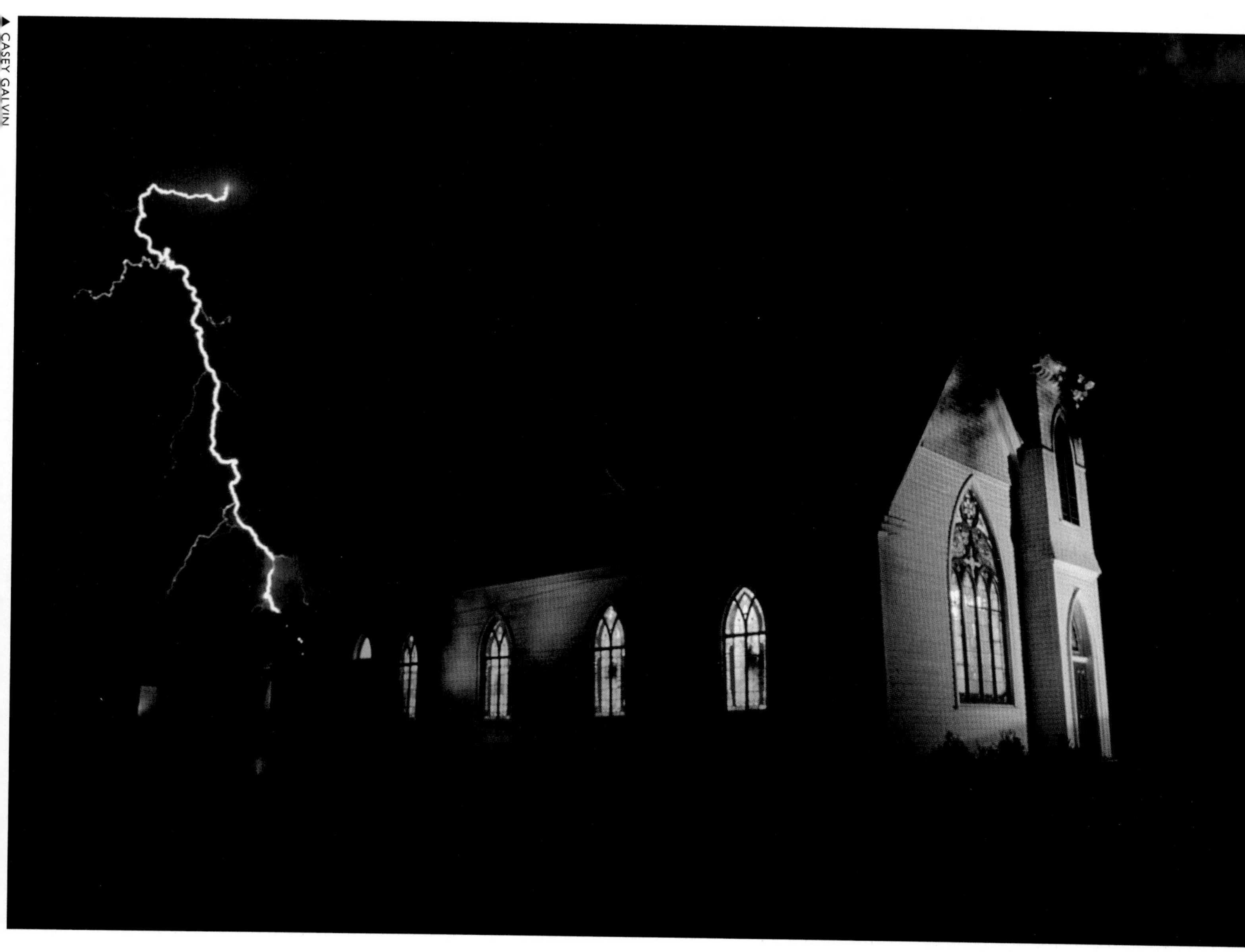

THE OLIVE CHAPEL AFRICAN Methodist Episcopal Church in Kirkwood withstands a storm.

▼ CASEY GALVIN

THE SLEEK, MODERN LINES of St. Anselm's Catholic Church are on display in west St. Louis County (LEFT). St. Louis has so many Catholics, even non-Catholics will ask what parish you live in.

THIS FOUNTAIN IS AN IRRESISTIBLE temptation to the students at St. Louis University. They love to fill it with soap and make it foam with bubbles.

The Fox Theatre was built in 1929 as a dream palace for the people of St. Louis. The splendid Siamese Byzantine interior is a show itself, but entertainers from Frank Sinatra to Liberace have graced the Fox's stage.

FOX
FOX THEATRE
KADI WELCOMES
THE
SOLD OUT

HONESTY

THIS FOUNTAIN IS AN IRRESISTible temptation to the students at St. Louis University. They love to fill it with soap and make it foam with bubbles.

THE FOX THEATRE WAS BUILT IN 1929 as a dream palace for the people of St. Louis. The splendid Siamese Byzantine interior is a show itself, but entertainers from Frank Sinatra to Liberace have graced the Fox's stage.

FOX
FOX THEATRE
KADI WELCOMES
THE
FABULOUS
FRI. FEB. 3 8
SOLD OUT

▲ JERRY NAUNHEIM, JR./REPERTORY THEATRE OF ST. LOUIS

ST. LOUIS ARTS ARE APPRECIATED beyond the city. The St. Louis Symphony is ranked in the top five in the country (OPPOSITE). The Repertory Theatre of St. Louis features productions ranging from "Madame Butterfly" (TOP LEFT) to "Fences," starring Avery Brooks (TOP RIGHT). The Opera Theatre of St. Louis is known as the darling of the New York critics (BOTTOM).

NAYSAYERS CLAIMED ST. LOUISANS would never abandon their cars for the new MetroLink light-rail system. They were wrong. We lined up the first day, and have been riding ever since.

RIGHT NOW, THE METROLINK runs from the airport through downtown St. Louis and across the Mississippi into Illinois, but there are even bigger plans for the future.

G. ROBERT BISHOP

G. ROBERT BISHOP

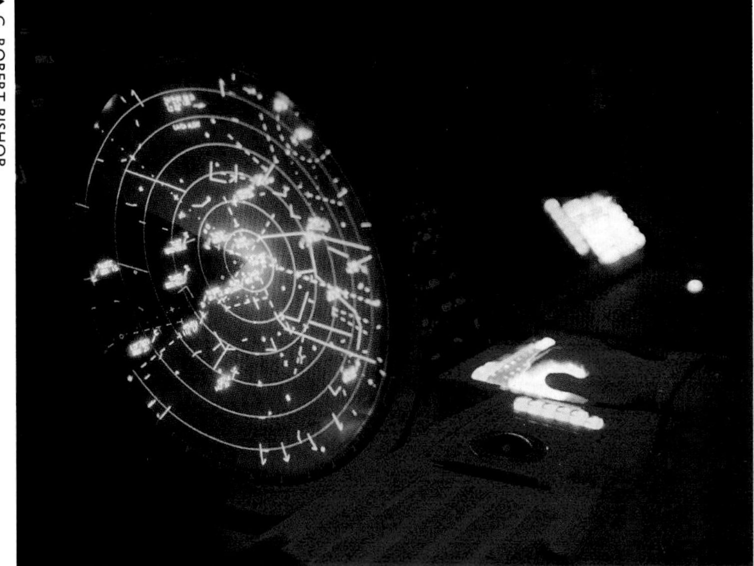

St. Louis has always had a special connection with aviation. Charles Lindbergh's historic flight was financed by St. Louis businessmen. Lindbergh flew across the Atlantic in the *Spirit of St. Louis*. A replica of his plane, which looks frighteningly small, hangs in the soaring Lambert St. Louis International Airport, one of the nation's most state-of-the-art passenger hubs.

▼ SPECTRA-ACTION, INC. / LEWIS PORTNOY

▼ G. ROBERT BISHOP

St. Louis manufacturing covers the spectrum from fibers to fighter planes. The McDonnell Douglas F-15 fighter is produced in the city (right).

THE FORD AEROSTAR, ONE OF the most popular minivans on the market, is another St. Louis product.

CATHY FERRIS

THE JEHOVAH'S WITNESSES' "quick build" program is the modern version of a barn raiser. After the foundation and other contractor essentials were put in, their Kingdom Hall was built mostly by volunteer labor.

▲ PAT DONOVAN

St. Louis keeps growing away from downtown and out to the suburbs. The metro area grew by almost 1 million residents between 1940 and 1990.

St. Louis County was once a long Sunday drive from downtown, a place for farms and woods. Now it has bold new buildings and thriving corporate centers such as the Maryville Centre (right; opposite bottom).

▼ SPECTRA-ACTION, INC. / LEWIS PORTNOY

▲ ANNIE MARSHALL

◀ SPECTRA-ACTION, INC. / LEWIS PORTNOY

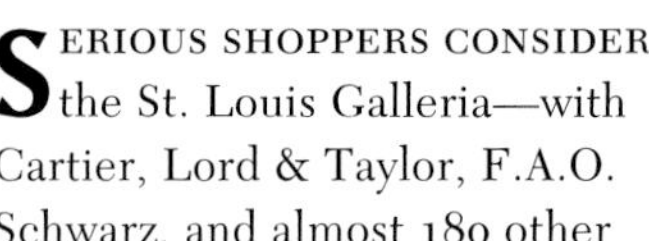
SERIOUS SHOPPERS CONSIDER the St. Louis Galleria—with Cartier, Lord & Taylor, F.A.O. Schwarz, and almost 180 other shops—as a tourist attraction in itself (LEFT). St. Louis Centre revitalized downtown shopping (RIGHT).

▲ SPECTRA-ACTION, INC. / LEWIS PORTNOY

▲ SPECTRA-ACTION, INC. / LEWIS PORTNOY

Crown Candy in North St. Louis has wonderful old-fashioned candies and ice cream (top left). Or, you can search for the most modern sweet treats at the Galleria (top right). Northwest Plaza, one of the area's largest shopping centers, even has miniature golf (bottom left). You can ride this 1920s hand-carved carousel in Faust County Park (bottom right).

Grant's Farm, maintained by the Anheuser Busch Companies, has 281 exotic acres. You can go to bird shows, feed young animals in the feeding area, and ride through a deer park with wild animals. The cabin was built by former President Ulysses S. Grant in 1856 (bottom).

▼ BRIAN GROPPE

THE CLYDESDALES, THE BEER wagon giants, are bred at Grant's Farm. The young colts frolic in one of the facility's pastures (BOTTOM).

DENISE SWEITZER-WINCHELL

ANNIE MARSHALL

TWO HUNDRED TONS OF SAND, sculpted into castles, are part of the fun at the annual Sand Castle Festival at Laumeier Sculpture Park (TOP). Fire and Ice is another lovely Laumeier event (BOTTOM).

▲ SUE FORD

LAUMEIER SCULPTURE PARK IS one museum where you can lie on the grass and admire the art works up close.

In summer, St. Louisans take time for a variety of old-fashioned concerts in the city's numerous parks.

▲ OPERA THEATRE OF ST. LOUIS

A SUMMER EVENING AT THE Opera Theatre of St. Louis often includes an elegant picnic.

◀ SPECTRA-ACTION, INC. / LEWIS PORTNOY

ST. CHARLES COUNTY (TOP) in the north and Chesterfield in the west (BOTTOM) are two of St. Louis' fastest-growing areas.

▲ SPECTRA-ACTION, INC. / LEWIS PORTNOY

St. Louisans like to brag that everything in our city is 20 minutes away. That's how we say it's a good place to live. But as St. Louis spreads out, we've expanded our definition. We now say places are 20 minutes from I-270. Kids get a day out of school for a field trip to the Missouri Botanical Garden (BOTTOM LEFT). Six Flags Over Mid-America, with more than 100 rides, draws kids like a magnet (BOTTOM RIGHT).

SPECTRA-ACTION, INC. / LEWIS PORTNOY

OUTLET MALLS, LIKE THIS ONE in Warrenton, lure young and old in the hunt for bargains (LEFT). But a brisk game of competition shuffleboard at the Senior Olympics is also exhilarating (RIGHT).

▲ PAT DONOVAN

THE SENIOR OLYMPICS IS A showcase for many of the city's mature athletes.

DAVID W. PRESTON

DAVID W. PRESTON

THE 1994 U.S. OLYMPIC FESTIVAL featured more than 3,000 athletes in 37 different sports. They all got a warm welcome from St. Louis County Supervisor George "Buzz" Westfall (TOP RIGHT).

▲ DAVID W. PRESTON

▲ DAVID W. PRESTON

St. Louis Mayor Freeman Bosley, Jr., read the opening proclamation for the Olympic Festival (top left). The torch ceremony is a moving one (top right). And speaking of moving, the bike races and kayaking events were fast-paced.

▼ SPECTRA-ACTION, INC. / LEWIS PORTNOY

ST. LOUIS IS A SPORTS TOWN.
We don't just watch, we play.

▲ SPECTRA-ACTION, INC. / LEWIS PORTNOY

▲ SPECTRA-ACTION, INC. / LEWIS PORTNOY

▲ LEON D. ALGEE, JR.

THE DEBATE RAGES WHETHER softball or baseball is better. One thing is for sure: anyone who calls this game softball has never been hit with one.

▼ RAY MARKLIN

▼ SPECTRA-ACTION, INC. / LEWIS PORTNOY

FOOTBALL IS A GAME OF MUSCLE, hope, and courage. St. Louisans flock to small neighborhood stadiums throughout the community to support their local gridiron heroes.

THE MIGHTY MUD MANIA IS a great way to get down and dirty. Some 2,000 kids crawl, climb, and jump through a messy obstacle course.

▲ CINDY WROBEL

A SYNCHRONIZED SWIM COMpetition in Clayton demonstrates the poetry of line and motion.

THERE ARE ANY NUMBER OF ways to chill out in a St. Louis summer, from a hammock to a cool pool.

▼ KRISTEN PETERSON

▼ CINDY WROBEL

▼ KRISTEN PETERSON

IT'S NOT THE SIZE OF THE POOL that counts, it's how well you put the cool water to use.

▶ PAUL MARSHALL

PAUL MARSHALL

SUMMER ON THE WATER CAN mean a slow, lazy sail or a swift jet ski.

CREVE COEUR MEANS BROKEN heart. However, Creve Coeur Lake Memorial Park is anything but heartbreaking for many of the area's sailing enthusiasts.

The National Charity Horse Show in Queeny Park features some of the region's finest equestrians.

▲ DAVID W. PRESTON

LOCAL GOLFERS ARE NOT trapped in dull courses. We even have courses designed by legends Hale Irwin and Arnold Palmer.

KATHLEEN M. O'DONNELL

FALL IS A FINE TIME TO LIVE in the Midwest. This youngster picked the perfect pumpkin at a produce and pumpkin farm in Chesterfield (RIGHT).

▲ LUBIC & LUBIC PHOTOGRAPHY / SHERRY LUBIC

St. Louis has all four seasons. Fall can be the most haunting, and the most enchanting.

▼ SPECTRA-ACTION, INC. / LEWIS PORTNOY

THE HUNTER AND THE HUNTED in the Missouri woods. For some hunters, this is more beer season than deer season.

NATURE IS CLOSE TO CIVILIzation in St. Louis. Deer come right into farms and yards, much to the delight or consternation of farmers, gardeners, and nature lovers.

▼ ANNE CASTRODALE

PEACEFUL PASTORAL SCENES such as these can be experienced in New Haven and other rural hamlets outside of town.

SOME OF THE MOST BEAUTIFUL nature walks are at the Arboretum at Gray Summit, about an hour from St. Louis. There are lovely views of wildflowers, plants, and trees on four square miles overlooking the Meramec River. Gray Summit is part of the Missouri Botanical Garden's outdoor resources.

▼ LUBIC & LUBIC PHOTOGRAPHY / BILL LUBIC

ANOTHER ENCHANTED SECTION of the Arboretum at Gray Summit. A common flicker and a robin feeding its young add to Missouri's natural beauty.

▲ LUBIC & LUBIC PHOTOGRAPHY / SHERRY LUBIC

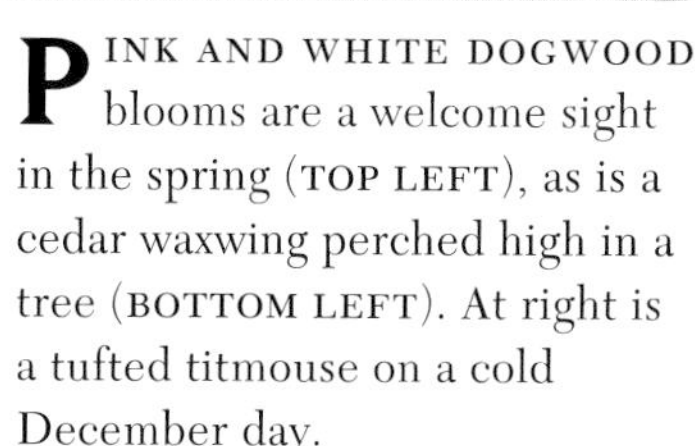

PINK AND WHITE DOGWOOD blooms are a welcome sight in the spring (TOP LEFT), as is a cedar waxwing perched high in a tree (BOTTOM LEFT). At right is a tufted titmouse on a cold December day.

◀ KRISTEN PETERSON

◀ QUINTA SCOTT

Augusta, Missouri, is St. Louis' wine country. German settlers chose this area in the 1880s because they thought it resembled the Rhine Valley. It is a pleasant drive from St. Louis, and a relaxing one at that.

▲ CATHY FERRIS
▼ QUINTA SCOTT

▼ QUINTA SCOTT

St. Charles was Missouri's first capital in 1821. State business was done in this brick and stone building (left). At right, the old river town's buildings on South Main have been lovingly restored.

FOLLOWING PAGES: REDBUD, Illinois, across the river from St. Louis, is dotted with farms and prairies perfect for grazing horses.
PHOTO BY QUINTA SCOTT

March 22, 1992, 4:40 p.m.

▼ QUINTA SCOTT

April 23, 1992, 3:30 p.m.

June 11, 1992, 8:02 a.m.

▼ QUINTA SCOTT

June 19, 1992, 10:10 a.m.

A wheat crop from sprout to harvest at a farm on North Prairie near New Minden, Illinois.

QUINTA SCOTT

MAY 12, 1992, 7:25 P.M.

JUNE 7, 1992, 3:15 P.M.

QUINTA SCOTT

JUNE 23, 1992, 5:45 P.M.

JUNE 25, 1992, 4:00 P.M.

QUINTA SCOTT

THE RICH ILLINOIS PRAIRIE makes it the nation's breadbasket. And as these pigs would surely attest, there's plenty of grain to go around.

▲ QUINTA SCOTT

THE ILLINOIS PRAIRIE IS ALSO oil country. Many farmers have oil wells that look like prehistoric beasts pumping in the fields. This one is at Worden, Illinois.

THE MYSTERIOUS CAHOKIA Indians built towering pyramid-shaped mounds (TOP). The tallest is 10 stories high, built out of earth hauled in with baskets and bare hands. When the Cahokian culture flourished from A.D. 850 to 1300, the people built a great city of perhaps 10,000. The charming French church came much later, with a different culture (BOTTOM).

Designated a World Heritage Site by the United Nations, the Cahokia Mounds are in a class with the Egyptian Pyramids and the Taj Mahal. Their civilization was highly developed. The Cahokians even had a complicated clock, built with poles (top). Unfortunately, the Cahokians had no system of writing, so we know little about them. By the time Columbus came to America, the tribe had disappeared.

▲ LORETTE BURKE

THOUGH THE CAHOKIAN TRIBE is somewhat of a mystery, St. Louis knows more about its other Indian cultures. We celebrate the real first families of North America—the Native Americans—with a host of festivals and ceremonies, such as American Indian Days at Jefferson Barracks.

▲ PAT DONOVAN

▲▼ JEFF VAUGHN

ALTON, ILLINOIS, IS A HISTORIC town near the confluence of the Missouri and Mississippi rivers (ABOVE). Just north of Alton, the limestone bluffs are high and handsome and the river is wide and beautiful. This is some of the area's finest river scenery (OPPOSITE).

LAURA BUILDING

ALTON IS A GOOD PLACE TO SPEND your money and your time: you can shop in the antique district, gamble at a riverboat casino, or simply fish and think about life.

THOSE WHO FISH THE RIVER are also philosophers who take time to contemplate the clouds and the meaning of life.

▲ JIM SOKOLIK

▲ QUINTA SCOTT

Each season, the Mississippi becomes a different river: swift and generous in the summer, cold and clogged in the winter.

"WELCOME TO THE ISLAND of St. Louis," commercial pilots greeted passengers as they flew into St. Louis during the Great Flood of 1993. The Mississippi River crested at a record-breaking 49.58 feet on August 2, drowning many towns in Missouri and Illinois.

▲ THOMAS WILLIAM MILLER

▲ THOMAS WILLIAM MILLER

PRESIDENT CASINO
THE ADMIRAL.
OPENING SOON.
RIVERFRONT
RIVERFRONT
RIVERFRONT

▲ DAVID HINKSON

On the St. Louis riverfront, the flood reached the steps of the Gateway Arch. The muddy brown waters literally brought the city to a standstill.

▼ QUINTA SCOTT

▼ QUINTA SCOTT

THE MISSOURI AND MISSISSIPPI rivers are working rivers, with a steady flow of barges hauling goods and grain.

Many St. Louisans remember the glowing Peabody Coal sign from youthful walks and cruises (top). To us, it is almost as romantic as the moon.

▼ DAVID W. PRESTON

THE RIVER BARGES ARE NO-nonsense on the outside, but inside they often feature some homey comforts.

DAVID W. PRESTON

THE GERMANS TURNED St. Louis into a brewery town. The river water was excellent for beer making and the city's limestone caves were ideal for storing cool beer. At one time, every neighborhood had its brewer; however, Prohibition destroyed most of them. Anheuser-Busch, pictured here, was a hardy—make that heady—survivor.

▲ DAVID W. PRESTON

SOME BEER DRINKERS REGARD the ornate, 19th-century Anheuser-Busch Brew House as the Sistine Chapel of beer.

▼ QUINTA SCOTT

THE OLD BRICK WAREHOUSES at the north end of Broadway maintain a simple, hardworking dignity.

▲ QUINTA SCOTT

THE RAIL YARDS, WITH THEIR promise of places to go, have their own romance as well.

▼ QUINTA SCOTT

THE OLD ST. LOUIS SOUTHWESTern Freight Depot and the Atlas warehouse and elevator facility (OPPOSITE) are long past their glory days. However, the deteriorating facades speak volumes about the city's colorful past.

▲ QUINTA SCOTT

Some see industry as an ugly growth on a city. Others find beauty and strength in its hardworking lines.

THE MONSANTO CARONDELET chemical plant in south St. Louis (TOP) overlooks the River Des Peres, a WPA project. This odd blue wall can be found on Chouteau Avenue.

▼ CASEY GALVIN

RIVERBOAT GAMBLING IS A new addition to the city's river scene. The Casino St. Charles has three decks of gambling in a 19th-century side-wheeler.

QUINTA SCOTT

The President Casino on the Admiral is a dockside casino at the foot of the Arch. Inside, the old riverboat looks like a Las Vegas casino, with bright lights, plenty of slots, and blackjack tables.

THE GATEWAY ARCH REMAINS the focus and fascination for St. Louis. Finished in 1965, it is a fairly new addition to the skyline. Now we can't imagine our city without it.

PAGES 236-237: QUINTA SCOTT

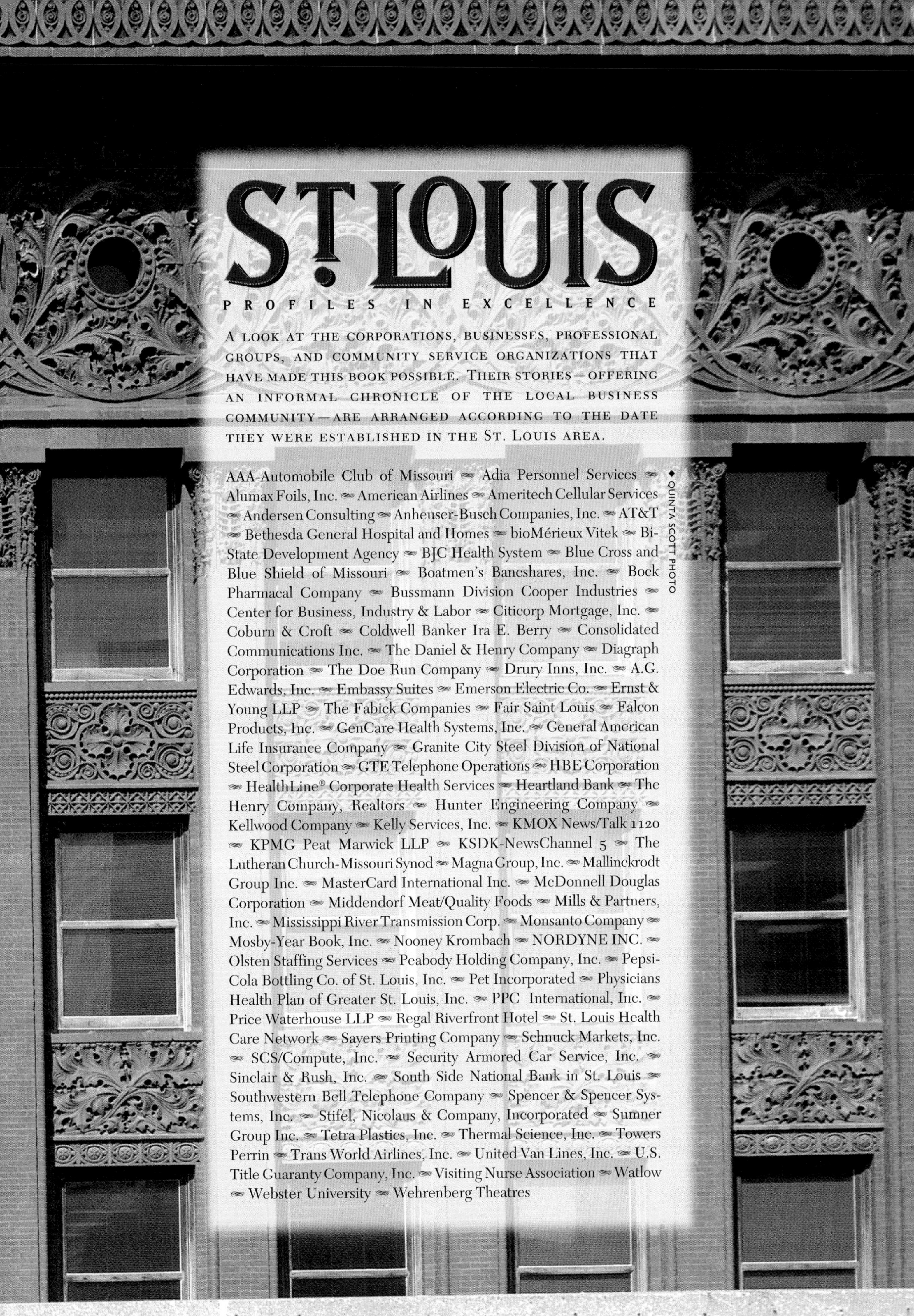

ST. LOUIS

PROFILES IN EXCELLENCE

A look at the corporations, businesses, professional groups, and community service organizations that have made this book possible. Their stories—offering an informal chronicle of the local business community—are arranged according to the date they were established in the St. Louis area.

AAA-Automobile Club of Missouri ⁓ Adia Personnel Services ⁓ Alumax Foils, Inc. ⁓ American Airlines ⁓ Ameritech Cellular Services ⁓ Andersen Consulting ⁓ Anheuser-Busch Companies, Inc. ⁓ AT&T ⁓ Bethesda General Hospital and Homes ⁓ bioMérieux Vitek ⁓ Bi-State Development Agency ⁓ BJC Health System ⁓ Blue Cross and Blue Shield of Missouri ⁓ Boatmen's Bancshares, Inc. ⁓ Bock Pharmacal Company ⁓ Bussmann Division Cooper Industries ⁓ Center for Business, Industry & Labor ⁓ Citicorp Mortgage, Inc. ⁓ Coburn & Croft ⁓ Coldwell Banker Ira E. Berry ⁓ Consolidated Communications Inc. ⁓ The Daniel & Henry Company ⁓ Diagraph Corporation ⁓ The Doe Run Company ⁓ Drury Inns, Inc. ⁓ A.G. Edwards, Inc. ⁓ Embassy Suites ⁓ Emerson Electric Co. ⁓ Ernst & Young LLP ⁓ The Fabick Companies ⁓ Fair Saint Louis ⁓ Falcon Products, Inc. ⁓ GenCare Health Systems, Inc. ⁓ General American Life Insurance Company ⁓ Granite City Steel Division of National Steel Corporation ⁓ GTE Telephone Operations ⁓ HBE Corporation ⁓ HealthLine® Corporate Health Services ⁓ Heartland Bank ⁓ The Henry Company, Realtors ⁓ Hunter Engineering Company ⁓ Kellwood Company ⁓ Kelly Services, Inc. ⁓ KMOX News/Talk 1120 ⁓ KPMG Peat Marwick LLP ⁓ KSDK-NewsChannel 5 ⁓ The Lutheran Church-Missouri Synod ⁓ Magna Group, Inc. ⁓ Mallinckrodt Group Inc. ⁓ MasterCard International Inc. ⁓ McDonnell Douglas Corporation ⁓ Middendorf Meat/Quality Foods ⁓ Mills & Partners, Inc. ⁓ Mississippi River Transmission Corp. ⁓ Monsanto Company ⁓ Mosby-Year Book, Inc. ⁓ Nooney Krombach ⁓ NORDYNE INC. ⁓ Olsten Staffing Services ⁓ Peabody Holding Company, Inc. ⁓ Pepsi-Cola Bottling Co. of St. Louis, Inc. ⁓ Pet Incorporated ⁓ Physicians Health Plan of Greater St. Louis, Inc. ⁓ PPC International, Inc. ⁓ Price Waterhouse LLP ⁓ Regal Riverfront Hotel ⁓ St. Louis Health Care Network ⁓ Sayers Printing Company ⁓ Schnuck Markets, Inc. ⁓ SCS/Compute, Inc. ⁓ Security Armored Car Service, Inc. ⁓ Sinclair & Rush, Inc. ⁓ South Side National Bank in St. Louis ⁓ Southwestern Bell Telephone Company ⁓ Spencer & Spencer Systems, Inc. ⁓ Stifel, Nicolaus & Company, Incorporated ⁓ Sumner Group Inc. ⁓ Tetra Plastics, Inc. ⁓ Thermal Science, Inc. ⁓ Towers Perrin ⁓ Trans World Airlines, Inc. ⁓ United Van Lines, Inc. ⁓ U.S. Title Guaranty Company, Inc. ⁓ Visiting Nurse Association ⁓ Watlow ⁓ Webster University ⁓ Wehrenberg Theatres

◆ QUINTA SCOTT PHOTO

1847

1847 Boatmen's Bancshares, Inc.
1847 The Lutheran Church-Missouri Synod
1852 Anheuser-Busch Companies, Inc.
1867 Mallinckrodt Group Inc.
1878 AT&T
1878 Granite City Steel Division of National Steel Corporation
1878 Southwestern Bell Telephone Company
1887 A.G. Edwards, Inc.
1887 Heartland Bank
1889 Alumax Foils, Inc.
1889 Bethesda General Hospital and Homes
1890 Emerson Electric Co.
1890 Stifel, Nicolaus & Company, Incorporated
1891 South Side National Bank in St. Louis
1893 Diagraph Corporation
1901 Monsanto Company
1901 Price Waterhouse LLP
1902 AAA-Automobile Club of Missouri
1906 Mosby-Year Book, Inc.
1906 Wehrenberg Theatres
1911 KPMG Peat Marwick LLP
1911 Visiting Nurse Association
1912 Sayers Printing Company
1913 Ernst & Young LLP
1914 Bussmann Division Cooper Industries

1914

◆ QUINTA SCOTT PHOTO

Boatmen's Bancshares, Inc.

In the early 1800s, St. Louis was a thriving steamboat town, its riverfront filled with adventure seekers—boatmen, trappers, settlers—who had no place to deposit their earnings since the city's sole bank catered only to the wealthy class. As a result, their income often disappeared in gambling and drinking excursions, and they could never get ahead financially. In 1847 an effort to change the plight of the laboring class took form in the creation of the Boatmen's Savings Institution. Its mission was to serve the "industrious classes."

Chartered in 1847

Since the Bank of the State of Missouri provided services mainly to the wealthy, a group of community leaders, led by George Knight Budd, began searching for a way to help members of the laboring class improve their lives through banking. "Experience has proved that savings institutions have been productive of great benefit to the laboring classes, inducing habits of economy and industry," Budd contended.

With this goal in mind, he and other community leaders launched a campaign to secure a bank charter from the state legislature. In 1847, after several failed petitions, a handful of trustees were granted the legal right to establish Boatmen's.

From the very beginning, the bank seemed earmarked for success. The 1855 passage of a new charter allowed Boatmen's to sell capital stock. All of its $100,000 offerings were purchased by noon on the first day. By the late 1800s the bank had gained national recognition and boasted deposits of nearly $4.5 million.

Today known as Boatmen's Bancshares, Inc., the organization is one of the 30 largest banks in the United States, with assets of more than $32 billion. Management points to four core values that have fueled such growth: quality in training and services, integrity of security and confidentiality, responsiveness to customer needs, and efficiency of operation.

Moving into the 20th Century

In 1897 Boatmen's erected a new building in keeping with the westward movement of the St. Louis business district. The building was completed on the corner of Fourth and Washington in time for the bank's 50th anniversary. Just 17 years later, a disastrous fire sent the bank packing again to new headquarters at Broadway and Olive, which served Boatmen's until 1976.

The World War I years ushered in a new era in banking, as female tellers were seen at the bank's windows for the first time. In 1926 Boatmen's established its Trust Division, which is currently among the largest trust institutions in the country.

Boatmen's provided extra service to its country during the World War II years. Staff members sold war bonds in all branches of the armed forces, as well as in U.S. Department of the Treasury organizations. Under the Treasury's direction, the bank established special facilities for personnel stationed at Fort Leonard Wood and Jefferson Barracks.

Until the late 1960s the bank grew by expanding its existing staff, thus forgoing acquisitions or mergers with other banks. But by 1969 the organization was ready to expand on a larger scale and formed a holding company. Known as Boatmen's Bancshares, Inc., the holding company initiated a series of acquisitions that have made it the dominant banking organization in the central United States.

Beginning with the 1983 acquisition of Metro Bancholding Corporation, Boatmen's made Missouri banking history several times. In 1985 CharterCorp was acquired, tripling the total assets of the corporation to more than $6 billion. Centerre Bancorporation's merger with Boatmen's in 1988 remains the largest ever recorded in Missouri.

The 1990s have also been active years, with Boatmen's expanding into Arkansas, Iowa, New Mexico, Kansas, and Texas. By year-end 1994, the organization had nearly $29 billion in assets and more than 400 locations in nine states. Boatmen's currently ranks among the nation's 30

The Boatmen's Plaza headquarters buildng (opposite) is located at One Boatmen's Plaza in downtown St. Louis.

Boatmen's was chartered in 1847 to serve the "industrious classes" of St. Louis—boatmen, trappers, and settlers—who had no place to deposit their earnings. Today, this superregional bank has more than $32 billion in assets.

largest bank holding companies and among the 15 largest trust institutions, with more than $36 billion in assets under management. Clearly, this superregional bank is a St. Louis success story.

A Civic-minded Organization

In the tradition of its founder, Boatmen's has maintained an ongoing commitment to its communities. During the Great Flood of 1993, for example, the bank's St. Louis and Des Moines operations displayed exemplary leadership by deferring loan and credit card payments, granting cash advances for emergency living expenses, and making home repair and cleanup loans with generous terms.

Already more than two-thirds of the company's banks have earned an "outstanding" designation by federal regulatory agencies for their dedication to the goals of the Community Reinvestment Act, a ranking far above the national average. While Boatmen's is proud of its commitment to the CRA, Chairman and Chief Executive Officer Andrew B. Craig III is quick to point out that the organization strives for more than mere compliance. Loans given through this program represent good business for Boatmen's.

Likewise, the organization's continuing interest in the historical and cultural heritage of St. Louis can be seen in its fine arts collection. Begun in 1938, the collection includes works by such noted artists as George Caleb Bingham, John James Audubon, and Frederic Remington. Many of the works are on permanent display in the Boatmen's downtown buildings.

Those buildings embody the healthy contrast that has become an important part of the bank's culture. Within their modern infrastructure thrives the old-fashioned belief in people and their integrity, a viewpoint that got Boatmen's started in 1847 and keeps it going today.

The Lutheran Church-Missouri Synod

THE LUTHERAN CHURCH-MISSOURI SYNOD, OFTEN REFERRED to as the Missouri Synod, has been a St. Louis cornerstone of culture and tradition for almost 150 years. Headquartered in St. Louis, the organization has 6,150 congregations and 8,800 pastors worldwide. The Missouri Synod's roots trace back to 1839, when a group of Saxon Lutherans fled the trend of rationalism, a reliance on reason instead of faith that had become the dominant belief of the Lutheran Church in Germany.

The group emigrated from Germany and settled near St. Louis to practice an orthodox Lutheranism more freely. Within eight years, the Saxons in Missouri had joined with Franconians in Michigan, Hanoverians in Indiana, and other widely scattered congregations to form a "synod"—from the Greek word for "walking together." The synod was organized on April 26, 1847, with 12 congregations and 22 ministers. By joining forces, the congregations were able to accomplish objectives that individually they would have been unable to achieve. Primary among these were the goals of providing greater mission work, education, and publishing, so that congregations could be supplied with faithful teachers, pastors, and church materials.

CLOCKWISE FROM ABOVE:
THE LUTHERAN CHURCH TRACES ITS ROOTS TO THE TEACHINGS OF MARTIN LUTHER, A RELIGIOUS LEADER IN 16TH-CENTURY GERMANY.

THE MISSOURI SYNOD CREATED THE CONCORDIA PUBLISHING HOUSE ON SEPTEMBER 11, 1869. TODAY'S CONCORDIA IS THE FOURTH-LARGEST RELIGIOUS PUBLISHER IN THE UNITED STATES.

THE INTERNATIONAL CENTER ON KIRKWOOD ROAD SERVES AS THE HEADQUARTERS FOR THE LUTHERAN CHURCH-MISSOURI SYNOD.

Membership Diversity

Its home in St. Louis, a community in which approximately 20 percent of the population claimed German ancestry, allowed the Missouri Synod to reach far into the new frontiers to spread its message and encourage others to join. The Missouri Synod grew quickly. By its 50th anniversary in 1897, it had become a national church body and was, at the time, the largest individual synod of American Lutheranism.

Today's Missouri Synod is diverse in its mix of ethnic groups and continues to expand into different cultures. In St. Louis alone, Missouri Synod congregations conduct services for Spanish-speaking, Vietnamese, and Cambodian residents, as well as for the deaf community. This diversity has also brought a variety of worship styles to the organization. Congregations range from the most traditional to the most contemporary. The musical styles vary from electric keyboard and guitar to some of the finest organs in the area accompanying adult and children's choirs.

Located at the International Center on Kirkwood Road, the headquarters for The Lutheran Church-Missouri Synod stands in a south-central corridor of metropolitan St. Louis' population of 2.5 million. The center houses the national offices of the denomination, its communications and other departments, the offices of the Board for Mission Services, the Concordia University System, and the Board for Parish Services.

The Board for Mission Services is the Missouri Synod's base for missionary work carried out by 250 missionaries and 30 partner churches all over the world. The Concordia University system unites the 10 colleges run by the organization. And the Board for Parish Services manages the Missouri Synod's 1,892 parish schools and 63 high schools, serving over a quarter million students. These services occupy the greatest part of the organization's energy and finances. Also affiliated with the Missouri Synod are 30 hospitals and 37 family and children's agencies.

The Lutherans of the St. Louis area also carry on a number of independent programs and services, apart from the Missouri Synod administration. These include the Lutheran Family and Children Services, which is engaged in counseling and social work; the Lutheran Ministries Association, which conducts ministry work for institutions such as jails, hospitals, and nursing homes; and Lutheran Altenheim and Laclede Oaks

Manor, nursing-care facilities for the aged.

Concordia Seminary and Concordia Publishing House

Standing as one of the best-known landmarks of The Lutheran Church-Missouri Synod is the Concordia Seminary. Founded in 1839 in Perry County, Missouri, the seminary came to St. Louis in 1850 and moved to its present 72-acre site in the St. Louis suburb of Clayton in 1926. The seminary, dedicated to educating men in the holy ministry of the Missouri Synod, has an average enrollment of 400 to 500 students. Since its inception, Concordia Seminary has provided more than 10,000 professional workers for the church. The Missouri Synod has a second seminary with the same mission located in Ft. Wayne, Indiana. The synod's radio station, KFUO, established in 1927, broadcasts religious programs locally and provides resource material to many congregations, organizations, and radio stations worldwide.

The Missouri Synod further expanded its outreach into religious education when it created the Concordia Publishing House on September 11, 1869. The publishing house immediately became a thriving business. At the close of the 1800s, Concordia was printing German bibles, hymnals, and textbooks, and was just starting to print material in English. Through the decades as the Missouri Synod grew and diversified, the publishing house changed as well. Today's Concordia is the fourth-largest religious publisher in the nation and is well known for its family and children's curriculum, music, and theological material.

The Lutheran Church-Missouri Synod, with more than 2.7 million members and over 6,000 congregations, now comprises one-third of all the Lutherans in North America. Through its mission work, educational institutions, publishing activities, and social services, it still strives—in St. Louis and around the world—to meet the goals set by the synod founders a century and a half ago.

Clockwise from below: Concordia Seminary has occupied its present 72-acre site in the St. Louis suburb of Clayton since 1926.

In addition to a number of administrative departments, the International Center houses this chapel.

Concordia Seminary, dedicated to educating men in the holy ministry of the Missouri Synod, has an average enrollment of 400 to 500 students.

Anheuser-Busch Companies, Inc.

Since its founding in St. Louis in 1852, Anheuser-Busch has been marked by a constant, intense focus on one concept: quality. From the company's choice of the highest-quality, freshest brewing ingredients, to its marketing efforts, to its environmental policies, Anheuser-Busch has always insisted on the highest standards. This tradition has enabled the company to grow to become the world's largest brewer, and to be a leader in the container manufacturing, recycling, and family entertainment industries.

Clockwise from below: Budweiser is brewed in St. Louis and 12 other U.S. cities, as well as in four overseas markets. It is currently exported to more than 65 other nations.

Several buildings at Anheuser-Busch's headquarters appear on the National Register of Historic Places.

Anheuser-Busch owns the St. Louis Cardinals and Busch Stadium, where the Cardinals play home games.

History

Anheuser-Busch traces its roots in St. Louis to the Bavarian Brewery, which in its first year of operation produced fewer than 200 barrels of beer. In 1860 the small, struggling brewery was taken over by Eberhard Anheuser, who, a few years later, brought his son-in-law, Adolphus Busch, into the business. It was Adolphus who began transforming the company into an industry powerhouse, and who is considered its founder.

A brilliant visionary and innovator, Adolphus dreamed of a national beer market and a national beer. As a first step in making that dream come true, he launched the industry's first fleet of refrigerated freight cars.

It was also under Adolphus, in 1876, that Budweiser was first brewed, using traditional brewing methods and only the finest barley malt, hops, and rice. Twenty years later, still under Adolphus' leadership, the company developed Michelob, which soon became the preeminent American premium beer.

Adolphus' son, August A. Busch, Sr., led the company through World War I and Prohibition. During Prohibition, the company survived and protected the jobs of its employees by making such products as baker's yeast, soft drinks, and Bevo, a nonalcohol malt-based beverage. One of Adolphus' two grandsons, Adolphus Busch III, guided the company through the end of the Great Depression and World War II. The other grandson, August A. Busch, Jr., then led the firm through the postwar era, during which the company first began establishing breweries outside St. Louis.

The King of Beers

Today Anheuser-Busch is led by Adolphus' great-grandson, August A. Busch III. Under his guidance, the company has widened its dominance of the beer industry, with a market share approximately twice that of its nearest competitor, while also becoming a growing force in international brewing. In addition, the company has major interests in food products and the entertainment industry.

Anheuser-Busch now operates 13 breweries, including the original one in St. Louis. Budweiser is not

only the best-selling brand in the nation, but the best-selling brand in the world. Besides Budweiser, Anheuser-Busch now produces more than 20 brands, including Bud Light, the nation's second-leading beer.

Budweiser is brewed in four overseas markets and is exported to more than 65 other nations. And new links are being forged abroad at a rapid rate, with recent investments and joint ventures in Mexico, China, and Japan as examples.

Over the years, Anheuser-Busch has established several subsidiaries related to its beer operations. Metal Container Corporation, for example, supplies more than half the cans used by Anheuser-Busch and is a significant supplier to the soft drink market as well. In 1978 Anheuser-Busch set up a recycling subsidiary, known as Anheuser-Busch Recycling Corporation, which has grown into the world's largest recycler of aluminum beverage cans.

Among the company's other subsidiaries are Campbell Taggart, the nation's second-largest producer of fresh-baked goods, and Eagle Snacks, which produces a line of high-quality salty snack and nut products.

Throughout its growth, Anheuser-Busch has been committed to environmental initiatives. At the turn of the century, Adolphus Busch began recycling spent brewer's grains for use as animal feed. Today, the company recycles enough grain to feed 4 percent of the U.S. dairy population, and is also involved in a wide variety of other environmental activities, including conservation of natural resources and preservation of wildlife.

Anheuser-Busch's highly regarded Sea World theme parks are leaders in animal research, rescue, rehabilitation, and breeding. The popular Busch Gardens Tampa theme park conducts one of the largest, most successful Asian elephant breeding programs in North America, helping to perpetuate a highly endangered species. In all, the company's family entertainment subsidiary, Busch Entertainment Corporation, operates 10 theme parks in the United States.

A Part of Life in St. Louis

St. Louis is widely known as a "baseball town," and each year millions of fans turn out to watch the St. Louis Cardinals, winners of more World Series championships than any other team in the National League. The team—and Busch Stadium, where they play—is owned by Anheuser-Busch.

A team of the world-famous Budweiser Clydesdales is housed at the St. Louis brewery in an ornate stable that has been designated a National Historic Landmark. The stable is open to visitors as part of the brewery's popular complimentary tour program.

Both St. Louis residents and tourists flock to Grant's Farm in St. Louis County. Once the home of August A. Busch, Jr., Grant's Farm today houses the only existing structure hand-built by an American president, Ulysses S. Grant. Bird and elephant shows, animal petting and feeding areas, and train rides through the farm's Deer Park are complimentary to visitors.

Anheuser-Busch is proud to be part of the fabric of life in St. Louis. Through its many philanthropic programs and other activities, the company seeks to be a part of all the communities where it operates. As it approaches the future, Anheuser-Busch will continue to emphasize that kind of responsible corporate citizenship, as it will continue to emphasize the bedrock of its success—its focus on quality.

Clockwise from left:
The Anheuser-Busch family of beers includes more than 20 brands of beer and two nonalcohol brews.

The company's family entertainment subsidiary, Busch Entertainment Corporation, is the nation's second-largest operator of theme parks, including four Sea World locations.

Residents and tourists flock to Grant's Farm in St. Louis County, where they can see the world-famous Budweiser Clydesdales, as well as the only existing structure hand-built by an American president, Ulysses S. Grant.

Mallinckrodt Group Inc.

Established in 1867 as G. Mallinckrodt & Company, Manufacturing Chemists, Mallinckrodt Group Inc. is today a strategically managed, technology-based Fortune 250 company with annual sales of $2 billion. Mallinckrodt and its three operating companies have more than 10,000 employees worldwide and more than 150 manufacturing, sales, and distribution facilities around the world. The companies provide over 2,500 human and animal health and specialty chemical products that are sold in more than 100 countries. International sales amount to 40 percent of the company's total business.

In St. Louis today, Mallinckrodt's presence—with six sites, including three headquarters operations, and 2,400 employees—is a measurable contrast to the company's beginnings. However, the tie to those early days remains highly visible, with one of two local manufacturing facilities still located in north St. Louis on the original site where Edward, Gustav, and Otto Mallinckrodt established the business to produce such staple chemicals as aqua ammonia,

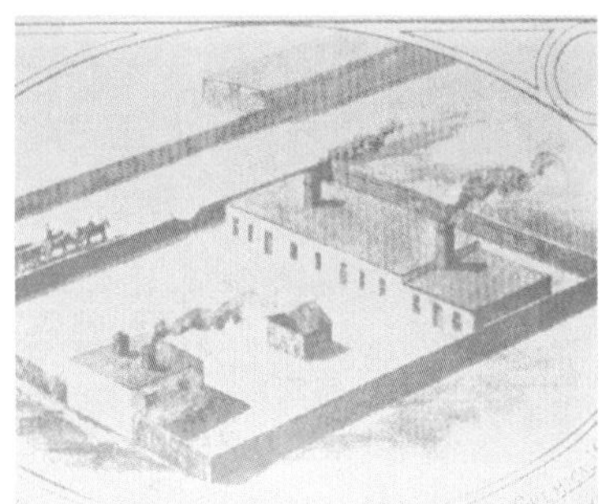

spirits of nitrous ether, chloroform, and acetic and carbolic acids. The meticulous attention to quality for which Mallinckrodt became known then remains today as the guiding principle for this global company based in St. Louis.

One of the proudest chapters in Mallinckrodt's history occurred during the early years of the atomic age. In 1942 the company was presented with a staggering technical challenge: to develop large quantities of uranium compounds on a purity level rarely achieved and to do so in a remarkably short period of time. Mallinckrodt's success led to the production of the first atomic bomb and, ultimately, to the end of World War II. The company remained a leading provider of nuclear feed materials for a quarter century.

Diversified Products

Throughout its 128-year history, Mallinckrodt has grown and expanded while remaining faithful to its original charter—supplying quality chemicals to the health care industry.

Mallinckrodt Chemical, headquartered in the St. Louis area, is a producer of high-quality specialty chemicals, including pharmaceuticals, catalysts, and laboratory and performance chemicals. About half of the company's business is related to pharmaceutical chemicals, and Mallinckrodt Chemical is the world's leading and lowest-cost producer of acetaminophen, the analgesic used in many over-the-counter pain relievers. The company also is a joint venture partner in Tastemaker, a worldwide flavors business.

Mallinckrodt Medical, also headquartered in St. Louis, provides technologically advanced products and services to five medical specialty areas: radiology, cardiology, nuclear medicine, anesthesiology, and critical care. Its primary mission is to improve the practice of medicine for physicians

and other health care professionals in those fields. Imaging agents, such as Optiray,® Albunex,® and OctreoScan,® help physicians diagnose and treat diseases and other abnormalities. The company also provides a variety of medical devices and monitoring systems to assist medical professionals during surgery and in intensive care.

Mallinckrodt Veterinary is one of the world's largest animal health and nutrition companies, providing some 1,000 brand products in more than 100 countries. Formerly

Clockwise from top right: A small stone building, an acid house, and a makeshift wooden shed comprised the original G. Mallinckrodt & Company plant, as it appeared in 1868.

Mallinckrodt Chemical is a leading worldwide supplier of catalysts, which are used in about 75 percent of all chemical processes to improve efficiency.

Hospitals around the world use Mallinckrodt's Optiray,® a nonionic X-ray contrast medium.

known as Pitman-Moore, the company joined the Mallinckrodt family in 1987 and is headquartered in Mundelein, Illinois.

A Leader in Many Areas

Ever protective of its workforce, Mallinckrodt Group implemented one of the industry's earliest industrial hygiene and safety programs. In fact, the company was a pioneer in the field of employee benefits, offering sick benefits and time off with pay as long ago as 1883. Employee development and reward remains an important value for the company's 10,000 employees.

A strong supporter of community and environmental causes, the company funds the Community Partnership Program, which allows Mallinckrodt Group's various sites to cultivate public trust and strengthen relationships with its neighbors. One such effort in St. Louis is the Earthtime Scholars program, which assists sixth, seventh, and eighth graders in working on environmental projects. In the older urban neighborhood surrounding the company's north St. Louis plant, Mallinckrodt Group is helping needy people with basics like food and shelter, as well as crime and drug-use prevention.

The company's philanthropic contributions to Washington University in St. Louis have been considerable. The university houses the Mallinckrodt Department of Pediatrics, the Mallinckrodt Department of Pharmacology, the world-renowned Mallinckrodt Institute of Radiology, and the Mallinckrodt Center for the Performing Arts. Washington University's chancellor, Dr. William Danforth, remarked on the occasion of the company's 125th anniversary, "The university would not be what it is today without the generosity of the Mallinckrodt family."

Two prominent St. Louis residents have played significant roles in Mallinckrodt Group's phenomenal growth. Harold E. Thayer, project manager for the early uranium work, followed Edward Mallinckrodt, Jr., as chairman in 1965. Raymond F. Bentele, who succeeded Thayer in 1981, continues as a member of the board of directors.

Mallinckrodt's past successes have prepared the company for its future. "We are steadfastly committed to the values that are important to us," says C. Ray Holman, chairman, president, and chief executive officer of Mallinckrodt Group. "We aim to be a leader in the markets we serve; to provide growth and development opportunities for our employees; to fulfill our social responsibilities; and to build long-term, extraordinary value for our shareholders."

From left:
C. Ray Holman is Mallinckrodt Group's chairman, president, and CEO.

Former Chairman Raymond F. Bentele serves on the company's board of directors.

Harold E. Thayer is a former chairman of Mallinckrodt.

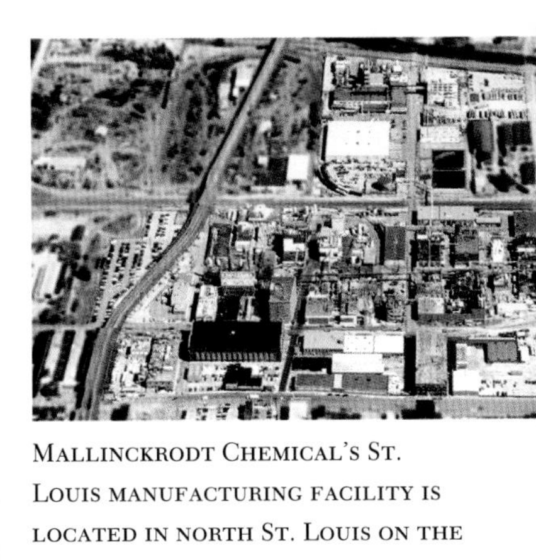

Mallinckrodt Chemical's St. Louis manufacturing facility is located in north St. Louis on the original site where the company was established (above).

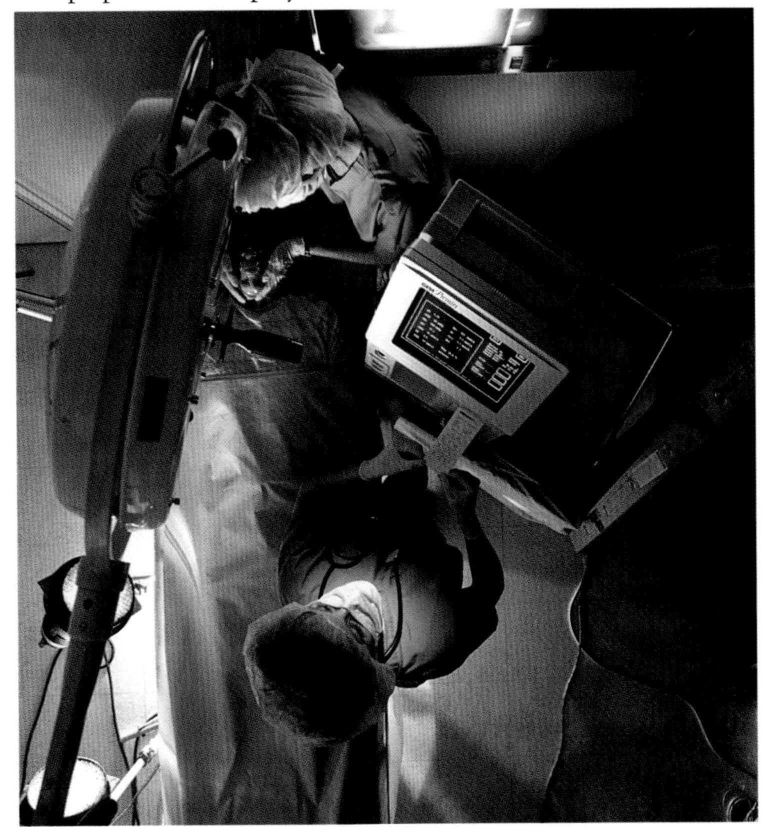

Mallinckrodt Medical's GEM Premier (left) allows hospitals to perform bedside analysis of blood gases and electrolytes in minutes.

Southwestern Bell Telephone Company

SINCE 1878, WHEN GEORGE DURANT'S TELEPHONIC EXCHANGE OPENED in St. Louis with 12 subscribers, Southwestern Bell Telephone has called the city its home. Today, as a wholly owned subsidiary of SBC Communications, Inc., Southwestern Bell offers its 10 million customers in five states a wide range of telecommunications products, backed by a high level of customer service.

Today's Southwestern Bell

When it comes to serving customers, Southwestern Bell Telephone does it in a big way: Every business day in St. Louis and its surrounding communities, Southwestern Bell Telephone handles some 16.6 million calls from area customers; its operators handle approximately 50,000 calls; and directory assistance responds to about 150,000 requests for information.

But Southwestern Bell's legacy of service goes beyond the big numbers: "We believe it's the little things we do each day that make the difference to customers," says Lea Ann Champion, vice president/general manager for Southwestern Bell in St. Louis. "That's why we're striving to give customers the services they want, when they want them. We're also making it easier for customers to do business with us."

For example, the company has recently extended weekday office hours in its residential service centers. In addition, new Saturday office hours allow customers more time to place new orders or make changes in service. Repair bureau operations are open 24 hours a day, 365 days a year.

THE COMPANY CONTINUES TO UPGRADE ITS NETWORK SO THAT ITS 10 MILLION CUSTOMERS RECEIVE THE TELECOMMUNICATIONS SERVICES THEY NEED TODAY AND IN THE FUTURE.

Both businesses and consumers are embracing new services provided by Southwestern Bell—including money-saving packages that appeal to the budget conscious. Calling plans have been especially popular with customers wanting to reduce expenses for nearby long-distance calls.

In addition, Calling Name/Caller ID is one specific service that has gained quick acceptance from St. Louis-area residents because it provides customers the sense of security that comes with knowing who's calling before they pick up their phone.

Southwestern Bell looks forward to the coming year thanks to the recent introduction of Integrated Services Digital Network (ISDN) to the St. Louis area. ISDN—which allows voice, video, and high-speed data to be transmitted simultaneously through a single phone line—benefits consumers and businesses alike. For example, ISDN makes it easy for telecommuters to tie into the office computer, for retail stores to check credit authorization, and for doctors to make video consultations or relay X-rays.

A Heritage of Service

Whether on the job or in their neighborhoods, the people of Southwestern Bell want to give something back to their communities. The Telephone Pioneers of America—a volunteer organization of current and retired phone company employees—provide charitable services. Nationwide, in 1993, Telephone Pioneers contributed more than 34 million hours of service to their communities—360,000 hours were worked in eastern Missouri alone. The more than 11,000 St. Louis-area members have taken on such projects as flood relief, reading and literacy programs, assisting at homeless shelters, and drug abuse prevention.

As these community activities and Southwestern Bell's spirit of service show, time and change have not altered the company's commitment to its customers.

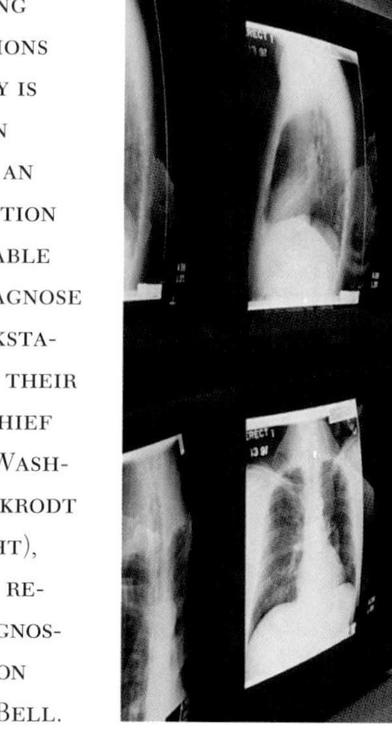
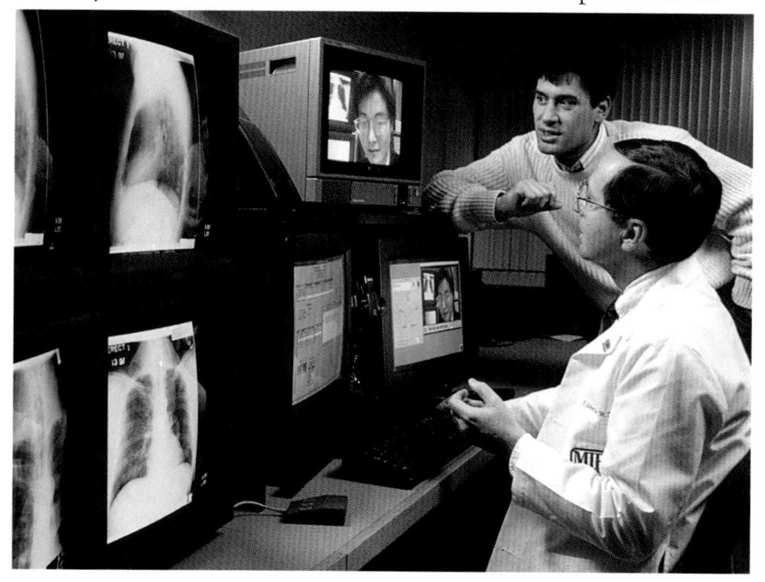

SOUTHWESTERN BELL IS HELPING BRING ADVANCED COMMUNICATIONS TO HEALTH CARE. THE COMPANY IS PART OF PROJECT SPECTRUM, AN ALLIANCE THAT IS DEVELOPING AN INTEGRATED MEDICAL INFORMATION SYSTEM. THE PROJECT WILL ENABLE NEARLY 5,400 PHYSICIANS TO DIAGNOSE PATIENTS FROM HOSPITAL WORKSTATIONS, THEIR OFFICES, OR EVEN THEIR HOMES. DR. R. GILBERT JOST, CHIEF OF DIAGNOSTIC RADIOLOGY AT WASHINGTON UNIVERSITY'S MALLINCKRODT INSTITUTE OF RADIOLOGY (RIGHT), AND MENELAOS KARAMICHALIS, RESEARCH ASSISTANT, EXAMINE DIAGNOSTIC IMAGES WITH TINA SIGARTO (ON SCREEN) FROM SOUTHWESTERN BELL.

Granite City Steel
Division of National Steel Corporation

When brothers Frederick G. and William F. Niedringhaus formed a tin shop in the 1850s, they could never have predicted the impact their business would have on the day-to-day lives of millions of Americans. In their pursuit of the American dream, they founded the community of Granite City, Illinois, developed new industries, and made the St. Louis area into one of the nation's largest steel producers. Their company is known today as the Granite City Steel Division of National Steel Corporation.

The Niedringhaus brothers, immigrants to St. Louis from northern Germany, began their careers in 1857 selling utensils made from handcut tinware. As the years passed, the brothers adapted to the new technologies available to produce their wares. By 1874 the business, known as the St. Louis Stamping Company, used ground granite as the basic material in the enamel of its products. The company developed and patented the process of making "graniteware," thus starting a major new industry.

A City Is Born

Shortly thereafter, the growing demand for sheet iron—the base material used to mold and enamel thin sheets of iron into various products—necessitated expansion. The farming community of Kinderhook, Illinois, proved to be an ideal location for a new plant. The Niedringhaus brothers purchased 3,000 acres of land in the early 1890s and hired the St. Louis city engineer to develop a new, industrial city and work production sites. The brothers named the site Granite City to commemorate the graniteware that was the basis of their business. Today, the 1,540-acre complex employs approximately 3,500 people and is still the largest employer in Granite City.

The brothers reached the peak of their careers in the early 1900s after their three plants—the St. Louis Stamping Company, the Granite Iron Rolling Mills, and the Granite City Steel Works—consolidated to form the National Enameling and Stamping Company. Eventually, the divisions separated into independent corporations. In 1927 the steel plant became a separate entity known as Granite City Steel. The company became a division of National Steel Corporation in 1971. And National Steel, in turn, became associated with the Nippon Kokan Corporation of Japan in 1984.

Today's Granite City Steel, led by General Manager Kenneth J. Leonard, has a $1 billion-plus annual net effect on the metro St. Louis economy. It is a leading supplier of high-quality, low-cost, flat-rolled carbon sheet steel products used for tubing, pipe, automotive, appliance, and construction applications. The division also produces galvanized steel roofing and siding under the names Strongbarn, Strongbarn II, Strongpanel, and Strongtrim.

At the 1,540-acre Granite City Steel complex, a slab emerges from the caster's final containment roll segment (above left).

Moving in from each side of the slab, twin torches, fueled by oxygen aided by natural gas, require less than 3.5 minutes to slice through an 80.4-inch wide, 8.7-inch thick slab (above right).

The Latest Technology

State-of-the-art technology is used throughout the mill, including a computerized distributed control system at the blast furnaces to automate firing and changing of stoves, and to improve efficiency of gas utilization. Continuous casting in all steel production, as well as the use of ladle metallurgy, ensures that products meet the exacting specifications of today's industries.

The Niedringhaus brothers' devotion to high-quality products, service, and cost-effectiveness was a hallmark of their business. That it remains a priority at Granite City Steel today ensures the ongoing fulfillment of the American dream the brothers started so many years ago.

AT&T

May 1, 1878, was a special day for St. Louis and the history of telephony. The date marked the opening of the state's first commercial telephone exchange, only the seventh in the country. These early telephone companies operated under licenses from Bell Telephone Company, founded in 1877 as the predecessor of AT&T. American Telephone and Telegraph Co. was incorporated in the state of New York in 1885.

A second milestone in telephony took place on June 24, 1896, when long-distance service opened between New York and St. Louis. And while many developments shaped the nation and the world in succeeding years, it would be a half century before St. Louis would again step into the communications spotlight—but in a big way.

With area offices at Clayton and Woods Mill roads and in downtown St. Louis, Network Systems is providing the foundation needed for the advanced intelligent telecommunications services of the future.

The Wave of the Future

On June 17, 1946, St. Louis became the site of the first commercial mobile telephone service, forerunner of today's high-technology cellular service. Mobile service has become the fastest-growing segment of a dynamic industry, and its importance was highlighted in 1994 by AT&T's merger with McCaw Cellular Communications. The merger was the biggest in telecommunications history and positioned AT&T as the nation's largest provider of wireless services.

Today, AT&T is no longer known as American Telephone & Telegraph Co. but simply as AT&T Corp. It is a global communications and computer company with annual revenues of $75 billion and 300,000 employees—more than 50,000 of whom are based in foreign countries.

Best known as a long-distance company, AT&T is a diversified corporation with significant revenues from equipment sales, leasing, and financial services. With 2.3 million registered shareowners, AT&T is the most widely held stock in America.

St. Louis Facilities

Nearly 3,000 employees work in the St. Louis area, with about two-thirds of these in the west St. Louis County facilities. The Network Systems Group at Clayton and Woods Mill markets major systems and equipment to communications service providers, principally to SBC Communications Inc. This five-state regional center also provides customer support, engineering, and installation for the group's product lines, including switching, transmission, cable, wireless, and operations systems. The main Network Systems sales

office is at 701 Market Street downtown.

The Clayton-Woods Mill complex is also the site of the AT&T Consumer Products National Service Center where customer service associates field consumer inquiries seven days a week from all over the United States. For homes and small businesses, Consumer Products also sells and leases corded and cordless telephones, cellular phones, answering systems, telephone accessories, and VideoPhones. Five retail stores, AT&T Phone Centers, are located throughout the metro area.

Nearby, at 14528 South Outer 40 Drive, Network Systems customer response members process equipment orders for all of the regional Bell operating companies and a host of equipment distributors. At 400 South Woods Mill Road, employees from several AT&T units perform work related to distribution and repair operations. These functions include logistics planning and engineering, warehouse and repair shop engineering, software development for repair services, and test set repair.

Global Business Communications Systems (GBCS), located at adjacent 424 South Woods Mill, sells multimedia communications applications and systems to both national and major accounts in a five-state area and also markets them internationally. For emerging markets, GBCS offers products such as DEFINITY,® Intuity,™ Group Video, Desktop Video (Vistium), TransTalk™ Wireless Systems, and Conversant Voice Response units.

From its strategic hub in Bridgeton, AT&T EasyLink Services technicians like Ben Aayach monitor a worldwide network of advanced messaging and electronic commerce services.

AT&T's Global Business Communications Systems offers advanced telecommunications products and services just right for any size business. Pictured at left is the new AT&T TransTalk™ Digital Wireless System demonstrated by Vanessa Garry, national accounts manager; Rich Cremona, general manager; and Tom Johnson, branch manager.

Also at 424 South Woods Mill, Business Communications Services markets AT&T Worldwide Intelligent Network services, providing competitive advantages through high-technology business solutions. AT&T's advanced network makes it possible to move and use information in new ways and to deliver it to conventional phones, computers, televisions, cellular handsets, and a new generation of wireless devices. Small- and medium-sized firms are served by the Commercial Markets group, which offers a wide range of inbound and outbound long-distance services.

The sales team for AT&T Global Information Solutions (GIS), formerly NCR, operates from west St. Louis County offices at 9811 South Forty Drive. AT&T GIS offers systems ranging from portable computers to massive parallel processors capable of handling very large databases. GIS also provides complete systems development and support.

AT&T EasyLink Services provides world-class advanced messaging and electronic commerce services to the business marketplace, including electronic mail, enhanced facsimile, electronic data interchange, and Telex. The Bridgeton facility, staffed by 250 employees, is a strategic, global hub for EasyLink worldwide offerings. This location serves as home for the Western Region sales team, all customer service and technical support operations, and the Global Network Operations Center.

A distinctive feature of the midcity St. Louis skyline is the AT&T tower atop the Toll Building at 2651 Olive. Some 600 employees from several AT&T units are involved here in maintaining and servicing the long-distance network. The Advanced Features Service Center, for instance, supports leading-edge features of AT&T 800 Service for business customers nationwide. With its powerful 4ESS™ electronic switch, the Toll Building serves as a major hub for the routing of telephone traffic throughout the United States.

AT&T employees—in St. Louis and around the world—are dedicated to being the world's best at bringing people together. To that end, AT&T provides its customers with easy access to each other and to the information services they want and need—anytime, anywhere.

More than 4 million calls come into AT&T's Consumer Products National Service Center every year and are handled by customer service associates like Bill Holt and Gail Pikey.

A.G. Edwards, Inc.

ONE OF THE COUNTRY'S MOST SUCCESSFUL RETAIL BROKERage firms was conceived and cultivated right here in St. Louis. With headquarters at Jefferson and Market on the western edge of downtown, A.G. Edwards, Inc., founded in 1887, is enjoying its 108th year of business. Far away from Wall Street, A.G. Edwards has built a reputation for excellence in the financial industry. A.G. Edwards' areas of expertise include securities and commodities brokerage; investment banking; and trust, asset management, and insurance services. Currently, nearly 2 million investors do business with A.G. Edwards, a testament to the firm's customer-friendly approach.

Putting the Client First

CEO Ben Edwards III has helped shape this friendly, yet productive work environment since he took the helm almost 30 years ago. Edwards' emphasis on listening to and serving the client is his mantra. "We should act as the client's agent, putting their interests before our own," he says. Edwards meets and greets clients at regular branch open houses and encourages open communication from employees. His practice of visiting branch offices is legendary—in 1994 he visited nearly 100 branches. For eight of the past 12 years, he has been named by the *Wall Street Transcript* as one of the top three CEOs in the securities industry.

The fourth-generation president believes that independence from the Wall Street scene is what helps the firm maintain its perspective. "We are not as likely to be influenced by the 'herd mentality' of Wall Street," says Edwards. One such example is A.G. Edwards' long-standing resistance to selling self-managed, in-house mutual funds and other investment products. The company avoids this practice so that its brokers can feel completely free from pressure to sell any products other than those they feel are in the best interest of their clients. With a sincere focus on the client and a conservative approach to the business, the firm has developed a unique formula for success.

BARBARA MARTIN

CLOCKWISE FROM TOP RIGHT: BENJAMIN F. EDWARDS III, GREAT-GRANDSON OF THE FIRM'S FOUNDER, IS CHAIRMAN AND CEO OF A.G. EDWARDS, INC.

THE FIRM IS HEADQUARTERED AT THE CORNER OF JEFFERSON AND MARKET STREETS ON THE WESTERN EDGE OF DOWNTOWN ST. LOUIS.

FOUNDED IN 1887 BY GENERAL ALBERT GALLATIN EDWARDS, A.G. EDWARDS, INC. IS CURRENTLY ONE OF THE LARGEST BROKERAGE FIRMS IN THE COUNTRY.

A Family Business

Since its inception in 1887, A.G. Edwards has been continuously managed in succession by five family members. Founder General Albert Gallatin Edwards served the Union during the Civil War, and was later appointed by President Abraham Lincoln to the post of assistant secretary of the Sub-Treasury Bank in St. Louis.

After retiring from this assignment, General Edwards opened a brokerage company with his son, Benjamin Franklin Edwards. Another son, George Lane Edwards, joined the partnership in 1890, and in 1898 they bought their first seat on the New York Stock Exchange.

George Edwards took over the reins at the company in 1891, and he became the first president of the St. Louis Stock Exchange. This legacy of leadership continued with another brother, Albert Ninian Edwards, who took command of the business in 1919.

With the record sale of liberty bonds during World War II, a new investor base had emerged. The company pursued the "individual" investor, carving a niche that would later expand to include smaller communities throughout the Midwest. Today, A.G. Edwards has more than 500 branch offices nationwide, with roughly 25 percent of the workforce concentrated at its headquarters here in St. Louis.

▶ RENE GREGG

ONE OF THE COMPANY'S MOST ACTIVE AREAS IS THE BOND DEPARTMENT, WHERE OCTAGONAL "TRADING PITS" AND AN OPEN SETTING ENABLE BOND TRADERS TO COMMUNICATE EASILY DURING THE PURCHASE AND SALE OF SECURITIES.

Measures of Success

The century-old firm is regularly and generously praised by others in the financial industry. In December 1993, *Smart Money* magazine published an analysis of the top seven U.S. brokerage firms for the individual investor. A.G. Edwards ranked number one overall, scoring highest in the areas of client satisfaction, reasonable fees, broker training and support, and freedom from pressure. And although Edwards' conservative approach to the brokerage business might be considered boring by some, it's a label the midwestern giant views as a compliment. If boring means stable, trustworthy, and a steady producer, then A.G. Edwards has rightfully earned the designation.

The firm believes strongly in enjoying its business and has incorporated these thoughts into its operating philosophy: "To enjoy what we are doing, we must like those with whom we work. In order to do this, we must respect each other and work together in mutual trust. We should try to do our jobs better each week and to have fun doing them."

This weaving of ambition, trust, and optimism characterizes the corporate culture at A.G. Edwards. Brokers are treated as team players rather than superstars, and they seem to like it that way. In 1993 A.G. Edwards was the only retail brokerage firm featured in the best-selling book *The 100 Best Companies to Work for in America*. Open communication with employees is encouraged. Monthly sessions with Chairman and CEO Ben Edwards via the firm's internal voice communications network is a ritual throughout the firm's branches.

Over the years, the firm has witnessed the commercial and industrial development of America, the birth of the Federal Reserve System, the Great Depression, World Wars I and II, and the globalization of financial markets. Yet, through all of its 108-year history, A.G. Edwards & Sons has maintained its uniquely midwestern character.

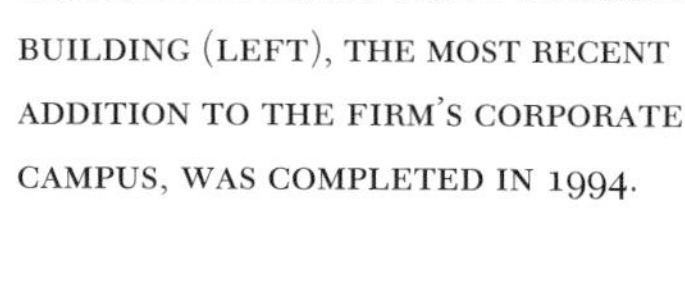

THE A.G. EDWARDS TRUST COMPANY BUILDING (LEFT), THE MOST RECENT ADDITION TO THE FIRM'S CORPORATE CAMPUS, WAS COMPLETED IN 1994.

Heartland Bank

HEARTLAND BANK HAS THE HONOR OF BEING ONE OF THE oldest financial institutions providing continuous service to its customers in the state of Missouri. The pragmatism and determination of its leadership have allowed Heartland to prevail during many economic downturns throughout its 108 years of business. Headquartered in downtown St. Louis, Heartland reflects a mixture of tradition and innovation—characteristics that distinguish it from its competition. In 1887, 13 area community and business leaders founded the financial institution that would one day become known as Heartland. With initial funding of $600,000, the bank was known as Economy Building and Loan Association. Economy's mission was to "accumulate a fund . . . to make loans for the purpose of enabling individuals to erect or purchase existing homes." The association gradually evolved into its present identity as Heartland Bank. Today, Heartland offers a full line of products and services to some 17,000 customers.

THE BANK'S LEADERSHIP INCLUDES (FROM LEFT) JOHN J. WUEST, PRESIDENT AND CEO; ANDREW S. LOVE, SECRETARY AND CHAIRMAN OF THE FINANCE COMMITTEE; AND LAURENCE A. SCHIFFER, CHAIRMAN OF THE BOARD.

Attention to the Depositor

From the beginning, this Missouri institution prospered because of its attention to the individual depositor. Evidence of the trust built with customers is found in one observer's comments: "Economy operated like a family group. Everyone knew everyone else, and they had accounts of the multiple generations of original account holders." Even during the Great Depression, when conditions were unstable for the association, no depositor suffered a loss. In 1934 Economy Building and Loan converted to a federal charter and changed its name to Economy Federal Savings and Loan Association.

During the post-World War II years, Economy was actively involved in the dynamic housing boom taking place. The association continued to grow during the 1960s and 1970s, opening new locations in the Missouri communities of St. Clair, Pacific, and Park Hills. Although assets had reached $125 million by this time, the hyperinflation of the 1970s and early 1980s caused the association to suffer. By 1985 a major infusion of capital was necessary.

A group of new investors, which included John and James McDonnell, Andrew S. Love, and Laurence A. Schiffer, formed the Love Savings Holding Company. They converted Economy to a stock company, with Love Savings owning 100 percent of the shares. The new leaders embarked on an aggressive plan to expand Economy's retail banking services.

One such expansion included a merger with Gravois Home Savings and Loan in 1987. Economy's special emphasis on single-family mortgage and commercial real estate loans helped build assets to an all-time high of $205 million. Also in 1987, newly hired President and CEO John J. Wuest oversaw Economy's name change to Heartland Savings Bank. At this time, senior management was restructured, and several new locations were opened. In January 1995 the bank's official name was changed to Heartland Bank.

Heartland currently operates 11 locations, with assets of $240 million and capital of $22 million. Structured as a full-service community bank, its owners, managers, and employees are committed to providing personalized quality service to their customers. With more than a century of expertise behind them, the people at Heartland Bank are well prepared for a successful future.

HEARTLAND'S NEWEST BRANCH IS LOCATED AT 1920 RICHARDSON ROAD IN ARNOLD, MISSOURI.

Bethesda General Hospital and Homes

FOLKS AT BETHESDA GENERAL HOSPITAL AND HOMES LIKE TO THINK of themselves as a 105-year-old family. The term "family" is an important one to Bethesda's staff—the company's full-service general hospital and numerous senior residential facilities were founded on a philosophy of caring. The name "Bethesda" even reflects this ideal. The term symbolizes healing and compassion in the Bible. ■ Since its founding, Bethesda has grown a great deal without sacrificing its original philosophy. Though the organization is today nondenominational, Bethesda was founded on Christian ideals, and residents, patients, and employees alike enjoy a legacy of lifelong caring and respect for the individual.

Current President John Norwood has been involved with the company's development since the 1960s. He is often reminded of the organization's rich history as he visits with Bethesda's elderly residents. What operated for years as a small hospital and home in midtown St. Louis is now a dynamic corporation with six campuses, serving thousands of people every day.

Bethesda General Hospital

Founders Elizabeth Hayne and Dr. Edward Saunders created the original Bethesda General Hospital as "a work of faith and a labor of love" in 1889. They saw a compelling need to care for the sick, the unfortunate, and the elderly in St. Louis. Hayne, Saunders, and countless volunteers gave their time and talents to the cause.

The hospital, located on Vista Avenue, is the true heart of the Bethesda organization, and it radiates the Bethesda philosophy to each patient and throughout the community. The 122-bed facility offers a full range of acute, diagnostic, and emergency care. It houses the Greater Midwest Epilepsy Treatment Center, PremierCare Neurorehabilitation Program, the Geropsychiatric Unit, and the Skilled Nursing Unit. Bethesda General also enjoys a cooperative relationship with its next-door neighbor, the St. Louis University Medical Center.

Focus on Retirement Living

Bethesda's evolution, however, has reflected its growing concern for the aging population. Blessed with longer life expectancies than ever before, members of the older generation are looking for support and security, while their children are often coping with busier, more stressful lifestyles. Rather than dwelling on the difficulties of a changing society, Bethesda is responding with progressive solutions to new challenges and patient needs.

CLOCKWISE FROM BOTTOM:
BUILT IN 1991, BETHESDA GARDENS OFFERS 92 TWO-BEDROOM, ONE-BEDROOM, AND STUDIO APARTMENTS WITH COMPLETE KITCHENS.

SHIRLEY CARUSO, R.N., IS ONE OF THE FRIENDLY FACES WAITING TO GREET RESIDENTS AND MAKE THEM FEEL AT HOME AT BETHESDA.

AT BETHESDA'S NURSING HOMES, THERE IS AN OVERRIDING RESPECT FOR THE DIGNITY OF RESIDENTS, REGARDLESS OF THEIR CONDITION.

Clockwise from right:
Bethesda West is a 210-bed, long-term care facility offering compassionate nursing suited to a variety of needs, including a unit for the care of Alzheimer's disease patients.

Conveniently situated in downtown St. Louis, Bethesda Town House was one of the city's first retirement communities.

Founded in 1889, Bethesda General Hospital offers a full range of acute, diagnostic, and emergency services, including neurorehabilitation, geropsychiatric care, and treatment of epilepsy.

The company's newest facility, known as Bethesda West, was built in 1990 to serve the rapidly expanding area of western St. Louis County. Located at 322 Old State Road in Ellisville, the 210-bed residence offers compassionate nursing care in a spacious and elegant setting. A special unit within Bethesda West serves the unique needs of Alzheimer's patients. With this resource, families of Alzheimer's patients are able to maintain a caring and productive relationship with their loved ones, despite the difficulties of coping with the disease.

Perhaps the largest and best known of all Bethesda properties is the Bethesda-Dilworth Memorial Home. Located in the greentree area of Kirkwood, the home is often referred to as "the finest in St. Louis." It all began in 1926, when Elizabeth Dilworth donated 26 acres of wooded property along Big Bend Boulevard. Since then the Bethesda-Dilworth site has grown into a state-of-the-art community for seniors.

While the original home housed 19 elderly women, the current complex serves almost 500 male and female residents requiring either assisted living or intermediate and skilled nursing. Homestyle meals are prepared onsite for residents, and the Bethesda-Dilworth kitchens also supply the local Meals on Wheels program with their nutritious fare.

Residents of the home participate in a special program that helps keep them young at heart. Since 1990, when the Bethesda Child Care Center was built on the property, seniors have enjoyed an exchange program with their young neighbors. Toddlers and preschoolers from the nearby center stop in for regular visits. On Tuesdays, for example, the three-year-olds work on craft projects with the seniors, while Thursdays are reserved for joint music sessions. Twice a month, toddlers bring their toys by to play among the home's residents. Holidays are always festive; preschool parades are not uncommon. And when the local humane society adds a few pets to the party, things really get lively. The interaction benefits young and old alike, as each generation shares time with the other. Some of the children "adopt" a

favorite senior friend and visit more often, along with their parents—just like an extended family.

Independent Solutions

A recent addition to the Kirkwood site is the Bethesda Oaks Retirement Homes. These single-story, condominium-style units are designed for seniors who prefer to live independently. Built in 1989, the full-service homes are the perfect solution for those looking to simplify their lives and enjoy a carefree retirement. Residents enjoy luxurious living without the worries of household maintenance or lawn care. They also have access to 24-hour emergency services. When seniors sign on with Bethesda Oaks, they are guaranteed a place in the Bethesda family for life. Long-term nursing care, if it becomes necessary, is available at Bethesda-Dilworth Memorial Home.

Administrator Fletcher Carter, who has been with Bethesda for 22 years, is convinced this is an ideal arrangement. "This type of living gives people the opportunity to do what they like to do, not just what they have to do," he explains. "We take care of the hassles, and they can enjoy themselves."

The success of Bethesda Oaks created a demand for more high-quality retirement living in the area. In response, the Bethesda Gardens apartments were built in 1991. Located in downtown Kirkwood, the 93-unit facility provides a family atmosphere for those who might otherwise be isolated in their retirement. Residents not only enjoy meals in a communal dining room, but also take advantage of regular group outings, shopping excursions, and other activities. A nurse is on duty 24 hours a day, and transportation is available, allowing residents to attend church and keep regular appointments. Bethesda Gardens offers residents the comfort and security of community living along with the privacy and independence of maintaining their own apartment.

For those who prefer city living, Bethesda Town House offers a gracious alternative. This fashionable high-rise building, nestled among the Plaza Square Apartments in downtown St. Louis, was one of the city's first retirement communities. Some 120 residents enjoy the cultural attractions and shopping that only downtown has to offer. With St. Louis' renowned Union Station just across the street and the Fox Theatre, Powell Hall, and Sheldon Concert Hall just blocks from home, it's easy to enjoy the good life at Bethesda Town House. And with around-the-clock security and support services, residents also feel safe.

Bethesda Town House uses a practical method of financial self-support—an endowment fund provided by the residents themselves. It is the only institution of its kind in St. Louis to offer lifelong care, regardless of changes in a resident's health or financial situation. These features make Bethesda Town House an excellent choice for an active retirement.

For more than 100 years, Bethesda General Hospital and Homes has been like an extended family to the community. It is no wonder that St. Louisans have been so generous to this institution. All Bethesda facilities have developed through private donations, a tribute to the quality of care they provide. Even in today's climate of change, Bethesda continues to lead the way in the health care industry. Its quiet, caring presence promises a better future for thousands of St. Louisans every day.

RETIREMENT LIVING AT BETHESDA SIMPLIFIES LIFE. RESIDENTS ARE FREE FROM DAILY CHORES, GIVING THEM THE PLEASURE OF INDEPENDENT, CAREFREE LIVING (LEFT).

BETHESDA DILWORTH (BELOW), LOCATED ON A BEAUTIFUL 18-ACRE CAMPUS, OFFERS RESIDENTIAL, INTERMEDIATE, AND SKILLED NURSING CARE TO ITS 465 RESIDENTS. BETHESDA OAKS RETIREMENT HOMES AND BETHESDA CHILD CARE CENTER ARE ALSO LOCATED ON THE SITE.

Alumax Foils, Inc.

JUST ABOVE THE BANKS OF THE MISSISSIPPI RIVER, THE INDUS-trial southern edge of St. Louis has been anchored for over 100 years by the nation's oldest manufacturer of aluminum foil, Alumax Foils, Inc. The sprawling mill on South Broadway produces light-gauge foil for a wide range of commercial applications. ■ Raw aluminum ingots, weighing 2,000 pounds each, arrive at the site to be melted, rolled, and precision finished into aluminum foil. Alumax sells its products to other companies, which in turn process the foil into flexible packaging used primarily in the food, beverage, and pharmaceutical industries.

A Longtime St. Louis Commitment

With 325 employees and over a century of history, Alumax Foils serves as one of Missouri's largest and most stable manufacturing employers. More than $55 million has been invested in capital at the St. Louis plant, including new technology for years to come.

ALUMAX PRODUCTS ARE OFTEN CONVERTED INTO FLEXIBLE PACKAGING USED IN THE FOOD AND BEVERAGE INDUSTRIES (RIGHT AND OPPOSITE).

RAW ALUMINUM INGOTS, WEIGHING 2,000 POUNDS EACH, ARRIVE AT THE ALUMAX SITE IN ST. LOUIS TO BE MELTED, ROLLED, AND PRECISION FINISHED INTO ALUMINUM FOIL (BELOW).

The company traces its founding to the Tin Foil and Metal Company, which was incorporated in 1889 by millwright James Johnston. The business prospered in the late 19th century, providing packaging for the St. Louis tobacco market. Today the operation is a major subsidiary of Alumax Inc., the nation's third-largest integrated aluminum company, headquartered in Norcross, Georgia.

Thomas J. Cleary, president and a 23-year Alumax Foils veteran, explains that the company's major customer base consists of "converters"—other manufacturers who take large rolls of foil and combine them on printing presses with film and paper. The finished products can be found on any supermarket aisle or fast-food condiment counter. Packets of ketchup, pouches containing seasonings, brick-pack coffee, packets of noodles and pasta, and the pull-off aluminum caps on yogurt cups or juices could contain foils produced in St. Louis. There also are multiple uses in the pharmaceutical field because of aluminum foil's flexible characteristics and its ability to hermetically seal tablet and liquid medications.

Alumax Foils has been a major supplier to the food service industry for over 20 years. Restaurants, schools, hotels, and institutions across the United States and abroad use Alumax food service foil with its unique Safety Cutter Edge. The company has consistently grown its customer base with long-term partnerships and superior service.

A separate Alumax production line produces tin and lead composition foils. Lead foil's unique characteristics continue to make it vital for some applications, such as ribbon solder and in battery and electronic components. The lead foil produced by Alumax Foils can be found in disposable dental X-ray packets.

Quality Manufacturing

The basic manufacturing process for aluminum foil begins by transferring the ingots to gas-fired furnaces that reach 1,900 degrees Fahrenheit. The aluminum is melted and transferred to a holding furnace. Next, the molten aluminum is filtered and then passes through continuous casters, where it is transformed into a quarter-inch-thick sheet that is then coiled into 20,000-pound rolls. Alumax Foils was among the first in its industry to introduce the continuous casting method of foil production, which greatly improves finished product quality.

The coils are next fed through various rolling mills that reduce the sheet thickness by approximately 50 percent per operation

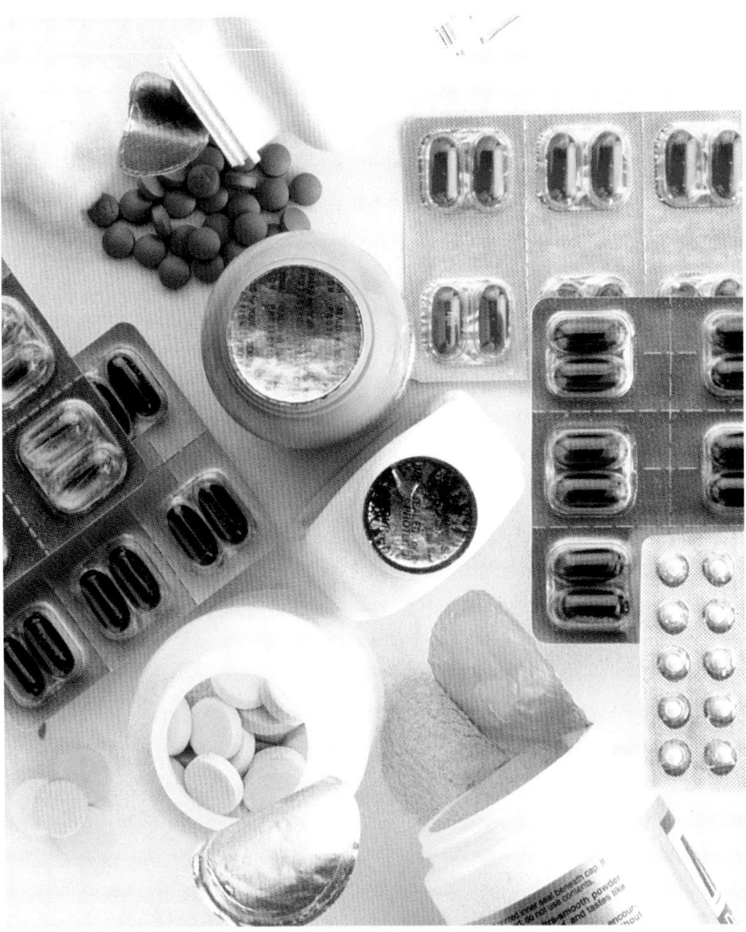

The company's products have multiple uses in the pharmaceutical field because of aluminum foil's flexible characteristics and its ability to hermetically seal tablet and liquid medications.

until it reaches the final gauge/thickness that matches the customer's specifications. One of Alumax's commercial foil products is the thinnest produced in America—just six microns thin, or eight and one-half times thinner than a human hair. The ability to produce a continuous roll of this super-thin material is a major technological achievement. Six-micron foil is found in products such as sandwich wrap used at fast-food restaurants and in beer bottle labels. The consistency of the thickness of Alumax's foils is achieved by what the industry calls automatic gauge controls. Although the standard industry tolerance is plus or minus 10 percent, the company achieves a range of better than plus or minus 5 percent, providing Alumax with a technological advantage.

The company's emphasis on quality has earned many awards from its customers. Eastman Kodak, for example, awarded Alumax Foils its coveted "Quality First Gold Award" for 100 percent on-time deliveries with no rejects. Also, Alumax Foils was named "Supplier of the Year" for two consecutive years by James River Flexible Packaging. According to Cleary, these awards are the kind of positive customer feedback that provides an important measure of quality. "Our customers tell us we're able to perform at a consistently superior level in terms of service, quality, and delivery," he says.

Alumax Foils has expanded its markets in recent years from the contiguous 48 states to Canada and Mexico, and is exploring new markets in Asia and Eastern Europe. Plans are currently being finalized for a multimillion-dollar expansion to meet these market opportunities. "I am optimistic about the future of the aluminum industry and of Alumax Foils," Cleary says. "Through continued innovation, expansion, and an emphasis on quality, Alumax Foils will maintain and strengthen its leadership position throughout North America and in new markets." No doubt, the future looks bright for St. Louis, with Alumax Foils leading the way to another 100 years of prosperity and growth in the aluminum industry.

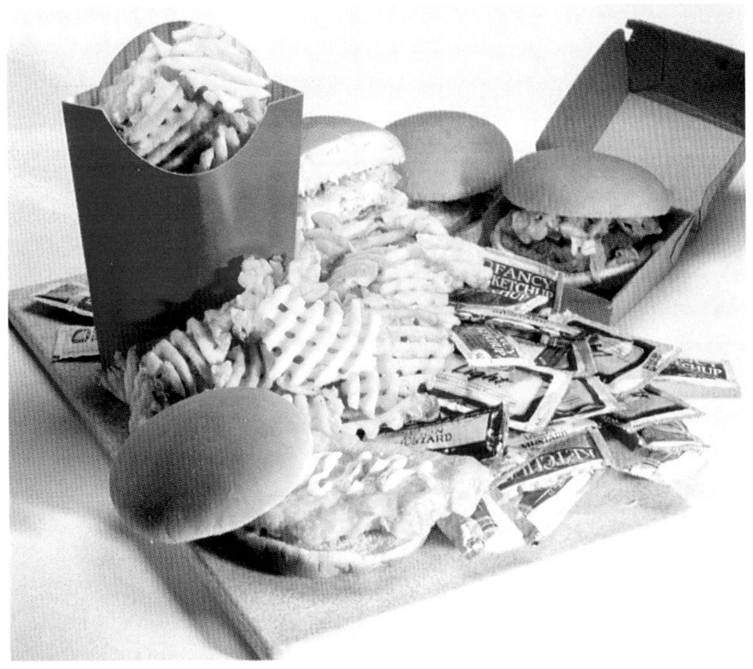

Emerson Electric Co.

FOUNDED IN ST. LOUIS IN 1890 AS AN EARLY PRODUCER OF ELECTRIC motors, Emerson Electric Co. today is known as one of America's best-managed corporations, distinguished by a record of financial consistency equaled by only a handful of other companies. ■ Manufacturing a broad range of electrical and electronic products and systems for industrial, commercial, and consumer markets, Emerson consists of 50 divisions with more than 70,000 employees, selling products in more than 150 countries through a network of 3,500 manufacturing, sales, and service locations.

Though the company is one of the world's leading manufacturers, products bearing its brand names are better known commercially than the company itself. In consumer markets, major products include Skil, Dremel, and Craftsman® power tools; White-Rodgers thermostats; and In-Sink-Erator waste disposers. In industrial markets, process control products designed and manufactured by Rosemount, Micro Motion, and Brooks are the clear global leaders, while Fisher Controls provides worldwide leadership in process control valves, systems, and regulators.

Emerson is also the world's largest producer of fractional and integral horsepower motors, manufactured under the Emerson, U.S. Electrical Motors, Leroy-Somer, CESET, and other brand names. In the heating, ventilating and air-conditioning, and appliance component markets, the company is a global leader with Copeland compressors, Fusite electric terminal assemblies, and Therm-O-Disc temperature control sensors and motor protectors. Additional examples of Emerson products synonymous with quality worldwide include ASCO solenoid valves, RIDGID professional plumbing tools, and Liebert uninterruptible power supplies.

A Century of Manufacturing

The circumstances of Emerson's founding more than a century ago were modest. The people of St. Louis in 1890, like most of America, were skeptical of electricity, which seemed a dangerous and unreliable energy source. But two Scottish-born brothers, Charles and Alexander Meston, who viewed electricity as a business opportunity, developed and patented a reliable alternating current motor and persuaded John Wesley Emerson, a former Union Army colonel, judge, and lawyer, to be the principal investor in their business.

As the company grew, it expanded its product line by attaching Emerson motors to newly developed products such as sewing machines, dental drills, player pianos, and hair dryers. In 1892 Emerson began selling the first electric fans in America—a product for which the company soon became renowned.

During World War II, as a supplier to the U.S. Air Force, Emerson became the world's largest manufacturer of aircraft gun turrets. In the postwar era, the company faced the dual challenges of rationalizing its highly seasonal fan product lines and responding to heightened competition from much larger electrical motor manufacturers.

Those issues were addressed head-on in 1954 when the company's new chief executive officer, W.R. "Buck" Persons, retooled and decentralized Emerson's manufacturing base and began an ongoing process of diversification. The company rapidly targeted high-growth markets and then made acquisitions to position Emerson favorably within those markets. Persons reaffirmed a long-standing company policy of component rather than end-product manufacturing, and also instituted a strong focus on cost

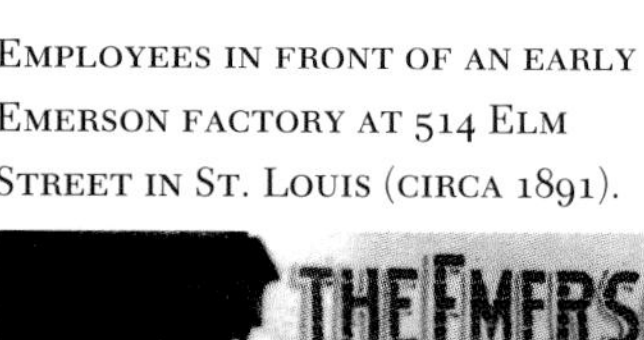

EMPLOYEES IN FRONT OF AN EARLY EMERSON FACTORY AT 514 ELM STREET IN ST. LOUIS (CIRCA 1891).

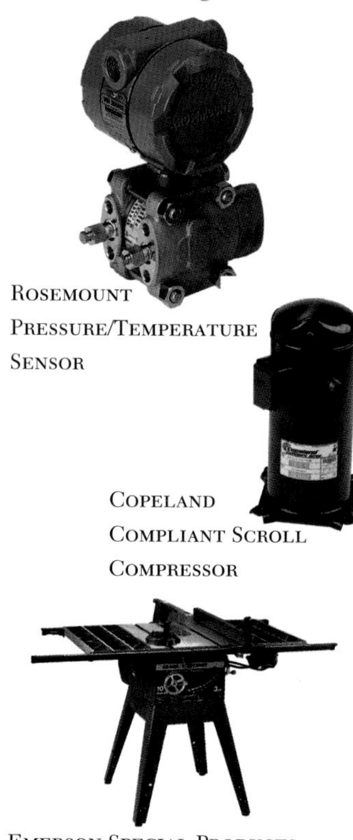

ROSEMOUNT PRESSURE/TEMPERATURE SENSOR

COPELAND COMPLIANT SCROLL COMPRESSOR

EMERSON SPECIAL PRODUCTS CRAFTSMAN® 10" TABLE SAW

reductions, quality improvements, and a formal planning process.

When Persons retired as CEO in 1973, Emerson had significantly expanded its operations from 4,000 employees in two plants in 1954, to 31,000 employees in 82 facilities. Product lines had grown from five basic products to hundreds, and in the process, Emerson had become a diversified corporation with nearly $1 billion in sales.

An automatic stator assembly line at Emerson's Paragould, Arkansas, appliance motor production facility.

Emerson Today

Under Charles F. Knight, who was named CEO in 1973, Emerson has become a global market leader in each of the businesses in which it competes. Annual sales now exceed $10 billion, including $2 billion in joint venture sales.

The company has continued to grow and prosper largely as a result of two central efforts: a strong focus on improving costs and adherence to a disciplined management process. Internal development of new products, attention to detail, and a strong system of control and follow-up have afforded the company remarkable stability amid periods of heightened international competition and worldwide economic instability. Emerson's record of consistency is evident in uninterrupted increases in earnings and dividends over the past four decades—a period that includes significant recessions in the mid-1970s, the early 1980s, and the early 1990s. This record is equaled by only four other publicly traded U.S. companies and no other American industrial manufacturing firm.

A major factor in Emerson's record performance has been its Best Cost Producer manufacturing strategy, formalized in the early 1980s. Under this program, long-standing commitments to lowering costs and increasing productivity were reemphasized, but with increased attention to ever-higher global competitive standards for quality.

Today, Emerson's technological commitment to research and development and its emphasis on new products continue to enhance the company's ability to meet customer needs and strengthen its market positions. More than 87 percent of Emerson's products hold the number one or number two position in U.S. end markets, and the company is leveraging this domestic strength to achieve similar market leadership worldwide. In implementing this strategy, international sales now represent 40 percent of total sales and constitute a key growth area for the company. Though its roots reach deep into St. Louis soil, Emerson is now a leader in serving its customers throughout the world.

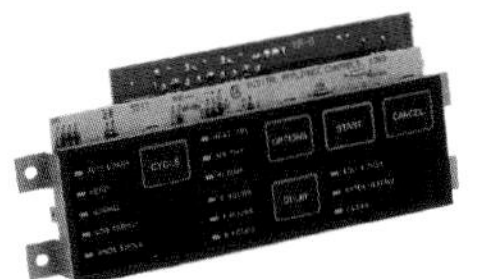

Digital Appliance Controls Electronic Washer Timer

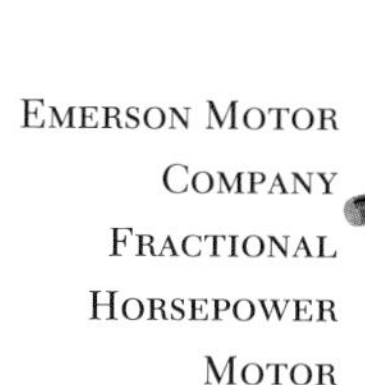
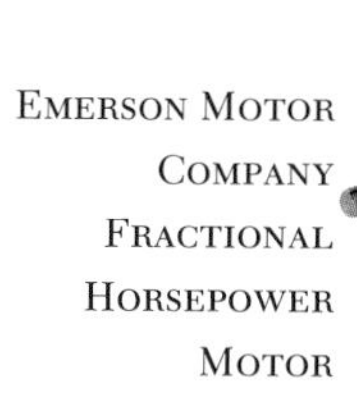

Emerson Motor Company Fractional Horsepower Motor

Branson Ultrasonic Welder

White-Rodgers Digital Thermostat

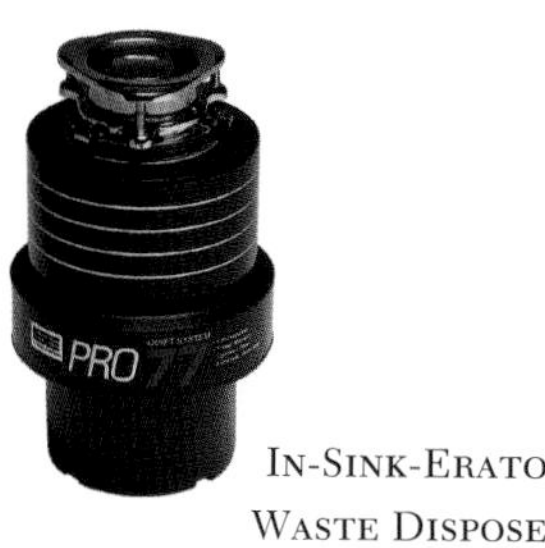

In-Sink-Erator Waste Disposer

Stifel, Nicolaus & Company, Incorporated

STIFEL, NICOLAUS & COMPANY, INCORPORATED, AN INVESTMENT banking and brokerage firm with Midwest roots, has reached far beyond the dreams of its founders. Established in St. Louis in 1890 as a general securities business, the company has grown to become one of the largest and most respected regional financial services firms in the nation, providing assistance to individuals, institutions, and businesses.

The Stifel, Nicolaus Family

Along with its impressive growth through the years, the firm always has maintained a sense of family. "Family" for Stifel, Nicolaus encompasses cherished longtime employees and welcomed new ones, including employees of companies acquired in the firm's ongoing expansion. But the most important members of the Stifel, Nicolaus family are the firm's customers.

Herman C. Stifel joined Stifel, Nicolaus in 1897 and helped lead the firm until his death in 1932. Stifel always affirmed the company's fundamental responsibility: safeguarding the money of others as if it is your own, a credo that remains the guiding principle of Stifel, Nicolaus today.

"We continue to strongly emphasize mutual trust and personal, individualized service in our customer relationships," says Gregory F. Taylor, president and CEO of Stifel, Nicolaus since 1992. "We do not consider this to be a sales organization. Our business is the creation and preservation of wealth. That is our mission—to create and preserve wealth, not to sell securities."

Complementing its general brokerage business, Stifel, Nicolaus began in the 1920s to assume a major role as an underwriter of public and private financings in St. Louis and, increasingly, in other locales. In 1929, for example, the firm arranged a $33 million refunding loan for Bolivia. Its reputation as an underwriter of municipal bonds grew substantially in the 1930s and even more dynamically during and after World War II. The company also became a pioneer in the underwriting of bridges and turnpikes. Underwritings for the Maine Turnpike, the Mackinac Bridge, and Chicago's O'Hare Airport were among the major transactions handled by Stifel, Nicolaus. Turnpikes financed by the firm were built in many states.

STIFEL FINANCIAL CORP., A HOLDING COMPANY OF WHICH STIFEL, NICOLAUS IS THE MAJOR SUBSIDIARY, HAS BEEN LISTED ON THE NEW YORK STOCK EXCHANGE SINCE 1986.

Acquisitions Fuel Growth

Throughout the company's history, the leaders of Stifel, Nicolaus have been growth-minded, expanding the firm through the acquisition of established companies. Among its major acquisitions have been Albert Theis & Sons, Inc. (1960),

"We continue to strongly emphasize mutual trust and personal, individualized service in our customer relationships," says Gregory F. Taylor (far left), president and CEO of Stifel, Nicolaus since 1992.

Chairman George H. Walker III (near left), who was president and CEO from 1978 to 1992, devotes most of his time to corporate finance and asset management.

Cruttenden, Podesta and Miller (1962), Milburn Cochran (1967), Dempsey-Tegeler & Co. (1970), Altofer, Podesta and Woolard (1981), Bacon Whipple (1982), Hendrick Urgo (1983), Scherck, Stein & Franc, Inc. (1985), Rowland, Simon & Co. (1988), and Todd Investment Advisors (1994).

Stifel Financial Corp., a holding company of which Stifel, Nicolaus is the major subsidiary, was formed in 1983 and became publicly held in that year. The holding company has been listed on the New York Stock Exchange since 1986.

Today's Stifel Financial Corp. is a fully integrated regional financial firm, which continues to emphasize retail investments. The retail side of the business accounts for over 80 percent of the company's annual sales of more than $80 million. Stifel has about 800 employees and operates 50 locations in 15 states, ranging from the Rocky Mountains to Ohio, from Canada to the Gulf Coast. The company's downtown St. Louis headquarters encompasses 80,000 square feet of office space on four floors.

Plans for Ongoing Growth

Taylor, who joined the Stifel, Nicolaus team in 1985 after working with brokerage firms in Chicago, Boston, and other cities, is in charge of the company's operations. Chairman George H. Walker III, who was president and CEO from 1978 to 1992, devotes most of his time to corporate finance and asset management. Stifel, Nicolaus continues to be very active in investment banking and underwriting, along with its retail brokerage services, and has become a specialist in financing for regional banks.

Taylor says the company has no plans to expand its geographic area of service, but most definitely intends to grow within its existing regional boundaries. "We have a huge geographic area to serve, and there is plenty of room for us to grow within that area. Our five-year plan calls for an increase in our number of brokers from the present number to 500, but we want to grow prudently."

Improvement within the company is regarded by Taylor as an ongoing responsibility. He points to staff additions within the past year in investment services, legal services, and compliance. The firm's public financing effort has been reorganized and strengthened, and a new research director promises to continue improvements.

This constant striving to make Stifel, Nicolaus a better company has helped create its outstanding reputation in the financial industry as one of the nation's strongest regional investment banking firms, with a sense of tradition and identity that separates it from the pack. The firm has shown dramatic growth in recent years and clearly has what it takes to go much farther.

Diagraph Corporation

EW MANUFACTURING COMPANIES CAN SAY THAT THEIR FIRST PRODuct is still in use by customers after 103 years. But with a dozen or so original Bradley stencil-cutting machines still in use, Diagraph Corporation can—even though the company probably would prefer to buy up the machines to display as historic items. As evidenced by the existence of these century-old cutting machines, Diagraph has a well-deserved reputation for stability. Originally founded to manufacture basic marking tools to identify cargo during shipment and upon arrival at the docks, Diagraph continues to produce and sell traditional marking and labeling products such as stenciling machines, markers, inks, and brushes. But the company has made its own mark on today's industry, manufacturing and marketing an array of sophisticated equipment that incorporates advanced programmable automation for scannable bar coding, as well as rapid ink-jet and laser label-printing systems.

Making Its Mark

Diagraph Corporation's presence in metropolitan St. Louis includes headquarters in the industrial suburb of Earth City; plants in Herrin and Energy, Illinois; and a plant in St. Peters, Missouri. Through this network, the company's 450 employees have helped establish Diagraph's reputation as the industry's leading supplier of industrial labeling systems and large-character, ink-jet coding.

Diagraph traces its history to an 1893 traffic jam on the St. Louis levee. While walking among heaps of cargo waiting to be hand addressed, inventor and entrepreneur Andrew Jackson Bradley knew there had to be a quicker way. The result of his efforts to speed the labeling process was the Long Bradley stencil-cutting machine, a piece of equipment that would revolutionize the process of marking.

Stephen Hartog, an employee of Bradley's, improved upon the concept by inventing a circular stencil-marking machine and offered his improvement to Bradley, who rejected it. Hartog left Bradley's employment and secured the backing of Theodore Remmers, owner of the largest machine shop west of the Mississippi. Remmers, who recognized the value of a great idea, invested in Hartog's circular design, stencil-cutting machinery and started the Diagraph Company. Remmers thus began a tradition of family involvement that continues today.

James R. Brigham, Jr., a direct descendant of Remmers, joined the company in 1989, following a successful career that included serving as New York Mayor Ed Koch's budget director. As president and CEO, his first directive at Diagraph was to add automated technologies to the company's product line. Diagraph's newer marking systems can be programmed by keyboard so they automatically print codes that include dates, time coding, and sequential numbering—information designed to be incorporated directly into a manufacturer's assembly line process.

Information contained in these codes, usually bar codes, keeps products moving continually along a distribution route. One significant economic advantage to this type of modernized product labeling is its contribution to the virtual elimination of the warehousing concept that for years has kept companies' funds tied up in inventory. Today, cargo trucks carrying goods arrive at a precise time and pull up to a cross-docking facility. Items are sorted mechanically by their codes and conveyed to waiting delivery trucks docked on the other side. "Items are never stocked. There's a tremendous reduction in inventory, so a great deal of cost has been taken out of the system," Brigham says.

Advanced product identification also economizes packaging. For example, Minute Maid, a major maker of frozen juice products, uses Diagraph's ink-jet printers to print scannable bar codes on its product containers. With dozens of product varieties, preprinting the codes could require storing many different boxes. Instead, Minute Maid preprints boxes with standard information, adding product-specific details as the box moves along the packaging line, including an internal date/time code and a specific product code.

A Growing, Global Market

Worldwide, Diagraph has achieved sales of approximately $75 million, and has turned primarily to Asian markets for growth. Newer operations are located in Hong Kong, China, Malaysia, Singapore, and Japan, as well as Australia and Mexico. Brigham says the company's global strategy is based on investing in the highest growth markets. Such emerging areas offer Diagraph a better return and faster growth rate, in part because customers in those markets tend to purchase the company's more advanced products, such as laser and ink-jet bar code printers. "We thought the traditional, old-line marking products would sell the quickest. Just the opposite has been true," Brigham says. "We're finding that globalization of the world economies is driving the very same marking, product identification, and bar code standards, whether you are operating in China, Mexico, or St. Louis."

The company's foreign expansion strives to incorporate local management. Its Asian subsidiaries, for example, are company owned but managed locally. The Asian managers come to St. Louis for extensive training in the company's products and culture, then return to run the business with a local flavor.

Closer to home, Diagraph supports a range of St. Louis-area civic organizations and is most proud of a recent contribution using its identification technology to assist the Missouri Botanical Garden. Diagraph set up a bar coding system to help track and identify the garden's extensive herbarium collection, which contains nearly 4 million plant species from around the world.

Whether abroad or working within the St. Louis area, Diagraph's products—both traditional and technologically advanced—are helping companies keep track of products from the early stages of production to the final phase of delivery.

Monsanto Company

MONSANTO CHEMICAL WORKS OPENED ITS DOORS IN 1901 WITH the goal to manufacture and market saccharin. Since then, the company's products have appeared in countless places. Its resins were used in the first fiberglass automobile bodies of the Chevrolet Corvette, and the company developed the world's most widely used herbicide, Roundup. ■ From artificial sweeteners to resins and herbicides, the next nine decades saw Monsanto become a $9 billion international corporation with facilities in Canada, Latin America, Europe, Africa, and the Asia-Pacific area, as well as more than 20 U.S. locations.

MONSANTO'S LIFE SCIENCES RESEARCH CENTER (ABOVE) IS LOCATED IN SUBURBAN ST. LOUIS.

THE COMPANY WAS FOUNDED IN 1901 BY JOHN F. QUEENY (RIGHT).

Founder John F. Queeny named his company in honor of his wife, Olga Monsanto. In recognition of the increasing diversity of its product portfolio, the company dropped the word "chemical" from its corporate name in 1964. By that time, Monsanto had expanded from a small plant on the St. Louis riverfront to an international enterprise and a major force in synthetic fibers, fabricated plastic products, and thousands of specialty and commodity chemical products serving agriculture, the automotive and housing markets, and the chemical process industry.

Research Propels Monsanto Forward

At the heart of the company's continuing quest for new and more effective products lies its commitment to research and development (R&D). Monsanto's annual R&D budget surpasses $600 million, placing the company among the top 30 research-based corporations in the United States. Nearly 2,000 Monsanto employees are engaged in R&D.

Dedicated in 1984, Monsanto's Life Sciences Research Center in suburban St. Louis is one of the world's largest and most sophisticated facilities devoted to using biotechnology and genetic engineering in the search for ways to improve health care and agriculture. Many of the scientists working from the center are recognized experts in their field.

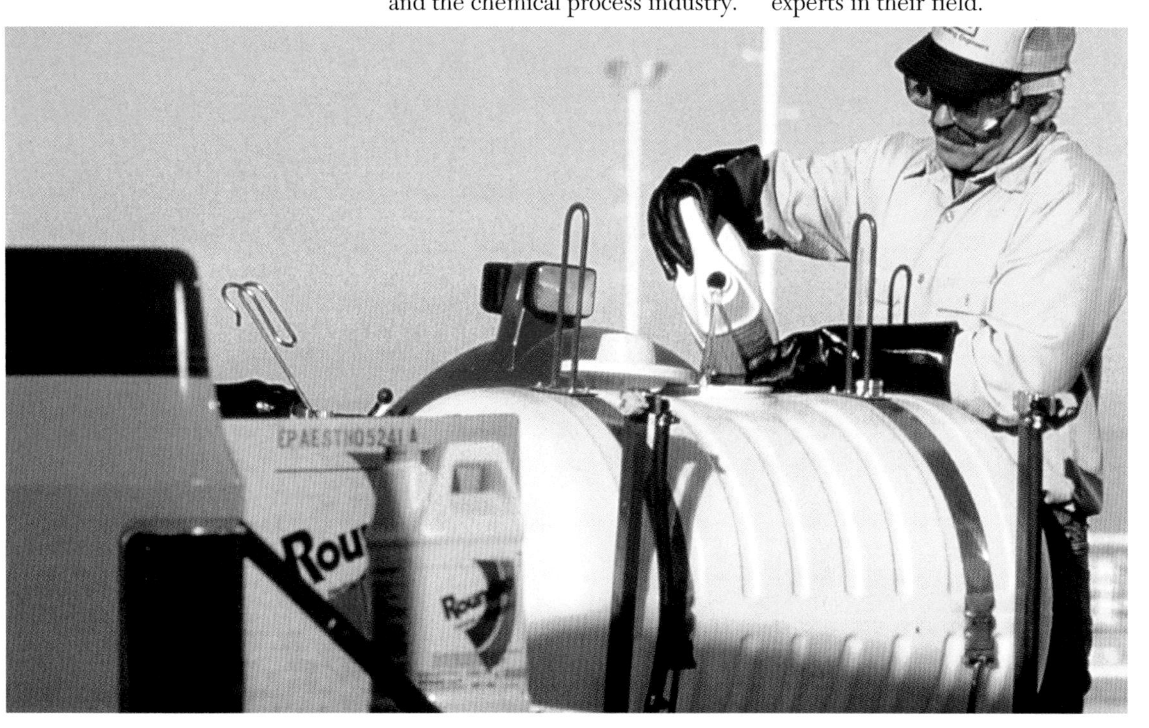

Monsanto's 30,000 employees worldwide devote their time and efforts to discovering, manufacturing, and marketing agricultural products, performance chemicals used in consumer products, prescription pharmaceuticals, and food ingredients. In addition to Roundup, some of the company's well-known brands include Ortho lawn-and-garden products, Wear-Dated carpet, Saflex plastic interlayer, Calan calcium channel blocker, and NutraSweet brand sweetener.

Today, Monsanto serves four broad markets. In the agricultural sector, the company supplies herbicides and products enhanced by biotechnology to improve food production and preserve environmental quality. Monsanto herbicides also are used in industrial markets, and its line of Ortho products is used by consumers in the lawn-and-garden market.

For chemical markets, the company manufactures a range of

performance materials, including fibers, plastics, Saflex plastic interlayer, phosphorus and its derivatives, and rubber and process chemicals. These materials are used by customers to make countless consumer, household, automotive, and industrial products.

In the pharmaceutical area, Monsanto develops and markets prescription pharmaceuticals. Its products include medications to treat infections, relieve arthritis pain, control high blood pressure, prevent ulcers, and ease insomnia.

And in food ingredients, Monsanto manufactures and markets sweeteners and other food ingredients, including NutraSweet brand sweetener, Equal and NutraSweet Spoonful brand tabletop sweeteners, and Simplesse all-natural fat substitute.

Environmentalism and Community Outreach

With an eye on the future, Monsanto has pledged to pursue a course of environmental stewardship that goes beyond what is required by law. The company's commitment to the environment is backed by annual expenditures in excess of $350 million.

In fulfilling its pledge, Monsanto has reduced air emissions of toxic chemicals by 92 percent worldwide, and by 85 percent in the United States. The company is preventing further pollution by generating less waste, reusing or recycling chemicals, and installing more effective treatment technologies. Monsanto also works to protect natural resources through promotion of sustainable agriculture and careful management of its facilities.

Monsanto ranks among the top 25 U.S. corporations in terms of philanthropic contributions. As a technology-based enterprise, the company focuses its grant-making efforts on science education. Since its creation in the mid-1980s, the Monsanto Fund has granted $6 million annually to education programs. The fund also aims to enrich the communities where Monsanto operates by supporting arts and cultural endeavors, as well as civic and community programs.

Likewise, Monsanto employees share their time and talents outside the job by volunteering with a variety of organizations through the Monsanto Volunteer Program. One of its most successful outreach efforts involves providing mentors for school science teachers and students.

Leading the Industry into the Next Century

Ideas, technology, and a dedicated workforce are propelling Monsanto into the 21st century as an innovative, global industrial leader in its chosen fields. As it develops the products for tomorrow, the company is guided by three fundamental business principles: Stop doing what you can't do well, do better what you do well, and start new projects for renewal and growth.

While the scope of Monsanto has changed over the years, the spirit and vision of its founding family continue to guide its leaders as they stand on the threshold of exciting biotechnology breakthroughs in health care, agriculture, and nutrition. That spirit and vision serve as a beacon for those who carry out Monsanto's mission today and into the future.

Some well-known company brands include Wear-Dated carpet (left), Roundup herbicide (opposite), and NutraSweet brand sweetener (below), which is used in thousands of products.

Another important Monsanto product area is prescription pharmaceuticals (above).

Price Waterhouse LLP

Mention the name Price Waterhouse to someone on the streets of St. Louis, and you are likely to get many different reactions. Some people, no doubt, will think first of the annual Academy Awards, where Price Waterhouse has, for years, tallied the winners revealed in "the envelope, please." Others may acknowledge the firm's role as one of the "Big 6" public accounting firms that serve the nation's major corporations. Still others may cite the firm's active community involvement, stretching from the 1904 World's Fair to the annual Fair St. Louis (formerly the V.P. Fair) and the 1994 Olympic Festival.

However people know Price Waterhouse, they all share a common perception: this international professional services giant is one of the city's most prestigious and respected professional services firms, with a well-earned reputation for quality, service, and innovation that goes far beyond the usual expectations of accounting firms.

Managing Partner P. Gregory Garrison (right) is a frequent visitor to Busch Stadium, home of the St. Louis Cardinals, a subsidiary of Anheuser-Busch Companies and a Price Waterhouse client for many years.

Beyond the Numbers

Like many public accounting firms, Price Waterhouse offers a wide variety of audit, tax, management consulting, and business advisory services to address clients' business opportunities and concerns. The firm distinguishes itself, however, through its ability to bring creative business ideas and effective solutions that help clients anticipate issues and transform problems into success stories. This approach has turned Price Waterhouse into one of the largest professional services firms in the city, with more certified public accountants on staff and more Fortune 500 clients than any other local firm. It also has resulted in long-term relationships with clients, some of which extend beyond 75 years.

From offices on the 20th floor of Boatmen's Plaza, Price Waterhouse management consultants gain a unique perspective on the St. Louis business community.

◄ James Visser

The success of the firm locally has helped establish the St. Louis office as a regional and national headquarters for many of Price Waterhouse's fastest-growing practices. For example, the St. Louis office houses Audit and Business Advisory Services, which takes clients beyond the basic audit to enhance financial management, strengthen controls, improve competitiveness, and plan for legislative and regulatory change. A National Tax Center of Excellence provides tax experts to address highly technical tax needs that arise in such areas as international tax, multistate tax, valuations, tax technology, personal finance, and employee benefits. Also based in St. Louis, the National Personal Financial Services Practice works with hundreds of executives from large and small companies to help them take full advantage of the compensation, benefits, and other income they receive.

Other practices located in St. Louis include a Regional Strategic Consulting Group, which assists organizations in such critical management areas as strategy development and implementation, organizational assessment, business reengineering, and operations improvement; a Regional Healthcare Industry Services Group, which helps many of the region's leading health care organizations find ways to reduce costs and create a more efficient health care delivery system; and a Regional Corporate Finance Group, which provides in-depth expertise and access to extensive domestic and international corporate finance resources to help clients capitalize on market opportunities.

A local staff or more than 350 professionals, including 27 partners, is supported by a global network of 400-plus offices in more than 100 countries. The St. Louis office is headed by P. Gregory Garrison.

Always First

The St. Louis office of Price Waterhouse, opened in 1901, mirrored the westward expansion of America. The local staff soon

became known throughout other Price Waterhouse offices as the "Beer and Beef Boys" because of their involvement with the brewing industry and the city's stockyards.

As the first accounting company in St. Louis, Price Waterhouse literally grew up with the city through its years as the nation's fur center, during the Great Depression, and through the resulting ups and downs in economic conditions. The company today serves clients in a wide range of industries, including food and beverage, health care, utilities, retail, and manufacturing. Among its current clients are such well-known names as Anheuser-Busch, Ralston Purina, Union Electric, Kellwood, Blue Cross and Blue Shield of Missouri, Harbour Group, and Saint Louis University.

The firm also has the distinction of serving most of the area's major sports franchises and teams, including the St. Louis Cardinals baseball team, the St. Louis Blues hockey team, and the Saint Louis University Billikens basketball team.

As the firm has grown, it has occupied space in some of the city's most prestigious corporate settings, including the Shell, Ambassador, Thomas Jefferson, and Gateway One office buildings, moving in the early 1980s to its present downtown location in Boatmen's Plaza at Eighth and Market streets.

Recognized for Excellence

Price Waterhouse takes great pride in its uninterrupted service delivery to long-standing clients and its ability to grow as their businesses have expanded and changed. The Price Waterhouse approach to service, summarized in its Client Bill of Rights, assures personalized attention, professional excellence, effective communication, and creative business ideas.

Price Waterhouse is the only large accounting firm to achieve the distinction of a perfect score (both in 1990 and 1993) in a critique by its peers. The Peer Review program is used by the U.S. public accounting profession to monitor and recommend improvements in the quality of accounting and auditing services provided to public companies. The program is one of the nation's major safeguards to assure the integrity and credibility of corporate financial reporting.

▶ JAMES VISSER

Throughout its history, the Price Waterhouse name has come to mean quality, excellence, objectivity, and reliability. These attributes are so well known by the public that Price Waterhouse has earned a special place in popular culture. *Sports Illustrated* magazine, in praising quarterback Joe Montana, noted, "He has the accuracy of Price Waterhouse." And columnist Erma Bombeck wrote, "Sadly, we have only a few national institutions of trust left. Among them—Walter Cronkite, penicillin, chicken soup, and Price Waterhouse."

▶ JAMES VISSER

Clockwise from above:
The St. Louis office is home to a National Tax Center of Excellence, providing in-depth knowledge and experience on a wide range of tax matters.

The firm regularly publishes industry-specific reports to help clients anticipate trends and plan for opportunities.

Proprietary accounting tools, such as PW Researcher, a CD-ROM-based compendium of accounting literature and regulations, allow Price Waterhouse staff to serve their clients more efficiently.

AAA-Automobile Club of Missouri

Since 1902, motorists have regarded the AAA-Automobile Club of Missouri as a friend on the road. Stranded motorists depend on the organization's legendary roadside service; travelers look to AAA's Triptiks, TourBooks, and Travel Guides. Although renowned for these membership benefits, a host of other services have now established the Automobile Club of Missouri as a multiservice resource for the motoring and traveling public.

Today, the organization features one of the largest full-service travel agencies in the Midwest. Members can take advantage of a car diagnostic service that identifies problems with their vehicles. And the organization provides an array of safety, consumer, and legislative programs that protect its individual members and the communities it serves.

Drivers Helping Other Drivers

The Automobile Club of Missouri began its long history of motorist assistance in 1902 when there were only 176 automobiles registered in the St. Louis area. The first Missouri auto club was organized by 16 St. Louis business leaders as an association of drivers helping each other. By 1904 the group had established its original headquarters at the Crowe Estate at Hanley and Clayton roads. It was also at that time that the club began its affiliation with the American Automobile Association, headquartered in New York City.

In those early days of automobiles, motorists were challenged by unpaved roads, poor or nonexistent road markings, and a complete lack of motorist services such as gasoline stations and repair facilities. Since then, the Automobile Club of Missouri has been concerned with providing programs and services to address the needs of its members and their communities.

One of these comprehensive programs is its Emergency Road Service, the first roadside service offered by any automobile club. When it was developed in 1915, Emergency Road Service consisted of five men on motorcycles who patrolled the main county road and offered assistance to any motorist needing help.

Another club first, AAA's Automobile Diagnostic Car Clinic opened in 1967 to provide members with an unbiased assessment of their car's condition. The clinic played an instrumental role in the nation's largest auto recall campaign in 1971, after diagnosticians at the clinic had discovered large numbers of defective engine mounts. Establishment of a worldwide travel agency in 1946 gave members access to domestic and international travel by air or cruise ship.

The organization's branch location on Lindell Boulevard in St. Louis is one of 42 offices now serving members.

Voice of the Motorist

Throughout its history, the Automobile Club of Missouri has shown remarkable leadership and insight in addressing the problems facing the motoring public. It has served as an advocate for motorists and travelers, while seeking reasonable and cost-effective solutions to driving problems.

As an example, the Missouri club has long provided a forum for the debate of speed limit issues. Beginning in 1909 when it boosted the state speed limit to nine miles per hour, and continuing into the 1980s with a challenge to the 55-mile-per-hour speed limit, the association has worked to protect the interests of drivers.

The Automobile Club of Missouri has also addressed issues such as mandatory seat belt use, air pollution controls, drunk driving legislation, motor vehicle inspection, highway funding, driver education, and school safety programs. Acting on behalf of its membership and the motoring public, the club is now identified as "the voice of the motorist."

Innovative Services to Meet Members' Needs

Today, the Automobile Club of Missouri serves more than 620,000 members through its

A pioneer in the field of traffic safety, the Automobile Club of Missouri sponsored safety lanes in the 1930s, where members' cars were given safety checks. Today, the Automotive Diagnostic Car Clinic continues this tradition.

ranch offices in Missouri, southern llinois, eastern Kansas, and Ar- ansas. As part of the extensive merican Automobile Association etwork, members have access to nore than 1,000 AAA offices ationwide, and are affiliated with nore than 36 million AAA mem- ers throughout the country.

Emergency Road Service is till a prominent feature of the ssociation, along with services uch as personalized travel ssistance; automobile financing; nsurance; the auto club's maga- ine, *The Midwest Motorist*; egislative activity; safety and esearch programs; and the Diagnostic Car Clinic.

Although the size and extent f services offered to its members as increased significantly over he years, the goals of the associa- ion have remained the same. Since 1902 when AAA began," ays Kenneth A. Johnson, presi- lent of the Automobile Club of Missouri, "we have been constant- y involved on behalf of our mem- ers and the motoring public. Our oal is to provide high-quality services with individualized attention."

As competition increases among auto assistance programs, the Missouri auto club has developed new and innovative programs to attract and retain its members. Recently, a category of membership was instituted for recreational vehicle (RV) owners, which includes emergency road service for RVs. In addition, AAA's insurance programs have been expanded to offer life, home owners, and health insurance, as well as the club's more familiar line of automobile insurance.

Most importantly, however, members can continue to rely on the Automobile Club of Missouri and its unparalleled level of service. "We have more employees per member than any non-AAA motoring organization, and each employee's job is directly concerned with service to the customer," says Johnson.

A century has passed since the automobile was introduced to the United States, and the auto club has been a companion to motorists for most of the journey. As the world continues to change, the AAA-Automobile Club of Missouri will keep evolving to serve new generations of motorists.

From its headquarters in St. Louis County, the Automobile Club of Missouri manages an extensive array of services for more than 620,000 members.

Mosby-Year Book, Inc.

MOSBY IS A COMPANY WITH GROWING MARKETS AND VISIONARY management. Founded in 1906, the St. Louis-based publisher has spent nine prosperous decades providing customers all over the world with superior health care publications and related products. ■ It all began when Dr. Charles Virgil Mosby noticed a shortage of quality texts for medical and dental students. Determined to meet the need, he spent his life building the company that continues to fulfill his vision of superior quality. Today, Mosby publishes over 5,000 book titles and more than 70 journals, and its texts and references are translated into 22 languages. In addition to its traditional books and journals, Mosby publishes software, videos, annuals, and continuing education programs for students and practitioners in medicine, dentistry, nursing, allied health, emergency medical services, and related college disciplines. The company also has a rapidly growing list of products for consumers. With a reputation for creativity and innovation, the company meets the demand for health science materials by researching market needs, carefully selecting authors for each project, and using its resources and expertise to ensure quality design, editing, printing, marketing, and distribution.

JOHN F. DILL (ABOVE) HAS SERVED MOSBY AS CHAIRMAN, CEO, AND PRESIDENT SINCE 1989.

TODAY, THE COMPANY PUBLISHES OVER 5,000 BOOK TITLES AND MORE THAN 70 JOURNALS, AND ITS TEXTS AND REFERENCES ARE TRANSLATED INTO 22 LANGUAGES.

Leading the Industry in Growth

Since merging in 1989 with Year Book Medical Publishers of Chicago, Mosby has enjoyed accelerated growth. To continue that trend in an era of uncertainty for the domestic health science industry, Mosby has pursued a dual strategy of domestic growth and international expansion. With the full support of Times Mirror, Mosby's parent organization since 1967, the company has made a series of bold moves that have positioned it to succeed in a global market.

In 1993 Mosby joined three of its Times Mirror sister companies in forming Times Mirror International Publishers (TMIP). Headquartered in London, TMIP currently has offices in 11 countries and provides a cohesive structure to facilitate international expansion for Times Mirror's rapidly growing professional publishing houses.

Mosby, however, has not let its international development overshadow expansion efforts at home. Domestic acquisitions have been equally impressive and have built on and expanded the markets served by the company.

As health care increasingly became a political and social issue in the early '90s, Mosby reorganized into three operating units to better position itself to provide health care information and new media to its customers. Traditionally a publisher for professionals, Mosby made a bold move into the consumer health care market by establishing Mosby Lifeline as an imprint in the late '80s and then as an operating unit in 1994. Lifeline creates products for the burgeoning consumer health care industry, publishes information for professionals in the pre-hospital emergency care and health occupation markets, and has valuable publishing agreements with the American, Canadian, and Australian Red Cross organizations.

The second of the units is the Professional and Academic Publishing unit, which focuses on the book publishing program in medicine, nursing, allied health, and college publishing. The third unit, Journal and Continuity Publishing, is responsible for Mosby's journal and continuity products in medicine, dentistry, nursing, and allied health.

Mosby has had a long series of successes in its history. Since 1989 Chairman, CEO, and President John F. Dill has initiated a program of strategic acquisitions balanced by in-house product development and has continued a tradition of excellence in the company's products. His positive management style encourages improvement by recognizing each employee's contribution to Mosby's higher goals, and during his tenure, sales have increased by 125 percent.

At Home in St. Louis

Mosby's recent focus on growth has meant expansion for its St. Louis operation as well. In 1994 the company purchased a building next door to its corporate headquarters. The structure has since been renovated and linked to Mosby's three existing buildings that house the headquarters.

Through all the profound changes it has undergone, Mosby remains committed to its hometown. Of its 1,400 employees around the globe, 750 are employed in St. Louis. It's a win-win situation for Mosby and St. Louis—the city values Mosby's exemplary corporate citizenship and support of local charities and universities,

while Mosby values the city's midwestern employee base and quality of life.

"I think the tradition of excellence that Dr. Mosby established has a lot to do with St. Louis," Dill asserts. "There is a sense of community and loyalty and value here that is instilled deep in the employee population."

Faster and Better

Today, Mosby's leadership strives to keep ahead of the changing forces that affect the publishing business. To manage an increasingly large amount of information, Mosby uses the latest technology and the best-trained employees.

And as the need for rapid information access grows, Mosby is planning its long-term strategy to meet that demand. The company prepared for the electronic exchange of information by storing digital forms of its titles.

The future promises to bring many changes on the national health care scene, which will greatly affect the way Mosby does business. But this innovative publisher is ready to face its domestic challenges by adapting its marketing strategy and relying on steady international growth. Dill is confident that Mosby will prosper through the coming years. "We will remain responsive, even nimble, despite our size," he says, "and we will continue to promote a state of mind that embraces change as a way of life."

As for the future, Dill plans for nothing short of greatness. "While you will see us continue to pursue the international agenda very aggressively, you will also see us pursue domestic growth just as hard and fast as we can. It is my dream for this company to be the unchallenged, preeminent publisher in health science worldwide." Indeed, Mosby is well on its way toward realizing its dream.

Clockwise from above:
Mosby employs 750 people at its St. Louis headquarters.

The company meets the demand for health science materials by researching market needs, carefully selecting authors for each project, and using its resources and expertise to ensure quality design, editing, printing, marketing, and distribution.

To manage an increasingly large amount of information, Mosby uses the latest technology and the best-trained employees.

Wehrenberg Theatres

The story of Wehrenberg Theatres has all the makings of a good movie script: what began as a humble neighborhood saloon in 1906 has become the oldest family-owned theater business in the country. Wehrenberg Theatres owes its success to the creative entrepreneurship and hard work of the Wehrenberg-Krueger family. From the early years when pre-talkies grossed $5 a day and founder Fred Wehrenberg's wife played the piano during each show, Wehrenberg Theatres has been an integral part of St. Louis' history. Today, Wehrenberg's grandson, company President Ronald Krueger, represents the third generation of his family to manage this St. Louis tradition. Ronald Krueger II, representing the fourth generation, joined the firm in 1994.

Company President Ronald Krueger (right) represents the third generation of his family to manage this St. Louis tradition.

Along with the theaters, the elder Krueger inherited his family's love of entertainment and the movies. As a boy in the 1940s, Krueger had his picture taken with screen idols Roy Rogers and Trigger, and as a teenager, he ran the miniature passenger train for the kids at his family's 66 Drive-In. He even conducted free pony rides at the drive-in. Krueger grew up entertaining St. Louis and believes Americans, now more than ever, need the escape that movies offer.

As part of Wehrenberg's commitment to providing top-quality entertainment and innovation to moviegoers, the newly expanded Des Peres complex houses 14 auditoriums with state-of-the-art DTS digital sound systems and superwide screens.

Douglas Abel

Pioneers in the Movie Theater Industry

Wehrenberg Theatres prides itself on providing top-quality entertainment and innovation to moviegoers in Missouri, Arizona, and Illinois. Always on the cutting edge of technology, the company was the first in St. Louis to create multiplex theaters. Wehrenberg was also the first in the region to install THX digital sound systems. As another example of this commitment to the latest technology, the newly expanded Des Peres complex in west St. Louis County houses 14 auditoriums with state-of-the-art DTS digital sound systems and superwide screens.

The most recent Wehrenberg innovation is a giant "video wall" in the Des Peres 14 Cine lobby. The wall, inspired by a similar one Krueger experienced in a Hong Kong shopping mall, features 25 television screens that can display single to multiple images of various sizes—all computer programmed to dance across the screens—showing what is playing in the auditoriums. Krueger's knack for entertainment has proved successful once again. The unique idea, combined with fast-paced and exciting programming, has made the video wall a popular attraction.

Leading the Way in St. Louis

As the entertainment industry rockets into the 21st century, Wehrenberg Theatres continues to lead the way. Future plans include continual modernization of the company's St. Louis theaters, along with the addition of many new sites—eight are currently on the drawing board.

Despite the fast pace of the movie business, Wehrenberg Theatres has always found time for community service. "We feel that St. Louis has been good to us," says Krueger, "and we try to reciprocate." From Fred Wehrenberg's Depression-era contests that awarded hams and household goods as prizes to Ron Krueger's present-day sponsorship of the Shriner's Hospital Salvation Army, Wehrenberg Balloon Festival, and numerous other activities, Wehrenberg Theatres gets involved. Like the company's commitment to top-quality, state-of-the-art entertainment, community involvement remains an important family tradition.

Douglas Abel

South Side National Bank in St. Louis

WALKING INTO THE LOBBY OF SOUTH SIDE NATIONAL Bank, there's an immediate sense of history. The bank is one of St. Louis' oldest institutions, and tellers continue to service customers from the original iron teller cages located on the open, second level with its marbled floor, high ceilings, and massive pillars. But something more important than architecture has been preserved.

"There is a sense of personal service that continues through all our modern consumer and commercial financial services," says Thomas M. Teschner, president and CEO. From its founding bank—the historic nine-story structure at Gravois and Grand avenues—as well as from five additional offices (four in south St. Louis and one in north St. Louis County), South Side National Bank is taking the lead in offering old-fashioned customer service mixed with modern conveniences.

A Century of Service to St. Louis

South Side National Bank traces its history to Adolphus Busch, founder of the internationally known Anheuser-Busch Companies. Busch opened South Side Bank in 1891 at Broadway and Pestalozzi to serve the prospering southside community in the vicinity of the brewery. A friendly merger in 1928 with South Side Trust Company and the Farmers and Merchants Trust Company, which in 1913 had built a three-story structure on the southeast corner of Grand and Gravois, created South Side National Bank in St. Louis. The bank needed a new home, which gave rise nearby to the present landmark building at 3606 Gravois Avenue.

In an age of banking mergers and acquisitions, South Side National Bank remains independent, and takes pride in its continuing ability to provide a comprehensive array of personalized banking services. South Side National Bank's own financial standing is strong. The bank's stock rose from $60 per share to over $160 per share in 1993. But one of the institution's greatest contributions to St. Louis is its ability to remain a community bank.

"Our goal is to keep aspects of community banking, which include greeting our customers by name," says Teschner. "We're also a growing organization and provide all the major products and services that can be found at the larger financial institutions—from a comprehensive line of deposit services to consumer and commercial loans to trust services."

The bank also has adopted as one of its operating principles an interest in the growth and development of the community it serves. There's extensive involvement and support for local civic and charitable organizations. South Side National also helps meet the credit needs of the community, including low- and moderate-income neighborhoods.

South Side's current direction assures its future role as a community bank, one that blends history, personal service, and modern banking services. "As the banking industry is constantly changing, and mergers and acquisitions continue to dominate our industry, this very environment creates continuing opportunity for South Side National Bank to offer a unique service," says Teschner. "We provide the personal touch that's so needed today."

▸ QUINTA SCOTT

THE BANK'S LEADERSHIP TODAY INCLUDES CHAIRMAN OF THE BOARD HOWARD F. ETLING (LEFT) AND PRESIDENT AND CEO THOMAS M. TESCHNER.

FROM THIS HISTORIC NINE-STORY STRUCTURE AT GRAVOIS AND GRAND AVENUES (LEFT), AND FROM FIVE ADDITIONAL OFFICES, SOUTH SIDE NATIONAL BANK IS TAKING THE LEAD IN OFFERING OLD-FASHIONED CUSTOMER SERVICE MIXED WITH MODERN CONVENIENCES.

KPMG Peat Marwick LLP

IN 1911 A MANAGER, AN ACCOUNTANT, AND A STENOGRAPHER OPENED AN accounting office in St. Louis. Few gave them much of a chance since two "Big 8" firms were already strongly entrenched in the St. Louis marketplace, but the upstart firm went about its business with energy, enthusiasm, and growing expertise. Today, that business—KPMG—is one of the largest and most successful global professional services firms, with more than 6,000 partners and 76,000 employees serving clients through 1,100 offices in 131 countries.

KPMG Peat Marwick's St. Louis office includes 250 employees with experience in serving clients in a full range of industry segments. The firm's financial services group and its manufacturing, retailing, and distribution group serve the bulk of KPMG's St. Louis clients, while the health care group is achieving rapid growth.

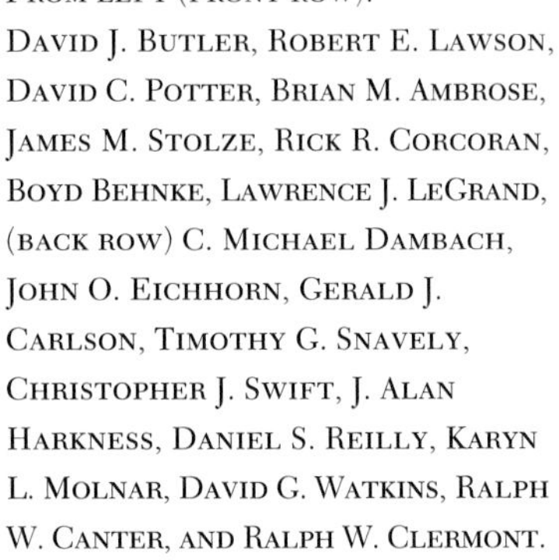

From left (front row): David J. Butler, Robert E. Lawson, David C. Potter, Brian M. Ambrose, James M. Stolze, Rick R. Corcoran, Boyd Behnke, Lawrence J. LeGrand, (back row) C. Michael Dambach, John O. Eichhorn, Gerald J. Carlson, Timothy G. Snavely, Christopher J. Swift, J. Alan Harkness, Daniel S. Reilly, Karyn L. Molnar, David G. Watkins, Ralph W. Canter, and Ralph W. Clermont.

The Client Speaks

Building on more than 80 years of growth and success, KPMG Peat Marwick recently looked to its clients for suggestions on how the firm could do an even better job of responding to their needs. "Clients told us they wanted KPMG to be advisers, to use in-depth understanding of their industries to provide creative solutions that address today's business problems and anticipate tomorrow's," explains Ralph Clermont, managing partner of the St. Louis office.

A KPMG leadership committee examined the firm's structure and developed a dramatic, innovative approach. "We decided to transform our organization along industries—what we call 'lines of business'—instead of being organized geographically or functionally, so that we could deliver more industry-specific expertise to our clients," says Clermont.

KPMG Peat Marwick's new organization includes five industry-based lines of business: financial services; health care and life sciences; information, communications, and entertainment; manufacturing, retailing, and distribution; and public services.

"As a result of this approach, which is unlike any other major professional services firm, we are always increasing our understanding of the industries in which our clients are operating," Clermont says. "We bring more specific expertise and better resources to address our clients' full range of needs, from consulting services such as performance improvement, systems integration, and sales force automation, to traditional accounting services.

"Our new structure also reflects the growing impact and demands of the global economy. While every company is concerned with minimizing the cost of doing business and maximizing performance, a fast-growing number are now facing direct competition from Europe, China, Canada, Mexico, South America, and elsewhere. The companies that are world-class in quality and efficiency will be the success stories of the 21st century, and KPMG will help ensure that our clients are among them."

KPMG's industry structure also allows it to mobilize quick responses to emerging issues. For example, the firm recently found its financial services clients facing additional regulations and elevated government scrutiny. KPMG's financial services line of business responded in short order by establishing the Regulatory Advisory Practice to help clients navigate the maze of regulations.

Now just over a year old, KPMG's reorganization is a success. "As our higher yields and quickly growing client base demonstrate, both our longtime and new clients are very positive about KPMG's innovative responses to their needs. It's a fitting way to build on 80 years of success," says Clermont.

Visiting Nurse Association

VISITING NURSE ASSOCIATION TRACES ITS ROOTS TO A group of nurses who traveled to St. Louis homes by horse and buggy in the late 1800s, arriving with only a washbasin and other basic medical supplies. Today, the not-for-profit organization provides the same high-quality home care that area residents have come to expect since the agency's inception in 1911. Caring for St. Louis-area families and their loved ones is all Visiting Nurse Association does. As the oldest home health provider in the area and the largest in the state of Missouri, Visiting Nurse Association provides more than 130,000 patient visits annually to homes in the city of St. Louis; the Missouri counties of St. Louis, Jefferson, and St. Charles; and the Illinois counties of St. Clair, Madison, and Monroe.

Comprehensive Care Meets Patient Needs

The Visiting Nurse Association nurse offers a wide spectrum of care, according to Susan Pettit, president and CEO. "Our nurses use comprehensive skills to evaluate each patient's condition from a broad perspective that goes beyond clinical issues. Our one-on-one approach to in-home care and evaluation ensures the patient's needs are met," she says.

Patients cared for by Visiting Nurse Association professionals are diverse—newborns, children, adults, seniors—creating a contrast from early days when all care was maternity oriented. The company's health care personnel assist patients with sophisticated medical equipment and self-care techniques, calling on the agency's specialized professionals for physical therapy, occupational therapy, social services, dietetics, or special services such as mental health.

Patients Benefit from Diverse Scope of Care

Visiting Nurse Association's home health services programs include Home Health Care, Hospice Care, Private Duty Care, Medical Equipment, and Infusion Services. Community wellness programs include an annual flu prevention campaign.

Intravenous therapy is one example of how home health care has changed in the past decade. The agency manages treatments that a few years ago would have required hospitalization, such as IV therapy with medications ranging from pain control and antibiotics to chemotherapy.

Visiting Nurse Association has also advanced home health services into the era of managed care insurance plans for St. Louis-area employees. The company's Case Management Consultants group works with many area employers to include home health services in their benefit packages.

An Eye on the Future

Visiting Nurse Association recognizes health care is ever-changing and true reform requires universal access to coverage and cost reduction, not just cost containment. As a key player in St. Louis' efforts to change the health care delivery system, the agency is on the front lines advocating change.

"We need to make health care affordable," Pettit says. "This means getting rid of excess or duplicate services in the industry. We also need programs emphasizing the importance of wellness in our community, programs that provide individual incentives for staying healthy."

Despite increasing changes throughout the health care industry, clinical professionals like Visiting Nurse Association will be caring for patients in their homes well into the 21st century. The aging population, the continuing need to control costs while maintaining quality, and ever-improving medical technology all foretell growth in the home health services arena.

"Visiting Nurse Association has been bringing quality health care home for 85 years," Pettit says. "St. Louisans will continue to feel right at home with our diverse, professional approach to home health now and well into the future."

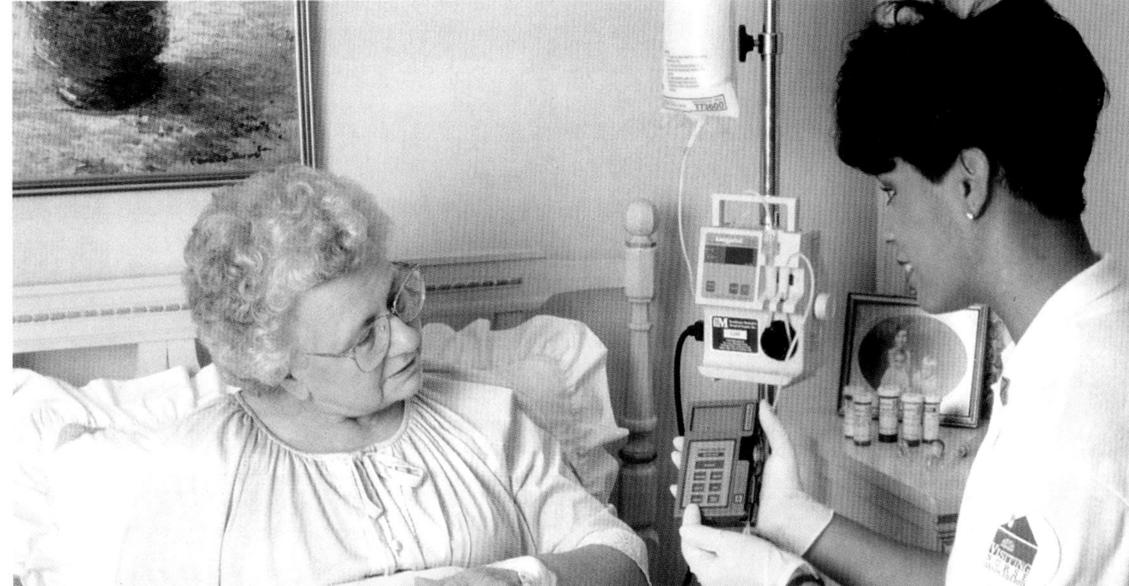

VISITING NURSE ASSOCIATION IS A LEADER IN BRINGING NEW HEALTH CARE TECHNOLOGY AND SOPHISTICATED MEDICAL TECHNIQUES INTO THE HOME—ALLOWING INDIVIDUALS TO RETURN HOME EARLIER, AND LESSENING THE STRESS AND COST OF HOSPITALIZATION FOR THEM AND THEIR FAMILIES.

Sayers Printing Company

HERBERT M. "SKIP" SAYERS, CHAIRMAN AND CEO OF SAYERS Printing Company, picks up a print advertisement for shoes and begins to make a quality assessment, checking to ensure the type is clean and crisp, that the colors register perfectly without shadows around the edges, and that the brown shoe has not faded to tan in later press runs. The evaluation is not just for the sake of quality assurance; it demonstrates the attention to detail that places Sayers Printing Company in a highly specialized business niche.

While "B-plus" work may be acceptable for some, Sayers is among an elite group of printers nationally that can be relied upon for "A-plus" reproduction. In terms of volume, the company ranks 98th among more than 54,000 U.S. printers. In terms of quality, it's among the top 20 printers based on a variety of industry standards.

CLARK KINCAID

CHAIRMAN AND CEO HERBERT M. "SKIP" SAYERS (TOP RIGHT) REPRESENTS THE THIRD GENERATION OF HIS FAMILY TO HEAD THE PRIVATELY HELD COMPANY.

CLARK KINCAID

CLARK KINCAID

SAYERS' TWO NEW SHEET-FED PRESSES ARE KNOWN AS YIN (RIGHT) AND YANG (ABOVE).

Skip Sayers represents the third generation of the Sayers family to head the privately held company, originally founded by Frank W. Sayers in 1912 to print accounting forms. His son, Herbert W. Sayers, became the second generation to take the helm in 1928, securing national printing contracts from many St. Louis-based companies like Brown Shoe Company, Pet Incorporated, and Monsanto.

The plant moved from its original riverfront location to the current site at 9600 Manchester in 1952. At the time, Skip Sayers was busy leading the company into the modern age of printing, including expanding its basic four-color press—an innovation in the 1940s—to a five- and then a nine-color press with modern high-speed web presses that print from a continuous roll for large runs.

CLARK KINCAID

Top-of-the-Line Technology

To further its quality mission, Sayers Printing has invested millions in advanced computerized equipment such as a start-up scanner that reads a printing plate, then sets hundreds of ink fountain keys within 2.5 seconds for perfect reproduction. Printing runs are continuously scanned for variations in color, hue, register, and consistency, with the results displayed in graph form on a screen. Skip Sayers illustrates the quality window acceptable for some printers by holding his hands wide apart. "For Sayers Printing, the parameters for quality are more like this," he says, moving his hands to a nearly closed position.

Another quality indicator—an impressive certification trophy from Hallmark Cards—stands on a pedestal under glass in the pressroom. Hallmark designated the company its first certified quality vendor, meaning that Sayers Printing can distribute products directly to Hallmark's 25,000 stores worldwide. The company is currently undergoing intensive training for ISO 9000 certification.

More than one-third of a million pounds of paper move in and out of the company's 100,000-square-foot printing plant every day. The process begins in the computerized composing room, a new multimillion-dollar investment, where an advertisement can be modified instantly to incorporate the perfect seashore, a change of model, or a change of product. The huge, spotlessly clean presses hum 24 hours a day and sport personalized nameplates. Two new sheet-fed presses are called Yin and Yang, while the massive web presses are known as Lightnin' Hawk and Screamin' Eagle.

Sayers Printing was the founding member of Graphic Innovators, a group of 12 printing companies nationwide noted for their unique techniques. Graphic Innovators helped develop three-dimensional advertisements that became popular in the 1960s. Newer innovations include scratch-off games, advertisements with scents, and endless variations in folding and cutting. Most recently, the company has been a leader in robotics, using equipment with the ability to print on both sides of a piece of paper, fold and cut it, insert or box it, and, finally, deliver it to the shipping room.

Sayers' central geographic location helps the company save on transportation costs for paper delivery and, therefore, keep client costs lower. In addition to its St. Louis operation, Sayers has sales offices in Charlotte, New York City, San Francisco, and Detroit. A sister company, Nova Marketing Services Inc., implements clients' creative projects, often taking a concept off a computer disc, handling the printing, and overseeing the job's distribution.

▶ CLARK KINCAID

Hallmark Cards designated Sayers as its first certified quality vendor, meaning that the company can distribute products directly to Hallmark's 25,000 stores worldwide (top left).

▶ CLARK KINCAID

With such a long history of growth and quality orientation, Skip Sayers credits the company's associates, as employees are called. "My grandfather had a saying: 'Any damn fool with money can buy iron, but it takes a lot of dedicated people to do anything with it.' We've been the beneficiaries of the best iron and machinery in the industry, but the thing that sets us apart is our dedicated people," he says.

The company's senior management meets quarterly with small groups of associates for open discussions about quality, the direction of the business, and suggestions for improvements. Charts depicting sales and growth margins are posted for all to see. Training, continuous improvement, and taking personal satisfaction from a job well done are emphasized.

The fourth generation of the Sayers family, Herbert M. Sayers, Jr., assumed a senior management position in 1995 as president and chief operating officer. He predicts Sayers Printing will play an innovative role in whatever form the printing industry takes in the future. "Our future strategies will be based on the basic concept that we are in the communications business, primarily printing. But whatever form communications takes in the future, we intend to be broad-minded enough to step into the forefront of the industry," he says. "We'll always be a leader, not a follower."

▶ CLARK KINCAID

Screamin' Eagle and Lightnin' Hawk (below left and right) are Sayers' massive web presses.

▶ CLARK KINCAID

Skip Sayers (left) and his son, President and COO Herbert M. Sayers, Jr., monitor quality in the St. Louis plant.

Ernst & Young LLP

Ernst & Young LLP is the largest professional services firm in St. Louis and a leader in the local business community. Today's Ernst & Young was created by the historic 1989 merger of two giants in the accounting industry: Arthur Young & Company and Ernst & Whinney. The firm's St. Louis office, established in 1913, provides auditing, tax, and consulting services for hundreds of clients, including individuals, corporations, and organizations in virtually every product and service category.

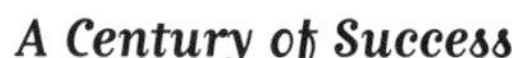

A Century of Success

Arthur Young was a Scotsman who came to the United States around the turn of the century to earn his fortune. In 1894, with $500 in capital and one stenographer, he founded an accounting firm in Chicago with an associate. After 12 years, the original firm was dissolved, and Young formed Arthur Young & Company with his brother, Stanley Young.

Meanwhile, A.C. Ernst had founded his firm in 1903 in Cleveland. Starting in 1923, the firm maintained a working agreement with Whinney, Murray & Co. of England, and the two firms conducted their international business under a third name: Whinney, Murray, Ernst & Ernst. In 1979 the entire operation merged to become Ernst & Whinney, establishing a single business name worldwide. The 1989 merger of Arthur Young and Ernst & Whinney created the preeminent professional services firm in the world, Ernst & Young.

Clockwise from above:
Ernst & Young professionals offer advice and input on client work.

Consultants discuss client projects.

Staff members access extensive software support in the Microcenter.

The firm now has more than 680 locations in over 125 countries, including 100 locations in the United States. With global revenues of $6 billion, Ernst & Young employs 66,000 people worldwide and ranks as one of the top three professional services firms in more major cities worldwide than any other firm, auditing almost 20 percent of the companies on the *Business Week* Global 1,000 and the *Fortune* Global 500 lists.

In the United States, Ernst & Young is the largest integrated professional services organization and has more total revenues from accounting, auditing, and tax services than any other firm. Nationwide, its clients comprise the full spectrum of companies, including 115 of *Fortune*'s 500 largest industrial companies; 17 of *Software* magazine's top 50 independent software companies;

16 of *American Banker* magazine's top 50 superregional banks; 74 of *AHA Guide*'s 200 largest multihospital systems; 41 of *AHA Guide*'s 100 largest nongovernmental hospitals; nine of Kurt Salmon's top 32 textile companies; 16 of *Builders* magazine's top 50 home builders; 22 of *Engineering News Record*'s top 100 construction companies; and 23 of *Business Week*'s 100 best small companies.

Serving a Diverse Array of St. Louis Industries

As part of its mission to be a full-service business adviser, Ernst & Young offers a host of audit, tax, and consulting services. The company's professionals work within distinct industry groups—health care, manufacturing, retail and consumer products, insurance, financial services, real estate and construction, and entrepreneurial services. This industry specialization allows Ernst & Young to serve clients' needs more efficiently and comprehensively by concentrating talent and focusing the experience, knowledge, and skills of its professionals on the industries they know best.

The St. Louis office of Ernst & Young has a staff of more than 500 that includes accountants and experts in audit, tax, entrepreneurial services, health care, human resource consulting services, information technology, performance improvement, corporate finance, restructuring and reorganization, valuations, litigation, capital markets, and cash management.

Like the national organization, the St. Louis office of Ernst & Young has a client list that includes the area's top businesses. One-third of the large companies with corporate headquarters in the St. Louis area are audit clients of Ernst & Young (more than any other St. Louis professional services firm), and many of the large companies in the area turn to the firm's management consultants for their consulting needs.

Ernst & Young continues to operate on a fundamental principle that long has been a company hallmark: "The successes of Ernst & Young and its clients are linked . . . and we understand that we must bring value to our clients for our mutual success to continue. We are committed to continuous improvement in all that we do. We seek to attract, develop, and retain high-performance people, and to deliver the highest quality work and value-added services responsive to our clients' needs and expectations." By meeting—and exceeding—these expectations, Ernst & Young looks forward to continuing its position as a leading local and worldwide integrated professional services firm.

Ernst & Young's location provides its professionals and visitors with numerous amenities (top).

Partners gather to discuss client needs (bottom).

Bussmann Division Cooper Industries

St. Louis is headquarters for the world's leading manufacturer of electrical circuit protection products—the Bussmann Division of Cooper Industries. Since its incorporation in 1914, Bussmann has enjoyed 80 years of steady and deliberate growth. Today the name Bussmann is synonymous with fuses. ■ "Most people don't realize how pervasive fuses are in their everyday lives," says Tom Guzek, vice president of product and market development for Bussmann. Over 35,000 different types of fuses exist, with a wealth of applications. There are fuses in every telephone and television set, every car, copy machine, and computer. And that's just the beginning. There are tiny electronic fuses (smaller than an ant) and there are giant four-foot fuses (used to power nautical icebreakers).

The Bussmann Division of Cooper Industries has provided almost every type of fuse imaginable to its diverse markets around the world. Of all Bussmann's circuit protection solutions, probably the most noteworthy are those used by NASA in its space shuttle program. As with NASA, the Bussmann team works to build partnerships with all its customers, designing specific products for specific applications as needed.

This Bussmann surface-mount fuse (right), known as the SMT 3216FF Chip Fuse, is smaller than an ant.

Bussmann's Optima™ line was developed using the company's Rapid Product Development Team concepts.

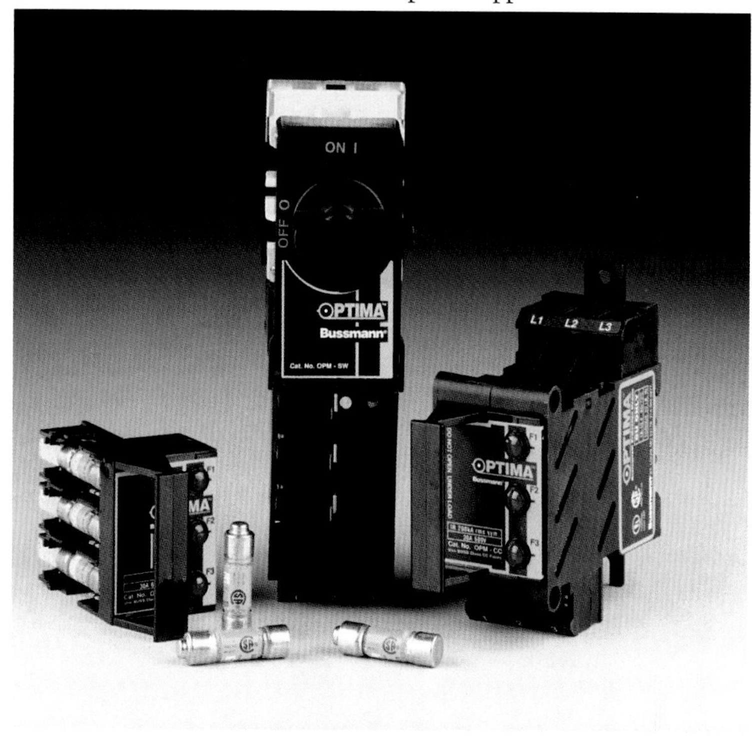

From the World's Fair to the World's Finest

The story of Bussmann's rise from family business to international leader is a story of inspiration and determination. The inspiration came when five sons of a German immigrant attended the 1904 World's Fair in their hometown of St. Louis. The Bussmann boys were thoroughly impressed by the spectacle of electric lighting at the fair. Their young minds concluded that electricity was the business of the future, and they were determined to get in on the ground floor.

They learned the trade by working for local electrical contractors, until brother Al saw an opportunity to invest in the fuse-making business. He bought the equipment from a former employer and set up shop in the Bussmann family basement in 1914. By 1915 the operation had moved to its first real factory. In 1916 the Bussmann business swelled in size and staff, due to its latest production line—fuses for the new "horseless carriages." The company grew steadily, and the five brothers sold their business in 1929 to McGraw Electric, which later combined with Edison to form McGraw-Edison. The brothers remained active in the company's management through the 1950s, when their sons—the second generation of Bussmanns—began to assume leadership. The last of the original clan to lead the business was Joe Bussmann, Jr., who died in 1976. By this time, the company had acquired several plants across the country, employing nearly 3,000 workers.

Moving Ahead with Cooper Industries

In 1985 Bussmann's parent company, McGraw-Edison, was acquired by Cooper Industries. The move has been profitable from both points of view. Cooper's acquisitions in the United Kingdom have helped Bussmann enter the European market and increase its exports. In turn, Bussmann is considered the "crown jewel" of the McGraw-Edison acquisition. Its proven product line is critical to the safety and viability of business and industry worldwide, and sales are well into the multimillion-dollar range. Bussmann's trademarks include Buss, Bussmann, SMD Tron, PC-Tron, Fusetron, Optima, Low-Peak, and many others.

The company's current headquarters is a newly constructed facility in Ellisville, Missouri, only 30 miles from its original location

In 1993 Bussmann opened the Paul P. Gubany Center for High-Power Technology. The testing center on the Ellisville, Missouri, campus includes three 20-million-volt-ampere custom-designed transformers (far left).

in downtown St. Louis. The facility serves as a worldwide distribution center, an automotive and subminiature fuse factory, and a stamping and final assembly stop. Everything about the 250,000-square-foot headquarters is state-of-the-art, including the corporate culture. President John Monter has initiated an upbeat management philosophy, and job satisfaction is at an all-time high. Dress is casual, and employees participate in cross-functional work teams that are committed to the pursuit of total customer satisfaction. The Bussmann workforce is encouraged to embrace change, strive for continuous improvement, share "knowledge wealth," and celebrate successes.

One recent success occurred in 1993 when Bussmann opened the Paul P. Gubany Center for High-Power Technology. Named for a former company general manager and industry leader, the center is the only one of its kind in the world. On the Ellisville campus, electrical products of all kinds are tested up to 300,000 amps. The generator used has enough power to light 50,000 homes at one time. The center includes three, 20-million-volt-ampere custom-designed transformers. This kind of investment shows why Bussmann is known for innovative solutions and quality products.

Growing Toward the Future

The future looks exciting for the Bussmann Division of Cooper Industries. On the domestic scene, the St. Louis team has plans to double its product development staff and resources, and to increase team member contribution. Bussmann also will continue to invest in its manufacturing plants in North Carolina, Kentucky, Illinois, Denmark, England, and Mexico. But the real push will be toward expanding international markets. With trusted products and progressive leadership, the company hopes to get a foothold in China and the former Eastern Bloc countries. Judging from Bussmann's track record, it's a sure thing.

The company's 250,000-square-foot headquarters facility is located in Ellisville, only 30 miles from its original location in downtown St. Louis.

GULF MOBILE
2

1915

1915 Webster University
1917 The Fabick Companies
1921 The Daniel & Henry Company
1921 Pet Incorporated
1922 Watlow
1925 KMOX News/Talk 1120
1926 American Airlines
1928 Mississippi River Transmission Corp.
1929 Pepsi-Cola Bottling Co. of St. Louis, Inc.
1929 Trans World Airlines, Inc.
1931 GTE Telephone Operations
1933 General American Life Insurance Company
1936 Blue Cross and Blue Shield of Missouri
1936 United Van Lines, Inc.
1939 Coldwell Banker Ira E. Berry
1939 McDonnell Douglas Corporation
1939 Schnuck Markets, Inc.
1943 Andersen Consulting
1945 Bock Pharmacal Company
1945 Nooney Krombach
1945 Towers Perrin

1945

◆ Quinta Scott Photo

Webster University

FOUNDED EIGHT DECADES AGO, WEBSTER UNIVERSITY IS TODAY a national and international network of campuses fulfilling its mission to provide relevant, forward-looking, and personalized education to its students. From its home in St. Louis to any of its more than 50 locations, this unique private university is committed to meeting the needs of its diverse student body and to responding to society's evolving needs.

FOUNDED IN 1915, WEBSTER UNIVERSITY HAS ALMOST 5,000 STUDENTS ENROLLED AT ITS ST. LOUIS CAMPUS (BELOW RIGHT) AND MORE THAN 10,500 STUDENTS WORLDWIDE.

GRADUATE STUDENTS TAKE ADVANTAGE OF THE INDIVIDUALIZED ATTENTION THEY RECEIVE IN SMALL CLASSES SCHEDULED TO FIT INTO THEIR BUSY SCHEDULES (BELOW LEFT).

"The size of our classes, the orientation of the faculty toward individualizing education, and our international focus provide students tremendous personal and professional growth opportunities," says Webster University President Richard S. Meyers.

A World of Opportunity

Accredited by the North Central Association of Colleges and Schools, Webster University offers both undergraduate and graduate programs in the arts and sciences, fine and performing arts, teacher education, and business and management.

The diversity of the student body reflects the changing demographics of contemporary university life. Webster University students range in age from the traditional 18- to 24-year-old group to adult learners who, for the most part, have full-time careers in addition to family and household responsibilities. The St. Louis campus has a 12 percent African-American population, and the university's overall minority population at all campuses is 20 percent. "We take pride in the fact that many Webster University students represent the first generation of their families to attend college or to earn master's degrees," says Neil J. George, executive vice president for academic affairs. "We make it exciting for students to explore the issues in their chosen field and understand them within the context of a world of competing, and sometimes conflicting, needs."

Webster University was recognized as one of the nation's "Top 10 Private Commuter Colleges and Universities" by the 1995 *Money Guide-Best College Buys*. Many students find a private education affordable at Webster University because they can continue to study and work close to home.

Pragmatic Learning

Making modern higher education relevant and useful is central to the mission and philosophy of Webster University. In addition to full-time faculty recognized as experts in their fields, the university incorporates executives, attorneys, artists, media professionals, writers, and computer specialists into its adjunct faculty to help provide a practical experience for students.

While class size averages between 15 and 25 students, the university's overall student population has grown to more than 10,500, of which almost 5,000 attend the St. Louis campus. "One of the reasons we're so successful with adult students is that they tell their friends and coworkers they are able to use classroom information the next day in their work," George says. "Likewise, our traditional-age students are exposed to the world outside the classroom when they apply what they have learned in internships, in performances, and by expanding their world view—through interaction

THE LEIF J. SVERDRUP BUSINESS/TECHNOLOGY COMPLEX (BOTTOM) HOUSES COMPUTER CLASSROOMS, THE MEDIA COMMUNICATIONS DEPARTMENT, AND THE SCHOOL OF BUSINESS AND MANAGEMENT.

with international faculty and students, and especially through travel opportunities."

Webster University is also located in 17 metropolitan areas, from San Diego to Chicago to Orlando, and on more than 30 military bases. International campuses are located in four European countries and Bermuda. These diverse locations reflect the university's philosophy of making higher education available at times and places accessible to the student. Meyers notes that one of the newest locations, Orlando, was opened to serve a burgeoning population where few colleges are available for working adult students. Similarly, the university offers advanced degrees for military officers on bases coast to coast.

Contributions to the Community

"Many people find themselves in responsible positions, yet in need of advanced education," says Robert A. Spencer, vice president for institutional advancement. "Webster University serves a large segment of the management and professional workplace in our various locations. By doing so, we are making an important contribution to the community.

"Beyond educating a sizable portion of the community's workforce, Webster University contributes significantly to the cultural life of St. Louis through its strong, nationally known theater and music programs, its photography and art exhibits, and its well-respected film series," Spencer continues. "The university's lecture series—featuring such notable speakers as Terry Waite, Shirley Chisholm, David McCullough, and John Naisbitt—is offered to the St. Louis community free of charge as a public service. In addition, The Repertory Theatre of St. Louis and Opera Theatre of Saint Louis present their season performances in the university's Loretto-Hilton Center for the Performing Arts, attracting some 200,000 persons annually."

International Outreach

Webster University's commitment to international education began in 1978 with the opening of its first European campus in Geneva, Switzerland. Three other campuses soon followed: Vienna, Austria; Leiden, Netherlands; and London, England. Currently, new partnerships are being pursued in the Pacific Rim, Latin America, South America, and Africa. The university is also working to establish a global network of classrooms linked with interactive video capabilities.

Articulating the university's vision and future direction, Meyers says, "The future of modern higher education is tied directly to its ability to adapt teaching and learning to stress the relevance of global interdependence to students. We live in an increasingly global economy, and our goal at Webster University is to give students better understanding of the world beyond themselves to help assure their success in the 21st century."

Clockwise from top left:
Faculty assist students in a variety of media production courses using the latest in equipment.

Demonstrating its commitment to international education, Webster University expanded its Geneva, Switzerland, campus in 1993 by constructing two new buildings.

The Loretto-Hilton Center for the Performing Arts hosts professional and student productions, lectures, and concerts. It also houses teaching spaces, workshop areas, a dance studio, and faculty offices.

The Fabick Companies

In the late 1800s while operating his family's livery stable, John Fabick astutely noted that America was moving away from the horse and carriage into the machine age. As a response to his observation, Fabick opened a small automobile dealership, Ideal Motor Company, in south St. Louis, beginning an enterprise that would become one of the world's largest and most remarkable machinery and equipment dealerships, the Fabick Companies. Since his move from horse-drawn carriage to car to the crawler tractor in 1917, Fabick has been involved in some of the greatest engineering feats of the modern era. Over the years, Fabick has been a part of many significant construction projects such as the Trans-Alaska and Trans-Alpine pipelines, the federal interstate highway system, Trans-Arabia pipeline, Forest Park Expressway, Bagnell Dam, "Little Inch, Big Inch" pipelines, and the Gateway Arch.

In 1917 John Fabick (above) established a business in south St. Louis that has grown into one of the world's largest and most remarkable machinery and equipment dealerships.

In the 1920s, Fabick became the exclusive Caterpillar sales and service dealership for the St. Louis area, a territory that now includes 73 counties in eastern Missouri and southern Illinois.

Meeting Customer Needs

The company's product line expanded from automobiles to earthmoving equipment as Fabick began to encounter the needs of his customers in what was then still an agricultural stronghold. The company added Cletrac "tank-type" tractors and Deere farm implements to its lineup, and in 1921, added two models of crawler tractors manufactured by C.L. Best. Fabick's early involvement with Best-produced equipment would provide yet another example of the forward-thinking business acumen that pushed the company to the top of its profession.

In 1925 C.L. Best merged with Holt Manufacturing Company, forming the Caterpillar Tractor Company. Shortly thereafter, Fabick became the exclusive Caterpillar sales and service dealership for the St. Louis area, a territory that eventually would expand to include 73 counties in eastern Missouri and southern Illinois. Today, with seven operational facilities, satellite stores, and crane and marine subsidiaries, Fabick has grown into a family of related companies with a worldwide reputation for dependable service.

New Territories and Services

Between 1938 and the early 1950s, Fabick opened four branches—one in Salem, Illinois; a second in Sikeston, Missouri; a third in Marion, Illinois; and a fourth in Jefferson City, Missouri. In a related move, in 1962 Fabick opened a crane operation, Gateway Machinery Company, to meet the needs of its building contractors in St. Louis and the surrounding area.

When the Eisenhower administration instituted the nation's interstate highway system, Fabick's location at the U.S. population center made it a natural to supply contractors with equipment for earthmoving and to supply materials such as sand, gravel, cement, and asphalt.

To provide better service to its customers, Fabick acquired its first aircraft in 1944. In the late 1940s, Fabick Aircraft Company was formed and received the dealerships for Beech aircraft and Bell helicopters. Although Fabick Aircraft Company was sold later in the 1950s, the company has maintained an aircraft to meet customer needs for the past 50 years.

The company has been twice recognized by the U.S. government with the coveted "E" award and "E" star award for excellence in foreign marketing activities and the promotion of the sale of U.S. products overseas.

In the early 1970s, the company's headquarters was relocated from the city of St. Louis to its present location on 80 acres in the suburb of Fenton (above).

During the 1980s, the company added two more facilities—Fabick Marine, which provides round-the-clock service for the large volume of barge traffic that travels the Mississippi River, and Fabick Power Systems, which services the extensive customer base of Caterpillar engines and generators.

Family Guides the Way

Today the Fabick family consists of 136 members. Fourteen of these members are active in the daily operations of the business. John Fabick, son of the founder, serves as the company's chairman of the board. His son, Harry, is president; and a nephew, Tom Dinkins, is executive vice president.

The Fabicks have led the growing family business through a variety of challenges, perhaps the most daunting of which was the construction and follow-up of the Alaska pipeline. "After completion of the project, we were the sole equipment dealer selected to inspect and appraise some 15,000 pieces of equipment scattered along 800 miles of rugged country, and complete the project in the short span of 90 days," recalls Harry Fabick.

In the early 1970s, the Fabicks decided to relocate the company's headquarters from the city of St. Louis to its present location on 80 acres in the suburb of Fenton where the availability of land allowed for greater expansion of its sales and service area.

People Remain the Focus

Whether in the pipeline industry, road construction, mining, farming, quarrying, or cogeneration engines, the center of Fabick's world is its customers and its 500 employees.

Throughout the company's growth, Fabick has looked after its customers' needs by offering a variety of equipment and parts complemented by top-notch

repair service. To keep equipment in full operation, the company employs more than 250 service people, 60 of whom are constantly on the move to service machinery on the job. Each year, the company invests thousands of man-hours in training service technicians.

The company has built more than 334,000 square feet of service area—137,000 in St. Louis— all of which is equipped with state-of-the-art diagnostic and tooling equipment. Fabick represents over 100 manufacturers of construction supplies and equipment, with Caterpillar, Inc. being the company's largest manufacturer. Fabick's facilities are stocked with nearly 90,000 individual parts. In all, the company provides its customers with ready access to an inventory of more than $12.5 million in replacement parts.

Throughout its history, the company has been governed by a single mission, expressed in founder John Fabick's motto: "To ever serve our customers better." That mission remains the company's guiding principle as it moves forward with confidence into the next century.

The Daniel & Henry Company

THE TIME WAS THE EARLY 1920S, AND THE DOWNTOWN ST. LOUIS business district was the hub of local commercial activity. During that era of civic progress, two St. Louis entrepreneurs, Carl P. Daniel and Jesse P. Henry, opened what ultimately would become the largest privately owned, independent insurance brokerage firm in Missouri—The Daniel & Henry Company. ■ The founders' vision was to operate a full-service insurance agency in a manner different from others of their peers. They sought to share common facilities, overhead, and expenses among a group of insurance brokers and local brokering houses that were subsequently acquired. The important distinction was that each broker owned and controlled his own book of business. The result was successful: Daniel & Henry created a cost-effective management style that continues to benefit both its customers and its brokers in a highly competitive industry. The original mission of being an economical and innovative insurance resource motivated the firm to adopt a motto in 1921 that is still in use today, "We're on your company's team; not on your company's payroll."

Daniel & Henry's headquarters building, located at 2350 Market Street, offers views of the Gateway Arch, Union Station, and the St. Louis skyline.

Growing with St. Louis

Daniel & Henry now has 190 employees and represents more than 40 top-rated insurance companies, including Commercial Union, Ohio Casualty, and USF&G, as well as having access to worldwide excess and surplus lines markets. The Daniel & Henry team maintains growth by building relationships with new brokers who have a viable book of business, or client base, that fits with the company's existing philosophy. The result is a corporate democracy that operates like a partnership and is managed by a nine-person executive committee. Directors chart the agency's needs and plan its growth rather than following the traditional route of implementing directives from a CEO or senior management.

Daniel & Henry's 74-year history of profitability and expansion includes not only insuring the St. Louis business community, but providing coverage for well-known local cultural and civic institutions. The beginning of this cultural symbiosis can be traced to an act of civic-mindedness at the outset, when Daniel & Henry led an initiative to restore the St. Louis childhood home of Eugene Field, the famous children's poet. The company, joined by the St. Louis Board of Education, encouraged the city's schoolchildren to collect pennies to help fund the restoration. This effort saved the historic home, which now stands as St. Louis' only museum of 19th-century childhood.

While maintaining and building on its roots as a St. Louis agency serving businesses in the greater metropolitan area, Daniel & Henry has reacted to global business trends and has been a longtime member of Assurex International. Affiliation with this universal insurance network has enabled the company to secure a full range of risk-management and insurance products to better serve its clientele, literally from London to Tokyo.

Above all else, The Daniel & Henry Company has always offered its customers professional knowledge and counsel, and has shared its practical experience in creating and implementing comprehensive insurance and risk management programs for all types of business at a reasonable cost. Today, as in 1921, The Daniel & Henry Company is a far-reaching and influential insurance agency that abides by its motto to work as a team member focused on its clients in a cost-effective manner. The future looks bright indeed.

Pet Incorporated

In 1884 a young Swiss immigrant named John Meyenberg settled into an enclave of the fertile farming and dairy country around St. Louis. He came to America to sell his idea of canning milk without adding sugar as a preservative. At a time when there was only primitive refrigeration and fresh food spoiled quickly, Meyenberg's idea proved to be a blessing. He wanted to start a "condensery" in Highland, Illinois. The following year, the Helvetia Milk Condensing Company was founded to produce Highland Evaporated Cream.

After some unsettling years of trial and error, the business moved to St. Louis in 1921. Two years later, the name was changed to Pet Milk Company, reflecting its most popular product, the "Our Pet" Evaporated Cream brand.

The organization became known as Pet Incorporated in 1966, characterizing its increasing diversification into other businesses. In 1969 the company established its international headquarters at Pet Plaza, a stunning downtown structure overlooking the Mississippi River and the renowned Gateway Arch.

In 1978 Pet was acquired by Chicago-based IC Industries, but in 1991 was spun off and again became a freestanding, publicly traded company listed on the New York Stock Exchange.

Fiscal year 1994 saw Pet Incorporated achieve net sales of $1.6 billion. More than 5,700 employees operated 18 domestic and eight international manufacturing plants, including subsidiaries in Canada, the United Kingdom, the Netherlands, Australia, and Venezuela.

Today, consumers recognize Pet's products under many well-known brand names, including Old El Paso Mexican foods, Progresso soups and Italian specialty foods, Downyflake frozen waffles, Van de Kamp's frozen seafood, Pet-Ritz frozen pie crusts and fruit cobblers, B&M baked beans, Underwood meat spreads, and the company's flagship brand, Pet evaporated milk. These items are sold in the grocery and frozen food sections of food retailers, and are distributed through food-service channels for restaurants and institutional customers.

As an independent company, Pet sharpened its focus on its major brands, primarily Old El Paso and Progresso. The company also achieved significant cost reductions and improved quality in operations through total quality principles. At the same time, Pet divested operations that did not fit its core businesses and long-term growth strategies. While these gains were significant, Pet found itself in an increasingly competitive marketplace.

In February 1995, Pet Incorporated was acquired by another venerable food producer, The Pillsbury Company, a subsidiary of London-based Grand Metropolitan PLC. In announcing the acquisition, Pillsbury commented that the addition of Pet would enable the company to build on its existing strengths while promoting further growth in Pet's leading brands.

It was that same vision of growth that also spurred a young 19th-century immigrant to pursue an idea. Even with his great aspirations, it's unlikely that John Meyenberg could have predicted his idea for canning preserved milk would mature into a global food manufacturer such as Pet Incorporated. The familiar products it nurtured and expanded will always trace their roots to Pet and the St. Louis area where it began.

Clockwise from left:
In 1969 the company made its international headquarters at Pet Plaza, a stunning downtown structure overlooking the Mississippi River and the renowned Gateway Arch.

Pet's many well-known products are sold in the grocery and frozen food sections of food retailers, and are distributed through food-service channels for restaurants and institutional customers.

In the early years, the company's most popular product was the "Our Pet" Evaporated Cream brand.

TODAY YOU ORDERED FRENCH FRIES AT A FAST-FOOD RESTAURANT, deposited your check in your bank's ATM, and watched a program on cable TV. Somehow a Watlow heater, sensor, and control made your life a little easier—from fast-food preparation to freeze protection on outdoor electronics to thruster heaters for a communication satellite. ■ Watlow Electric Manufacturing Company began in St. Louis more than 70 years ago manufacturing electric heaters for industries that had been dependent upon costly steam and hazardous gas heating. The age of electricity was still young in 1922 when Louis Desloge, Sr., founded Watlow, a name derived from a word play on "low wattage." The company originally designed and manufactured heaters for the shoe industry. The next year Watlow engineers developed electric heaters for brick presses, and thereby began a series of expansions into new industries.

Today the company is still making electric heaters, plus the sensors and controls needed to complete the thermal system. Watlow's ability over the years to keep up with rapidly changing technology has brought about its expansion into numerous markets found worldwide including plastics processing, medical, aerospace, semiconductor manufacturing, food equipment, and petrochemical. Today's Watlow employs more than 1,500 people around the globe and generates over $150 million in annual sales.

Leadership in a Changing Marketplace

Company leaders of the post-World War II Watlow realized new products were required for the new era. One architect of the modern Watlow was Desloge's son George, who joined the firm in 1948. George Desloge engineered many successful products for the company, also designing the equipment to manufacture them. In 1950 he invented a band heater with a patented clamping strap that found widespread use in the young plastics industry. He invented, and later patented, the FIREROD® cartridge heater in 1954, an innovation that improved heat transfer efficiency in industrial applications. The FIREROD heater quickly propelled the company to prominence and became the industry leader in its class.

George's brother, Louis Desloge, Jr., joined the company in 1963, bringing with him international sales and marketing expertise. He is credited with establishing Watlow's global sales and distribution network that allows the company to provide product service and support worldwide.

Watlow flourished under the

CLOCKWISE FROM ABOVE:
IN 1922, WITH ST. LOUIS AS ONE OF THE SHOE PRODUCTION CAPITALS OF THE WORLD, LOUIS DESLOGE, SR., FOUNDED WATLOW TO MANUFACTURE ELECTRIC HEATING ELEMENTS FOR SHOE STEAMERS AND DRYERS.

IN 1991 GARY NEAL (LEFT) BECAME PRESIDENT OF WATLOW, GEORGE DESLOGE (RIGHT) BECAME CHAIRMAN OF THE BOARD, AND LOUIS DESLOGE, JR., BECAME VICE CHAIRMAN.

WATLOW GOES TO EXTREMES IN ELECTRIC HEATING, MEETING TEMPERATURE REQUIREMENTS UP TO 2,300 DEGREES FAHRENHEIT.

brothers' leadership. The company's main facility, located in the Westport area of St. Louis, expanded numerous times to its present size of more than 180,000 square feet. In 1972 Watlow opened its first facility outside of the United States in Weiher, West Germany. Another facility was opened in Hannibal, Missouri, later the same year.

In 1976 Watlow purchased Waynco, Inc., of Winona, Minnesota, further expanding its product line to include sophisticated electronic temperature control expertise. The company also purchased the Claud S. Gordon Company of Richmond, Illinois, in 1985, the nation's leading manufacturer of temperature sensors.

Today Watlow produces heating system components in 11 manufacturing locations in the United States as well as six locations in Europe and Asia—England, France, Germany, Italy, Shanghai, and Singapore.

Since 1991 Watlow has been guided by company president Gary Neal, while George Desloge and Louis Desloge, Jr., have headed the company's board of directors.

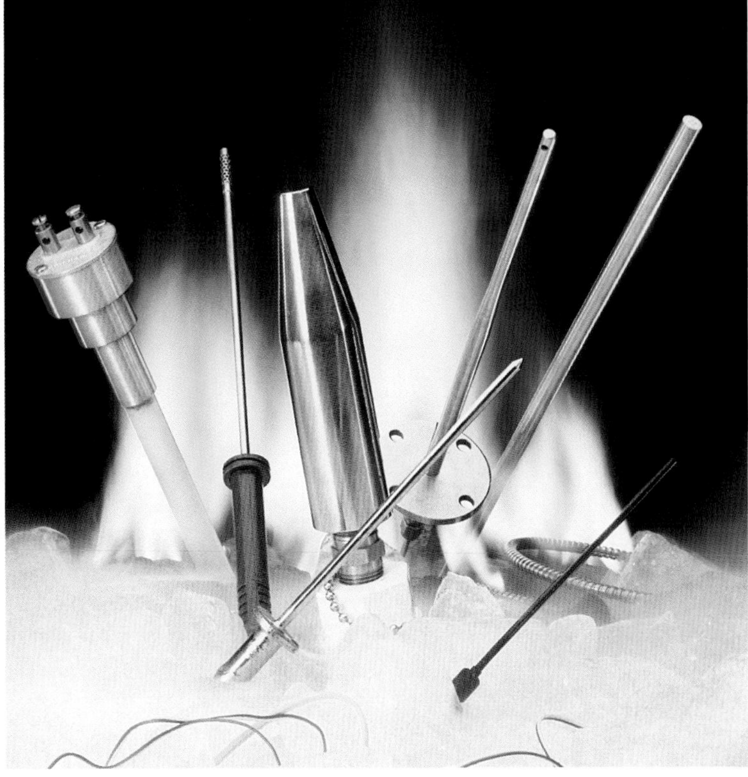

The Difference Is Engineering and Application Know-How

"Only by understanding the end use of applications can we be sure to provide the best product," says Neal. "Our engineers become a part of the customer's design team, working directly with them to understand not only their needs, but also their customers' needs."

Watlow often partners with customers to create new products and processes. Each Watlow plant is equipped with its own research and development department to constantly test new designs, construction methods, and materials. Customer R&D services also include prototype development and quality certification.

Because Watlow designs and manufactures all of the components of a thermal system, the company can provide single-source performance accountability. More importantly, this capability enables Watlow engineers to recommend, develop, and deliver the best heat solution for a customer's specific application.

"By being involved with all of the thermal components and understanding diverse applications, Watlow engineers help build better products, with shorter time to market and lower overall cost," Neal explains. "Watlow's experience with different markets allows solutions from one industry to provide fresh ideas in another."

Setting Goals for the Future

Being the best means continued new-product development, encouraged through a company requirement that 20 percent of sales must come from products developed within the preceding five years. To support this goal Watlow dedicated a facility to long-term research to identify new technologies and develop the required thermal support components.

The company adopted ISO 9000 procedures as the quality standard throughout its facilities worldwide. It has also organized employees into teams for greater creativity and productivity, trained team members in the use of total quality management tools, and empowered those teams to make operating improvements.

"By merging our technical expertise and customer need with innovative new products," Neal explains, "Watlow will continue our leadership role—providing our customers with the very best heaters, sensors, and controls for the competitive advantage they need in today's global markets."

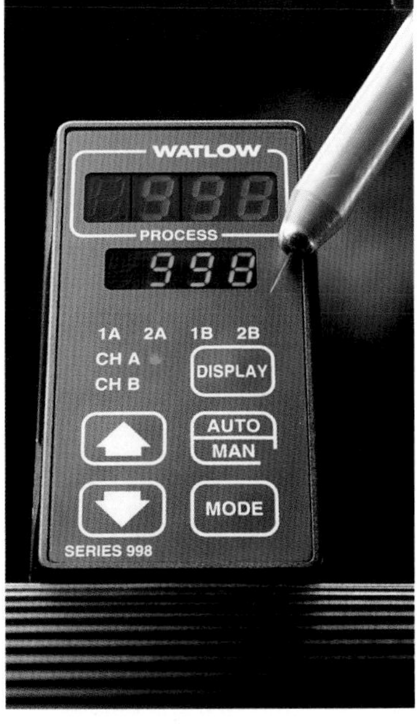

Clockwise from above:
Watlow controls are built to withstand hostile environments, including heat, electrical noise, static discharge, humidity, and vibration.

Watlow temperature sensors can handle anything from cryogenic -328 degrees Fahrenheit to refractory temperatures of 4,200 degrees Fahrenheit.

In 1954 George Desloge invented the FIREROD® cartridge heater, an innovation that improved heat transfer efficiency.

KMOX News/Talk 1120

IT IS ONLY FITTING THAT THE OFFICES OF KMOX NEWS/TALK 1120 command a panoramic view of the downtown St. Louis waterfront. Known as "The Voice of St. Louis," KMOX has provided the city with the best in up-to-the-minute news, issue-driven talk shows, play-by-play sports, and entertainment for the past 70 years. The station's innovation and refinement of the talk show format have led the way in maintaining its number one position in the marketplace. KMOX has served the needs of the St. Louis community well.

KMOX dominates the market in many ways. Its 50,000-watt signal is picked up in 44 surrounding states, and it remains the dominant radio station in the top 50 U.S. markets based on audience share. "KMOX is St. Louis. We reflect this community in all our programming and community events," says Rod Zimmerman, vice president and general manager of the station.

The CBS-owned station first went on the air December 24, 1925. KMOX established its leadership in radio by becoming the first to editorialize and endorse a political candidate. From the early days of broadcasting mostly news, music, and network programs, KMOX, under the guidance of Robert Hyland, went on to pioneer the talk show format. It was February 28, 1960, and the show was "At Your Service," a dialogue talk show on community issues. It was the first of its kind, and through 35 years of development and refinement KMOX has used this talk format to serve the needs of the city by providing informative programming. Today, Kevin Horrigan, Charles Brennan, Charles Jaco, and Dianna Proffitt, along with veteran hosts Jack Buck and Jim White, have been instrumental in continuing the tradition of issue-driven talk radio that has kept KMOX in the number one position.

The Best in News and Sports

Also known as "Mid-America's Most Trusted Source for News," 1120 on the AM dial is where St. Louis residents turn for the latest in local, regional, and global news coverage. With "Total Information-AM," Wendy Wiese and Bill Wilkerson provide the most comprehensive look at the day's news, sports, traffic, and weather. KMOX has the ability to cover news events around the world, relying on its own reporters and the worldwide news-gathering organization of the CBS Radio Network. KMOX has broadcast live from such hot spots as the Middle East and Moscow. On the way home, St. Louis residents depend on "Total Information-PM" with Doug McElvein and Barbara Whitesides.

The station's garnering of numerous annual awards attests to its success. KMOX has won three Marconi awards from the National Association of Broadcasters—Major Market Station of the Year, News/Talk Station of the Year, and Legendary Station of the Year. Other awards include three Peabody awards for investigative journalism and five National Headliner awards.

No other radio station gives St. Louis the degree and depth of sports coverage that KMOX provides. Trademarked "America's Sports Voice," the station is legendary in its coverage of local, regional, and national sports. Sports Director Jack Buck, one of the nation's most admired sports broadcasters, heads the lineup of KMOX sports personalities and reporters. The station's past and present voices in sports include such prominent figures as Bob Costas, Dan

◂ BILL COBY

CLOCKWISE FROM ABOVE: COHOSTED BY BILL WILKERSON, "TOTAL INFORMATION-AM" PROVIDES THE MOST COMPREHENSIVE LOOK AT THE DAY'S NEWS, SPORTS, TRAFFIC, AND WEATHER.

CHARLES JACO, FORMER CNN CORESPONDENT, HOSTS "KMOX NEWSMAKERS."

KMOX'S ON-AIR PERSONALITIES INCLUDE (SEATED, FROM LEFT) DIANNA PROFFITT, BARBARA WHITESIDES, WENDY WIESE, (STANDING) JIM WHITE, CHARLES BRENNAN, JACK BUCK, DOUG MCELVEIN, AND KEVIN HORRIGAN.

Clockwise from top left: During a November 1960 broadcast of "At Your Service," host Jack Buck and Senior Vice President and General Manager Robert Hyland welcome former First Lady Eleanor Roosevelt.

KMOX sponsors the annual Great Forest Park Balloon Race.

The KMOX/Cardinals broadcast team includes (from left) KMOX Sports Director Jack Buck, Mike Shannon, and Joe Buck.

Dierdorf, Harry Caray, and Joe Garagiola. Boasting one of the largest and most experienced sports departments in radio, KMOX broadcasts play-by-play for St. Louis Cardinals baseball, St. Louis Blues hockey, NFL Monday Night Football, and the University of Missouri at Columbia football and basketball.

Technology and Research

KMOX is always looking for ways to improve programming and provide its listening audience with the finest radio has to offer. Its current 24-hour programming is broadcast from six state-of-the-art studios. The views and attitudes of the listeners are constantly monitored and researched for new ways to improve upon the product.

Fulfilling the Needs of the Community

KMOX stays in tune with the world and the St. Louis community through station-sponsored programs such as '90s diversity seminars, safety seminars, and town hall meetings, plus scholarship and intern programs. KMOX is renowned for its leadership in philanthropic efforts in the St. Louis community, raising millions of dollars through charitable sponsorships and fund drives. One example that characterizes the station's efforts was its response to the Great Flood of 1993. The station was a source of vital information for millions of affected people, coordinating volunteer efforts throughout the flood zone. It also created the Flood Relief Radio Network, which raised more than $145,000 through radio stations across the country for the relief of flood victims. Charitable support throughout the years has been given to agencies such as Cardinal Glennon Children's Hospital, St. Patrick's Center for the Homeless, Entrepreneur of the Year, American Red Cross, Mathews-Dickey Boys Club, and March of Dimes, to name a few.

"KMOX is constantly evaluating where we've been and where we're going in order to keep pace with the views and issues important to our listeners and advertisers," explains Zimmerman. It is this dedication to being the dominant voice in radio, as well as the meeting place for its listening audience, that will continue to ensure KMOX's role as "The Voice of St. Louis."

Mississippi River Transmission Corp.

Mississippi River Transmission Corp. (MRT), the largest transporter of natural gas to the St. Louis region, provides gas transportation and storage services for natural gas distribution companies and municipal utilities throughout southeastern Missouri and southern Illinois. Laclede Gas Company, MRT's largest customer, serves an area that includes the city of St. Louis and St. Louis County with approximately 600,000 customers. MRT's vital gas delivery services and its history of aggressive investment in the natural gas industry have placed the company in a key behind-the-scenes role in the development of the St. Louis region, according to Michael T. Hunter, company president.

In all, the company has 2,100 miles of pipeline running from Louisiana west into Texas and north through Arkansas into Missouri and Illinois. MRT directly supplies natural gas to many of the region's largest industrial concerns. Names like Granite City Steel, Laclede Steel, Shell Oil, Cerro Copper Products, and others have long-held relationships with MRT.

"Over the years, we've worked closely with those industries to craft contracts that are very plant specific and to everyone's mutual benefit, and perhaps have even helped those industries remain viable contributors to the area's economy during leaner times," Hunter says.

Louisiana to St. Louis

The company traces its founding to 1928 when a business consortium formed Mississippi River Fuel Corp. to build a pipeline from Monroe, Louisiana, to St. Louis. This 1929 vintage "main line number one," originally intended to supply fuel for the St. Louis region's steel industry, is still in service. By 1947 Laclede Gas Company had begun utilizing natural gas exclusively in its distribution system.

In response to regulatory changes, MRT has evolved in recent years from a wholesale merchant of natural gas to a transporter and storage operation. The company also operates a growing subsidiary, MRT Energy Marketing, that provides an array of gas sales and related services, including serving as agent to procure supplies for customers and the management of their natural gas supply and transportation portfolios.

Since 1986 MRT has been a wholly owned subsidiary of NorAm Energy Corp., of Houston, the nation's third-largest distribution company in terms of customers. NorAm provides natural gas transportation or distribution services through MRT and other operating units in a geographic region stretching from the border of Canada to the border of Mexico.

A Bright Future

Although the MRT name may not be as readily recognized in the community as some of its customers, the company and its employees actively support St. Louis-area civic, charitable, and philanthropic causes.

Hunter is optimistic about the company's future based on projected growth in the use of natural gas—both in residential, commercial, and industrial settings and in newer, nontraditional applications. He anticipates one day seeing fleets of vehicles fueled entirely by natural gas. Hunter also expects further changes in the regulatory environment to create new energy service opportunities for the company. "MRT stands first and foremost on the bright future of natural gas," he says. "The company has the ability and flexibility to provide energy services that the marketplace demands over time."

Clockwise from top right:
MRT began operating in 1929 just after the bottom fell out of the stock market. It took the company five years to declare a dividend.

MRT's fifth anniversary dinner was held at the Melbourne Hotel on November 2, 1934.

From its St. Louis headquarters, MRT today provides gas transportation and storage services for natural gas distribution companies and municipal utilities throughout southeastern Missouri and southern Illinois.

American Airlines

AMERICAN AIRLINES AND ST. LOUIS HAVE HAD A LONG AND historic relationship, and it all began with a young aviator named Charles Lindbergh. One April morning in 1926, Lindbergh flew into St. Louis in a single-engine biplane. He was carrying a bag of mail from Chicago, and his flight represented the first mail run for a company that was later to become American Airlines.

Today, St. Louis and American Airlines continue this special partnership, although these days the airline is committed to providing the best in passenger air service. Jane Swift, general manager for American Airlines in St. Louis, says, "Our role in St. Louis is to offer the traveling public a choice. We are the premier carrier for both domestic and international travel. With our partner, American Eagle, we offer service to 237 cities worldwide."

American Airlines and its parent company, AMR Corporation, have headquarters in Fort Worth. Today, there are more than 94,000 employees who wear the uniforms of American Airlines. Some 100 of those employees can be found working in St. Louis at Lambert Field's three American Airlines gates, ticket counter, Admirals Club, and nearby AA cargo facility.

An Innovator among Airlines

With 650 aircraft in its fleet and almost 900,000 departures per year, American Airlines is the nation's largest air carrier. As befitting a leader, American has also led the industry in pioneering new services to meet the needs of its expanding customer base.

The company developed the first program to reward customers for their loyalty by introducing the AAdvantage® Program in 1981. The program remains the largest and most comprehensive frequent flyer program in the industry. SABRE, the company's travel information network, was created to provide automated ticketing and travel information through computer systems worldwide. According to Swift, "SABRE is the system that everyone else has tried to duplicate." Super Saver fares, coast-to-coast service, and VIP lounges (American's Admirals Clubs) are all innovations for which American Airlines can take credit.

And there's more to come. "We were the first airline to offer telephones in every row of coach class," Swift explains. "Soon, we'll provide incoming phone calls and faxes, too."

Serving St. Louis—and the World

American offers 15 flights that originate from St. Louis each day and connect with Nashville, Chicago, and Dallas to provide service around the globe.

With four hubs in operation around the country—Chicago, Dallas/Fort Worth, Miami, and Nashville—as well as San Juan, American is equipped to transport its customers to almost any destination on earth, whether it's Buenos Aires, Barbados, or Boston.

American's partner in regional airline service, American Eagle, expands the level of service offered. American Eagle provides frequent flights between American Airlines' hubs and smaller communities throughout the country.

American is proud of its longstanding affiliation with St. Louis and demonstrates this pride by providing superior customer service. "Our passengers benefit from a very positive experience—flights that are on time, safe, and pleasant," Swift says. "Customer service is what differentiates American from other airlines, and it's what makes us 'Something Special in the Air.'"

CLOCKWISE FROM ABOVE:
CHARLES A. LINDBERGH WAS A PIONEER AIR MAIL PILOT FOR ST. LOUIS-BASED ROBERTSON AIRCRAFT CORPORATION, A PREDECESSOR TO AMERICAN AIRLINES.

AMERICAN'S AWARD-WINNING INTERNATIONAL FLAGSHIP SERVICE,® INTRODUCED IN 1990, IS SETTING NEW STANDARDS INTERNATIONALLY.

WITH 650 AIRCRAFT IN ITS FLEET AND ALMOST 900,000 DEPARTURES PER YEAR, AMERICAN AIRLINES IS THE NATION'S LARGEST AIR CARRIER.

Pepsi-Cola Bottling Co. of St. Louis, Inc.

Young North Carolina pharmacist Caleb Bradham could not have imagined the $25 billion soft drink empire he was creating when he mixed kola nuts, vanilla extracts, rare oils, and soda water together during the hot summer of 1898. Originally designed as a cure for dyspepsia—or indigestion—Pepsi-Cola today is the flagship soft drink of a worldwide drink and food conglomerate.

As the new beverage, originally dubbed "Brad's Drink," became increasingly popular, Bradham renamed it Pepsi-Cola as an allusion to its potential for curing dyspepsia. Bradham formed his own company to market his soda in 1902. Now known as PepsiCo, Inc., it has become the world's second-largest producer of soft drinks, as well as the largest snack foods company and the largest restaurant system in the world.

The Total Beverage Company

Pepsi-Cola Bottling Co. of St. Louis is owned and operated by Pepsi-Cola North America, part of the PepsiCo organization. Founded in 1929 as Hygrade Soda Water Co., the St. Louis facility operates within Pepsi's Gateway Market Unit, one of 103 such market units in the United States.

"The Gateway Market Unit serves 11 Missouri and Illinois counties," notes Dan Trott, general manager. "We are the second-largest of Pepsi's company-owned market units in the United States, but we are at the top in market share. As the largest beverage company in the St. Louis area, we deliver about 20 million cases of Pepsi beverages a year and have net sales of $120 million. Our area is truly the heartland of Pepsi."

Pepsi produces a wide range of beverages in cans and bottles, in addition to its soda fountain products. The legendary Pepsi-Cola and its several varieties are joined by Mountain Dew, Slice, and other brands. Pepsi also distributes Lipton ready-to-drink teas, Ocean Spray juices and lemonades, and the new Allsport drink.

"Our company considers us to be 'The Total Beverage Company,'" Trott says, "and our mission is to supply consumers around the world with beverages of all types,

The legendary Pepsi-Cola is shown in some of the latest packaging success stories.

excepting only alcoholic beverages and milk."

A Long History

Pepsi's road to global success has been a long one. During the Depression years, the company was owned by Loft, Inc., a candy manufacturer. Striving for a marketing advantage, Loft sold "giant" 12-ounce bottles—twice the size of competing soft drinks—for the standard price of a nickel. Pepsi sales immediately jumped and have soared ever since. Today, Pepsi-Cola is the most-purchased brand item in grocery stores.

In 1965 Pepsi-Cola merged with Frito-Lay, a thriving snack food manufacturer, to form PepsiCo. Snack food sales had reached $7 billion by 1993, about one-third of the company's total sales. In 1977 PepsiCo expanded into food service with the purchase of Pizza Hut and its 2,600 restaurants (now more than 10,000). The Taco Bell restaurant chain was acquired in 1978, and Kentucky Fried Chicken (now known as KFC) was added in 1986. Acquisition of additional food service companies has continued into the 1990s.

Pepsi-Cola originally was distributed in the St. Louis area under a franchise granted to the family-owned Hygrade Soda Water Co. The Pepsi-Cola Co. purchased Hygrade in 1958 and created the Pepsi-Cola Bottling Co. of St. Louis, which continued to operate in Hygrade's 647 Tower Grove Avenue plant. Beginning in 1975, the company was owned by MEI Corp. of Minneapolis until Pepsi-Cola North America reacquired it in 1986.

With sales burgeoning in the late 1980s, Pepsi-Cola Bottling Co. of St. Louis began making plans to build a new facility for the 21st century. That dream came to fruition on March 29, 1994, with the dedication of a $35 million production and distribution facility in the Union Seventy Center business park in north St. Louis.

"We intensively considered whether to remain in the city of St. Louis or move out to the suburbs," Trott says, "but we had been in the city for more than 60 years and we are strongly committed to its future. We found an attractive and cost-effective site, and we knew it was right for us."

An Industrial Anchor

The Pepsi facility, credited by city officials with revitalizing development in north St. Louis, anchors a business park built on the old site of the General Motors St. Louis plant. A 165-foot-high water tower, described by Mayor Freeman Bosley, Jr., as a beacon of hope for St. Louis, proudly displays the Pepsi logo.

Pepsi's 263,000-square-foot facility is located on 27 acres. The plant's 124-valve can line fills about 1,600 cans per minute, and its 96-valve bottle line fills about 300 two-liter bottles and 750 twenty-ounce bottles per minute.

Trott notes that Pepsi's 500 employees had significant input in the design of the new facility. Warehouse loaders and production operators visited vendors, tested equipment, and approved equipment shipments. Office personnel visited other facilities to test the workstation proposed for the St. Louis plant.

"Our new operation confirms our commitment to provide the beverages that our customers and consumers prefer," Trott says. "This is truly a total beverage operation, not just a soft drink plant. We're also pleased that its construction created significant jobs in the city of St. Louis and that our decision to locate here has helped bring other substantial operations to this area."

In 1994 Pepsi-Cola Bottling Co. dedicated its new, $35 million production and distribution facility in the Union Seventy Center business park. The company's presence in the area is credited for revitalizing development in North St. Louis (above).

This 165-foot-high water tower, described by Mayor Freeman Bosley, Jr., as a beacon of hope for St. Louis, proudly displays the Pepsi logo (below left).

Trans World Airlines, Inc.

A lengthy history of pioneering firsts has lifted Trans World Airlines, Inc. to a position of aviation leadership—both in St. Louis, where the airline has its corporate headquarters, and worldwide, where TWA is a readily recognized name in passenger aviation. From its emergence in the 1930s as the nation's first coast-to-coast carrier, to its recently established employee-owned operational structure, TWA has been an industry leader. The senior U.S. air carrier continues to set standards of safety, travel speed, comfort, and operating efficiency.

GREG KIGER

Jeffrey H. Erickson is TWA's president and chief executive officer.

TWA and Trans World Express (TWE), the airline's network of regional commuter carriers, serve more than 100 destinations in the United States and the Caribbean, as well as 12 cities in Europe and the Middle East. St. Louis' Lambert International Airport is the domestic hub, with more than 400 daily departures. Nearly 12 million passengers fly TWA in and out of St. Louis yearly. Most international flights originate at New York's John F. Kennedy International Airport. The airline operates 184 jet aircraft on domestic and international routes, including McDonnell Douglas DC-9s and MD-80s; Boeing 727s, 747s, and 767s; and Lockheed 1011s.

From Famous Ownership to Employee Ownership

TWA's historic ties to St. Louis reach back officially to 1929. Transcontinental and Western Airways (T&WA) was known as the "Lindbergh Line"—after famed St. Louis aviator Charles A. Lindbergh, who served as chairman of the carrier's first technical committee.

Renowned personality Howard Hughes directed much of TWA's early progress. As an accomplished aviator in his own right, Hughes became TWA's principal stockholder by 1939 and was instrumental in bringing the Lockheed Constellation into service. This four-engine aircraft was used extensively overseas between 1946 and 1967, and remains a hallmark of aerodynamic design.

TWA pioneered commercial use of the DC-2 and later the DC-3, the aircraft models that brought passenger aviation to millions. The airline was the first to demonstrate, with the consultation of Douglas Aircraft, the safety of twin-engine flight. This confidence in its aircraft fleet enabled TWA to establish efficient, reasonably priced flights. In 1961 TWA became the first airline to offer all-jet service on

This MD-83 aircraft, known as "Wings of Pride," is sponsored by the employee-owners of TWA.

international flights, followed by all-jet domestic flights in 1967—heralding the development of today's high-speed, highly reliable passenger service.

TWA holds most of the firsts in aviation passenger comfort as well. The airline was among the first to fly "air hostesses" aboard DC-2 flights in 1935. TWA began inflight motion pictures in 1961, and was the first airline to set aside nonsmoking sections aboard all flights in 1970.

TWA continues to provide leadership to its industry, emerging from an old style of airline management to the new employee-equity management structure, which became effective in 1993. A number of other airlines have followed. The establishment of TWA's employee-owner management team was influenced by Donald F. Craib, Jr., the company's former chairman of the board. Current Board Chairman John Cahill, formerly of British Aerospace, brings positive direction in his nonexecutive position. The management team responsible for labor agreements with all three of TWA's unions was assembled by Jeffrey H. Erickson, the company's president and chief executive officer. That team has also implemented an aggressive business plan to remake the airline into the nation's first low-cost, full-service carrier.

Working with St. Louis

The city of St. Louis has played a key role in the airline's recent development. For example, the city provided TWA with incentive packages to aid in its financial restructuring, a factor that influenced the airline's decision to move its world headquarters and its reservations unit to St. Louis in 1994. By adding these departments to the existing operations at Lambert, plus a maintenance facility in Kansas City, the number of TWA employees in Missouri reached 11,000. The airline's total U.S. workforce is 22,249, complemented by about 900 overseas employees. The St. Louis hub facilities include the Trans World Travel Academy, with full training for reservations staff and flight attendants. TWA also offers recurrent training for pilots in high-tech flight simulation units.

The airline has a unique St. Louis community involvement program. TWA adopted one of the city's public schools, Eliot School, through the School Partnership Program. TWA flight attendants, flight service managers, pilots, and reservation clerks provide classroom programs on topics ranging from effective communications to good grooming. The program models awards for student excellence after TWA's own employee recognition program. Classes adopt TWA destination cities, and company employees who fly there share with the class their personal observations, snapshots, and postcards.

Erickson is optimistic about TWA's future in St. Louis and beyond. He says the airline will continue to build on the strengths of employee ownership to provide superior service in a market that's increasingly delineated between no-frills, low-cost carriers and full-service, high-cost carriers. He believes that TWA's employee-owner structure can present the marketplace with a better alternative. "We are a full-service airline, yet we do it at low cost," says Erickson. "So, we're continuing to pioneer ways to present what the marketplace needs at a price it can afford."

TWA and its network of regional commuter carriers serve more than 100 destinations in the United States and the Caribbean, as well as 12 cities in Europe and the Middle East.

GTE Telephone Operations

For thousands of home owners and businesses around the St. Louis area, GTE is their telephone company. In fact, GTE and its predecessors have served much of St. Charles and surrounding counties since the 1930s. Today's Missouri businesses and residents have additional uses for telecommunications services—transmission of information, "telemedicine," education, and video services.

GTE, the nation's largest provider of telecommunications products and services, brings these services to the Missouri communities of O'Fallon, St. Peters, Lake Saint Louis, Defiance, and Wentzville in the metropolitan St. Louis area. GTE and its nearly 1,700 employees statewide provide information superhighway solutions for today's business and residential communication issues.

From fiber rings to network construction to telephone service for the local pizza shop, GTE provides access to the information superhighway or clear, crisp connections for voice-grade circuits. The company also is a leader in deployment of fiber-optic circuits for its customers, as well as serving as a contractor for businesses and government applications of specialized communications circuitry.

And for in-state vacationers, travelers, and students, GTE is a familiar site, serving much of the Missouri heartland in such communities as education-minded Columbia and fast-growing Branson.

Throughout the world, GTE is the fourth-largest publicly held telecommunications company and the largest United States-based local telephone company. The firm provides telecommunications services to areas such as Tampa, Dallas, and suburban Los Angeles. Even Hawaiian vacationers are provided GTE telecommunications service. The company also is the second-largest cellular telephone service provider in the United States. GTE's cellular and telecommunications operations serve nearly 30 percent of the country's population. Travelers from St Louis' Lambert Field can call home while in the air via GTE's Airfone service. The company is a leader in government and defense communications systems and equipment, aircraft passenger telecommunications, directories, and telecommunications-based information services and systems. GTE's Directory Company quality service was recognized in 1994 as a Malcolm Baldrige award winner.

In St. Louis, GTE soon will become more of a household name as the company assumes its responsibility as official telecommunications supplier to the National Football League, a role it has played for nearly 10 years. The company has been the exclusive supplier of thousands of communications lines and equipment to stage one of the largest sports spectacles in the world—the Super Bowl.

Founded in 1918 in Richland

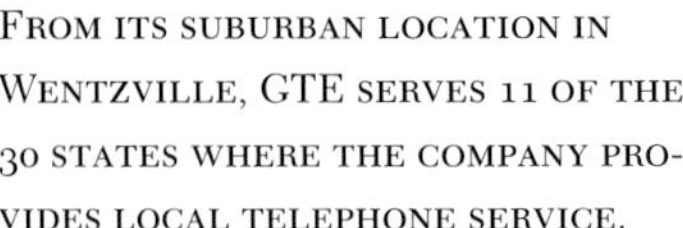

From its suburban location in Wentzville, GTE serves 11 of the 30 states where the company provides local telephone service.

CHUCK FISHMAN

Center, Wisconsin, the company has grown into a worldwide provider of telecommunications. In 1993 GTE's revenues were nearly $20 billion. The company's operations include 22.1 million access lines in British Columbia, Quebec, Venezuela, and the Dominican Republic, as well as serving portions of 33 states. It employs some 117,000 people worldwide, providing a variety of telecommunications services in 70 countries. In Missouri, GTE provides telecommunications products and services to some 365,000 access lines in more than 200 communities. The company employs nearly 1,000 people in the St. Louis area, and that number is growing. From its suburban location in Wentzville, GTE's service order center serves 11 of the 30 states where the company provides local telephone service. And its operator service center handles calls and directory assistance for its own customers, as well as customers of other companies. Requests for telephone numbers as far away as the state of Washington are fulfilled at the company's Wentzville campus.

Telecommunications has become the economic development tool of choice as more and more communities rely on GTE's technical expertise to connect their businesses, homes, and schools to the information network of the future. And, within the next five years, every community in Missouri will be served by information-age digital technology, gaining access to the opportunities provided by the information superhighway. The company expects that orders for access to this new information superhighway will be handled at its Wentzville facility, providing economic growth and employment opportunities for the St. Charles County area.

As part of the company's service and growth strategies, all public and educational facilities within its operating area will have access to the information superhighway. This high-speed network will be provided through a high-speed T-1 network or fiber optics. Both provide highly accurate, reliable information superhighway access.

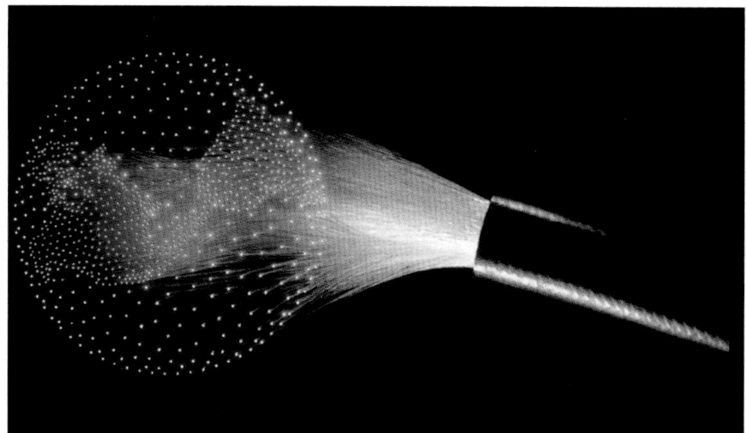

The telecommunications leader recently entered into a partnership to test applications of telecommunications in medical applications within the state. Other telecommunications utilities, the Missouri Public Service Commission, and the University of Missouri are all partners in the test designed to bring diagnostic and treatment capabilities to various parts of the state.

GTE is a leader and partner in business, economic development, and educational applications of telecommunications products and services in Missouri, the nation, and the world. Its vision is to continue leadership in the areas of voice, video, and data services in local, national, and international markets.

GTE employs some 117,000 people worldwide, providing a variety of telecommunications services in 70 countries.

GTE Telephone Operations and its nearly 1,700 employees in Missouri offer information superhighway solutions for today's business and residential communication issues.

General American Life Insurance Company

FOUNDED IN 1933, GENERAL AMERICAN LIFE INSURANCE COMPANY has come a long way in six decades. The company began during the Great Depression when a group of New York investors took over the Missouri State Life Insurance Company, which the courts had declared insolvent. Today, General American has a reputation for financial strength, integrity, quality products, and superior service. A Fortune 50 life insurance company, it ranks in size among the top 1 percent of all U.S. life companies. General American attributes its growth to having provided "products to value, people to trust" throughout its history. Of course, its approaches to providing financial products and services have become increasingly sophisticated over the years. But its mission of helping individuals and groups of employees meet their needs for financial security has not changed since the company's inception.

RICHARD A. LIDDY, CLU (RIGHT), IS CHAIRMAN, PRESIDENT, AND CHIEF EXECUTIVE OFFICER OF GENERAL AMERICAN LIFE.

The Rugged Climb to the Top

After the New York entrepreneurs gained control of the failed Missouri State Life, they placed a lien on half the reserve value of each individual life insurance policy. Almost all the policyholders accepted the idea, and General American Life began the climb to financial stability.

The company's early days were not easy. Besides the predictable challenges of starting a new company, General American had to fight off corrupt politicians who demanded tribute, and struggle through the hardships caused by the nation's troubled economy. With its focus on establishing profitability, General American examined every aspect of its operations—boosting the value of its real estate holdings, for example, through improvement of its farmland and rehabilitation of its urban properties.

JOSEPH HOFFMANN, CLU, CHFC (BELOW, AT RIGHT), IS A MEMBER OF GENERAL AMERICAN'S PROFESSIONAL SALES FORCE.

As part of their commitment to build "soundly, conservatively, and permanently," company officers decided to turn ownership of the company over to its policyholders. By 1946 General American had become a mutual company, owned by its individual policyholders.

Soon after World War II, General American restored all losses incurred by the original Missouri State policyholders—two years ahead of schedule. By this time, all death claims had been paid in full. "This piece of work," said a leading industry analyst at the time, "is the most remarkable that has ever been carried through in the life insurance world."

More remarkable changes were on the horizon. Sales skyrocketed as new products hit the marketplace; for example, new major medical and group policies and price-competitive individual policies bolstered General American's product line. Established agents from around the country were attracted to St Louis' rising star, and during the 1960s the company's growth exceeded that of the 27 previous years.

Bursting at the seams, General American built two new facilities in the mid-1970s: the architecturally distinctive National Headquarters downtown and the sprawling National Service Center in south St. Louis County. Today, more than 2,500 General American associates work at the two sites. They, along with 1,700 other employees nationwide, work together to meet the needs of clients worldwide.

Sound and Innovative Products

After a recent reorganization, General American now focuses on five major lines of business: group life and health insurance, which offers insurance protection to groups of employees; General American Investment Company, which provides a full range of investment services to both General American and outside clients and is responsible for the sales and marketing of qualified pension plans; Reinsurance Group of America, which shares risks with the nation's top-quality life insurance companies and explores ventures overseas; a new company (as yet unnamed), which offers a broad range of employee benefit products and administrative services; and individual life insurance. Individual life has been restructured to accommodate an operat-

ing unit for the development of new products; Security Equity Life Insurance Company for large, corporate-owned life insurance business; General Life of America for sales through brokers; and GenMark for sales and marketing of insurance and investment products through general agents and representatives of Walnut Street Securities, General American's broker-dealer subsidiary.

For individual sales and service, General American relies on its agency distribution system to meet the needs of each policyholder. Independent agents offer whole life, term, universal life, variable universal life, and annuities. Clients are primarily business executives and professionals who require large amounts of insurance.

More than 2,000 group insurance clients rely on General American for coverage. Well-known clients include Anheuser-Busch, McDonnell Douglas, Phillips Petroleum, and Southwest Airlines. However, product flexibility is such that the company can serve many smaller organizations as well. These clients come to General American for many types of coverage, including life, medical care, and long-term disability insurance. The company offers plans that range from traditional funding arrangements—whereby General American assumes most of the risk—to those in which the employer takes on most of the risk, relying on the insurance company for administration.

The group pension unit provides investment, plan design, and administrative services for more than 600 pension and profit-sharing clients. Although large, well-known corporations are among its clients, the company offers a range of services that appeal to organizations of all sizes. To meet their investment needs, General American allows group pension clients to select from an array of investment options, including special-purpose funds. A wide range of choices is particularly attractive to participants in defined contribution plans, such as 401(k).

General American's subsidiaries offer related financial services. These subsidiaries include Consultec, which supports the administration of state and federal government welfare programs, and Paragon Life Insurance Company, which provides low-cost combined life insurance and investment programs for employer-sponsored groups.

The largest insurance company with headquarters in Missouri, General American recently surpassed the $235 billion mark for life insurance in force. The qualities that have always served General American—strength, stability, and flexibility—will ensure its continued growth and success in the 21st century. As Chairman, President, and Chief Executive Officer Richard A. Liddy expresses it: "After six decades of uninterrupted progress, we've only just begun."

Clockwise from above:
For many years, General American's home office was located at 15th and Locust in the former Missouri State Life headquarters.

Today, the company's distinctive National Headquarters, designed by Philip Johnson and John Burgee, is located in downtown St. Louis.

Located on a 100-acre tract in south St. Louis County, the National Service Center features modular construction that facilitates expansion.

Blue Cross and Blue Shield of Missouri

CHANGE, CARING, AND—FIRST, LAST, AND ALWAYS—AN ABSOLUTE DEDICation to customer satisfaction are the milestones on the nearly 60-year path to success carved by Blue Cross and Blue Shield of Missouri (BCBSMo). With some 900,000 members, BCBSMo and its for-profit, publicly traded Alliance Blue Cross Blue Shield subsidiary are the largest health insurers in the state of Missouri. "So long as we satisfy the customer, we succeed," says Roy Heimburger, president and chief executive officer of BCBSMo and Alliance Blue Cross Blue Shield. "Satisfy the customer, and growth and gain follow."

Customer satisfaction in the hard-charging health insurance industry of the 1990s requires that a company be ready and able to change to meet the shifting needs of its customers and its market. Change holds no terrors for BCBSMo and Alliance Blue Cross Blue Shield. "We had our genesis in change," Heimburger says. "We thrive on change."

Roy Heimburger (right) serves as president and CEO of Blue Cross and Blue Shield of Missouri and of Alliance Blue Cross Blue Shield.

▼ DOUG McKAY

The company's headquarters, located at 1831 Chestnut Street in St. Louis, houses a team of 1,500 employees dedicated to providing customers with better health and better value through managed care.

Tradition of Caring and Change

Started in 1936 with borrowed money, its handful of employees working without pay on orange-crate desks in a one-room office, St. Louis Blue Cross (BCBSMo's predecessor company) brought Missouri the then-revolutionary concept of prepaid health care benefits—that is, health insurance that meant that illness or injury need not carry the additional fear of financial ruin. Over the next half century, caring for customers meant expanding benefits and expanding the kinds of care available to the customer: family coverage, 1937; medical-surgical through St. Louis Blue Shield (BCBSMo's second predecessor company), 1945; prescription drug, 1945; major medical, 1959; dental, 1970; hospice care, 1980; and major organ transplants, 1985.

Caring for the customer did bring growth and gain. By 1986 the two companies were serving more than 750,000 members in a service area that stretched out across the state. But also by 1986, a new wave of change was about to hit the health insurance industry, and the company had to be ready to catch that wave. St. Louis Blue Cross and St. Louis Blue Shield merged in 1986 to form BCBSMo, and the new company began to reinvent itself as a managed care company.

Customer satisfaction has been formally embraced as the organization's corporate goal.

Over the next eight years, BCBSMo put together the complex blend of mechanisms that make up managed care—benefit design, provider contracting, customer and provider education, utilization management, and product design. The company's Alliance preferred provider program was recast and today is the most successful PPO in Missouri; the company created a new BlueCHOICE health maintenance organization out of the whole cloth and brought it to the market in record time.

By 1994 BCBSMo had been totally transformed from a claims-processing and claims-paying company to a managed care company. Customer satisfaction was formally embraced as the corporate goal. Once again growth and gain followed, and once again the company moved to reinvent itself to meet another wave of change.

Alliance Blue Cross Blue Shield

In 1994 BCBSMo made the biggest single change in its six decades of change. Its managed care business was spun off into Alliance Blue Cross Blue Shield, a for-profit, publicly traded subsidiary.

BCBSMo is the parent company and majority stockholder of Alliance Blue Cross Blue Shield. In addition, BCBSMo retains the company's traditional indemnity business, the Federal Employee Program members, participating national account groups, and the company's low-cost BasicBlue program, as well as administration of the state's Missouri Health Insurance Pool and the charitable Caring Program for Children.

"We knew that the political and business dynamics of today's health insurance market required an absolute concentration on managed care and access to capital," Heimburger says. "Alliance Blue Cross Blue Shield gives us both. It is a managed care company and, as a publicly traded company [NYSE: RIT], it gives us access to the equity capital markets."

Alliance Blue Cross Blue Shield offers a broad spectrum of managed care products, including the company's Alliance preferred provider program, the Alliance-Choice and BlueCHOICE POS Plus point-of-service programs, and the BlueCHOICE health maintenance organization.

"With Alliance Blue Cross Blue Shield we have a new mission to enhance customer satisfaction and lower total health costs by improving the health status of our members through the most efficient provision of superior health care services. We are going to provide our customers with better health and better value through managed care," says Heimburger. "Our strategy is to provide high-value products, cost-effective product delivery, and superior customer service.

"Our mission and strategy, in short, is to satisfy the customer. No matter how much we change, that will never change. Customer satisfaction is this company's goal today as it was in 1936 and in 1986, and as it will be in 2036."

United Van Lines, Inc.

EVER IN SEARCH OF A BETTER LIFE, HUMANS HAVE BEEN ON THE MOVE since the dawn of history, setting out for the unknown carrying their possessions with them—at first on their backs and later in wagons, ships, and railroad cars. With the arrival of the motorized vehicle in the early years of the 20th century and the development of paved roads, the modern moving business began to evolve. ■ Out of this evolution, United Van Lines began in 1928 in Cleveland, Ohio. Originally known as Return Loads Service, Inc., the company's founding group of farsighted entrepreneurs saw that the two-way motor transport business could be profitable, but only if vehicles were kept loaded a high percentage of the time. Accordingly, early movers began to secure shipments for their trip home by forming cooperative return-load ventures—a concept that proved successful for Return Loads Service.

"Our goals for the future include expansion of our lead in the marketplace, maximum use of emerging technology, and building upon our quality service process to further differentiate ourselves from the competition," says President Robert J. Baer.

The company relocated to St. Louis in 1936 and was reorganized into its current structure in 1947, considered the founding year for today's United Van Lines. It occupied its current headquarters location in 1963. Today, United Van Lines is the largest household-goods carrier in the nation and among the largest in the world, with 1,050 agents around the globe from Afars to Zimbabwe.

Serving a World on the Move

United's customers include individual shippers of household goods, as well as thousands of corporations for which the company performs a wide range of transportation services. United agents, while benefiting from their association with a van line recognized worldwide, retain their own operating authority and identity as local and regional moving companies.

Within the United States, approximately 4,400 tractor-trailer units and 1,600 "straight" (single-unit) trucks are qualified for United Van Lines service. The vast majority are owned by United's affiliated agents, who lease them to the van line because of the centralized operating and dispatching coordination that United provides.

According to the Fortune Service 500, United Van Lines ranks as the 34th-largest transportation company in the country. Total revenues for United and its sister companies reached a record $995 million in 1994, and the van line handled 326,000 shipments comprising over 2 billion pounds. United Van Lines currently employs more than 900 people at its 39-acre world headquarters complex in Fenton, a suburb of St. Louis.

Innovation and Safety

United has long been recognized as an innovator—first among all movers with a number of features and services to aid the shipping public. Topping the list is the company's quality service process—a comprehensive, five-step approach to ensuring quality consistency throughout the company's system. The steps include a service pledge, specific standards of performance, measurements of adherence to those standards, advanced professional training, and recognition of top performers.

In safety, United Van Lines is also known as an industry leader. In 1991 the company became the first van line ever to receive the American Trucking Associations' President's Trophy, the highest industry safety recognition available to motor carriers. For five consecutive years, United has received the highest quality score among major carriers from the General Services Administration's Performance Index. The Safety Council of Greater St. Louis also recognized United by bestowing upon it the Outstanding Achieve-

TODAY, THE COMPANY IS THE LARGEST HOUSEHOLD-GOODS CARRIER IN THE NATION AND AMONG THE LARGEST IN THE WORLD, WITH 1,050 AGENTS AROUND THE GLOBE FROM AFARS TO ZIMBABWE.

ment in Safety and Best Sustained Vehicle Accident Frequency Rate for Large Fleets awards.

A Family of Companies

United Van Lines is the principal operating activity of UniGroup, Inc., a parent company owned by a number of equally partnered agents of the van line. In addition to United Van Lines, there are three principal operating companies of UniGroup: United Leasing, Inc., founded in 1969, is devoted to the sale and leasing of trucks, trailers, in-van equipment, and supplies required by the professional mover; Vanliner Group, Inc., which originated in 1978, provides a variety of insurance coverages and services tailored to meet the specific operational needs of agents, independent van owner-operators, and independent trucking concerns; and United Capital Services, Inc., a captive finance company, was created in 1988 to assist the van line, its agents, and United Leasing with their financial requirements.

UniGroup and United Van Lines are governed by a board of directors composed of shareholder agents elected by their peers. The board employs a professional management team headed by nonagent President Robert J. Baer. Members of the board, as well as members of senior management, are active in the industry, occupying key positions in a number of trade associations.

During the 1980s, after the federal government deregulated the moving industry, every major van line except United underwent at least one ownership change. United has proudly retained the same ownership structure and direction since its founding, with many of its agencies now managed by second and third generations of the same families.

The company is also proud of its community service efforts in its hometown and elsewhere. Across the nation, United's agents are respected corporate citizens within their communities, participating in civic organizations and donating services to charitable causes. In times of natural disasters, such as the Midwest floods in 1993 and Hurricane Andrew in 1992, United vans have been volunteered to haul donated goods to displaced families.

"Our goals for the future include expansion of our lead in the marketplace, maximum use of emerging technology, and building upon our quality service process to further differentiate ourselves from the competition," Baer says. "Our slogan, 'The Quality Shows in Every Move We Make,' continues to describe our company as we move toward the 21st century."

TRACING ITS ROOTS TO 1928 IN CLEVELAND, OHIO, UNITED VAN LINES HAS PLAYED AN IMPORTANT PART IN THE EVOLUTION OF THE MODERN MOVING BUSINESS (LEFT AND OPPOSITE).

Coldwell Banker Ira E. Berry

One out of every nine homes sold in America in 1994 involved a Coldwell Banker sales associate. The residential real estate company operates more than 2,300 offices with over 53,000 sales associates and employees serving the United States, Canada, and Puerto Rico. Since its establishment in San Francisco after the earthquake of 1906, Coldwell Banker has grown to become one of the largest real estate companies in North America.

During the Great Depression, another real estate firm was born. In 1939 St. Louis resident Ira E. Berry formed the company that was to bear his name. Berry opened his first office in the suburb of Kirkwood, Missouri. The Ira E. Berry Real Estate Company became a leader on the St. Louis and national scenes. Ira Berry sales associates distinguished themselves by their productivity and by their practice of the Golden Rule. Associates were encouraged to "Do unto [clients] as you would have them do unto you." The policy is still in effect today.

Although the two real estate firms hailed from different regions, they matured, met, and finally merged. In 1985 Coldwell Banker acquired Ira E. Berry Real Estate in St. Louis. It was a sound relationship from the beginning. The combination of 50 years of Berry's success with the national presence of Coldwell Banker boosted sales potential dramatically.

Clients from throughout the St. Louis metropolitan area have learned to "Expect the Best™" from Coldwell Banker.

A Powerful Alliance

Today, the St. Louis real estate market benefits from the stability of this powerful alliance. Known as Coldwell Banker Ira E. Berry, the local firm continues to follow the Golden Rule. Its management team is composed of St. Louis natives, including President and Chief Operating Officer Joe Riley, Chief Financial Officer Jim Dohr, and Senior Vice President Steve Spehr. The company's competitive edge lies in its ability to service the entire metropolitan area, including nearby Illinois communities. "While most companies operate in a niche market," Spehr says, "Coldwell Banker is the only one that services buyers and sellers in all areas. We have an office in Belleville, Illinois, and will continue to add offices in fast-growing areas beyond St. Louis County."

Thorough training for its sales staff is just one of the reasons Coldwell Banker Ira E. Berry has grown. "The Golden Rule is a timeless philosophy, but we provide lots of practical support for our agents as well," explains Riley. The firm, for example, requires extensive training for its new sales associates. There is also ongoing training for all sales personnel, giving Coldwell Banker a reputation for professionalism that is unsurpassed. In addition to its exceptional Coldwell Banker University program, the company offers a number of enrichment opportunities for its associates. For several years, agents have attended local retreats featuring networking time with top agents. The International Elite Retreat, held annually, is designed to challenge the top performers com-

panywide and prepare them to increase their business and quality of life.

Sales Manager Ellen O'Brien has been with Coldwell Banker in St. Louis for 20 years. Her longevity is evidence of the company's practice of promoting from within. "I have truly been allowed to grow over the years. I started working for Mr. Berry as a transaction closer, and I worked my way up to management," she says. One of O'Brien's favorite training events is the annual Coldwell Banker convention, which is held in a different city each year. "It's wonderful. We network with people from across the country; we work with the top educators; and we have breakout sessions to share our expertise," O'Brien explains.

The company is also tops in the relocation market. A separate relocation department functions within the St. Louis company. The director assists agents with a national computer referral service and an exclusive annual home-pricing index. The index posts average home prices across the country, allowing clients to make important comparisons. Widespread newspaper, television, and radio advertising gives Coldwell Banker sales associates and clients yet another advantage.

Customers Have the Final Word

Customer feedback is a regular part of the company's transactions. After each closing, a comprehensive survey is mailed to the clients involved. Currently, 94 percent of the respondents have been satisfied with the service they received. With results like these, Coldwell Banker Ira E. Berry builds steadily on referrals and repeat business.

The St. Louis residential real estate market includes many high-quality competitors. Transactions are becoming more complicated and technical than ever before. As American consumers become more sophisticated, they also demand better service. "We earn everything we get," says Spehr. Coldwell Banker Ira E. Berry is proof that hard work coupled with consideration for others is a dependable formula for success.

Sales associates at Coldwell Banker Ira E. Berry offer "Support You Can Count On.™"

McDonnell Douglas Corporation

Born before the Wright brothers' first flight, James Smith McDonnell and Donald Wills Douglas were captivated by aviation at an early age. Devoting their talents and energies to building machines that fly became their life's purpose. The extent of their success can be measured in the company that today bears their names—McDonnell Douglas Corporation, a giant in the aerospace industry. McDonnell started McDonnell Aircraft in 1939 in a rented office at St. Louis' Lambert Field. In 1967, after almost three decades of growth, he purchased Douglas Aircraft Company, a California venture founded in 1920 by Douglas. That merger formed McDonnell Douglas Corporation, which has become the world's leading producer of military aircraft, the third-largest commercial aircraft manufacturer, and the nation's largest defense contractor.

Clockwise from top right: Says President and CEO Harry C. Stonecipher, "It is impossible to conceive of a growing world economy that does not include a vibrant and growing aerospace industry. Our future is aerospace, and the future of aerospace is bright."

The company's F/A-18 Hornet is the fighter plane of choice in the international marketplace.

McDonnell Douglas is one of the largest contractors in the International Space Station program, and the manufacturer of the world's most reliable launch vehicle, the Delta II.

Superlatives Reflect Company Spirit

Among the many firsts attributed to McDonnell Douglas are the first jet plane designed to take off and land on an aircraft carrier, and the first spacecraft to carry an American into orbit around the Earth. McDonnell Douglas manufactures an array of equipment used by the U.S. Navy, including fighter planes, antiship missiles, and pilot training systems.

The F/A-18 Hornet is the fighter plane of choice in the international marketplace. Praised for its combat versatility, effectiveness, high reliability, and low operating costs, the Hornet is the only tactical fighter currently in production for the U.S. Navy and will remain so through the 1990s.

Since entering service, the F-15 Eagle has attained a perfect air combat record. In fact, F-15s shot down 33 of the 35 fighters lost by Iraq in air combat during Operation Desert Storm. The other two were shot down by McDonnell Douglas Hornets. The March 1991 issue of *Barron's* magazine aptly summed up the company's contribution to the effort: "The first month of the Gulf War was basically McDonnell Douglas versus Iraq."

The company's Harpoon antiship missile is designed to be launched from aircraft, surface ships, submarines, and land-based installations. After more than 20 years of service, it is still deployed as the navy's basic antiship missile. In addition to these McDonnell Douglas products, the navy uses the T-45 Training System, which gives new pilots the most effective training possible while reducing overall training costs.

The newest addition to the AV-8 Harrier family of aircraft is the Harrier II Plus. This aircraft features a combat-proven radar system that brings multimission capability to the Harrier's vertical/short takeoff and landing features that allow it to operate where other fixed-wing aircraft cannot.

Beyond the Defense Industry

In addition to its proven record in the defense industry, McDonnell Douglas has long been in the forefront of manned space exploration and the commercial use of space. The company is one of the largest contractors in the International Space Station program, and the manufacturer of the world's most reliable launch vehicle, the Delta II.

In 1991, to position itself for new opportunities in an environment of shrinking defense budgets, McDonnell Douglas formed the prototype development center known as the Phantom Works. Located in St. Louis, the Phantom Works focuses the company's best talents on high-tech engineering,

Clockwise from left:
Company founder James Smith McDonnell started McDonnell Aircraft in 1939 in a rented office at St. Louis' Lambert Field.

Today, with 65,000 employees worldwide—24,000 of whom are in St. Louis—McDonnell Douglas has become a giant in the aerospace industry.

Since entering service, the F-15 Eagle has attained a perfect air combat record, including critical service during Operation Desert Storm.

lean production, new materials, flexibility, and security for highly classified programs. In addition, the Phantom Works enhances the performance of current produc-

tion programs by transferring new methods developed in the center to other production programs.

A Major Presence in St. Louis

In terms of both number of employees and annual sales, McDonnell Douglas is the largest company in St. Louis. With 65,000 employees worldwide—24,000 of whom are in St. Louis—the company currently has revenues of approximately $14 billion annually.

Founder James McDonnell chose St. Louis as his base because of its central location and the midwestern work ethic of its people. Over the years, the local community has strongly supported McDonnell Douglas. In return, the company and its employees support their communities through the McDonnell Douglas Foundation and Employee Community Funds, which support educational programs, as well as programs for the disabled, troubled youth, and many others.

Looking to the company's future, President and CEO Harry C. Stonecipher believes that the shrinking U.S. defense market poses no threat to McDonnell Douglas. "Our sales to allied nations continue to grow, and there are ample opportunities for the company within the aerospace industry," he says. "It is impossible to conceive of a growing world economy that does not include a vibrant and growing aerospace industry. Our future is aerospace, and the future of aerospace is bright."

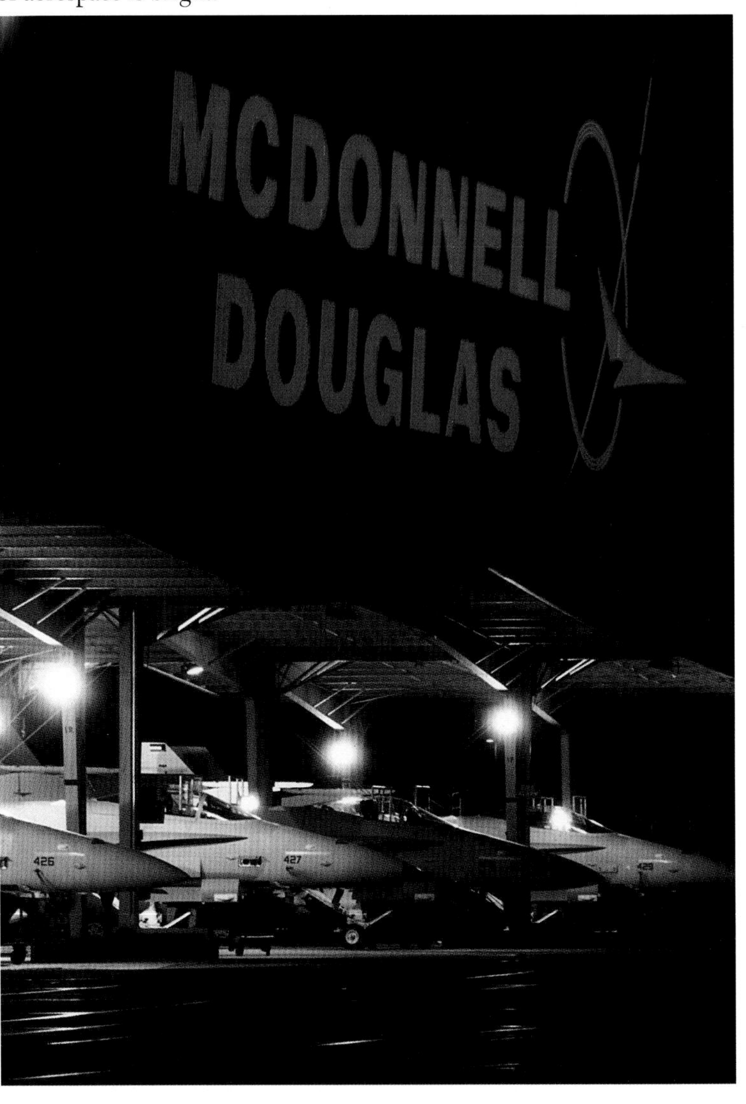

Schnuck Markets, Inc.

FOUNDED IN 1939 AS A FAMILY CONFECTIONERY IN NORTH St. Louis, Schnuck Markets, Inc. has grown to a position of leadership in the Midwest. Advocating customer service, value, and quality as the formula for success, the Schnuck family's values and commitment to the community have helped make St. Louis one of the most sophisticated supermarket cities in the nation. ■ The first Schnucks store, a 1,000-square-foot corner confectionery, was run by Anna "Mom" and Edwin H. "Pop" Schnuck, a couple who shared a strong work ethic and an ambitious dream. Their store offered staples such as bread, canned goods, and coffee, plus extras like hand-packed ice cream. Homemade deli items were carefully prepared in Mom Schnuck's kitchen.

Pop Schnuck had been in the meat business since 1928; he used his expertise to establish the family's meat department in a small back room of the store. Schnucks quickly earned a reputation for supplying superior meat products at attractive prices. This integrity set a standard of excellence and value that remains a hallmark of Schnucks today.

Making the Transition

The Schnuck children—Edward, Donald, and Annette—played an active role in the family business. By 1947 Schnuck family members individually owned seven different stores. During the postwar economic boom, the company expanded steadily; Schnucks made a successful transition from neighborhood-based grocery stores to the large, self-service supermarkets of today. In 1961 Schnucks adopted the pledge of being "The Friendliest Stores in Town." Even today, this old-fashioned philosophy is the cornerstone of the company's loyal customer base.

During the 1960s, Schnucks began its emergence as a national leader in the supermarket industry by creating new services, developing new merchandising techniques, and fostering technological growth while always keeping customers first. In fall 1970, Schnucks completed what was then its largest single expansion by purchasing 26 Bettendorf-Rapp stores from Allied Supermarkets of Detroit. That year Schnucks topped the $100 million sales mark. From the 1940s until their deaths in 1987 and 1991, respectively, brothers Ed and Don Schnuck made an unbeatable management team as they built their parents' dream into a billion-dollar business. Their partnership provided a successful model followed today by Don's five sons: Craig, Scott, Terry, Mark, and Todd.

MATT PISKULIC

CLOCKWISE FROM RIGHT:
ON JANUARY 16, 1995, CRAIG SCHNUCK ANNOUNCED PLANS TO PURCHASE MOST OF NATIONAL SUPER MARKETS.

TODAY, THE COMPANY'S LEADERSHIP IS PROVIDED BY THE THIRD GENERATION OF SCHNUCKS. FROM LEFT: BROTHERS TODD, TERRY, MARK (STANDING), SCOTT, AND CRAIG (SEATED) ARE FLANKED BY PORTRAITS OF COMPANY FOUNDERS EDWARD J. SCHNUCK AND DONALD O. SCHNUCK.

COLORFUL FLORAL DEPARTMENTS ARE A RECENT STORE ENHANCEMENT, ALONG WITH BAKERY, GOURMET PREPARED FOOD, DELI, SEAFOOD, AND VIDEO DEPARTMENTS.

Consistently, Schnucks has demonstrated its strength as an innovator through early moves to combination food and drug stores, electronic checkouts, and such in-store changes as fresh bakery departments, fresh gourmet prepared foods, outstanding deli and seafood departments, floral and video operations, and other customer favorites. Schnucks' integrity and commitment to customer service have been demonstrated in many ways, including consumer information programs and its 1994 "World-Class Service" recognition by the Better Business Bureau.

Deeply Involved in the Community

Despite work demands, Ed and Don Schnuck made time to focus on a wide variety of community programs and organizations. They were particularly drawn to charities that helped feed the needy, care for children, support family life, and enhance educational efforts. This corporate commitment to the St. Louis community was expressed initially by Ed, who volunteered with efforts ranging from the Better Business Bureau and its consumer advocacy focus to the Boy Scouts and Salvation Army.

By the late 1970s, with both Ed and Don leading the company's efforts, Schnucks' involvement had grown dramatically. Don led a number of special campaigns, including those which preserved the Missouri Historical Society Museum and saved the Girl Scouts from the disaster that struck their 1984 cookie drive.

Ed and Don became the only

brothers in the nation to receive the supermarket industry's highest honor, the Sidney R. Rabb Award, in 1978 and 1983, respectively. The award from the Food Marketing Institute recognized each Schnuck brother's "statesmanlike contribution to the food industry and service to his community."

Schnucks' tradition of community involvement remains alive today, fostered by the present generation of family members. All five sons of the late Don Schnuck work together to run the business. Like their predecessors, brothers Craig, Scott, Terry, Mark, and Todd are involved in helping organizations such as the United Way, Urban League, Salvation Army, NAACP, local area food banks, St. Louis Children's Hospital, Boy Scouts, and Junior Achievement.

While many corporations discourage family members from working together, Schnucks holds the opposite view. Numerous extended families, spanning many decades, have built careers as Schnucks associates. Schnucks takes pride in being "a company of families and a family company."

A Bold Acquisition

Marking its 50th anniversary in 1989, Schnucks consolidated four offices into one new headquarters facility in St. Louis County and moved its dairy to a larger plant. Geographic expansion was also under way; by 1990 Schnucks had entered the central Illinois market. By 1994 the company owned several stores in Kansas, Indiana, and Missouri, plus 50 supermarkets in metropolitan St. Louis. Employees numbered more than 12,000.

In January 1995, Chairman and CEO Craig Schnuck surprised the community by announcing the firm's purchase of National Super Markets, a Canadian-owned competitor. The acquisition included 57 stores, with 50 in the St. Louis area. Schnucks pledged to pass anticipated savings on to its customers. Once again, the family-owned firm proved its tenacity—this time amid the stiff competition of membership club stores and discount chains.

While growth as a regional supermarket company is key to Schnucks' business strategy, value to customers is the motivation. "We focus on providing value through quality, variety, service, competitive pricing, and friendliness," notes Craig Schnuck. "With every change, we intend to reinforce our performance and reputation as 'The Friendliest Stores in Town.'"

Clockwise from top left:

By 1947 Schnuck family members individually owned seven different stores, including this one located at Manchester and Newstead.

Pop Schnuck's knowledge of meats from his years with Swift & Co., and then as proprietor of his own wholesale meat business, was helpful in establishing Schnucks as "meat masters."

The company's slogan, "The Friendliest Stores in Town," is exemplified by its checkers of the year, pictured here along with Scott and Craig Schnuck.

Schnucks' store-brand products have increased in variety and earned widespread appeal.

Andersen Consulting

Since its inception, Andersen Consulting has grown to be the largest management consulting firm in the world. With an international network of 152 offices in 47 countries and more than 32,000 employees, its global resources are vast. Applying a strong blend of industry knowledge and technical expertise, Andersen Consulting helps clients, from small businesses to Fortune 500 giants, manage the complex process of changing to be more successful.

The Business Integration Approach

The firm has been the leader in technology management since 1954, when it installed the first computer application for commercial use at General Electric. Andersen Consulting also pioneered the use of artificial intelligence, image processing, relational database management systems, and client/server and open systems architectures. Complementing its technology management capabilities, the firm has built a solid reputation in change management.

The St. Louis office management team includes C. Robert Farwell (left), who leads Andersen Consulting's manufacturing practice in the Midwest, and Managing Partner James S. Reed.

Professionals at Andersen Consulting combine business knowledge with technology expertise to help clients change to be more successful (below).

Andersen Consulting believes organizations must have enough pride in themselves to have the courage to change. "Change is inevitable and may not always be viewed as positive," says Jim Reed, managing partner of the St. Louis office. "Our role is to help our clients benefit from a changing marketplace."

Andersen Consulting offers a powerful approach to serving clients: business integration. Bob Farwell, who leads the firm's manufacturing practice in the Midwest, explains, "To achieve business integration for our clients, we align an enterprise's strategy with its technology, people, and business processes so they all work to attain the best business performance. We consider the entire business enterprise, including the client's suppliers and customers, to create and sustain value while managing costs." Adding further value to this approach is a strengthened industry initiative that provides highly skilled professionals in every major industry group.

Partners in Success

Andersen Consulting partners with many of the world's largest public companies to help them sustain a competitive advantage. However, the firm also works with innovative smaller companies to further increase their success. "One of the things that makes Andersen Consulting distinctive is our emphasis on partnering with our clients," says Reed. "Some firms stop earlier in the process, after providing the client with ideas. We are more than advisers to our clients; we are their partner. In that capacity, we are both 'thinkers' and 'doers' throughout the entire process of change." With more than 200 professionals in the St. Louis office, the firm is uniquely capable of providing clients with total business solutions.

A Knowledge Network

Andersen Consulting links its consultants worldwide with the firm's Knowledge Xchange™ knowledge management system. The system includes a series of interactive databases that track client engagements, consultants' experience, and general market information for each of Andersen Consulting's major industry practices. "We want to make it easy to access and reuse information to the benefit of our clients—bringing a wealth of knowledge that is unparalleled in our field," explains Reed. Through the Knowledge Xchange and Andersen Consulting's ability to assemble a team of world-class

The Center for Professional Education, a 151-acre campus facility located in St. Charles, Illinois, demonstrates the firm's commitment to the continuous education and training of its consultants.

experts, local clients—such as Anheuser-Busch, Monsanto, Ralston Purina, and Peoria-based Caterpillar—receive the collective expertise of the global organization.

Reed emphasizes that while the need to absorb change is a common denominator for most Andersen Consulting clients, every organization has a unique journey along its road to change. "Many times we work with clients on the front end to make sure their vision links business strategy to operational realities. The next step is to help rethink their processes, evaluate the ability of their organization to change, and then define the people, skills, organization, technology, and infrastructure needed to turn a client's vision into reality."

Many times, new systems and technologies are necessary to help companies transform. However, companies can struggle with new technology. So, Andersen Consulting offers its business integration approach to ensure that every part of a client's business is part of the change process. Reed adds, "Transformation is the process, not the goal. We work to enable each client's organization to better manage change, rather than be a victim of changed circumstances."

A Commitment to Excellence

In all of its efforts, Andersen Consulting relies on a solid base of creative, well-trained professionals. Each year, about 6 percent of the firm's revenues are spent on training—a considerable sum since 1994 revenues totaled $3.45 billion. "As a firm, we are committed to hiring and training the best and the brightest," Farwell explains. "We hire people who will make a difference to our clients and to our organization. Our business is delivering the highest-quality service. To be successful, we must develop and nurture our resources—our people."

To make this possible, Andersen Consulting operates the Center for Professional Education in St. Charles, Illinois. All Andersen Consulting professionals worldwide attend, and sometimes teach, classes at the campus facility, which occupies 151 acres and has 135 classrooms to accommodate more than 2,000 participants.

A Journey of Change

Increasingly, companies recognize that being an industry leader demands more than just improving their organization. Now more than ever, companies must rethink and transform their core business—creating a change journey.

"Andersen Consulting is well positioned to help businesses on their journey," says Reed. "Through our partnering with clients, we work with them to make all parts of their business work synergistically—their strategy, people, processes, and technology—to help them reach new pinnacles of success."

Andersen Consulting partners with local clients, such as Peoria-based Caterpillar, to achieve business integration.

Bock Pharmacal Company

Bock Pharmacal Company represents the classic American business success story. The privately owned company has experienced phenomenal success in distribution and sales of its pharmaceuticals to health care professionals. In fact, a black line on a sales graph would head almost due north off the page, illustrating a growth in sales from \$2.7 million in 1985 to nearly \$100 million today.

Clockwise from right: The company's current leadership includes Chairman Lawrence B. Moskoff (left) and President William B. Moskoff.

The company differentiates its respiratory care products by emphasizing their pleasant taste and smell to enhance patient compliance.

Bock was founded in 1945 by pharmacist Boris L. Moskoff.

Bock's leadership credits its success to a superior, professional sales force; a niche marketing approach; a continual search for new opportunities; and a dedication to achievement. As co-owners of the company, brothers Lawrence B. and William B. Moskoff do not concern themselves with boardroom corporate strategy, concentrating instead on finding the right market positions. "The best description of this company," says William Moskoff, "is a blending of people, products, and opportunity with careful focusing of all those vital components."

From its corporate headquarters in St. Louis County, Bock specializes in the marketing, development, sales, packaging, and distribution of specialty pharmaceuticals, particularly in respiratory and women's health care. Its sales force calls on physicians, nurses, pharmacists, and other health care professionals in the 48 contiguous states, Hawaii, and Puerto Rico.

Bock was founded in 1945 by the Moskoffs' father, pharmacist Boris L. Moskoff, as a regional provider of antibacterial triple sulfa. Over the years, growth was the norm, and the sons assumed leadership positions after their father's death in 1963. Today, Lawrence is chairman of the board and chief executive officer, while William serves as president and chief operating officer.

The company's 240 sales representatives, complemented by an administrative and marketing support staff, comprise the Bock Pharmacal team. In addition, the company operates Highland Packaging, also owned by the Moskoff family. Highland packages all of Bock's pharmaceutical products, as well as providing packaging services for other pharmaceutical companies.

Phenomenal Growth

Bock's growth—an average annual sales growth of 61 percent from 1990 to 1994—is particularly

► Rich Murphy

impressive in light of current market conditions in the pharmaceutical industry. Company officials attribute the increase to expansion of the sales force, development of new markets, and, most importantly, deeper penetration into existing markets.

"We've stayed focused," Lawrence Moskoff says. "We're not trying to conquer the world, but only our mountain. A sales force of our size can't go after the whole pharmaceutical market, so we remain focused on the right positions within the right markets."

Bock strives to differentiate its products from other brands and works to help physicians, pharmacists, and managed care providers understand the differences. By design, the firm does not manufacture its own pharmaceuticals. However, Bock does provide input toward improved versions of existing products by paying attention to the needs of the consumer and adding extra value to the products.

A prescription cough syrup that looks bad and tastes bad, for instance, might get pushed to the

◄ Bill Leslie

back of the home medicine cabinet—something doctors call "poor patient compliance." To alleviate this problem, Bock developed its Poly-Histine® syrups in a fruit basket of flavors. Other tactics to surmount the competition include enhancement of a tablet's visual appeal or of its shaping to make swallowing easier. All of these nuances have become trademarks of Bock.

At the same time, the company strives to continually reformulate its pharmaceuticals based on the latest medical recommendations. One of Bock's leading women's health care products, Prenate 90,® is a vitamin-mineral supplement to be taken during pregnancy. Prenate 90® has had several formulation changes that have kept it at the leading edge of the prenatal care market, as well as the number one prescribed prenatal vitamin in the United States.

Trained Professionals

Beyond developing superior niche products and looking for markets within markets, the Moskoffs are passionate about the role of the firm's employees in achieving success. They note that the company strives to hire sales professionals who possess good sales skills and who share in the company's attitudes, values, and beliefs.

Acknowledging that all companies claim to support employees, the Moskoffs place Bock above the norm. "Bock walks the talk," says William Moskoff. "We sincerely recognize that people are our single largest asset. This company has thrived on the talents of a group of people and a lot of little efforts that have snowballed into one enormous success."

Where does Bock go from here? The strategy encompasses maximizing sales of current products and marketing new ones. This includes marketing successful products that are no longer strongly supported by other companies. Bock also is looking to market new FDA-approved products from international pharmaceutical companies that do not have a U.S. presence.

According to Lawrence Moskoff, the Bock vision is based on looking for day-to-day opportunities. "This company reacts to change, because inside change you find opportunity," he says. "While we react to change, the vision remains constant. We continue to provide an extremely high-quality product and a great working environment, as well as allow the people of Bock to expand their horizons. That combination is our vision, and will keep this company operating at a very high level well into the next century."

▶ RICH MURPHY

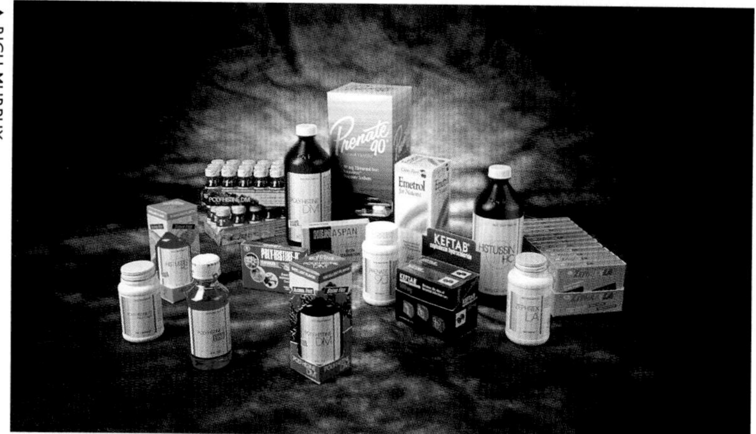

◀▶ RICH MURPHY

CLOCKWISE FROM LEFT:
BOCK MARKETS ITS BRANDED PHARMACEUTICAL PRODUCTS IN THE 48 CONTIGUOUS STATES, HAWAII, AND PUERTO RICO.

LOCATED IN WEST ST. LOUIS COUNTY, THE COMPANY'S CONTEMPORARY HEADQUARTERS IS REPRESENTATIVE OF BOCK'S COMMITMENT TO HIGH-QUALITY VALUES, ATTITUDES, AND BELIEFS.

TO SUPPORT ITS NATIONAL SALES AND DISTRIBUTION SYSTEM, BOCK HIRES HIGHLY TRAINED AND MOTIVATED PEOPLE TO BE PART OF ONE OF THE COUNTRY'S FASTEST-GROWING PHARMACEUTICAL COMPANIES.

Nooney Krombach

As the end of the 20th century approaches, the commercial real estate industry is experiencing some of its best years. For five decades Nooney Krombach has been a forerunner in this changing industry. Today the firm retains its position as a real estate leader through its commitment to clients, dedication to employees, and determination to provide the best in information resources.

Clockwise from above:
The Lakes townhouse and garden apartment complex is managed and leased by Nooney Krombach.

The firm has managed and leased the landmark Hampton Village Shopping Center in south St. Louis since 1955.

In the 1960s, Nooney Krombach developed Pierre Laclede Center in Clayton, home of its corporate headquarters. The firm continues to manage and lease the 650,000-square-foot, two-tower complex, owned by CIGNA.

Photos by Alise O'Brien

The year 1995 marks the 50th anniversary of St. Louis-based Nooney Krombach, a full-service commercial and industrial real estate organization that is a leader in brokerage, asset and property management, development, appraisal, consulting, research, and financial analysis.

50 Years of Service

Nooney Krombach, founded in 1945 as G.J. Nooney & Co., today handles nearly $300 million in annual transactions. The company annually leases or sells approximately 7 million square feet of property and currently manages more than 12 million square feet of space for financial institutions, corporations, pension funds, and individuals.

Some of the nation's financial companies that rely on Nooney Krombach to represent owners' interests include CIGNA, the Equitable Life Assurance Society of the United States, John Hancock Mutual Life Insurance Company, and General Electric Credit Equities. St. Louis-based corporations also use Nooney Krombach to manage their corporate headquarters, including Mallinckrodt Group Inc., Kellwood Corporation, Boatmen's Trust Company, and Belden Inc. Others use the firm's representation in acquisition of headquarters properties, including Edward D. Jones & Company and Enterprise Rent-A-Car.

Company Leaders Set the Pace

Chairman of the Board Gregory J. Nooney, Jr., and President Peter B. Krombach head the company, which has over 200 employees and branch offices in Columbia (Missouri), Chicago, Indianapolis, Minneapolis, Kansas City, and Cincinnati. Corporate headquarters is in Clayton's Pierre Laclede Center.

During Nooney Krombach's early years, commercial real estate deals were made on the backs of envelopes and finalized with a handshake. Today, every transaction demands intricate data, research, complete knowledge of

OFFICERS AND DIRECTORS OF NOONEY KROMBACH ARE (SEATED, FROM LEFT) ROBERT E. KRESKO, VICE CHAIRMAN; GREGORY J. NOONEY, JR., CHAIRMAN; PATRICK A. BYRNE, EXECUTIVE VICE PRESIDENT; (STANDING, FROM LEFT) PETER B. KROMBACH, PRESIDENT; AND PATRICIA A. NOONEY, SENIOR VICE PRESIDENT.

the market, and sophisticated accounting. Nooney points to the company's progressive role in research and analysis as a source of accomplishment. "Decision makers today require timely, comprehensive, and accurate information and financial data," he explains. "We were one of the first in our industry to set up a research department to provide this type of information, and we're continuing to expand and improve in this area, setting new levels of service."

Krombach agrees, pointing out that companies today need a complete detailing of their selected property and comparisons of other properties to justify real estate transactions. There is a need in the market for complex information on properties related to environmental, health, safety, and telecommunications issues, but companies specifically want alternative site and financial comparisons as well. "It's not only the larger institutions that want this type of information," Krombach notes. "All companies need to be able to look in a file and say, 'This is why we made that decision.' "

The firm has also developed expertise in tenant representation. "We're frequently asked to represent firms in renewing or executing new leases, as well as to consult on conditions of the current market," Krombach adds. "This provides tenants with an objective comparison and analysis of their location options."

The firm's senior management is particularly proud of the level of professionalism and integrity the industry has achieved, with Nooney Krombach setting progressive examples. The firm and its employees are active in numerous professional and trade organizations at the local, state, and national levels. These include the Society of Industrial and Office Realtors; the Commercial Investment Real Estate Institute; the Institute of Real Estate Management; the Appraisal Institute; and the National, Missouri, and St. Louis Associations of Realtors. The company is certified as an Accredited Management Organization by the Institute of Real Estate Management.

In addition, employees of Nooney Krombach take active roles in St. Louis-area civic and charitable organizations. The company also provides support for major cultural entities, such as the Missouri Botanical Garden, St. Louis Zoological Park, Science Center, and Art Museum.

Employee Dedication

A distinguishing aspect of Nooney Krombach is the average time employees have been with the company. Current managers and brokers have spent, on average, at least 10 years with the company. This is an extremely high average in an industry where frequent movement is common. A contributing factor to employee loyalty is Nooney Krombach's unique man-

THE FIRM MANAGES AND LEASES THIS INDUSTRIAL BUILDING LOCATED AT 13700 LAKEFRONT DRIVE IN EARTH CITY (BOTTOM LEFT).

agement structure. The company's managing principals do not compete with the firm's brokers and salespeople for assignments and commissions. This differs from most commercial and industrial real estate firms nationally.

As chairman, Nooney also has an open-door policy that fosters a culture of teamwork and openness. There are no extra layers of management. Everyone gets into the trenches on every deal, with senior executives using their expertise to provide extra attention to assure top quality. As Nooney Krombach celebrates its 50th anniversary, the firm is looking to utilize its extensive experience to achieve even greater levels of superior client service.

"We're dedicated to holding our commanding lead in the St. Louis market, to be aggressive and on the leading edge of continuing change," Nooney says. "But even more important, we're extremely interested in assuring that the professionalism and integrity we've achieved for the commercial and industrial real estate industry continue to grow."

NOONEY KROMBACH MANAGES AND LEASES THE 31-STORY LACLEDE GAS BUILDING IN DOWNTOWN ST. LOUIS FOR JOHN HANCOCK MUTUAL LIFE INSURANCE COMPANY.

PHOTOS BY ALISE O'BRIEN

Towers Perrin

Many St. Louis employers rely on Towers Perrin for consulting expertise in all areas of human resources management. ■ A total of 125 Towers Perrin professionals based in the Interco Tower in Clayton serve public and private corporations, as well as not-for-profit and government entities, which find outside expertise increasingly necessary as employee benefits and compensation programs grow more complex.

Towers Perrin's St. Louis clients include Anheuser-Busch Companies, Inc.; Boatmen's Bancshares, Inc.; Edison Brothers Stores Inc.; Emerson Electric Co.; Mercantile Bancorporation Inc.; McDonnell Douglas Corporation; Monsanto Company; and Union Electric Company. Worldwide, nearly 700 of the largest 1,000 companies use the firm's services.

Building on Decades of Tradition

Incorporated in its present form in 1934, Towers Perrin traces its roots back through several predecessor firms to the late 1800s. In 1917 the organization designed one of the first pension plans in the United States.

The St. Louis office, part of the New York-based firm's global network, is the seventh-largest of Towers Perrin's 34 U.S. offices and the 10th-largest among its 74 offices worldwide. The local office established its St. Louis presence in 1945 through a predecessor company, Nelson & Warren, which later became Tillinghast, Nelson & Warren.

In 1986 Tillinghast, Nelson & Warren merged with Towers, Perrin, Forster & Crosby. Since 1991 the firm has been known as Towers Perrin. Tillinghast, Nelson & Warren retains its identity as Tillinghast, a Towers Perrin company.

As the company celebrates its 50th anniversary in St. Louis in 1995, F. Michael J. Lackey, principal and manager of the St. Louis office, sees Towers Perrin as a highly visible local presence. "We view ourselves as a partner in the St. Louis marketplace," Lackey says, adding that the firm sponsors informational business briefings and executive forums on a regular basis. The firm encourages employee service on local civic boards and supports such organizations as Art St. Louis, Provident Counseling, St. Louis Art Fair, and St. Louis Symphony.

Towers Perrin is a privately held corporation; it is owned by active employees known as principals, who make up approximately 12 percent of the total workforce. "Our independence of vested interests is among Towers Perrin's prized attributes," says John T. Lynch, chairman and chief executive officer of Towers Perrin.

"It allows us to deliver superior service that is client-oriented. Our solutions to client needs are unique rather than 'off the shelf.'"

John T. Lynch serves as chairman and chief executive officer of Towers Perrin.

THE FIRM'S ST. LOUIS PRINCIPALS INCLUDE (STANDING, FROM LEFT) ABRAHAM GOOTZEIT (TILLINGHAST), THOMAS P. CARNEKA, JOSEPH M. VOGL, CRAIG L. KAINTZ, (SEATED) MARTIN J. ZIGLER, F. MICHAEL J. LACKEY, AND JAMES E. DRENNAN.

In differentiating Towers Perrin, Lackey also cites a superior workforce and ongoing employee education and training. "Only through a high degree of professionalism can we maintain the level of service we offer our clients," he explains. "Our success as a firm is entwined with our clients' success. We're proactive in helping them to achieve that success, and we challenge them in the counseling process."

A Broad Base of Services

Towers Perrin services encompass employee benefits programs in areas including retirement plans; health and welfare plans; compensation, including employee pay, executive compensation, and sales compensation; employee communications; benefit administration; organizational effectiveness; people strategy; risk management; and workers' compensation.

Tillinghast, a Towers Perrin company, provides counsel and actuarial services to life and casualty insurance entities. Tillinghast actuaries develop financial, operational, and profitability projections for insurance companies; analyze insurance products; and develop marketing programs for those products.

Towers Perrin's growth, according to Lackey, is attributable to superior, broad-based service. Contributing factors are a number of management trends—notably the burgeoning of technology.

"For instance," Lackey says, "technological advances have made efficient the outsourcing of the benefit administration function." Companies increasingly are using tools such as Towers Perrin's retirement planning software and its sophisticated computer- and telephone-based benefit communication tools.

Globally, Towers Perrin helps multinational companies address complex human resource issues—particularly in Latin American, European, and Pacific Rim nations.

Towers Perrin's mission, in summary, is to be the premier provider of quality and value in human resource management counsel. "Our success in realizing that mission," Lackey says, "depends on our success in contributing to the growth and prosperity of the St. Louis business community."

As Towers Perrin moves into its second half-century of St. Louis citizenry, its partnership with its "home on the river" remains strong and energetic.

NO
LEFT
TURN
30

1 9 4 6

1946 Hunter Engineering Company
1947 KSDK-NewsChannel 5
1949 Bi-State Development Agency
1949 Coburn & Croft
1949 Sinclair & Rush, Inc.
1955 Peabody Holding Company, Inc.
1955 Sumner Group Inc.
1956 Kelly Services, Inc.
1958 Falcon Products, Inc.
1960 HBE Corporation
1961 Kellwood Company
1962 Middendorf Meat/Quality Foods
1964 Tetra Plastics, Inc.
1967 Security Armored Car Service, Inc.
1967 Thermal Science, Inc.
1968 Olsten Staffing Services
1970 MasterCard International Inc.
1972 Citicorp Mortgage, Inc.
1972 SCS/Compute, Inc.
1974 Magna Group, Inc.
1974 PPC International, Inc.
1975 Adia Personnel Services

1 9 7 5

◆ CATHY FERRIS PHOTO

Hunter Engineering Company

Hunter Engineering Company owes its beginnings to a discharged automobile battery. Lee Hunter, Jr., a 23-year-old St. Louis architecture student, found himself frequently confronted with recurring car battery failure in his Packard convertible. At the time, in 1936, it took several days to recharge a battery. Hunter was determined to find a better, faster way, and he began exploring new methods of charging a battery quickly.

With the help of a former Washington University electrical engineering professor, Hunter's experiments paid off. He developed the first quick-charge battery recharger, based on a diverter pole generator, and put the new product on the market. But Hunter's innovative spirit did not stop with his first product. Over the 50-year history of Hunter Engineering, the company has become known worldwide for its state-of-the-art automobile service equipment. Ever on the cutting edge of automobile technology, the company computerized its automotive diagnosis and repair equipment and currently offers the international market computerized wheel alignment software written in 21 languages.

From top right:
Hunter's electronic circuit boards are designed using state-of-the-art software.

More than 1,000 digital photos are stored in Hunter software to help mechanics make a diagnosis.

Aligners are inspected prior to shipment from Hunter's St. Louis facility.

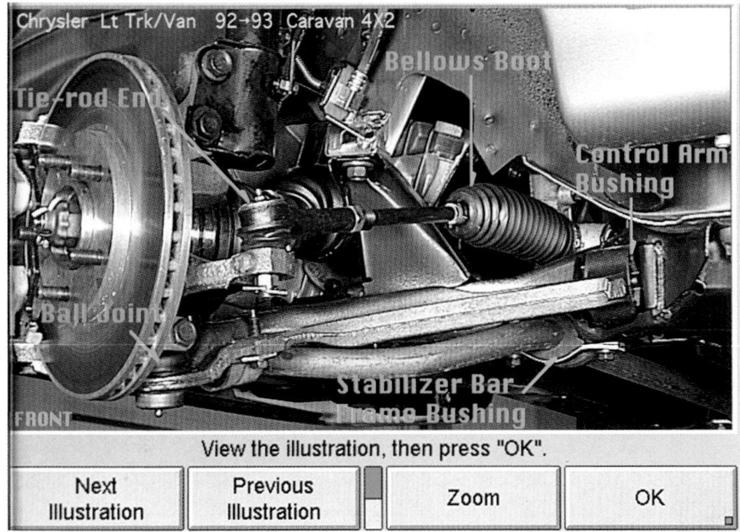

A History of Innovation

During the Great Depression, Lee Hunter, Jr., Manufacturing Company, as the business was first known, was selling the $497 Kwikurent charger as fast as it could make them. After serving in both the Engineer Corps and the Ordnance Corps during World War II, Hunter returned to St. Louis in 1946 and reopened his business under the name Hunter Engineering.

The new company manufactured another Hunter invention, the "Tune-In," which balanced automobile wheels while they were spinning on the car. In 1955 Hunter developed a new system for aligning automobile wheels called "Lite A Line," which became the industry standard. Over the years to follow, Hunter refined his inventions, developing a revolutionary system for rapid and accurate diagnosis of wheel alignment problems in the late 1960s. The F60 dynamic aligner, as the product was known, calculated all readings from the point at which the tire meets the road, with the wheel in motion. Hunter's four-wheel alignment technology followed, and remains in use around the world today.

Hunter Engineering also pioneered the use of computer aids for automotive service, starting in the 1970s with wheel alignment equipment that featured digital displays and printouts. In 1980 came the use of the CRT, another industry first. Today, the company designs and manufactures its own printed circuit boards in its electronics plant in Raymond, Mississippi.

Hunter also has branched out to manufacture brake testing equipment used in automobile safety inspections. The company's tester is designed to detect small problems before they become big ones. With Hunter's equipment, it takes less than two minutes to assess front-to-rear and side-to-side balance of the brake system, and to determine if all four brakes

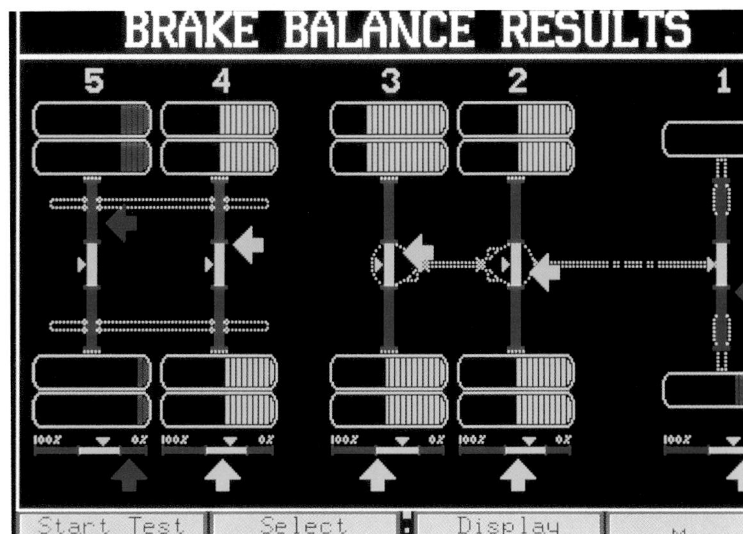

Electronic truck brake testing is a recent Hunter venture that promises tremendous growth.

are working as designed. The company also has built a truck and bus safety center in St. Louis, used for research and development, which provides brake inspections and wheel alignments for large vehicles.

Keeping the Customer in Mind

Reflecting its history of growth and expansion, one-fifth of Hunter's sales today are international. The company has exclusive distributors in 50 countries, as well as a wholly owned subsidiary in Canada, each with complete electronic and mechanical service capabilities. In addition to offering its software in 21 languages, Hunter's CD-ROM version aligner shows mechanics digital photographs and gives live audio-visual demonstrations of alignment techniques via MPEG technology.

Such devotion to pleasing the customer has made Hunter Engineering the automotive service industry leader. Hunter is a growing, privately held company headquartered in St. Louis with additional plants located in Mississippi. Four hundred of Hunter's 700 workers are located in the St. Louis area. In the United States, the company also has a 200-person sales force and a corps of 220 service technicians who install systems, conduct training, and handle repairs, carrying a complete inventory of replacement parts in their vans. Finally, Hunter has established a network of 11 training centers throughout the United States where service technicians teach more than 10,000 people per year how to use the company's equipment.

Hunter Engineering continues to strive for the best in customer service through creative new products that remain the cornerstone of its success. Continuing Lee Hunter's tradition, company engineers are an energized, highly creative group. "A passion for creativity is what we look for in prospective engineers," says Stephen F. Brauer, president of Hunter Engineering since 1979. "Creative new products have fueled the company's phenomenal growth, rather than mergers and acquisitions."

Hunter Engineering reaches the world from its St. Louis base, exporting not only top-quality automotive service equipment, but Yankee ingenuity—in the Lee Hunter tradition.

A mechanic prepares to align a car using Hunter's latest radio frequency cordless sensors.

Hunter's 23-acre, campus-like headquaters is located at the intersection of I-70 and Lindbergh Boulevard in Bridgeton.

KSDK-NewsChannel 5

KSDK-NewsChannel 5 has a long tradition and history as a national and local television leader. When it signed on the air in 1947 as St. Louis' first television station, Channel 5 was one of only seven stations in the country. Joseph Pulitzer II, of the famous Pulitzer publishing family, recognized the future in television and brought what was then KSD-TV to the St. Louis airwaves on February 8, 1947. Just six days later, Channel 5 televised the first play-by-play sports event in the Midwest, broadcasting a basketball game between Saint Louis University and Oklahoma from Kiel Auditorium (the precursor to today's Kiel Center).

The Early Days

NewsChannel 5 was originally known as KSD-TV. The station's first telecast was a program called "News and Views." The show boasted 90 minutes of variety—covering everything from ballroom dancers to baseball stars.

As television's popularity and presence grew nationally, KSD's momentum began to build as well. In 1949 the station started its long-standing affiliation with the NBC network.

Fabulous '50s and '60s

The '50s and '60s brought about the emergence of national programs, including soap operas like "Love of Life" and evening programs such as the comedy "Life of Riley" and the drama "Dragnet." For the young baby boomers, "Howdy Doody" and "Kukla, Fran, and Ollie" became hits.

Viewer favorites also included locally produced programs like "To the Ladies," which brought local stardom to Charlotte Peters, Stan Kann, and Marty Bronson. One of KSD's biggest successes and one of the station's longest running shows, "St. Louis Hop," also got its start during this time. The program, geared toward teenagers, was sort of a local version of "American Bandstand."

News operations began to take the number one priority spot in the 1960s. The station gave more air time to the news and featured staff, including well-known St. Louis newscasters Chris Condon, Max Robey, Bob Chase, and John Roedel, as well as weathercasters Clif St. James and Howard DeMere.

'70s and '80s Bring Changes

As technology changed the way news was presented, KSD-TV was at the forefront of acquiring the most up-to-date information then as it is now. Local programs expanded to include live broadcasts of Cardinals baseball. One of the St. Louis community's top assets, anchor Karen Foss, also came to the area, joining the station in 1979.

In 1983 the station was sold by the Pulitzer Publishing Company to Multimedia, Inc. At this time, its name was changed to KSDK-TV. Multimedia is a diversified communications company based in Greenville, South Carolina. Formed in 1968, the firm now has five divisions—Newspapers, Broadcasting, Cablevision, Entertainment, and Security.

Sally Jessy Raphael is a name

NewsChannel 5's number-one-rated news team includes (from left) anchors Deanne Lane, Rick Edlund, Karen Foss, and Dan Gray.

NEWSCHANNEL 5'S "SPORTS PLUS" SHOW, HOSTED BY KSDK SPORTS DIRECTOR MIKE BUSH, IS THE TOP-RANKED LOCAL SPORTS PROGRAM IN THE MARKET. THE STATION'S SPORTS TEAM INCLUDES (FROM LEFT) FRANK COSUMANO, MIKE BUSH, MALCOLM BRIGGS, AND TREY WINGO.

familiar to national television audiences. The "Sally" show got its start in St. Louis at KSDK's studios during the mid-1980s. After three years of production locally, "Sally" moved to New York and is today just one of the programs syndicated nationally by Multimedia Entertainment. Others include the Phil Donahue, Rush Limbaugh. and Jerry Springer shows.

The station regularly receives Emmy awards for local programs, and consistently has the top-rated news programming in the nation's 30 largest markets.

KSDK is consistently recognized for its emphasis on local news; virtually every NewsChannel 5 newscast is rated number one in its time period. According to Vice President and General Manager John Kueneke, the station's slogan also serves as its mission statement. "Where the News Comes First" is a credible claim; KSDK-NewsChannel 5 broadcasts approximately 40 percent more local news coverage than its closest competitor in the St. Louis market. Aside from the usual evening news programs at 5:00, 6:00, and 10:00, the station airs 90 minutes of news at the crack of dawn, one hour of news at noon, and morning newscasts on Saturday and Sunday. KSDK was also the first station in St. Louis to feature a weekly Sunday night sports wrap-up show, "Sports Plus." The show consistently delivers higher ratings than other network affiliates' nightly newscasts.

A Philosophy of Helping the Community

Community outreach is another component of KSDK's mission and an important factor in its success. The station's Volunteer 5 program, started in January 1993, has successfully linked people in the community willing to volunteer with organizations needing help. The project provides more than $5 million annually in volunteer services to the community and hundreds of thousands of hours of volunteer time to area service organizations. Volunteer 5 features a different charitable group each week, publicizing its activities and volunteer needs.

As a salute to the tremendous response from local viewers, KSDK airs an annual prime-time Volunteer 5 awards program. It is produced in conjunction with the National Jefferson Awards, which honor outstanding public service.

NewsChannel 5 is at the forefront in serving the community by supporting many organizations with their major projects, including United Way, Boy Scouts "Scouting for Food" project, Salvation Army Tree of Lights holiday campaign, AIDS Foundation, St. Louis Art Fair, Lifeskills Foundation, Mathews-Dickey Boys Club, United Cerebral Palsy, Ronald McDonald House, and Senior Olympics. KSDK also airs the annual Muscular Dystrophy Association Labor Day Telethon.

For nearly a half century, KSDK-NewsChannel 5 has provided outstanding programming to the metropolitan St. Louis area. In 1989 the station expanded its broadcast time to 24 hours a day to better serve the public. Not only has the station emphasized quality journalism, but also it has been a leader in broadcast technology.

But the station's employees are KSDK's greatest asset; they keep things running smoothly, both on and off the air. Without the dedication of its staff, NewsChannel 5 might be just another station. Instead, it is a valuable resource to the St. Louis community.

THE NEWSCHANNEL 5 WEATHER TEAM KEEPS AN EYE ON THE SKIES FOR ST. LOUIS' EVER-CHANGING WEATHER WITH THE LATEST IN TECHNOLOGY AND FORECASTING TOOLS. THE WEATHER TEAM FEATURES (FROM LEFT) METEOROLOGISTS MARY BETH WROEBEL AND SCOTT CONNELL, CHIEF METEOROLOGIST JOHN FULLER, AND METEOROLOGIST PAUL WILLIAMS.

Bi-State Development Agency

EVEN THOUGH THE LAST STREETCAR TURNED OFF ITS POWER IN 1966, talk of reviving the electric railway continued among transit advocates who were vowing someday to renew rail lines around the St. Louis region. The perseverance of those supporters, and action by the Bi-State Development Agency, resulted in the introduction of MetroLink, the region's new light-rail system, which began operations July 31, 1993.

MetroLink has been praised by the president of the United States, who made an inaugural ride on it, and by the U.S. Secretary of Transportation, who called it a national model for light-rail transportation. "One of the most significant contributions MetroLink has made to the St. Louis metropolitan area was turning abandoned and decaying infrastructure into a highly useful product for the community," says Milton F. Svetanics Jr., chairman of the Board of Commissioners for the Bi-State Development Agency, which owns and operates the system.

MetroLink was made possible by a commitment of federal funds, an innovative bridge swap, donated rights-of-way on existing rail lines, and three years of fast-track construction. One of the major pieces required to make MetroLink possible was the city's exchange of the McArthur Bridge for the Eads Bridge, owned by Terminal Railroad. The bridge, railroad rights-of-way, and associated property were then donated to Bi-State to provide the local match for the federal funds and the route for MetroLink.

The Bi-State System

The Bi-State Development Agency was created through a compact between the states of Missouri and Illinois that was ratified by the U.S. Congress and signed by President Truman in September 1949. The agreement gives Bi-State the authority to implement or assist with regional programs and activities, crossing boundaries between both states, the City of St. Louis, six counties, and more than 200 municipalities and taxing districts.

Bi-State employs more than 1,900 people and is governed by a board of 10 commissioners, five each from Missouri and Illinois, appointed by the governors of the respective states. An executive director is hired by the board to oversee the agency's activities. "Our guidance from the board is to strive toward being the best transit system in the nation," says John K. Leary Jr., Bi-State's executive director, "and to be a consensus developer for the region in projects where our Bi-State powers prove most effective."

In 1963, 15 privately owned transit companies became the property of the Bi-State Development Agency through a $26.5 million revenue bond issue. The Bi-State Transit System was formed as an operating entity of the agency and was responsible for shaping a unified and modernized transit network.

Bi-State Today

Bi-State now owns and operates the metropolitan area's public

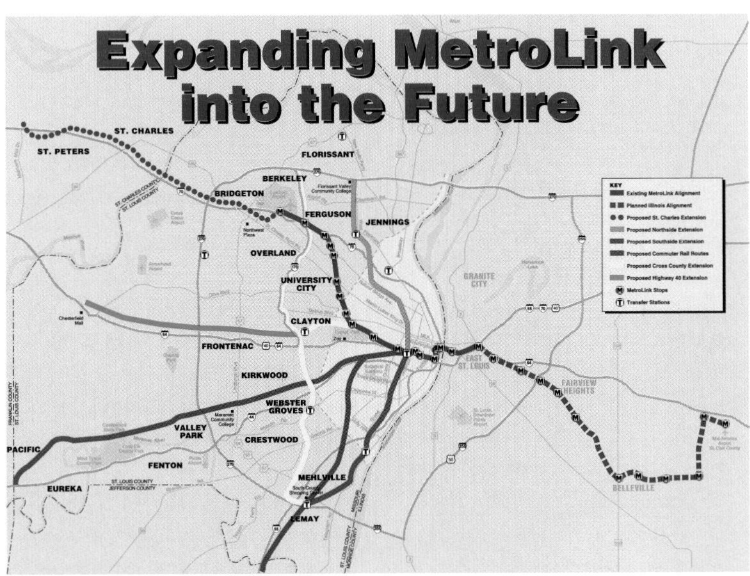

transportation system, which includes MetroLink, buses, and paratransit vans; St. Louis Downtown-Parks Airport and the surrounding business/industrial park; three station/garages from which buses are dispatched; a central bus and van repair facility; and a light-rail maintenance complex. The agency also operates the Gateway Arch transportation system, Arch Odyssey Theatre, and Arch parking facility.

The crowning glory of Bi-State's 46 years is its 18-mile, state-of-the-art light-rail system and multimodal transportation network. The area's entire system of 126 bus routes was redesigned to allow connection of many routes with MetroLink stations. The system includes 644 buses and 71 vans in addition to 31 light-rail vehicles. Synchronized transfer centers have added to the popularity and ease of riding MetroLink.

"The MetroLink investment has sparked development all along the rail line," Leary says. "And attractions such as the new Kiel Center for hockey and basketball, Busch Stadium for baseball, and the almost-completed domed stadium for football are being served, as are our customers. MetroLink frequently carries 10,000 people or more to sporting events and to other special activities."

Following the introduction of MetroLink, Bi-State received the American Public Transit Association's most competitive and prestigious award and the "Oscar" of the transit industry—the Management Innovation Award. The agency was commended for its customer-focused approach to service and its well-tailored marketing techniques.

Agency Growth

The Bi-State system carried more than 45 million commuters in fiscal 1994, a 21 percent increase over the previous year. Leary attributes much of the increase to the popularity of MetroLink, but also credits the redesigned system, which is more convenient and cost efficient for commuters. In addition, Call-a-Ride Plus vans provide demand-responsive, curb-to-curb service reserved exclusively for disabled persons. All MetroLink vehicles and most buses are wheelchair-lift equipped.

The Bi-State Vision

"There is a new transportation vision for the St. Louis region," according to Svetanics. "We see a $1.5 billion, 25-year period of extending MetroLink into several new corridors; placing accessible, clean-air buses into service; adding more paratransit vans for persons with disabilities; and making a number of enhancements to better serve our customers." Bi-State has already begun to take action on the agency vision, which has been made possible as a result of Missouri voters' overwhelming support in 1994 of a one-fourth of 1 percent increase in the local sales tax. In addition to providing a 21st-century transportation network, the Bi-State Development Agency looks forward to performing many roles throughout the metropolitan area. After all, "development" is its middle name.

OPPOSITE PAGE:
THE AGENCY'S LEADERSHIP INCLUDES MILTON F. SVETANICS JR. (LEFT), CHAIRMAN OF THE BOARD OF COMMISSIONERS, AND JOHN K. LEARY JR., EXECUTIVE DIRECTOR FOR BI-STATE.

BI-STATE OWNS AND OPERATES THE REGION'S LIGHT-RAIL SYSTEM AND MULTIMODAL TRANSPORTATION NETWORK, WHICH INCLUDES 126 BUS ROUTES, 644 BUSES, 71 VANS, AND 31 LIGHT-RAIL VEHICLES. A 25-YEAR EXPANSION PROGRAM IS EXPECTED TO EXTEND METROLINK INTO SEVERAL NEW CORRIDORS (LEFT).

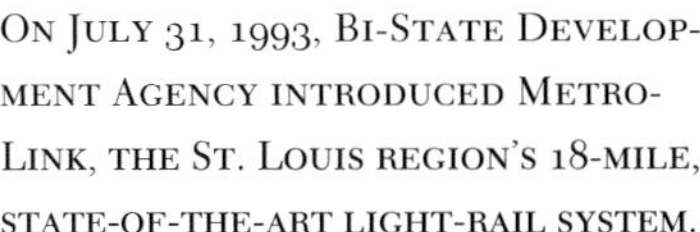

ON JULY 31, 1993, BI-STATE DEVELOPMENT AGENCY INTRODUCED METROLINK, THE ST. LOUIS REGION'S 18-MILE, STATE-OF-THE-ART LIGHT-RAIL SYSTEM.

RICHMOND COBURN SAID, "DO A GOOD JOB, KEEP THE CLIENT INformed, and send a fair bill." With those words as their motto, and a couple of railroads as their clients, Richmond Coburn, Clem Storkman, and Tom Croft started the firm of Coburn & Croft with the goal of becoming the premier litigation firm in St. Louis. Forty-five years and 80 lawyers later, it appears that their goal has been realized.

QUINTA SCOTT

Unique for its size in St. Louis, Coburn & Croft specializes in high-profile litigation across the United States—even to the remote island of Guam, where two years ago the firm successfully defended one of its clients in a seven-week trial. Also unique for a litigation firm is the fact that Coburn & Croft will represent both plaintiffs and defendants in lawsuits—generally representing defendants in product liability cases, but representing either plaintiffs or defendants in commercial cases.

The only St. Louis law firm listed in the *Guinness Book of World Records*, Coburn & Croft tried the longest jury trial in the history of the United States. That trial lasted three years and nine months in front of the same jury, and resulted in a defense verdict for the firm's client.

A Solid History

Not prone to moving from building to building, Coburn & Croft spent its first 26 years in the Ambassador Building and the last 20 years at its present location in the Mercantile Center. What started as one-half of a floor in the Mercantile Center has now expanded to four floors, and the firm is in the process of finishing a complete renovation of its space. In addition to its St. Louis office, Coburn & Croft has offices in Belleville, Illinois, and Houston, Texas.

Several noteworthy events have made Coburn & Croft the preeminent firm that it has become: Storkman's elevation to the Missouri Supreme Court gave the firm statewide notoriety; a 1959 $4 million verdict against two insurance companies, at a time when million-dollar verdicts in Missouri were rare and $4 million settlements were unheard of; a lawsuit, ultimately decided by the Missouri Supreme Court, that paved the way for Monsanto's world headquarters in St. Louis County; and Coburn's invitation from U.S. Senator Stuart Symington and President John F. Kennedy to go to Washington, D.C., to become the general counsel for a Senate committee investigating the stockpiling of war material, a job that kept Coburn out of St. Louis and in Washington for one year.

The firm's successful representation of Standard Oil of Indiana in its trademark lawsuit against Standard Oil of New Jersey gave Coburn & Croft nationwide notoriety. As a result of this judgment, the defendant had to change its name—choosing "Exxon."

QUINTA SCOTT

Croft's victory in a separate commercial case set the record at the time for the highest jury verdict in the state of Missouri.

During all this time the firm continued to represent the largest railroads in the country, and Coburn served as president of the Bar Association of Metropolitan St. Louis and the Missouri Bar.

The firm's win in the longest jury trial in history opened doors across the country for toxic tort litigation, followed by Coburn & Croft's representation of major corporations in litigation outside

PARTNERS LINDA L. SHAPIRO (TOP) AND DEAN L. FRANKLIN (RIGHT) ARE HELPING COBURN & CROFT BUILD ON ITS 45-YEAR HISTORY IN ST. LOUIS.

THE FIRM'S MANAGING PARTNERS ARE (FROM LEFT) KENNETH R. HEINEMAN, J. WILLIAM NEWBOLD, AND JOHN R. MUSGRAVE.

▶ QUINTA SCOTT

of St. Louis in all types of personal injury and commercial cases. In fact, the firm has now handled cases in 33 states across the country.

Presently, Coburn & Croft has three partners who are Fellows of the American College of Trial Lawyers and three partners who are members of the American Law Institute.

▶ JAMES VISSER

Building the City

Although the firm specializes in litigation, the transactions side of the practice has also been successful at Coburn & Croft. For example, construction of high-rise office buildings in St. Louis had been thwarted by a city ordinance requiring that all buildings be constructed of brick. When the ordinance was repealed in the early 1960s, Coburn & Croft did all the legal work for the construction of the first modern office building in St. Louis, the Executive Office Building on Olive Street.

Coburn & Croft then did all the legal work for the construction of Busch Stadium, as well as the parking garages and buildings that were built as a part of the Civic Center Redevelopment Corporation.

Today, the firm represents a multitude of corporations in their transactional work in the United States and overseas.

What is next for Coburn & Croft? As Jack Musgrave, the firm's managing partner says, "The business of law is in a state of flux, but our goal is to continue to provide the type of services that our clients need at a cost commensurate with the nature of the work. We have developed the staff and technology to handle those cases, and we want to continue to be the firm you go to when you have a tough case that you need to win."

The late Richmond Coburn could not have said it better himself.

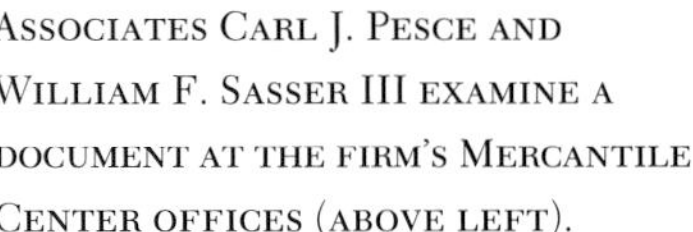

Associates Carl J. Pesce and William F. Sasser III examine a document at the firm's Mercantile Center offices (above left).

Associates Daniel J. Carpenter and Nicholas B. Clifford, Jr., join Partner Anne-Marie Keinker to discuss a client matter (above right).

The Partners of Coburn & Croft celebrate founder Richmond C. Coburn's 92nd birthday on May 5, 1992 (left).

Associate Stacey L. Stater takes advantage of the firm's technological capabilities (left).

Sinclair & Rush, Inc.

FOUNDED IN 1949 AS A DIP MOLDER OF VINYL PLASTISOL PRODucts, Sinclair & Rush is a "big-little" company with large aspirations and a global view. A bottom-line management style, combined with an aggressive marketing approach and a freewheeling entrepreneurial spirit, has propelled Sinclair & Rush to the top of the industries it serves. ■ Headquartered in St. Louis County, Sinclair & Rush has two plants in the St. Louis area and manufacturing facilities in Los Angeles; Sydney, Australia; and Maidstone, England. The company has sales offices in Kobe, Japan; Paris, France; and Monterrey, Mexico. Future plans call for a plant in Japan and another new, state-of-the-art manufacturing plant in Missouri.

As the world's largest dip molder of vinyl plastisol products, Sinclair & Rush offers tremendous employment opportunities. The operations manager for the company's St. Louis dip molding business, the most profitable operating unit, is 30 years old and formerly ran the United Kingdom operation.

"People can move up quickly here if they are willing to work hard and accept a lot of responsibilities," says Frank A. Forst, president and chief operating officer of Sinclair & Rush.

Two-thirds of the company's employees are located in the St. Louis area, spread among the corporate headquarters, a modern extrusion/injection facility in west St. Louis County, and a dip molding and printing facility in Jefferson County.

Chairman and CEO Vincent Gorguze (left) and President and COO Frank Forst are leading the company's expansion into global markets.

Modest Beginnings

Following World War II, two young engineers, George Sinclair and Wayne Rush, saw the potential of a remarkable new material, vinyl plastisol. Because the material could be easily dip molded in many different shapes, formulations, and colors at a very low price, it became an instant substitution for rubber.

From that modest beginning, Sinclair & Rush now has more than 15,000 customers worldwide. In 1978 the company was purchased by Vincent Gorguze, former president and vice chairman of Emerson Electric Co., and John Henry, former executive vice president of Rockwell International. Gorguze serves as chairman and chief executive officer of Sinclair & Rush; Henry is vice chairman. Gorguze, Henry, and Forst are the company's only stockholders.

A Melding of Marketing and Bottom-Line Management

Gorguze installed an aggressive growth style of management in which marketing, cash flow, and financial control are paramount to the business. Forst, who has been with Sinclair & Rush more than 25 years, has a marketing background and works closely with Executive Vice President Brad Stack, who directs all worldwide marketing.

"It is tough to combine a bottom-line orientation with aggressive marketing, but it has worked extremely well," says Forst.

Sinclair & Rush's St. Louis-area operations include executive offices in west St. Louis County and a state-of-the-art manufacturing facility completed in July 1995 in Jefferson County.

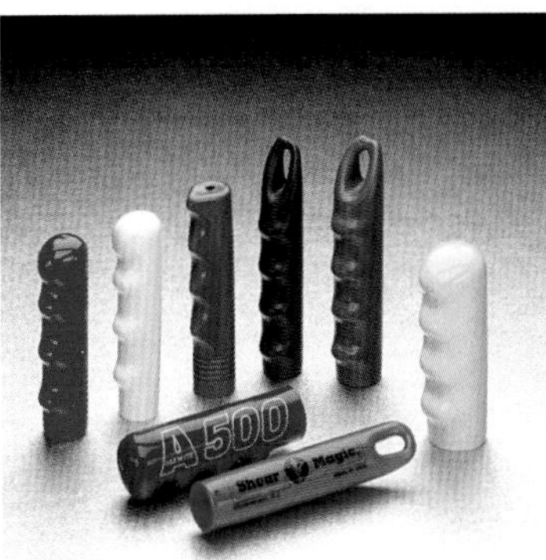

"Few companies of our size have our financial and operational expertise. We run this entire operation worldwide with only four accountants in St. Louis, and they are all CPAs."

Gorguze and Henry took advantage of the firm's strong marketing position by adding manufacturing processes and products. In 1981 the company entered extrusion manufacturing and followed that with an entry into the injection molding business in 1984.

Several new marketing divisions and brands were created in the early 1980s. Sinclair & Rush's stockCap™ is now the leading supplier of industrial closures and custom moldings to original equipment manufacturers throughout the world. GripWorks™ manufactures handgrips for bicycles, exercise equipment, tools, and other industrial consumer items. VisiPak® is a leading supplier of clear, extruded packaging.

For its first 32 years, Sinclair & Rush sold products only to other manufacturers. In 1982 the management team decided to extend the dip molding process to consumer products and formed the Sundance line. Sundance now manufactures and markets dip molded, injection molded, and extruded sports bottles, can holders, and other leisure beverageware. Sundance products are shipped worldwide and are on the shelves of many of the large retailers, including Wal-Mart and Kmart.

Swinging into Golf Accessories

In 1991 Sinclair & Rush swung into golf accessories by creating the Castle Bay line of golf club head covers. The company developed radically designed iron and wood covers from a rubberized flexible vinyl plastisol, known

as Softex.® Castle Bay's products provide complete protection for golf club heads, an important issue with the advent of expensive graphite shafts. Castle Bay golf accessories are now sold in 22 countries.

The company entered the European market with the acquisition of a dip molder in Sittingbourne, Kent, England, followed by the 1993 acquisition of another dip molder in Sydney, Australia, positioning Sinclair & Rush to service the expanding markets of the Pacific Rim.

The Cameron Connection

While Vince Gorguze was overseeing the growth of Sinclair & Rush, he also acquired other companies through Cameron Holdings Corporation (a Gorguze Investment Company), which has offices in St. Louis and San Diego. Lynn Gorguze, a Duke University graduate with a master's degree in business administration from Washington University in St. Louis, is president of the company. Prior to forming Cameron Holdings Corporation, Lynn Gorguze was very instrumental in acquiring several other companies in the Gorguze portfolio. Cameron Holdings Corporation has controlling interest in communications firms, playground and recreational companies, and other golf industry investments. Gary Feigenbutz is executive vice president of Cameron Holdings Corporation and was formerly vice president and chief financial officer of Sinclair & Rush.

Cameron Holdings Corporation utilizes the broad acquisition, operations, marketing, and financial experience of Vince Gorguze and his partners to acquire companies and point them on a similar growth path as Sinclair & Rush.

As Sinclair & Rush has proven, the formula works. The "big-little" plastics manufacturer is now in the major leagues of worldwide business.

Sinclair & Rush markets its diverse plastic products to consumers, as well as other manufacturers.

As the world's largest dip molder of vinyl plastisol products, the company offers tremendous employment opportunities (above).

Sinclair & Rush has invested heavily in talented people and the best equipment to become the leader in the industries it serves (left).

Peabody Holding Company, Inc.

EVERY DAY, 365 DAYS A YEAR, PEABODY HOLDING COMPANY, INC. SUBsidiaries and affiliates mine an average of 411,000 tons of coal, making the Peabody Group of companies the largest coal producer in the United States. From mines across the United States and in Australia, the more than 150 million tons of coal Peabody Group companies will mine each year go to customers in 28 states and 14 foreign countries, producing annual revenues exceeding $2 billion. Fifty-seven percent of the electricity in the United States is generated from coal, and about 6 percent of all electricity in the nation is generated by using Peabody Group coal. Twenty-one of the 25 lowest-cost power plants in the United States are fueled by coal.

CLOCKWISE FROM RIGHT:
IRL F. ENGELHARDT, CHAIRMAN, PRESIDENT, AND CEO OF PEABODY HOLDING COMPANY, INC.

ROCHELLE MINE IN WYOMING'S POWDER RIVER BASIN IS THE MOST PRODUCTIVE COAL MINE IN THE UNITED STATES AND ONE OF THE SAFEST.

AT RAWHIDE MINE IN THE POWDER RIVER BASIN, COAL SEAMS TOTALING 110 FEET OF THICKNESS MAKE IT EASY TO MINE COAL EFFICIENTLY USING TRUCKS AND SHOVELS.

Leadership for Changing Times

Peabody Holding provides policy management and strategic planning for more than 50 coal mining, marketing, trading, and related corporations in the United States and Australia. Today's highly automated coal operations are a far cry from the original Peabody Coal Company started in 1883 by 24-year-old Francis S. Peabody with a $100 loan.

Miners now operate complex machinery and follow sophisticated mining plans to maximize production while ensuring safety. In underground mines, for example, longwall mining units, with panels 1,000 feet wide or more, remove coal continuously to a conveyor for transportation out of the mine. These high-technology machines produce up to 3,000 tons of coal per hour. In surface mines, draglines uncover coal seams with large buckets that extract as much as 155 cubic yards of rock and dirt with each swing of the boom.

Miners, too, have changed. Peabody Group people are highly skilled and experienced, with an average age of 47 years and with an average 20 hours of training per year. A miner's average wages and benefits exceed $55,000 per year. The wages of Peabody's 8,000 employees contribute strongly to an overall economic impact that totals about $1.5 billion annually in wages, taxes, purchased materials, and services in the nine principal states in which its subsidiaries operate.

Modern coal mining reclamation has changed drastically as well. For example, today's coal operations return land after mining to its original or better condition, using detailed reclamation and revegetation practices. At a cost of $7,000 to $20,000 per acre, depending on local conditions, Peabody Group subsidiaries have restored tens of thousands of acres, returning the land to premining uses such as recreation and wildlife areas, forests, crop and grazing lands, and home sites. In 1994, for instance, Peabody Group's midwestern subsidiary, Peabody Coal Company, turned over management of a 64,000-acre tract in Kentucky to the state, to protect wildlife

resources and open postmined lands to the public for hunting, fishing, and other outdoor recreation. In Illinois, just a 45-minute drive from St. Louis, the 1,800-acre Peabody River King Wildlife Area provides recreation opportunities for thousands of users.

Quality and Safety First

Another focus is coal's quality—its content measured in precise tolerances for sulfur, Btus, ash, and moisture. Seventy-five percent of the coal sold annually by Peabody Group companies is low-sulfur coal. Emission requirements for electric power plants mean that utilities must demand precise specifications. To meet these stringent standards, many Peabody Group operations have installed multimillion-dollar analyzers that test and blend coal before it leaves the mine. For Peabody customers, the better the coal quality, the more efficiently it burns, and that lowers the kilowatt-hour cost to consumers.

Mine safety always has been a critical concern for the coal industry and for the Peabody Group. In 1994, having already reduced accidents by more than 66 percent since 1990, the Peabody Group launched a safety initiative called "One Future—Safety through Teamwork" with the ultimate goal of achieving industry leadership in safety. The program enlists all employees as team members in adopting zero tolerance for safety hazards that could lead to a workplace accident. The One Future program also features wellness activities and health screenings at mines and business units.

The Peabody Group has expanded its business base dramatically, with annual sales increasing from nearly 87 million tons in 1989 to a projected level of 155 million tons in 1995. More than a decade into its second century, the Peabody Group of companies looks forward to continued growth in the United States and overseas. With nearly 12 billion tons of high-quality coal reserves worldwide, the Peabody Group remains the industry leader.

Clockwise from below:
Five Peabody Group underground operations in West Virginia mine coal using highly productive longwall machines.

At Caballo Mine in Wyoming, workers remove coal from a 70-foot-thick seam with trucks and shovels.

Peabody's longtime commitment to reclamation of surface-mined lands has created thousands of acres of public recreation and wildlife areas, such as this one in Illinois.

Sumner Group Inc.

FORTY YEARS AGO, A MAN WITH A STRONG WILL TO SUCCEED and an ardent entrepreneurial spirit purchased the St. Louis distributorship of a mimeograph and supply company. What began in 1955 as a local distributor for A.B. Dick Company has evolved into Sumner Group Inc., one of the premier independently owned office equipment dealerships in the United States. ■ Along the way, the entrepreneur, E.G. "Bud" Sumner, passed on his business acumen to his family. Today, Sumner Group is still a family business, led by Bud's sons. Steve Sumner holds the position of president and chief executive officer; Ed Sumner is executive vice president of Sumner Group and president of Copying Concepts, a division of the company.

The company's leadership includes (from left) Randy Jung, president of Datamax Graphics Systems and Document Management Services; Carl Bergauer, president of Datamax Office Systems; Ed Sumner, executive vice president of Sumner Group and president of Copying Concepts; Fred Weaver, chief financial officer of Sumner Group; Kevin Laury, vice president of Copying Concepts; and Steve Sumner, president and chief executive officer of Sumner Group.

Sumner Group has grown into a corporation with multiple operating divisions, all directed toward a goal of providing the best in office equipment, printing equipment, computer networks, and related services to companies in the Midwest. It offers clients a single source for all equipment placements, network connections, supplies, service contracts, billing, and customer service.

"Our core strength is our ability to rely on the vast resources of our Sumner Group partners," explains Steve Sumner. The seven independent operating divisions that compromise the group are Datamax Graphics Systems, Document Management Services, Copying Concepts, SGI Financial Services, and Datamax Office Systems of St. Louis, Arkansas, and Texas.

"Collectively," Sumner explains, "we can address our customers' immediate and long-term document management needs. From toner to a fully integrated digital color output device or a four-color printing press—our combined knowledge, services, and product lines allow us to provide solutions for our customers."

Sumner Group offers several advantages over its local competition, one of the most important being local control. As the largest locally owned, privately held company of its kind in the metropolitan area, its eight officers have more than 128 years of combined experience. Decisions are made locally and, therefore, more quickly—each division is accessible to its customers, enabling them to provide effective solutions.

Although divisions of the company represent different facets of business, each subscribes to the Sumner policy: "Our customers are our partners in business. We will succeed only when they succeed." Sumner Group emphasizes this commitment to its customers by providing them with a commitment of its resources: stability based on consistent growth, quality people, and superior products. The commitment has been successful by any measure. Employing more than 450 people among the company's divisions and corporate office, Sumner Group lists annual sales of more than $60 million.

Sumner Group brings a long tradition of commitment to St. Louis, and has earned a reputation as a concerned corporate citizen. Its commitment to the community includes helping local organizations, such as United Way, Cystic Fibrosis Foundation, American Red Cross, Boy Scouts of America, National Council of Alcohol and Drug Abuse, and Children's Miracle Network.

Sumner Group will continue to assume a leadership posture as it looks toward the 21st century. The company has long recognized that flexibility and quick response are keys to continued growth in this rapidly changing industry. Sumner Group is determined to meet these challenges by offering even more innovative products and services in the years ahead.

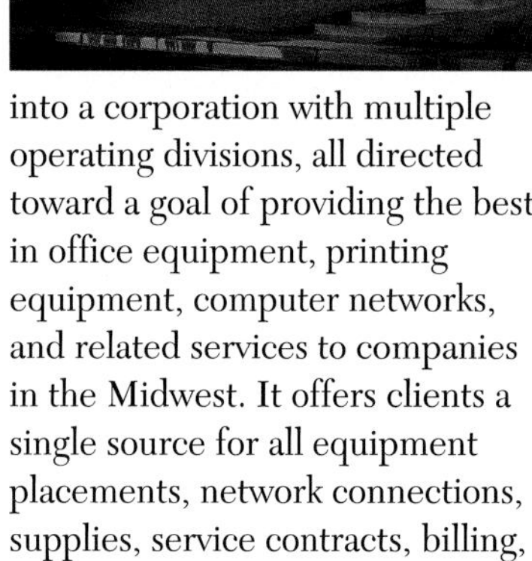

SGI Financial Services handles leasing contracts and billing for all equipment represented by the Sumner Group divisions (above).

Administrative functions are executed from Sumner Group headquarters at 2121 Hampton Avenue in St. Louis (above right).

Copying Concepts

One of the largest independent dealers in the country, Copying Concepts has experienced a continuous 10 percent annual growth since its inception in 1975. Today, Copying Concepts employs more than 100 individuals in sales and support of products that include

Mita and Minolta copiers, Muratec and Mita facsimile machines, Digital Color, Digital Black & White, Novell Operating System, Network Fax, Fax on Demand, Compaq Computer Systems, and Hewlett-Packard laser printers and computer systems.

Copying Concepts continues to be the innovator when it comes to programs based around customer satisfaction. It is the only company in St. Louis to provide a five-year, unconditional replacement guarantee; five-year fixed pricing; and guaranteed uptime—all written into its service contract. In 1995, in an effort to enhance customer satisfaction even further, Copying Concepts created a Customer Development Department that is responsible not only for resolving customer service issues, but for preventing problems from ever occurring.

The philosophy of Copying Concepts is that its success depends on absolute commitment to each and every customer. "We define success as ongoing, profitable growth for the customer, the employee, and the company," says Kevin Laury, vice president of Copying Concepts. "Our goal is to provide quality products, outstanding service, fair pricing, and team expertise that employs the highest levels of integrity, professionalism, and sincerity." Living up to its slogan, "We keep things humming, day after day after day," Copying Concepts was named one of 1994's Top 50 Office Equipment Dealers in the country for service and support, progressive leadership, ongoing staff training, quality products, and integrity.

Clockwise from top right: Copying Concepts warehouses an extensive inventory of equipment and supplies.

One of the largest independent dealers in the country, Copying Concepts is located at 6691 Manchester Road in St. Louis.

Copying Concepts offers a full line of equipment available for in-house demonstrations.

To keep things humming, the Customer Development Department ensures an ongoing "no hassles" relationship with its customers.

Computer-aided service dispatching means rapid response.

Datamax Office Systems

Datamax Office Systems, formerly A.B. Dick Products of St. Louis, acquired its new name when it expanded to become the St. Louis dealership for the Canon line of products in 1980. Canon has ranked first in placements of copiers worldwide for more than a decade, and of plain paper facsimile machines for the past five years. As Canon is regarded as an industry leader, so is Datamax. Since its establishment more than 40 years ago, Datamax has become one of the top 10 independently owned Canon dealerships in the nation.

Besides Canon, Datamax represents Kyocera, Hewlett-Packard, Novell, and Laser Optical Systems, while providing complete service and support for all the products it represents. Datamax-St. Louis president Carl Bergauer credits the company's unique structure for its success. "We believe that each operating division must remain exceptionally close to its customers in order to provide world-class service and support. This philosophy recognizes the unique needs of each customer and the importance of meeting those needs while taking advantage of our size to provide economical solutions."

Similar in structure to the St. Louis operation, offices are also located in Little Rock, Dallas, and Fort Worth.

These combined locations of Datamax Office Systems comprise the largest component of Sumner Group, employing almost 300 people. With more than 10,000 customers, Datamax is clearly meeting the needs of today's office. "Our unique selling proposition," Bergauer explains, "is built on our strength in listening to our customers and exceeding their expectations. We are always communicating with our customers. We need to know what we do well. But, more importantly, we must know where we need to improve our performance." A testament to the company's commitment to customer service is Datamax's recent nomination as a finalist in the 1994 *Inc.*/MCI National Customer Service Award competition. "We're very proud of our nomination," says Bergauer. "It means a lot to our entire team."

Never forgetting its roots, Datamax believes in giving back to the community. Bergauer was recently quoted, "On the field, at the fair, and in your office, Datamax is always there." A major sponsor of the St. Louis County Fair and Air Show benefiting local children's hospitals, the M.A.C. Sports Foundation National Collegiate Soccer Players of the Year benefiting local amateur athletics, and numerous other local charities, Datamax is committed to its "home on the river."

Clockwise from above:
Datamax is a Canon factory authorized training center.

Datamax provides total solutions to document management needs, from creation to storage and final output.

Datamax Office Systems, located at 6717 Waldemar Avenue, is one of the largest independently owned Canon dealerships in the nation.

Datamax Graphics Systems

"Our company's mission is to improve the productivity and profitability of our customers," emphasizes Randy Jung, division president of Datamax Graphics Systems, a full-service/full-line supplier of graphics solutions in St. Louis.

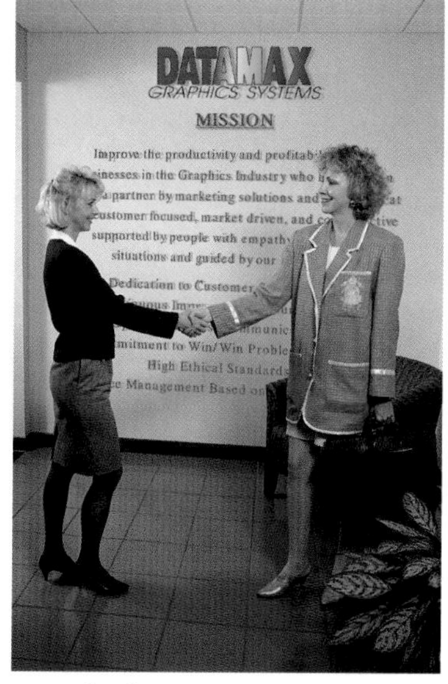

The division represents a wide variety of offset presses, collators, binders, folders, cutters, digital output devices, and duplicators from some of the most reliable names in the graphics business. Datamax Graphics Systems' product line is continually evolving to meet the changing needs of its customers.

One aspect that remains constant, however, is Datamax's commitment to offering the very best reprographics solutions on the market. "We look for equipment and supplies that will satisfy the particular needs of the clients we are working with," says Jung. "Once we've identified our customers' needs, we thoroughly research all possible solutions before recommending the proper one, and we test each thoroughly—so there are no surprises for our customers."

To respond quickly to customer problems, the company stocks many different products. "We keep a large inventory so that we can resolve these issues immediately," stresses Jung. "We recognize that it's critical for them to remain operational, and our local supply helps them to do that."

Through its telephone support service, the division is able to answer questions about problem issues, orders, pricing, and shipments within minutes. Jung believes that open communication is essential to customer satisfaction. "Our goal is to remain one of the most innovative graphics service companies in the St. Louis metropolitan area," Jung adds. "We are dedicated to partnering with our customers and assuring their total satisfaction."

Document Management Services

The newest division of Sumner Group, Document Management Services (DMS), was introduced in 1994 to serve the needs of a growing customer base. As the processing of information on paper becomes more and more sophisticated, many businesses are finding it cost-prohibitive to own high-tech equipment and to employ a highly skilled workforce to operate it.

"DMS represents an innovative approach to meeting our customers' comprehensive needs," says Jung, who also heads DMS. "It represents the ultimate partnering arrangement; we not only provide the equipment, but we also supply the operators in our customers' facilities."

For customers, the benefit is simple: it allows them to focus on doing what they do best. "By inviting DMS in-house," Jung explains, "our customers are not preoccupied with technology management. It lets them attend to their core businesses."

Under a single contract, DMS will provide the equipment and personnel necessary to operate a company's entire information output network, including computers, laser printers, fax machines, stand-alone copy centers, offset printing, color copying, and even mailroom and delivery services.

Although a new idea, facilities management was a natural step for Sumner Group. "Our mission in creating DMS was to build on the synergy derived from the other Sumner Group divisions," says Steve Sumner. "By focusing all our resources, we are able to create unique, customized, cost-effective solutions to our customers' copy and facilities management needs."

Clockwise from below:
Document Management Services is located at 2133 Hampton Avenue in St. Louis.

As shown in the DMS slide presentation, the joint resources of the Sumner Group divisions help provide cost-effective solutions for DMS customers.

Datamax Graphics Systems Account Representative Brenda Melton (left) welcomes customer Mary Holder of The Lutheran Church-Missouri Synod.

Datamax Graphics Systems is located at 2149 Hampton Avenue in St. Louis.

Kelly Services, Inc.

IN RECENT YEARS, AS WORKPLACE NEEDS HAVE CHANGED, STAFFING services companies have changed the way in which they meet customer needs. For instance, Kelly Temporary Services, a division of Kelly Services, Inc., offers customized staffing services to assist customers in remaining productive and competitive. In addition, Kelly® provides a broad range of employment opportunities to individuals to meet customers' staffing needs in the areas of office services, marketing, light industrial, technical, accounting, and other professional services through its worldwide network of directly owned and operated offices.

Since 1956 the St. Louis Kelly Temporary Services office has provided staffing services and employment opportunities to meet the needs of employers and employees alike. Today, the St. Louis-area Kelly offices include eight full-service staffing offices, in addition to a recruiting office in Fairview Heights, Illinois, which conducts testing and training for applicants and employees.

Customized Staffing

Today's highly competitive business environment has led many businesses to seek more efficient operating techniques. In turn, Kelly is offering many new staffing services to businesses to help them meet their needs.

"For many businesses, having more efficient operating techniques means concentrating on their core business and seeking alternative methods of handling administrative functions," says Judy Schahn, district manager of the St. Louis Kelly Temporary Services offices. "To maximize their business potential, more and more employers are turning to staffing services companies to develop and implement customized services that effectively address quality, training, cost, and productivity issues."

For example, with the Partnered Staffing® program, Kelly will act as an extension of a company's human resource department, managing the temporary help needs at a customer location, thus allowing the customer to concentrate on its core business.

Due to the close partnering relationship Kelly has established with its customers, the company also developed a temp-to-full-time program, KellySelect.® KellySelect provides customers the opportunity to evaluate an employee's performance and "fit" while on assignment before making a long-term hiring commitment.

And, with Kelly Managed Services, Kelly can assume operational responsibility for functional activities the customer has decided to outsource. With its specialty in Managed Mail Services, Kelly can optimize a customer's operations in areas ranging from express management to shipping and receiving.

Training Employees for Changing Technology

Kelly Temporary Services' commitment extends to its employees as well. Kelly realizes that the advanced technology used in business today requires employees to have a working knowledge of a variety of software packages. Kelly monitors workplace trends and develops customized training programs that allow employees to expand existing software skills and enhance productivity or learn new, marketable workplace skills.

"At Kelly, we believe that training is the key to professional development," says Schahn. "As a result, we commit considerable resources to develop proprietary training programs to ensure our customers receive qualified employees to meet their specific workplace needs."

For nearly four decades, the St. Louis Kelly offices have played a vital role in the local economy. "Temporary employees are a cost-effective way to achieve workforce flexibility," says Schahn. By staying on top of the latest technological advances and changes in the business environment, Kelly Temporary Services will continue to provide St. Louis employers with well-trained employees to fill many challenging positions.

Among the local Kelly staff members are (from left) Sherry Thein, account manager; Kathy Garcia, branch manager; Judy Schahn, district manager; and Rick D'Arcangelis, branch manager.

Kelly monitors workplace trends and develops customized training programs that allow employees to expand existing software skills and enhance productivity or learn new, marketable workplace skills.

◄ HILLARY LEVIN

Falcon Products, Inc.

The St. Louis Convention Center stands there now, but in 1958, at Broadway and Franklin, a young man started a tiny company to supply the emerging hospitality industry. With only $500 and no employees, he nonetheless had an unswerving mission statement—give customers what they want, when they want it, and if something is wrong, fix it quickly. ■ The hospitality industry has grown dramatically since then, and Falcon Products, the company that CEO Franklin A. Jacobs built, has grown with it. Now 1,300 employees make furniture and equipment for the hospitality market, posting annual sales of $78 million. In addition to the St. Louis corporate headquarters and factory in Olivette, the company operates factories in five states and three foreign countries. Showrooms are in Chicago, Paris, Hong Kong, Macau, and Tokyo.

Early Supporters

In the beginning, Jacobs, a young St. Louis resident, did not have money—just an idea. Fortunately for him, companies in the metropolitan area were willing to back him financially. They believed in what he was trying to do and allowed him to pay for dies and patterns as he sold the products made with them.

Jacobs' first product was a pedestal table base cast in Belleville, Illinois, and painted in south St. Louis. Sales were made to restaurant equipment distributors as far away as Oklahoma and Texas. With new restaurants opening daily, distributors were looking for vendors like Falcon that would support them and deliver goods when promised. "It is crucially important that commercial ventures be able to open on time and that if something is wrong, it gets fixed quickly," says Jacobs. "If you make it easy to do business with you, you will succeed."

Full-Circle Provider

Falcon started out as a manufacturing, sales, and marketing operation, but when its suppliers couldn't meet deadlines, the company became a vertically integrated manufacturer—one that controls the entire cycle from gathering raw materials to shipping the finished product.

Today, Falcon builds entire restaurant interiors, which are test-assembled in the plant, then broken down, shipped to the site, and efficiently installed by Falcon experts. Sophisticated computers and computer-aided design systems interpret drawings of existing buildings to ensure that the new interiors will fit.

The acquisition of Kaydee Metal Products in 1992 and the Charlotte Company in 1993 complemented Falcon's existing product line with metal furniture and upscale office furniture. Acquisition of the Czech Republic's Miton Company in 1994 moved Falcon into the center of Western Europe. Once Falcon technology has been implemented at the Czech facility, it will become the center of the company's European operations.

The explosive growth in the hospitality industry that occurred in the United States in the 1960s and 1970s is happening today all over the world, and Falcon Products is at the forefront supplying that industry. In fact, all company literature is printed in five languages and uses metric measurements. This international growth, coupled with Falcon's commitment to excellent customer service, will ensure that its decades-old mission statement remains fulfilled.

CEO Franklin A. Jacobs (far left) established Falcon Products in 1958.

In addition to the St. Louis corporate headquarters and factory in Olivette (near left), the company operates factories in five states and three foreign countries.

Today, 1,300 Falcon employees make furniture and equipment for the hospitality market, posting annual sales of $78 million.

HBE Corporation

SOME 20 YEARS AGO, AN ARTICLE IN *Harvard Business Review* DEscribed traditional construction as a fragmented effort, "with architects in charge of some activities, contractors in charge of others, and seemingly, the fates in charge of the rest." Apparently, the author had not heard about Fred S. Kummer, a young civil engineer and construction executive who, in 1960, embarked on a path to end this fragmentation.

With $25,000 he had scraped together, Kummer established Hospital Building and Equipment Company, an integrated planning/design/construction firm specializing in the medical field. He was banking on a belief that his single-source approach would save substantial amounts of both money and time for his clients.

The firm Kummer started 35 years ago has grown into multi-divisional HBE Corporation headed by Kummer, president and chief executive officer. Combining an integrated, single-source philosophy with a highly centralized, hands-on management style, HBE has established standards of efficiency and value unmatched in the construction industry.

HBE CORPORATION HAS DESIGNED AND BUILT MORE THAN 650 PROJECTS IN 49 STATES, INCLUDING THE 911-ROOM ADAM'S MARK HOTEL IN ST. LOUIS.

The company is known nationally for executing complicated projects on time and within budget by using innovative techniques and an intense focus on project detail. Says Kummer, "The detail is where you deliver the product." Kummer, who is deeply involved in every project, supervises the work of the project team and coordinates input from an experienced, professional staff.

HBE now has over 6,000 employees, including more than 450 architects, engineers, interior designers, and construction professionals. More than 500 employees work at HBE corporate headquarters in the St. Louis suburb of Creve Coeur. With an annual payroll in excess of $100 million, the company currently has over 70 projects under construction throughout the United States.

Expansion Fosters Growth

What began as Hospital Building and Equipment Company has now become one of six divisions of HBE Corporation, which expanded over the years beyond the medical field. The hospital division and the financial facilities division have planned, designed, and built more than 650 projects in 49 states, totaling in excess of $3 billion. Individual projects have ranged from $1 million to $100 million, including hospital facilities as large as 1,000 beds.

In 1973, when the company was ready to expand, Kummer, who grew up in New York City the son of a hotel engineer, felt comfortable with the hospitality industry and ventured in with a new division called Adam's Mark Hotels. Today, HBE's Adam's Mark Hotel Division encompasses 14 major hotel properties with more than 7,000 rooms. The flagship of the chain is the 911-room Adam's Mark in downtown St. Louis across from the world-famous Gateway Arch.

Several years ago, in recognition of its hospitality industry expertise, the Minneapolis Community Development Agency selected HBE to own and develop, as well as design and build, that city's 814-room downtown convention hotel that opened in 1992, several months ahead of schedule.

HBE Financial Facilities was established in 1975 to provide quality planning, design, engineering, and construction services to the financial community. HBE Financial Facilities specializes in satisfying unique facility needs through close relationships and intimate knowledge of its customers. This enables HBE to achieve maximum value and results when partnerships are formed with clients to meet their expansion needs. A continued commitment to customer satisfaction has allowed HBE Financial Facilities to design and construct over 3.5 million square feet of space for financial institutions in 44 states.

HBE's world-class Adam's Rib Recreational Area in Colorado—representing a third corporate division—is a 3,000-acre, four-season resort featuring a special-use permit for downhill skiing in 3,000 additional acres of the U.S. Forest Service. Develop-

The flagship of HBE's Adam's Mark hotel chain is the 911-room Adam's Mark in downtown St. Louis across from the world-famous Gateway Arch.

ment of the resort as a self-contained village with commercial, entertainment, and recreation venues is continuing.

Other divisions of HBE Corporation are the Medical Buildings Division and the Properties Division (which owns and manages over 500,000 square feet of commercial office space in four cities).

Efficiency and Aesthetics Ensure Future

With the health care industry under intensive pressure to cut costs, the demand for HBE's integrated approach continues to grow. Working on the basis of a guaranteed price, the company consistently has demonstrated its ability to maximize cost-efficiency in the building or expansion of hospitals and medical centers, as well as the hotels, banks, credit union headquarters, and diverse buildings constructed by other HBE divisions.

In its zeal to provide maximum value to its clients, HBE has not forgotten the importance of aesthetics. A project in San Antonio transformed a decaying, 82-year-old railroad station into a striking, 20,000-square-foot headquarters for the San Antonio City Employees Federal Credit Union. The magical renovation brought a National Preservation Honor Award to the client and to HBE Financial Facilities, praised for "outstanding restoration and innovative reuse" of the historic depot.

"I think the one thing that I have done in this industry better than most, maybe better than anybody," Kummer says, "is to integrate the totality of all the disciplines. Today you have to know the financial consequences of every decision you make. I believe this company is capable of extracting substantially more value out of a dollar than most firms, and it is all in the way we go about it. All the disciplines come together."

HBE Financial Facilities was established in 1975 to provide quality planning, design, engineering, and construction services to the financial community.

Kellwood Company

KELLWOOD COMPANY IS A LEADING MARKETER, MERCHANDISER, and manufacturer of apparel. From its headquarters in west St. Louis County to its many operations across the globe, Kellwood is known for value-oriented, quality products and quick response to changes in retailer and consumer demands. The company's diversified merchandising capabilities, state-of-the-art production facilities, computer design systems, and worldwide sourcing make it an attractive business partner for the retail industry.

The rise to the top began in 1961. Kellwood was formed by a merger of 15 of Sears, Roebuck and Co.'s soft goods suppliers. Two former Sears executives, Charles H. Kellstadt and Robert E. Wood, lent their names to the enterprise. The new company had 22 plants in 10 states, and employed 7,000 people. Original product lines included a wide variety of apparel, camping equipment, and bedding. At that time, Sears represented the bulk of Kellwood's business, but gradually reduced its stake in the company. Kellwood branched out to other customers.

PREDOMINANTLY A MARKETER OF WOMEN'S APPAREL, WITH 75 PERCENT OF ANNUAL SALES VOLUME COMING FROM THIS AREA, KELLWOOD ALSO PRODUCES APPAREL FOR MEN AND CHILDREN.

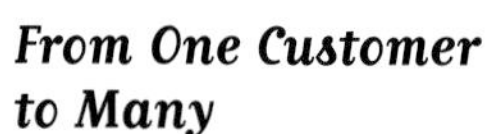

From One Customer to Many

Fred W. Wenzel, Kellwood's president from 1965 to 1976, and chairman from 1964 to 1991, is credited with reorganizing the company and steering it through the stormy 1970s. At the time he took over the presidency, Wenzel moved the company's headquarters from Chicago to St. Louis, where Kellwood had existing operations. By his retirement in 1991, Wenzel had seen Kellwood evolve into a giant of the apparel industry. Sales in 1995 reached $1.4 billion, and Kellwood expects to surpass the $2 billion sales mark before the year 2000.

Today, the company markets a myriad of more than 170 labels through its multidivisional business units. Some of Kellwood's most recognizable brands include Cricket Lane,® Melrose,® Sag Harbor,® Northern Isles,® Plaza South,® David Brooks,® and Robert Scott.®

Known for diversity, Kellwood's divisions offer a wide range of apparel products from outerwear to sportswear to lingerie. Predominantly a marketer of women's apparel, with 75 percent of annual sales volume coming from this area, Kellwood also produces apparel for men and children. American Recreation Products, Inc., an exception to the other apparel-product-driven business units, markets and manufactures recreational camping products and is headquartered in St. Louis.

Success in a Niche Market

Kellwood credits its success to diversification, internal growth, and acquisition. In today's changing retail climate, it is often easier to fill a specific niche than to satisfy an entire segment of the

market. By concentrating on these niche markets, Kellwood has been able to focus on and deliver what the customer really wants. This policy carries over into acquisitions as well. Kellwood's family of companies continues to expand as a result of acquiring healthy, niche-oriented firms designed to add variety and broaden consumer appeal. Vice Chairman and Chief Financial Officer James C. Jacobsen says, "We are a growth company looking for growth opportunities."

Kellwood strengthened its presence in the discount store market with the acquisition of Halmode Apparel, Inc., a multidivisional women's apparel maker. The company also added David Dart, Inc. in 1994 to its family of companies. Winner of the 1994 California Designer of the Year Award, David Dart is Kellwood's first entree into the contemporary bridge sportswear arena.

Under the leadership of William J. McKenna, current chairman and chief executive officer, Kellwood expanded its customer base to serve more than 25,000 stores in the United States, as well as a growing number of outlets in Mexico, Canada, Japan, and China. The company sells to all major department and specialty stores, national chains, mass merchandisers, discount operations, and mail-order catalogs. McKenna says, "Kellwood is riding the wave of recent retail consolidations, filling the demand for branded products and store-label goods to satisfy the value-conscious consumer."

Through its family of companies and vast product offerings, Kellwood differentiates itself from others in the apparel industry by its ability to develop specific apparel product lines for retailers, and also to provide them with current designs from existing branded product lines. President and Chief Operating Officer Hal J. Upbin describes the process: "Our management and merchandising teams meet with retailers individually to assess their needs. After determining their merchandising directions and requirements, we can do a line adaptation from current products or create an entirely new merchandise program for the store." Responsiveness—and focusing on numerous niche markets, one at a time—brings satisfied customers and greater profitability, Upbin believes.

Clockwise from top left: According to President and Chief Operating Officer Hal J. Upbin, responsiveness—and focusing on numerous niche markets, one at a time—brings satisfied customers and greater profitability.

Vice Chairman and Chief Financial Officer James C. Jacobsen says, "We are a growth company looking for growth opportunities."

Fred W. Wenzel, Kellwood's president from 1965 to 1976, and chairman from 1964 to 1991, today serves the company as chairman emeritus.

Under the leadership of William J. McKenna, current chairman and chief executive officer, Kellwood expanded its customer base to serve more than 25,000 stores in the United States, as well as a growing number of outlets in Mexico, Canada, Japan, and China.

Clear Vision for the Future

Kellwood is a company with a clear vision of what it is and where it is going. Future goals include several key strategies. Among the top priorities is to develop sales in the international market, especially in the Far East. Another goal is to increase overseas sourcing of Kellwood's merchandising mix. Global sourcing through owned plants and contractors provides the company with the flexibility to alter the production mix to satisfy the customer's specific merchandise requirements. The company also plans to continue its growth through acquisitions, which is part of its overall design for success.

With an aggressive acquisition strategy and continued growth in a consolidating industry through niche marketing, Kellwood will succeed in focusing on opportunities both now and in the future.

Tetra Plastics, Inc.

Tetra Plastics was built on challenges. In the late 1960s, the company developed plastic components for the production of plastic kites and explansion tubes for construction of nuclear power plants. During the 1970s, it developed specialty materials for snow skis and water skis. In the 1980s, Tetra teamed up with NIKE and played a critical role in the development of the NIKE Airsole® cushioning system that revolutionized athletic footwear. But in the Great Flood of 1993, Tetra Plastics took on its biggest challenge to date—salvaging its machinery from a factory inundated with seven feet of muddy water. When the Missouri River burst through a levee and drowned Tetra's Chesterfield plant, the ingenuity that led to the company's numerous innovations in plastics stepped in to guide it through the crisis.

The determination needed to rise above the flood reflects the technological creativity that Tetra thrives on today. A 30-year-old firm, now an independently run subsidiary of NIKE, Inc., Tetra solves difficult problems using innovative engineered technology. "We seek customers who need plastic products that require innovation and engineering not available in the standard marketplace," says Paul H. Mitchell, president and CEO. What Tetra is not, explains Mitchell, is a company that produces commodities in large volume similar to those offered by other companies. "We're in the specialty thermoplastics business," he explains. "We listen to customers' needs and develop innovative solutions to meet those needs."

As a result of this strategy, Tetra is growing rapidly. With a staff of more than 300, the company reported 1995 annual sales of $44 million, up from $30 million the previous year. A large portion of the growth comes from Tetra's non-NIKE customers, although NIKE remains the company's biggest client.

Early Successes

Tetra's growth began in 1964, when F. Lee Hawes purchased Sycraft Plastics, a small company with two extruders, in University City. In 1965 it moved to nearby Maplewood and changed its name to Tetra Plastics. The Greek word for four, "Tetra" signifies the four values the company is built on: quality, service, innovation, and engineering.

The company built a new plant in 1968 in Chesterfield and developed an innovative extrusion process to produce explansion tubes for Combustion Engineering's use in nuclear power plant construction. Several hundred of these tubes, loaded with detonating cord, were connected together and exploded, swagging the Inconel® tubing into the boiler plate instantly, instead of mechanically swagging one tube at a time. That same year, Tetra engineered a process that applied hot melt adhesive to a square tube used as

In 1981 Tetra began work with NIKE to develop the NIKE Airsole® cushioning system. Today, the St. Louis company is the only supplier of Airsole® cushioning materials to NIKE worldwide (right).

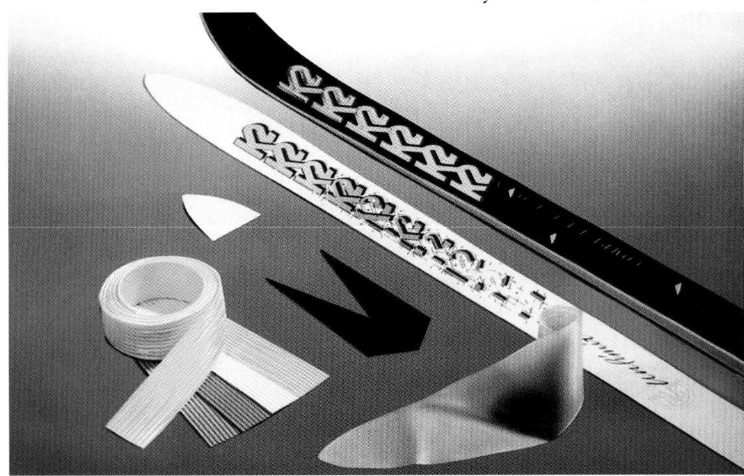

During the 1970s, Tetra developed specialty materials for snow skis and water skis (above).

In mid-1995 Tetra moved into a new 220,000-square-foot plant located in the Missouri Research Park in St. Charles (right).

wing sticks on plastic kites.

In 1972 Tetra became the only U.S. company to successfully develop and manufacture plastic top surface, sidewall, internal parts, and base materials for the production of snow skis. Previously, all materials were supplied from Europe. The company also developed the original predecorated ABS plastic top for fiberglass water skis.

But in 1980, events beyond the company's control eliminated a substantial portion of its business. Three winters of virtually no snow shut down most of the nation's snow ski manufacturing. The water ski industry also suffered from low lake levels caused by the lack of snow. Because of the Three Mile Island disaster, nuclear reactor construction came to a halt. Tetra's workforce shrank from 105 employees to 28, and, faced with yet another challenge, the company began searching for new markets.

In 1981 Tetra began work with NIKE to develop the NIKE Airsole® cushioning system. A proprietary extrusion process was developed by Tetra engineers to produce the polyurethane film for the original Airsoles® used in the early 1980s. In 1986 the company developed another proprietary process for production of a heel-cushioning Airsole® that was visible through windows in the shoe. In 1991 Tetra developed a proprietary blow-molding process that produces an air system totally visible in the heel and creates maximum cushioning. Tetra is the only supplier of Airsole® cushioning materials to NIKE worldwide. When Hawes retired in 1991, NIKE purchased Tetra to ensure the company's continued support of NIKE Air®.

In Deep Water

Although solving problems is what Tetra does best, the Great Flood of 1993 presented a huge challenge. The company was faced with the physical damage to the Chesterfield plant and the possibility that production of NIKE Air® shoes might be forced to shut down, as well as other Tetra customers. Drawing on the strengths that have kept Tetra at the leading edge of its industry, the company set out to keep NIKE and its other customers' plants running.

Mitchell used his Army experience to conduct a helicopter airlift through a hole in the plant roof. This approach worked for small equipment, but for heavier items Tetra turned to another innovative solution. Knowing a diesel engine will run without an electrical system after it is started, the company used a flatbed diesel truck with its air intakes raised above water level to drive through water five feet deep to evacuate the plant. After moving the equipment to a temporary leased plant in Earth City, restarting production required more innovations—such as portable power generators, using ice cubes to cool process water until chillers could be rebuilt, etc. Initial production resumed just 27 days after the levee broke. It was a close call—the disaster came within two weeks of shutting down NIKE, and within days of shutting down other customers.

In making a decision regarding a new facility, Tetra considered moving to Oregon, where it would be closer to NIKE and other major customers. But the company decided to relocate locally to retain its St. Louis employees. "Our biggest asset," says Mitchell, "is our workforce. We can buy buildings anywhere."

In mid-1995 Tetra moved into a new 220,000-square-foot plant located in the Missouri Research Park in St. Charles, just across the Missouri River from the old plant, a reminder of Tetra's longtime dedication to rising above the challenge.

During the Great Flood of 1993, Tetra took on its biggest challenge to date—salvaging its machinery from a factory inundated with seven feet of muddy water. Thanks to the company's innovative spirit, production resumed in temporary quarters just 27 days after the Missouri River burst through a nearby levee.

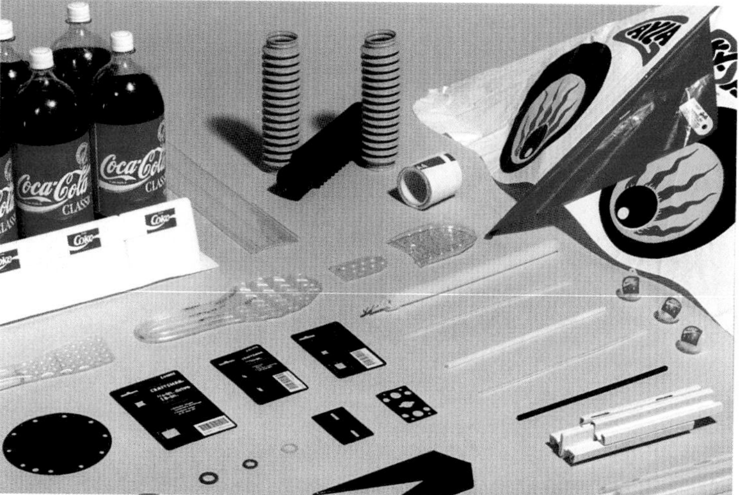

The company provides plastic products that require innovation and engineering not available in the standard marketplace.

Security Armored Car Service, Inc.

THE TRUCKS OF SECURITY ARMORED CAR SERVICE, INC. MOVE along the streets and highways of metropolitan St. Louis on a daily basis, transporting money from retail businesses to banks or delivering currency to automatic teller machines. Security Armored Car has been providing this vital service to the St. Louis area for nearly three decades, growing from a single armored vehicle to today's fleet of 40 trucks.

The family-owned business, founded in 1967, has 120 employees providing pickup, counting, and delivery of currency services for many of the area's largest corporations, plus the growing riverboat gaming industry and the Federal Reserve's St. Louis district operations.

A Family-Owned and -Operated Business

Security Armored Car President and Treasurer Janet L. Schanzle has headed the company since the death of her husband, John C. Schanzle, Jr., in 1983. She also has provided professional leadership in the security business arena, serving as president of the Independent Armored Car Operators Association, Inc., an international organization. The Schanzle children have grown up with the family business. Jill L. Schanzle and John C. Schanzle III serve the company today as vice presidents.

As a native of St. Louis, Janet Schanzle is proud that her company has become an integral part of the area's commerce and of its community activities. Security Armored Car donates its services to a number of charitable organizations, including the Muscular Dystrophy Association, Shriners' Circus, Newsboy Day, and American Diabetes Association, as well as natural disasters such as the Great Flood of 1993. Public service efforts also include providing security expertise to help reduce community crime. Janet Schanzle, for example, is on the board of the Third Police District Business Association, a business association that supports the local community and police in fighting crime.

The company's pride in St. Louis extends to its customer service philosophy. "This is a great city and we're very proud to be a part of it," Janet Schanzle says. "Our customers are the most important aspect of our business, and as an independent firm, we can offer personalized service. We can give the customer immediate attention, answers to questions, and personal assistance because we are family and locally owned."

Security Armored Car was launched nearly three decades ago with one customer, St. Louis-based Schnuck Markets. Today, its client list includes more than 1,200

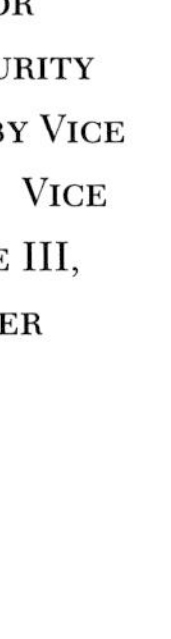

A FAMILY-OWNED BUSINESS FOR NEARLY THREE DECADES, SECURITY ARMORED CAR IS TODAY LED BY VICE PRESIDENT JILL L. SCHANZLE, VICE PRESIDENT JOHN C. SCHANZLE III, AND PRESIDENT AND TREASURER JANET L. SCHANZLE (SEATED).

◆ QUINTA SCOTT

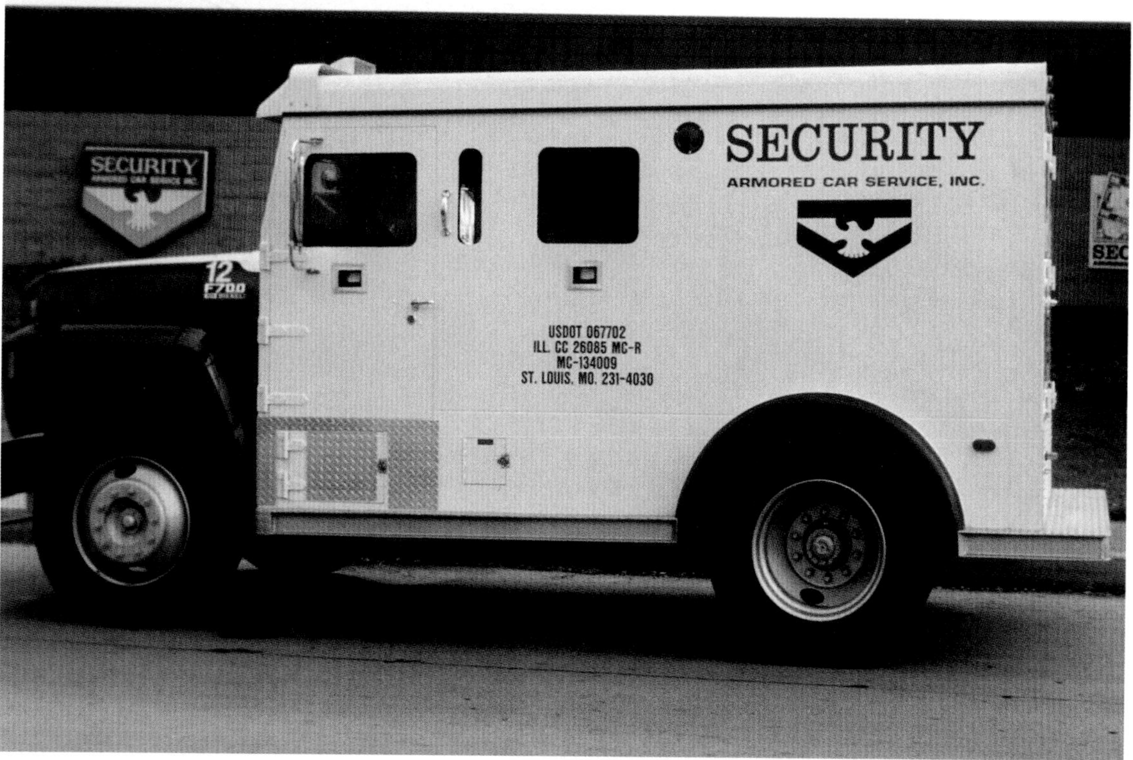

SINCE ITS FOUNDING IN 1967, THE COMPANY HAS GROWN FROM A SINGLE ARMORED VEHICLE TO TODAY'S FLEET OF 40 TRUCKS.

names, mostly St. Louis businesses of every size. In addition to currency, Security Armored Car transports other valuables such as jewelry, rare works of art, or other articles of extremely high value. From its security-conscious, windowless headquarters south of downtown St. Louis, the firm has a large coin room where coins are counted and wrapped by machine into over 20 million rolls per year to be delivered to customers.

Security Armored Car's second-highest business expense is insurance on its transactions. All pickups and deliveries are totally insured by Lloyd's of London. In fact, this internationally recognized insurance firm visited Security Armored Car to learn about American armored car services because similar operations in Europe have distinct differences. Security guards in England, for example, are not licensed to carry firearms.

Keeping Security First

Strict procedures are in place to ensure the safety of the company's employees and their cargo. Pickup and delivery of currency occurs in a timely manner, but never at the same time. As an added precaution, a security guard rides inside the truck, in addition to one or two in the cab. Drivers never shut off the engine, enabling the truck to react immediately in the event of a threat. All Security Armored Car trucks are custom built at a cost of $60,000 to $120,000 per truck, depending on size. The bodies are made of reinforced steel and bullet-proof glass. Each vehicle travels 100 to 500 miles a day and then undergoes an exacting in-house service check.

As Security Armored Car plans for the future, a major growth market exists in servicing automatic teller machines (ATMs). Currently, the company provides 24-hour and holiday cash replenishing for freestanding ATMs and those on banking premises. Contrary to some futuristic predictions of a cashless society, Janet Schanzle believes trends point toward continued reliance on cash as the basic tool for everyday transactions. Security Armored Car sees a strong future in metropolitan St. Louis as new entertainment venues like the emerging NFL football franchise, the domed stadium, and the Kiel Center create even more need for services from Security Armored Car in an area that enjoys a rich heritage as the midwestern hub of commercial trading.

Thermal Science, Inc.

THERMAL SCIENCE, INC. IS A COMPANY OF PEOPLE AND resources dedicated to the creation of new and better passive fire protection products designed to save lives and property in the event of fire. ■ Thermal Science is a Missouri-based corporation whose activities literally span the globe. It is engaged in the manufacture, development, and distribution of thermal protection and thermal insulation materials, high-temperature polymers, and fire retardants. This product line has been an important factor in the thermal protection market for almost 34 years. Growth in sales and product acceptance has been significant due to the proven, reliable performance under actual fire conditions of the company's fire-resistive and fire-retardant products.

Background

The company is a spin-off of the former Thermal Sciences Division of Emerson Electric, dating its origin to 1956. This division pioneered the use of sublimation for hyperthermal protection. Its notable successes include heat shielding for the Pegasus, Little Joe Space Capsule, Minuteman Payload System, Polaris A-2, Saturn rocket, X-15 airplane, the Mariner, and communication satellites.

Thermal Science was organized as an independent entity in August 1967 under essentially the same leadership team still heading the company today. Over the years the company has built a substantial capability based on a patented proprietary line of subliming fire-resistive and fire-retardant products. The background and resources available at Thermal Science are essential in advancing the state of the art of thermal protection and formulating new materials systems with substantially improved and customized thermal protection efficiencies.

The company recognized the adaptability of the aerospace-derived technology to fill the growing commercial and industrial needs for truly advanced fire-resistive materials. The unique thermal protection provided by its extensive line of heat shield, subliming, fire-resistive, and fire-retardant products has been used for three decades, making Thermal Science one of the world's leading suppliers of thermal protection materials.

THIS LIQUEFIED NATURAL GAS STORAGE VESSEL IN AUSTRIA IS PROTECTED WITH THERMO-LAG.

Global Applications

Thermal Science's thermal protection products are sold to a wide variety of users on a global basis. The materials have been used in the United Kingdom, Sweden, Norway, Germany, France, Austria, Italy, Spain, Saudi Arabia, Kuwait, the United Arab Emirates, Australia, Japan, Taiwan, China, Korea, Indonesia, Malaysia, Canada, Mexico, and elsewhere. The company's family of subliming products is marketed under the trademark THERMO-LAG.

Thermal Science's subliming materials have been used extensively for the fire protection of offshore oil- and gas-producing platforms, commercial buildings, industrial plants, electrical transmission systems, power generating plants, ships, televisions, storage tanks for compressed liquefied flammable gases, and over-the-road and railroad tank cars, among others. They have seen worldwide use under many different environmental exposures and have provided a high level of performance dependability.

The company's fire protection systems have an extensive and highly successful track record in North Sea applications, and have been selected for major new offshore platform construction projects such as Troll Gas, Troll Olje, Marathon's East Brae, Elf Froy, and Hibernia (the world's largest offshore platform ever to be built). Thermal Science also provides technical field support for the product line on an international basis through the company's Field Service Group. Thermal Science services its international customers from sales offices in London, Scotland, Dubai, and Mexico, as well as through its extensive network of sales representatives throughout the world.

Comprehensive, Independent Testing

In addition to its own state-of-the-art testing, the company's products are rigorously tested by an

Thermal Science's headquarters, executive offices, sales, research and development, engineering, marketing, and manufacturing facilities are located in the St. Louis area in a 60,000-square-foot building on a 10-acre tract (far left).

The structural steel at the Hyatt Regency Hotel in Chicago relies on THERMO-LAG for protection (near left).

impressive list of agencies, including Underwriters Laboratories, Inc.-UL (USA), Lloyd's Register of Shipping (UK), Det norske Veritas (Norway), SINTEF-Norwegian Testing Laboratory (Norway), Bundesanstalt Fur MaterialprufungBAM (Germany), Fulmer Yarsley (UK), Industrial Risk Insurers (USA), and many leading oil and petrochemical companies.

Facilities

Thermal Science's headquarters, executive offices, sales, research and development, engineering, marketing, and manufacturing facilities are located in the St. Louis area in a 60,000-square-foot building on a 10-acre tract.

The company's research and development laboratory consists of a closely knit group of research scientists, working in a modern research laboratory. It is complemented by strong analytical and quality control laboratories that are equipped with the latest state-of-the-art instrumentation and test equipment, as well as a fire research testing laboratory capable of performing a wide range of fire-endurance tests recognized by many of its users.

Thermal Science's production facilities are equipped with large-capacity mixing mills, continuous forming presses, extrusion molding and processing lines, surface grinders, and high-temperature curing capabilities.

The company has been a member of the St. Louis community for more than three decades. Its management supports higher education for area youth by sponsoring a variety of programs. Thermal Science also has been a strong supporter of the Regional Commerce and Growth Association (RCGA), Missouri Chamber of Commerce, Better Business Bureau, various technical associations, St. Louis Arts, and other community-oriented service programs.

This 22,000-ton Troll Gas offshore platform is protected with THERMO-LAG 440.

Middendorf Meat/Quality Foods

It would have been impossible for Orville Middendorf to know back in 1962 that the meat company he was starting would one day become a major food distributor to St. Louis metropolitan-area restaurants. He founded the business with no money, made deliveries out of the trunk of his car, and worked a night job to support his family. "I put all the money I made back into the business, always improving," Middendorf says. "What I gave my customers back then is what we still focus on today—personal service."

By ensuring the highest-quality product and providing exceptional care to fine dining establishments, Middendorf Meat has grown to 130 employees who service more than 2,500 accounts. The 30 to 40 items the company carried in 1962 have increased to more than 5,000 food-service products.

"We customize our meat cuts to the client's needs," Middendorf explains. "Commercial kitchens of today need more conveniently packaged products than they did in the past. We constantly look for ways to improve our services, thereby improving theirs." For instance, the company employs a full-time chef to assist clients with selections and preparation.

In 1967 Don Middendorf, the founder's brother, joined the company, bringing with him knowledge and experience in purchasing and sales. Under his direction, all members of the Middendorf sales force have spent time working in the meat processing/packaging department, giving them the experience needed to have an advantage with clients.

Middendorf's reputation for the personal touch also extends to staff members like Gene Porter, the company's first employee and original meat cutter, and Rich Dillon, its original driver. Both men are still with the business. "We have an open-door policy here," says Orville Middendorf. "Anytime anyone needs to talk, they know my door is always open."

Although the company's mainstay is supplying Certified Angus Beef, Middendorf expanded its service line in 1983 to include Middendorf Quality Foods. This new food-service division offers everything from dry goods, paper goods, canned goods, and frozen goods to bakery items. But growth has not affected the company's ability to focus on individual client needs.

General Manager Steve Weissler, a 22-year veteran of the company, views Middendorf's emphasis on client relations as its strength. "Our clients have a partnership with us; that's why we have to go the extra length to maintain quality."

"In this industry, reputations are earned, not given," adds Rick Naber, company controller. "We've worked hard to keep our reputation on top."

Orville Middendorf's involvement in the local food-service industry has further enhanced the company's solid reputation. "He's always been a big part of the food-service industry," says Larry Hults, executive chef of Bellerive Country Club. "He's been an associate member and a big help to St. Louis Chefs de Cuisine [a professional chefs organization]."

As has been the case for more than 30 years, fine kitchens around St. Louis continue to depend on Middendorf Meat/Quality Foods for updated service and high-quality products. Certainly, Orville Middendorf can see no other vision. "All my life," he says, "this is all I've done—work to improve the St. Louis food industry and, therefore, Middendorf Meat/Quality Foods as well."

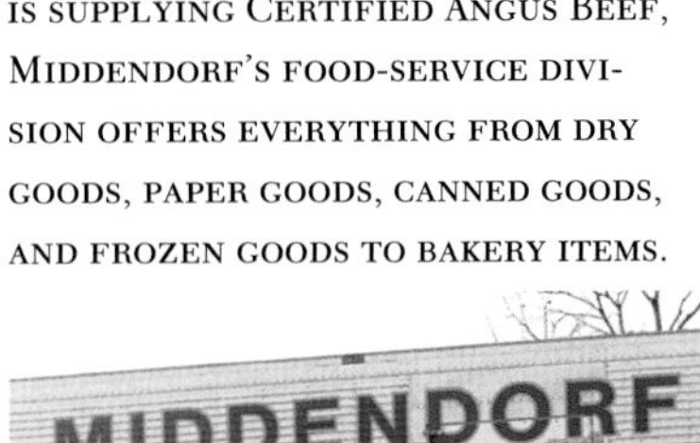

Although the company's mainstay is supplying Certified Angus Beef, Middendorf's food-service division offers everything from dry goods, paper goods, canned goods, and frozen goods to bakery items.

Olsten Staffing Services
Olsten Kimberly Quality Care

IN TODAY'S COMPETITIVE BUSINESS MARKET, COMPANIES MUST USE every asset to their best advantage. When hiring a temporary employee is more advantageous than hiring a permanent one, St. Louis companies of all sizes look to Olsten Staffing Services to strengthen and maintain organizational efficiency. ■ "We're a locally owned and nationally affiliated part of the largest staffing service in the United States, and the second-largest in the world," says William C. Young, CEO of the St. Louis franchise. Through this affiliation, Olsten has been able to develop fresh ideas to meet the changing demands of local businesses.

Keeping Labor Costs Down

Young established Olsten's first St. Louis office in 1968, the year he returned to the area to raise his family in the city he grew to love while working here in the 1950s. Olsten Staffing Services today employs an average of 1,300 to 1,500 assignment personnel in the St. Louis metro area. Clark Young, vice president in charge of staffing services and son of the CEO, says, "We're proud to be a contributor to the corporate solution. Managers are looking for ways to keep costs down. A qualified assignment employee from Olsten enables them to utilize our staffing resources without creating a permanent cost."

To ensure compatibility and help companies with affirmative action and equal opportunity employment plans, Olsten uses a personnel evaluation process validated by ETS (Educational Testing Service). "Our clients' needs are constantly changing," says Clark Young. "That's why our evaluations are so extensive. With help from the resources provided by the worldwide Olsten Corporation, our testing remains unique."

Not only do St. Louis businesses reap the benefits of Olsten's services, but the firm offers its temporary staff advantages as well. "For assignment employees, Olsten offers an attractive package that other temporary staffing services can't," says Clark Young. This includes a weekly pay schedule, a child care plan, and a child care discount.

▶ QUINTA SCOTT

New Offices Facilitate Growth

One of Olsten's major strengths has been its ability to continually change and grow. In 1976, for example, the firm added a home health care division, Olsten Kimberly Quality Care. The division has helped make Olsten one of the largest integrated managed health care and staffing service organizations in St. Louis today.

"The home managed health care aspect that we provide has grown through the turbulent market of health care because we have remained inexpensive while improving our clinical standards," says William Young. Olsten has been a leader in the care of AIDS patients since the 1980s and has provided speakers at seminars dealing with AIDS.

In 1988 the St. Louis organization added a technical staffing office, and in 1992 it opened a professional accounting office. Olsten currently has 11 offices located throughout the St. Louis area, including four staffing offices (St. Peters, downtown St. Louis, Sunset Hills, and Westport) and seven health care offices (in Westport, Washington, downtown St. Louis, Brentwood, and St. Peters; and in Alton and Belleville, Illinois). With these facilities, Olsten continues to expand its strong presence in St. Louis and surrounding areas.

▶ QUINTA SCOTT

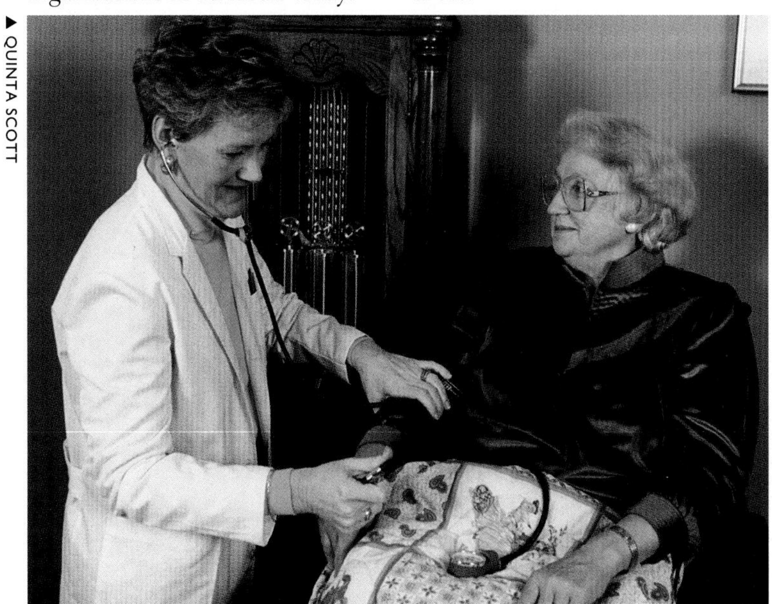

▶ QUINTA SCOTT

CLOCKWISE FROM ABOVE:
THE COMPANY'S LEADERSHIP INCLUDES CEO WILLIAM C. YOUNG (RIGHT) AND HIS SON CLARK YOUNG, VICE PRESIDENT IN CHARGE OF STAFFING SERVICES.

THE FIRM'S HOME HEALTH CARE DIVISION, OLSTEN KIMBERLY QUALITY CARE, HAS HELPED MAKE OLSTEN ONE OF THE LARGEST INTEGRATED MANAGED HEALTH CARE AND STAFFING SERVICE ORGANIZATIONS IN ST. LOUIS.

OLSTEN STAFFING SERVICES TODAY EMPLOYS AN AVERAGE OF 1,300 TO 1,500 ASSIGNMENT PERSONNEL IN THE ST. LOUIS METRO AREA.

MasterCard International Inc.

IN THE TECHNOLOGY-DRIVEN WORLD OF BANKING, SPEED AND RELIability have become the rule of thumb. For example, when a St. Louis resident traveling in Sydney, Australia, makes a purchase using a MasterCard® credit card, the sale transmits electronically around the world and back in seconds, with 100 percent reliability virtually every time. The MasterCard® payment network offers a level of dependability that has become expected on a worldwide basis. Why and how the process works so quickly and reliably is what MasterCard's St. Louis Operations Center is all about.

Building Value through Technology

While MasterCard International is headquartered in New York, the association's nerve center is centrally located in St. Louis, where the attractive cost of living and midwestern work ethic appeal to the more than 1,000 Operations Center employees.

The St. Louis facility is open around the clock, seven days a week to handle network operations, member services, product support, emergency card replacement, and software development, among other things. While technology is at the core of the Operations Center, it is the St. Louis staff who make it all come together—and they are among the world's best technology and payment operations specialists. MasterCard and its St. Louis employees are dedicated to the community in which they work and live. On various levels, the association participates in organizations such as the Missouri Special Olympics, the St. Louis Symphony Orchestra, the St. Louis Science Center and Art Museum, and a host of charities.

At the heart of MasterCard's evolving systems is Banknet,® a private, global transaction-processing network. Banknet provides banks, merchants, and consumers with unsurpassed speed, reliability, security, and flexibility for the authorization, clearance, and settlement of credit card transactions. In 1994 alone, the MasterCard network handled 4.5 billion transactions in more than 150 currencies worldwide and maintained its record for unsurpassed reliability throughout the year. It is Banknet that provides MasterCard's foundation for delivering technology that is second to none, and St. Louis is where this all takes place.

Network flexibility also means that MasterCard can offer value-added technology and services to its member financial institutions. For example, St. Louis operates a voice service center to identify cardholders and manages a file for lost and stolen credit cards. It also controls the MasterCard Automated Point-of-Sale Program (MAPP®), which provides point-of-sale (POS) credit and debit card processing for its members. The MasterCom program, the industry's first imaging system, offers an unparalleled imaging and retrieval process that allows an actual copy of a sales receipt to be passed over the network from anywhere in the world to verify that a sale occurred.

In addition to MasterCard's consumer and commercial credit card products, the association offers a variety of payment options with the Complete Debit Program,™ MasterCard's fully integrated package of ATM card enhancements that give consumers worldwide access to their checking accounts. Inclusive in this program is MasterMoney,™ an off-line POS debit program; the MasterCard/Cirrus® ATM Network, one of the world's leading ATM and cash access networks; and Maestro,® the first global on-line debit card program.

THE ASSOCIATION'S ST. LOUIS OPERATIONS CENTER (BELOW) IS OPEN AROUND THE CLOCK, SEVEN DAYS A WEEK TO HANDLE NETWORK OPERATIONS, MEMBER SERVICES, PRODUCT SUPPORT, EMERGENCY CARD REPLACEMENT, AND SOFTWARE DEVELOPMENT, AMONG OTHER THINGS.

Technology on the Horizon

As a leader in the payments industry, MasterCard must continuously look to the future to identify new and better technologies for payment methods. MasterCard has provided leadership to the payments industry by committing

IN 1994 ALONE, THE MASTERCARD NETWORK HANDLED 4.5 BILLION TRANSACTIONS IN MORE THAN 150 CURRENCIES WORLDWIDE AND MAINTAINED ITS RECORD FOR UNSURPASSED RELIABILITY THROUGHOUT THE YEAR.

to microchip-based payment products—or smart cards—for its entire global payments system. Having identified smart cards as a dynamic technology for the future, MasterCard estimates that virtually all MasterCard-branded payment products and acceptance locations will include chip technology in some form by the year 2000.

Because of their advanced memory and calculation capabilities, smart cards have virtually limitless applications in the payments industry. For example, a cardholder could transfer money from a checking account to the smart card and then give the card, instead of cash, to a college-bound student. A smart card also has the ability to store personal information such as frequent flyer numbers, electronic coupons, and vital medical information that could be accessed only by medical or emergency personnel.

MasterCard's Beginnings

In the late 1940s, a number of U.S. banks began issuing their customers scrip that could be used as cash in local shops. As the practice caught on, groups of banks started to form networks to accept each other's local "credit cards." In 1966 one such group formed the Interbank Card Association (ICA), to manage the interchange functions of authorization, clearing, and settlement of transactions.

Subsequently, ICA expanded beyond the United States to form global alliances and acquired exclusive rights to the MasterCharge name with its familiar, interlocking circle logo. Computerization came in 1973 with the development of the Interbank National Authorization System (INAS), designed as a central hub to connect members electronically, replacing the need for verbal authorization by telephone. In 1974 the magnetic stripe was standardized on all credit cards, further enabling electronic transaction. In 1979 ICA became MasterCard International, and the association's trademark was changed from MasterCharge to MasterCard.

MasterCard has evolved into a global payments franchise of nearly 22,000 member financial institutions worldwide. Through its family of brands, MasterCard offers a full range of credit and debit products and services supported by a global transaction processing network. The MasterCard®/Cirrus® ATM network, which is composed of 200,000 ATMs in 68 countries and territories, provides cash access to more than 420 million credit and debit cards worldwide. In addition, MasterCard offers the Maestro® POS program, with more than 149 million committed European debit cards and Maestro debit cards, of which more than 85 million are live cards. In 1994 MasterCard's credit and debit cards were accepted at more than 12 million locations worldwide.

As the payment needs of consumers and merchants continue to evolve, MasterCard is committed to fulfilling its mission: to be the world's best payments franchise by enabling members to provide superior value and satisfaction to their customers, thereby building member profitability.

Citicorp Mortgage, Inc.

One of America's most comprehensive consumer credit and mortgage servicing operations calls St. Louis home. Citicorp Mortgage, Inc., a subsidiary within Citicorp's global network of banking and financial services operations, provides consumer services for an array of mortgage and consumer credit products in continental U.S. markets from its home on the river. ■ Citicorp Mortgage employs 1,900 people in its St. Louis headquarters to process, maintain, and service nearly all of the parent company's domestic mortgage and consumer credit products. Mortgages and other loan products originate at branch bank locations or anywhere nationally via Citibank's toll-free application-by-phone services.

Resting on the shoulders of its team in St. Louis are comprehensive administrative responsibilities for Citicorp's mortgages, personal lines of credit, certificate of deposit loans, and other consumer credit products. Responsibilities begin with reviewing the application, underwriting, and setting up the mortgage or consumer credit product on the company's servicing system. In addition, St. Louis-area personnel maintain escrow accounts, pay property taxes and insurance premiums, and close the account upon payoff.

Citicorp has led the financial services industry in consolidating consumer credit processing operations in one location. Centralization of servicing functions traditionally done at branch locations assures high-quality, rapid service. Citicorp founded the mortgage subsidiary in 1972, locating its headquarters in west St. Louis County. In addition to the St. Louis County operation, Citicorp Credit Services, Inc. in Kansas City, Missouri, opened in 1986 as a collection facility for Citibank credit card customers. This north Kansas City operation employs nearly 850 people.

Citicorp Mortgage receives customer payments from around the country and posts them through a high-speed process that reduces paper flow and increases efficiency. In all, Citicorp Mortgage has service responsibilities for more than 1.5 million customers in the United States. To assure that services are provided

Top to bottom:
Mark J. Devine, president and COO of Citicorp Mortgage.

To assure services are provided "anytime, anywhere, anyway" the customer wants, the company values the can-do work ethic of its St. Louis-area employees.

Citicorp Mortgage has assisted numerous civic and charitable groups, such as Habitat for Humanity.

"anytime, anywhere, anyway" the customer wants, the company values the can-do work ethic of its St. Louis-area employees.

Although Citicorp Mortgage's servicing operations are domestic in scope, the parent company, headquartered in New York City, provides financial services worldwide to consumers and businesses in more than 90 countries. Citicorp's customers benefit from the company's global expertise, and its reputation for service excellence begins with professionalism and dedication that characterize the Citicorp team in Missouri.

Community service is a logical extension of the value Citicorp Mortgage places on its employees. The company believes that good business and community investment go hand in hand. Under a strategy that emphasizes support to education and children's needs, Citicorp Mortgage has assisted numerous civic and charitable groups, including Habitat for Humanity, March of Dimes WalkAmerica, Boys Hope/Girls Hope, Annie Malone Children's and Family Service Center, St. Charles Boys Club and Girls Club, William Clay Scholarship Fund, United Way, 100 Neediest Cases, and Toys for Tots. Citicorp Mortgage employees give their time as volunteers and also support St. Louis organizations with their own contributions, which the company matches dollar for dollar.

Growth for Citicorp Mortgage is geared toward Citicorp's national strategies to acquire more consumer accounts and mortgages. The St. Louis-area operation will reach for this goal by improving service to ensure consumer satisfaction. The mortgage subsidiary also seeks cross-selling opportunities—that is, locating existing customers interested in newer or additional Citicorp products. Citicorp Mortgage also plans to grow its portfolio by acquiring mortgages and mortgage-servicing rights from other companies that may lack servicing expertise or may be reducing their servicing portfolios. Citicorp Mortgage generates additional revenues from servicing these acquired accounts, which is good for the company and for St. Louis.

Looking to the future, Citicorp Mortgage has extensive potential to service additional customers through growth and development of its workforce, facility expansions, and continued innovation in technology. Growing businesses are the best assets any community can have.

Clockwise from top left: Citicorp Mortgage has extensive potential to service additional customers through continued innovation in technology.

Citicorp Mortgage employs 1,900 people in its St. Louis headquarters to process, maintain, and service nearly all of its parent company's domestic mortgage and consumer credit products.

Professionalism and dedication characterize the Citicorp team in Missouri, including these top service award winners.

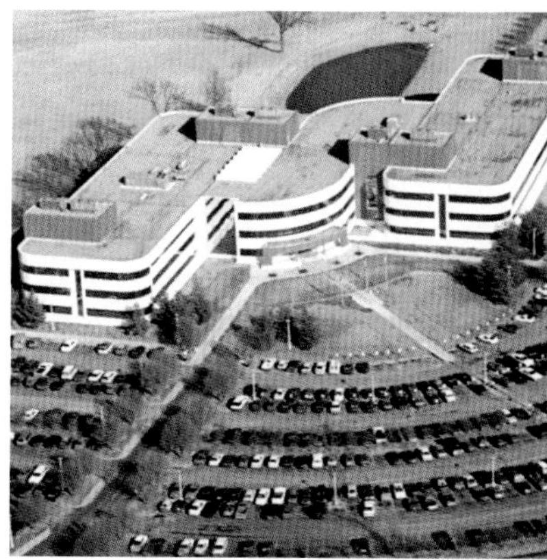

Magna Group, Inc.

Although it is now a major financial institution with assets of $4.5 billion, Magna Group, Inc. has never strayed far from its roots in community banking. The St. Louis-based company operates more than 70 banking centers in the bistate metropolitan area, plus 20 centers in central Illinois and 14 more in southern Illinois. Its Magna Trust Company subsidiary offers asset management and financial counseling.

"We think of ourselves as what bankers call a super community bank," notes G. Thomas Andes, chairman of the board. "Our focus remains on the individual communities we serve and on the customers who define the quality of our products and services. But our size enables us to offer a full range of banking services and cost efficiencies not available to the smaller bank. We regard it as the best of both worlds, and our customers reap the benefits."

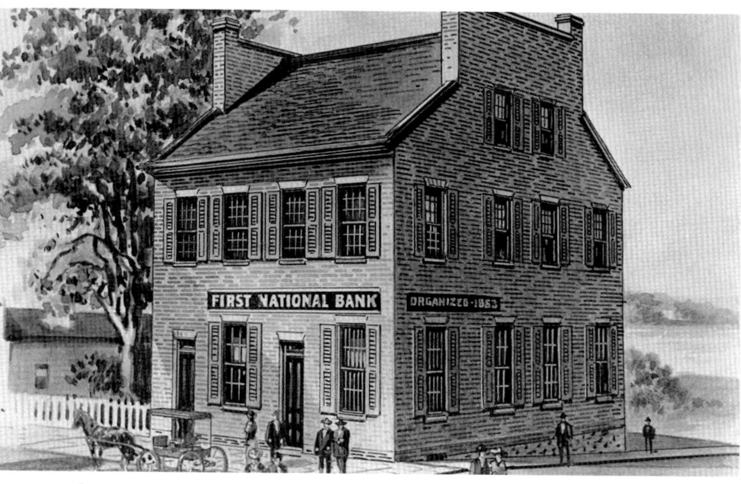

A predecessor to today's Magna Group, this St. Charles bank has been operating at its original location since 1863 (right).

Former Chairman of the Board William S. Badgley (below, left) and Chairman, President, and CEO G. Thomas Andes.

A Long Record of Community Service

Since it was formed two decades ago, Magna Group has steadily acquired community banks, mostly in Illinois, and folded them into the holding company while retaining the strong local roots and civic ties of years past. The holding company was established in Belleville, Illinois, in 1974, adopting the Magna name in 1983. However, some of the organization's individual banking centers have far longer histories. The St. Charles, Missouri, bank, for example, has been operating on the same site since 1863. The First National Bank of Belleville, the bank from which the company grew, was chartered in 1874. Another Magna cornerstone, the Millikin National Bank of Decatur, was chartered in 1860.

The steady growth of Magna Group over the years took a giant leap forward in 1991 with the acquisition of the 10-bank Landmark Bancshares Corporation of St. Louis, a transaction valued at more than $70 million. Magna Group now is the third-largest St. Louis-based bank holding company.

A Change of Command

The rapid development of Magna Group—driven by consistent internal growth and the acquisition of 43 other financial institutions in less than 20 years—has been guided

One of Magna Group's Super Money Markets is located in a Schnuck's grocery store in St. Louis County.

since the company's founding by former Chairman of the Board William S. Badgley. Starting out as a clerk at Belleville's First National Bank in 1954, he earned a college degree after attending night school, and became president of the bank by 1968. Badgley also headed Magna Group when it was formed in 1974. The esteem in which he is held by his peers was acknowledged in 1992 when Badgley was elected president of the Illinois Bankers Association.

At the end of 1994, Badgley began his transition to retirement. In January 1995, he turned over his post as chairman and chief executive officer to G. Thomas Andes, a colleague of 30 years. Andes previously had served as Magna Group's president and chief operating officer.

Despite this change in leadership, the future of Magna Group will remain strongly tied to retail banking, with an emphasis on individual customers and small to mid-sized businesses. That has always been the primary niche of Magna's community banks, and company leaders see no reason to change that successful focus. Although Magna Group serves many large corporate customers and welcomes their business, smaller businesses and individual customers are regarded as the foundation of the company's future.

A Friendly Banking Atmosphere

Friendly service and community involvement have long been hallmarks of Magna Group's banking centers. "Our strong community involvement certainly will continue," emphasizes Andes, "and we will put a great deal of effort into improving our services to our customers. Our staff will receive intensive training in customer service and customer relations. We feel this has always been a strong point with Magna, but we believe it can always be improved."

In addition, many banking centers will be given a new look to make the Magna facilities more inviting to customers. The changes will range from new wallpaper and carpeting at some centers to major renovation at others. "We want to get away from stereotyped ideas of banks as cold, formal, unfriendly places," Andes says. "The old-time atmosphere of marble columns and unsmiling bank officials has no place in today's scene. We're looking at many different ways to make the entire banking experience as easy, friendly, and convenient as possible."

Magna Group and its employees participate in the annual Arthritis Foundation Mini Grand Prix.

Magna Group's emphasis on convenience has meant some nontraditional locations for banking. The company, for example, opened four full-service supermarket banking centers in 1994.

Amid all its success and growth, Magna Group continues to make customer and community service its first objective. From the executive who meets with a customer on Sunday morning to approve a home mortgage application, to company-sponsored classes in sign language that help employees better serve hearing-impaired customers, the spirit of service pervades Magna Group.

PPC International, Inc.

As a young noncommissioned officer serving with the U.S. Air Force in England in the early 1970s, Carl R. Tisone was finishing his master's degree in counseling psychology and working with military personnel who were experiencing job-related problems. Many of those problems resulted from alcohol or drug abuse and emotional or family concerns. Tisone believed that the same counseling techniques he was using in the military could be put to use with businesses in the private sector.

With this in mind, Tisone and Richard Hellan, a social worker specializing in family counseling, founded Personal Assistance Consultants (PAC) "on a shoestring" in 1974 in the basement of Tisone's house in University City. When three new partners joined with Tisone and Hellan in 1975, PAC changed its name to Personal Performance Consultants (PPC) and opened its first commercial office in Clayton. PPC set about to demonstrate to businesses how troubled employees could be counseled as part of their employee benefits.

By the late 1970s, PPC had begun to expand in the Midwest, first to Cincinnati and Dayton, and then to Detroit and Chicago. In the early 1980s, the company began developing operations throughout the United States. Today, PPC, Inc., with Tisone as chairman, is the corporate division of Medco Behavioral Care Corporation and has a network of thousands of counselors in hundreds of offices in metropolitan and rural communities. PPC, Inc. serves as the exclusive U.S. service provider for PPC International (PPCI), of which Tisone is president and chief executive officer. PPC, Inc. is the largest of a network of PPCI national companies providing culturally specific services in the Americas, Europe, and the Pacific Rim. Hellan retired in 1992.

Cofounder Carl R. Tisone today serves as chairman of PPC, Inc., and president and chief executive officer of PPC International.

A Concept Becomes Reality

Since their introduction, employee assistance programs (EAPs) have grown from a daring new idea into an accepted institution. Today, more than 85 percent of large employers have implemented EAPs, and these companies are finding that an effective program does far more than provide help for troubled employees. Besides reducing costs associated with personal problems, a well-designed EAP helps managers deal better with human performance issues; enhances employee benefits programs; and demonstrates a company's concern for employee well-being.

Services offered by PPCI companies include comfortable, off-site counseling centers that are equipped with private waiting rooms; managed mental health care; on-site supervisor orientation; continuous case monitoring; rigid clinical peer review; case follow-up; critical incident intervention; data reports and analysis; and a consumer evaluation system. Emergency counselors are available 24 hours a day, seven days a week. The company has specialized crisis teams for detraumatizing victims of events such as plane crashes, robberies, natural disasters, and workplace violence.

St. Louis-based Monsanto was PPC's first client. Today the company's client roster reads like a who's who of Fortune 500 and global enterprises. It includes such giants as AT&T Information Systems, Arthur Andersen, Asea Brown Boveri, British Steel, Boehringer Mannheim, Ciba-Geigy, Citicorp, Coca-Cola, Federal Express, Ford Motor Company, ICL, IBM, Kleinwort Benson, Loral Aerospace, McDonald's, NEC, Nissan, and Procter & Gamble. Other clients include professional sports teams, unions, clergy, military, and many small and medium-sized companies and professional firms.

Culture-Specific Assistance

PPCI companies design EAPs specifically to an organization's needs and employee population. Each program is carefully coordinated with the human resources

PPCI's St. Louis headquarters reception area (bottom right).

Promotional posters inform employees of the availability of personal assistance (below).

philosophy and practices of the client company. Service reflects each country's health care delivery system and national practice regarding counseling and mental health issues. "In today's global economy, all companies need to make the most of production capabilities," Tisone explains. "Personal problems are frequently the cause of an employee's inability to be productive. That happens in every culture."

Most employees who participate in PPC programs do so of their own accord, but sometimes, when an employee's job performance continues to suffer because of personal problems, a supervisor may refer the individual. Discussions with employees, however, are kept strictly confidential and records are secured in locked files.

From its headquarters in St. Louis, the corporate management team of PPCI maintains a hands-on relationship with all PPC national companies to ensure quality and consistency for its many multinational clients. Each national PPC associate organization is responsible for assuring that services are appropriate for the local culture, health care system, and employment practices. This global network of culture-specific service providers is unique in the world of counseling.

Tisone believes PPCI's success is the result of attention to detail and willingness to go the extra mile for its clients. "We have established a strong record of successful programs for results-oriented employers," he says, "and we owe that success to a tradition of one-to-one caring. Each associate company in the PPCI family must employ the very best people available who are steeped in the world-class PPC practices that our multinational clients demand." But equally important, according to Tisone, is "the ability of the provider to understand *within a specific cultural arena* how each individual's problem interferes with job performance. Only then can counseling or personal consultation be effective."

PPC is credited with introducing the short-term counseling, or "brief therapy," model to EAPs. It has also become the leading provider of integrated EAP and managed mental health care programs. In addition to being a past director of the Employee Assistance Professionals Association (EAPA), in 1994 Tisone was inducted in Montreal into the prestigious EAP Hall of Fame. He has authored numerous publications on EAPs and managed mental health care.

PPCI Executive Vice President Vincent T. Volpe.

Since its founding in 1974, the firm has won a number of local and national honors (left).

PPCI offers comfortable, off-site counseling centers that are equipped with private waiting rooms.

TECHNOLOGICAL ADVANCES OVER THE YEARS HAVE PROVED TO be the key to the future as well as sources of constant change. Robert W. Nolan, Sr., chairman, CEO, and founder of SCS/Compute, has used his tax preparation technology to change the way companies and firms across the country manage their tax and accounting software solutions now—and for the future.

PRESIDENT AND CEO ROBERT W. NOLAN, SR., FOUNDED SCS/COMPUTE IN 1972.

Back in 1969, accounting practices were fairly simple operations. But Nolan, then a young CPA, was looking for opportunities to gain a foothold over more recognized accounting firms and practices. Nolan focused on computer tax processing, and in 1972 he founded SCS/Compute as a St. Louis-based regional center for tax firms to process claims quickly and accurately. In the 1980s, SCS/Compute became one of the largest processing centers for tax and accounting firms in the Midwest. Processing services generated a record $23 million in revenue in 1990.

Changing with New Technology

While the company grew, so did the tax and accounting software industry, making mainframe processing obsolete. In order to compete amid this software shift, SCS/Compute altered its focus and created innovative software packages for its customers' needs. This transition from processing to multiple configuration software was a difficult task, but through teamwork SCS/Compute was successful. The result was a St. Louis-based software company, a rarity in the Midwest.

Through open communication and superior customer service, SCS/Compute guided its customers through the transition. "We see ourselves as partners in our customers' firms. We were ready to provide them with tax preparation software when the processing business declined. And we continue to listen to them and deliver solutions that address their changing business requirements," Nolan says.

SCS/Compute describes its tax and accounting software as driven by speed and efficiency. The company develops packages to solve simple and complex individual or business tax preparations on multiple platforms, including DOS, Unix, and Windows. All SCS/Compute software has been designed to interface either directly or indirectly with the IRS through electronic filing. On the accounting side, the company provides a suite of products—client accounting, fixed-asset management, and payroll—for the professional accountant. The ability to integrate the tax and accounting software gives many customers a real advantage.

Theodore W. Schroeder, vice president of sales and marketing, stresses the importance of integration among products. "Our customers save more than time by using our compatible software packages. Our complete software solutions also improve their bottom line."

SCS/Compute looks to the future with great expectation and anticipation. "We have recently introduced a line of accounting software for our customers' clients that interfaces with our core products, thus helping to solidify their relationships," comments Nolan. "It's not enough in this competitive business merely to have a great product. You have to offer and deliver both high-level software and high-level services to keep pace with the constantly changing business environment."

THE COMPANY'S EXECUTIVE TEAM INCLUDES (FROM LEFT) CHIEF FINANCIAL OFFICER CHARLES G. WILSON; VICE PRESIDENT OF SALES AND MARKETING THEODORE W. SCHROEDER; VICE PRESIDENT OF PRODUCT DEVELOPMENT AND OPERATIONS ROBERT W. NOLAN, JR.; AND PRESIDENT AND CEO ROBERT W. NOLAN, SR.

◆ CATHY FERRIS PHOTO

1976

1977 bioMérieux Vitek
1977 Drury Inns, Inc.
1980 The Henry Company, Realtors
1980 Spencer & Spencer Systems, Inc.
1981 Fair Saint Louis
1983 HealthLine® Corporate Health Services
1984 Ameritech Cellular Services
1984 The Center for Business, Industry and Labor
1985 Consolidated Communications Inc.
1985 GenCare Health Systems, Inc.
1985 Mills & Partners, Inc.
1985 Physicians Health Plan of Greater St. Louis Inc.
1986 The Doe Run Company
1987 NORDYNE INC.
1991 Embassy Suites
1993 BJC Health System
1993 Regal Riverfront Hotel
1993 U.S. Title Guaranty Company, Inc.
1994 St. Louis Health Care Network

1995

◆ CATHY FERRIS PHOTO

Drury Inns, Inc.

IT DIDN'T HAPPEN BY ACCIDENT. DRURY INNS, INC. BECAME A TOP PERFORMER in the lodging industry through 30 years of hospitality experience and a consistent record of profitability. The company traces its roots to Lambert Drury, who started with a residential plastering company in southeast Missouri shortly after World War II. As the company prospered, his four sons expanded the business in different directions, including commercial real estate and construction. By the 1960s, the company had invested in the hospitality industry. As Drury's group of hotels grew, the concept of tailoring a hotel's services directly to the needs of its customers was developed.

Drury eliminated the standard lounges, dining rooms, and banquet facilities found in traditional full-service hotels, enabling the company to offer first-class, rooms-only accommodations at rates 20 to 30 percent below the competition. The first Drury Inn opened in 1973 in Sikeston, Missouri, featuring the new, rooms-only concept.

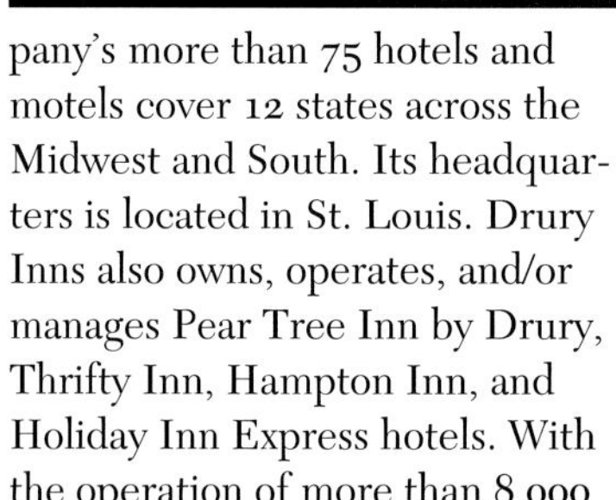

CLOCKWISE FROM RIGHT: THIS ARTIST'S RENDERING DEPICTS A PROTOTYPE DRURY INN UNDER CONSTRUCTION IN SEVERAL LOCATIONS ACROSS THE MIDWEST AND SOUTH.

MODERN DESIGN, QUALITY CONSTRUCTION, AND A COMMITMENT TO GUEST SATISFACTION HAVE MADE DRURY INNS A LEADER IN THE LODGING INDUSTRY.

AN ARRAY OF BREAKFAST ITEMS—INCLUDING FRESH FRUIT, PASTRIES, BAGELS, JUICES, HOT AND COLD CEREALS, TOAST, MILK, COFFEE, TEA, AND MORE—IS AVAILABLE DAILY AT THE FREE QUIKSTART® BREAKFAST BAR.

A Different Kind of Success Story

Today, with Charles L. Drury, Jr., as president and CEO, the company's more than 75 hotels and motels cover 12 states across the Midwest and South. Its headquarters is located in St. Louis. Drury Inns also owns, operates, and/or manages Pear Tree Inn by Drury, Thrifty Inn, Hampton Inn, and Holiday Inn Express hotels. With the operation of more than 8,000 rooms, expansion plans call for another 25 hotels to be built in the next three years.

Business travelers make up over half the company's guests, and Drury offers unique services to ensure their stay is a pleasant one. One accommodation is the free QUIKSTART® breakfast, which delivers a fast and nutritious meal to begin the day. Another highly touted benefit is a membership program for frequent travelers called the Preferred Customer program. Members have the opportunity to earn free nights and enjoy the use of many other special services geared toward this group.

The consistently crisp, clean appearance of all Drury Inns is due to the strong emphasis placed on maintenance and housekeeping. Drury employs its own team of inspectors to evaluate each hotel for quality standards. In addition, corporate policy dictates that each facility's decor be completely renovated every five to six years.

Drury Inns' hospitality is not confined to guests. The company's corporate giving programs provide a helping hand to several goodwill organizations in the community, including the St. Louis Zoo, United Way, Missouri Special Olympics Inc., and American Red Cross.

Drury has made excellent service a priority for its employees. To emphasize this commitment, each employee is empowered with the authority to guarantee guest satisfaction on the spot. Any problem brought to staff attention is handled swiftly. The guarantee offered to guests is simple: "We'll make things right, or that night's stay is free." This accent on service has earned Drury its reputation in the lodging industry as a top performer.

Adia Personnel Services

Adia Personnel Services has been filling St. Louis' personnel needs since 1975. One of the only firms in the industry to provide both temporary and permanent employees, Adia has six offices in metropolitan St. Louis—downtown, Creve Coeur, Chesterfield, south St. Louis County, St. Peters, and Fairview Heights—and places more than 3,500 employees annually in both temporary and permanent positions.

"The growing trend toward the use of an integrated, flexible workforce has been a significant factor in Adia's success," says Karen Keller, area vice president for Adia St. Louis. "Our business is now firmly established as part of our customers' human resources strategy. The performance of our temporary labor force is integral to the success of our clients—making our service, quality, and cost effectiveness increasingly critical. We have addressed these trends through partnership programs that create closer relationships with our clients. Automation and innovative technological developments are also allowing us to meet the needs of customers in better and exciting new ways."

Passion, Dedication, Commitment

Founded in 1957 in Lausanne, Switzerland, Adia grew quickly, expanding to other European countries and later to Asia, Australia, and the United States. Today, Adia has offices in 29 countries worldwide. In the United States, Adia has more than 570 offices and employs more than 300,000 individuals each year. Adia Personnel Services and its subsidiaries—Accountants on Call, Adia Information Technologies, Lee Hecht Harrison, and Nursefinders— are among the industry leaders in filling positions in the secretarial, clerical, technical, light industrial, data processing, word processing, health care, banking, and financial services fields.

Adia's impressive history of growth can be attributed to three factors: dedication to innovation, commitment to employees, and a passion for quality. Within Adia's corporate mission statement is a modest sentence: "Adia will be known as the easiest personnel services company to do business with." For Adia St. Louis, this straightforward approach to doing business has paid big dividends. "At Adia we are dedicated to removing barriers between ourselves and our customers," says Keller. "Our customers expect the very best in personnel services. They understand that we have a commitment to provide them with a consistently high level of service."

Adds Keller, "At Adia, we like to do more than provide our customer with the right employees. We want to share our expertise in the human resources field." Since 1990 Adia has sponsored complimentary half-day seminars on topics of interest to human resources professionals. The Adia Seminar series was designed to help its clients keep informed on new employment laws, issues, and trends.

Throughout the years, Adia's commitment to St. Louis has involved more than supplying the best personnel for its workforce. The firm is committed to its role as an active supporter of local and national foundations. In community support, as in all its endeavors, Adia consistently displays a high level of excellence.

From word processing to spreadsheets to graphics, Adia's temporary employees and full-time candidates put technology to work.

Adia's commitment to computer-based candidate testing and training delivers people who can step in and be productive immediately (above).

Adia values the diversity represented by its permanent and temporary workforce (left).

bioMérieux Vitek

IN THE 1960S, WHEN THE NATIONAL AERONAUTICS AND SPACE Administration (NASA) was planning an unmanned space flight to Mars, it hired McDonnell Douglas to develop and build an onboard instrument to monitor the growth of microorganisms in zero gravity. This instrument—known as the MLM or Microbial Load Monitor—was created for a space flight that never took place. But the MLM's creation instead spawned a company, known today as bioMérieux Vitek, maker of the VITEK® system, and the world leader in automated microbiology.

With the first half of its name stemming from the Latin root word "vita" meaning life, and its second half a derivative of the word "technology," the VITEK is a completely automated instrument and data management system for bacterial and yeast identification, antimicrobial susceptibility testing, and urine screening.

In January 1989, Vitek Systems was acquired from McDonnell Douglas by the bioMérieux Group, an international company dedicated to microbiology, serology, clinical chemistry, and hemostasis. Its North American division is made of facilities in Rockland, Massachusetts; Canada; and Mexico, in addition to bioMérieux Vitek in Hazelwood, a suburb of St. Louis.

Formed in 1897 by Marcel Mérieux, a disciple of the famous French scientist Louis Pasteur, bioMérieux Group is today headquartered in Marcy-l'Etoile, France, a suburb of Lyon, the sister city to St. Louis. Alain Mérieux, grandson of the founder, is president and chief executive officer of the privately held company, and Phillippe Archinard, president of bioMérieux North America, oversees the day-to-day operations in Hazelwood.

While still a division of McDonnell Douglas, Vitek Systems experienced strong growth during the 1980s, growth the bioMérieux Group expects to continue due to Vitek's research and development capabilities. One of the most recent new products to emerge from bioMérieux Vitek is the VIDAS® (Vitek ImmunoDiagnostic Assay System). VIDAS detects bacteria, viruses, toxins, hormones, and antibodies directly from patient specimens and food samples.

With more than 3,000 employees worldwide, bioMérieux Vitek employs 550 people in its Hazelwood facility plus 200 throughout the United States. BioMérieux's product line is produced in eight research and manufacturing sites worldwide, and is sold through 20 subsidiaries and more than 130 distributors. Technical specialists and field engineers staff a 24-hour hotline seven days a week, resolving most customer concerns within 20 minutes.

Economizing Labor, Reducing Waste

Always on the cutting edge of technology, bioMérieux Vitek has set industry standards with its complete line of manual, semi-automated, and fully automated products for the microbiology laboratory. Hospitals and public health institutions around the

CLOCKWISE FROM RIGHT:
PHILLIPPE ARCHINARD, PRESIDENT OF BIOMÉRIEUX NORTH AMERICA, OVERSEES THE DAY-TO-DAY OPERATIONS IN HAZELWOOD.

WITH MORE THAN 3,000 EMPLOYEES WORLDWIDE, BIOMÉRIEUX VITEK EMPLOYS 550 PEOPLE IN ITS HAZELWOOD FACILITY.

THE VITEK TEST CARD IS THE SIZE OF A PLAYING CARD AND CONTAINS 30 MICROWELLS, WHICH REPLACE THE MORE TRADITIONAL TEST TUBES.

The VITEK is a completely automated instrument and data management system for bacterial and yeast identification, antimicrobial susceptibility testing, and urine screening.

world use bioMérieux Vitek instruments for infectious disease testing. Many food, dairy, cosmetic, and pharmaceutical companies use bioMérieux Vitek products for testing meats, seafood, poultry, frozen and dried foods, candies, cosmetics, and pharmaceuticals.

The automation provided by the VITEK means less hands-on time for technicians, freeing them to perform other laboratory functions. Featuring an easy-to-use, compact-sized test card, the VITEK enables the lab technician to load the test card into the reader/incubator and move on to other tasks. The VITEK test card is the size of a playing card and contains 30 microwells, which replace the more traditional test tubes. These microwells hold the bacterial mixtures for testing. Since the card is a sealed container, there is no chance of spillage during testing, thus minimizing potential staff contamination. The test card's small size reduces the amount of disposable waste, an important consideration in today's environmentally conscious society.

Components of the VITEK include the test card; the filler/sealer, which permanently vacuum seals the cards; the reader/incubator, which provides a controlled environment for simultaneous incubation and hourly readings of the cards; the CC1 Constellation Center, which is a state-of-the-art workstation designed to handle sophisticated data management programs, as well as interface with other instruments and departments within an institution or company; and a printer, which automatically prints test results as soon as they are available. With the VIDAS and the VITAL,® an automated system for testing blood cultures (pending FDA submission), bioMérieux Vitek offers a complete solution to the microbiology laboratory.

Through the manufacture of the VITEK and its components, bioMérieux Vitek helps keep medical costs down, reduce medical waste, and protect the environment. In 1994 bioMérieux Vitek's overall performance was judged "World Class" by Garwood & Associates, Inc., an Atlanta-based consulting firm that evaluates planning and operating procedures of manufacturing companies. The company also has been honored by the prestigious International Standards Organization (ISO), which sets standards of quality management for manufacturers worldwide.

"Our considerable investment in research and development puts us in a position to continue developing and acquiring new technologies and producing new products that will improve the quality of care," says Archinard.

"Together, Building a Healthier World" is the motto of bioMérieux Group, upheld by each employee and shared with clinical pathologists and technologists worldwide, expressing a mutual dedication to the universal quest for health.

The VITEK test card moves through the production line.

Spencer & Spencer Systems, Inc.

Husband-and-wife team Bob and Linda Spencer, owners of Spencer & Spencer Systems, Inc., have been providing quality computer information services for 15 years to a large number of Fortune 500 companies. The design of their headquarters in west St. Louis County reflects the progressive and congenial attitude that drives not only the way they run their organization, but also the way they treat their staff and clients.

Spencer & Spencer consultants are full-time employees who primarily develop and maintain custom computer software for clients. They also provide personal computer training and MIS consulting to businesses. Companies typically use Spencer & Spencer when they need special expertise not available within their own organization. They can "staff up" with Spencer & Spencer consultants during peak work periods without facing the subsequent problems associated with terminating employees after a project is completed. Most of the consultants' time is spent at the client's office, unless space constraints make this impossible. In some cases, clients set up shop at the Spencer & Spencer branch offices until a project is completed.

Since its founding in 1980, the firm has grown steadily—from a single office with 14 employees to four midwestern branches with a total of 170 professionals. The St. Louis location serves as corporate headquarters. In 1985 a second office opened in Cincinnati, followed in 1991 and 1992 by new branches in Indianapolis and Kansas City, respectively.

Spencer & Spencer's sales have climbed from the first year's $400,000 to a current annual figure of $12 million. After its first five years in business, the ambitious young firm ranked 200th on *Inc.* magazine's list of the 500 fastest-growing companies in the United States. In 1985 *St. Louis* magazine featured Spencer & Spencer in its article highlighting 20 of the best companies to work for in St. Louis.

The company's leadership includes (from left) Co-chairman Robert W. Spencer, Co-chairman Linda S. Spencer, and President David T. Pieroni.

Creating the Right Environment

Success like this is no accident; Spencer & Spencer planned a unique strategy, and the company has stuck with it. The Spencers, computer specialists in their own right, knew the pitfalls of the industry firsthand. Both were employed with major corporations before setting out on their own to create better career opportunities for themselves and others like them. The Spencers designed their business with the objective of attracting and retaining the most talented people in the industry, and they succeeded.

Along with former Ernst & Young management consultant David T. Pieroni, who joined the company as president in 1991, the Spencers manage an environment where employees and clients alike are treated with dignity and respect. They also encourage fun and enthusiasm as a vital part of the corporate culture. Employees have flexible schedules and significant input into major decisions. In 1994, for example, staff members designed their own benefits package within a budget established by the company.

Quality Staff with Staying Power

Job security is a fact of life at Spencer & Spencer. "In two major recessions we have never laid off a technical software consultant," says Bob Spencer. "Our recruiting process is lengthy, but we're hiring people for careers, not for just a project or two. It has to be a good fit both ways." In an industry notorious for high turnover, Spencer & Spencer has earned the loyalty of its staff, many of whom have been with the company for a decade or more. The quality and longevity of Spencer & Spencer's consultants are the key to attracting high-caliber clients. The firm builds repeat business easily, because clients feel more comfortable coming back to an organization that offers continuity as well as quality.

With a proven record of hiring the right people for the job, Spencer & Spencer retains a number of prestigious clients. Among its client list are giants like

In an industry notorious for high turnover, Spencer & Spencer has earned the loyalty of its staff, many of whom have been with the company for a decade or more.

Anheuser-Busch, McDonnell Douglas Corporation, Monsanto Company, SmithKline Beecham, and Southwestern Bell. "The reputation of the company is reflected upon our employees," Bob Spencer says. "But in reality, they're the ones who have created the reputation."

Bringing Quality of Life to the Community

Because of their workable office environment, Spencer & Spencer staff members are free to pursue a balanced lifestyle. "We are not a one-dimensional group," says Linda Spencer. "Most of us are active in the community, and the company is involved in a number of local charities."

Dave Pieroni, for example, is active on a number of charitable boards, including United Way of Greater St. Louis. For the past seven years, Spencer & Spencer has received the Standard of Excellence Award for its participation in the United Way campaign. And since 1990, the firm has been host sponsor for the St. Louis Food Pantry Association's Walk for Hunger, which raises funds to help feed needy families.

Besides volunteering for well-established charities, the employees of Spencer & Spencer began a blood and platelet donation drive in 1994 to benefit the pediatric ward of St. John's Mercy Medical Center in St. Louis County. According to Bob Spencer, community service is seen as an extension of the firm's successful business philosophy. "Quality of life is what we're all about," he says. Clearly, Spencer & Spencer has become a credit to the community it serves.

Spencer & Spencer consultants are full-time employees who primarily develop and maintain custom software for clients.

The Henry Company, Realtors

FIFTEEN YEARS AGO IN ST. LOUIS, HENRY J. AYDT FOUNDED THE Henry Company, Realtors on the premise that "Behind every agent stands another Henry Company agent." ■ "There is a camaraderie and spirit. If you're a Henry Company agent you can feel comfortable going to another agent to ask for input," explains Luanne Zwolak, daughter of the founder, and vice president of advertising and marketing. "Real estate is a very competitive field, but we ask our agents to be competitive only with themselves, not with fellow agents."

▶ MARXER PHOTOGRAPHY

CLOCKWISE FROM ABOVE:

HENRY J. AYDT FOUNDED THE COMPANY ON THE PREMISE THAT "BEHIND EVERY AGENT STANDS ANOTHER HENRY COMPANY AGENT."

THIS PHILOSOPHY OF SUPPORT FROM WITHIN HAS HELPED ENSURE THE FIRM'S MANY SATISFIED CUSTOMERS.

HENRY COMPANY AGENTS, NOW MORE THAN 130 STRONG, HAVE CONSISTENTLY PROVIDED ST. LOUIS WITH THE FINEST IN RESIDENTIAL REAL ESTATE SERVICES.

In this supportive environment, the firm's agents, now more than 130 strong, have consistently provided St. Louis with the finest in residential real estate services. The company has a three-faceted corporate relocation department that offers comprehensive relocation services for corporations, incoming buyers, and outgoing sellers.

Support and Training Spell Success

It is as important for buyers and sellers to feel comfortable with their agent as it is for that agent to be totally conversant with market conditions. In addition to agents supporting each other, The Henry Company itself stands firmly behind its agents. Its support services and training programs are among the most thorough in the St. Louis market. "It is my opinion that there has been inadequate training given to the average real estate agent," says Aydt. "We want our agents to be well-versed and the best-informed, and we provide this service through in-house training and weekly sales meetings."

▶ MARXER PHOTOGRAPHY

Support services include two in-house attorneys, a CPA, participation in the Multiple Listing Service, state-of-the-art computer systems, and sales packets and brochures for buyers and sellers.

▶ MARXER PHOTOGRAPHY

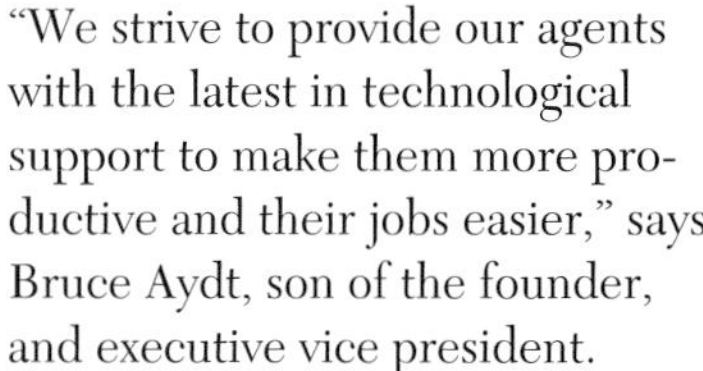

"We strive to provide our agents with the latest in technological support to make them more productive and their jobs easier," says Bruce Aydt, son of the founder, and executive vice president.

"We do everything we can to provide full service to our agents with the maximum return to them," adds Henry Aydt. "We look at each agent as a business within a business. It's important for them to market themselves as well as The Henry Company, because our business functions in partnership with our agents."

The Henry Company also believes a well-managed business must rely on the input and team effort of the entire company. "The Agents Council is one way we put this principle into action," says Henry Aydt. Regularly scheduled meetings of elected agent representatives provide input to management. Another vehicle is weekly meetings of the management team, which provide information about the company and industry trends.

Dedicated to the service of the real estate profession, The Henry Company has provided two presidents of the local association of Realtors and one president of the state association within the past eight years.

This philosophy seems to be working. In fact, the company has carved out a place among the area's top real estate agencies. Proud of its continued status as an independently owned and family-operated business, The Henry Company looks forward with confidence to ongoing prosperity.

Ameritech Cellular Services

WHEN CELLULAR TELEPHONE AND PAGING CAPABILITIES were introduced in the St. Louis area in 1984, the technology opened new channels of communication for both businesses and individual consumers. The world of cellular communications in St. Louis is available through an industry leader, Ameritech—the company that first brought cellular phone service to the nation.

The Ameritech name is new to St. Louis, but the company's roots have been known in the area for decades under the name CyberTel. In 1991, Ameritech, eager to expand its wireless network to Missouri, purchased CyberTel. The Ameritech predecessor started operations as a paging company in the 1970s and, in 1984, became the first company to introduce cellular service to St. Louis.

A leader in the growing communications industry, Ameritech provides paging, cellular telephone, and other wireless services in the St. Louis metropolitan area, as well as central and southeast Missouri, and parts of Illinois, Indiana, Michigan, Ohio, and Wisconsin. With additional cellular interests in Norway and Poland, Ameritech serves more than 1 million cellular customers and half a million paging customers.

Tip of the Iceberg

Americans have more access to modern technology than ever before. Even so, the growth of cellular telephone service has been extraordinary. "A few years ago, we thought the market for cellular service might reach 2,000 customers a year," recalls Ameritech Cellular Vice President Bill Gibson. "Now we sign that many St. Louis-area customers in a week."

About 22 percent of St. Louis adults use a cellular telephone, with a recent study estimating that another 13 percent plan to purchase a cellular phone soon. These numbers are consistent with the explosive growth in wireless communications nationwide. Today, nearly 20 million people use cel-

lular phones in the United States, and analysts predict cellular use to continue growing at a rate of 10 to 30 percent a year.

Nationally, two out of every three new telephone numbers is assigned to a cellular phone. By the year 2000, Ameritech estimates between 25 and 30 percent of all U.S. household telecommunications expenditures will be wireless.

The cellular industry's growth means employment growth in St. Louis. Ameritech now employs 450 people throughout Missouri, and expects to maintain an annual growth rate of more than 10 percent. This growth in staff has allowed the company to keep up with customer demand.

A Link to Better Communications

The industry's growth has spurred demand for more powerful, more sophisticated cellular services. With the goal of being the community's link to better communications, Ameritech has built a wireless infrastructure in the St. Louis region as powerful as the most modern landline telephone networks. Based on the AT&T Autoplex 5Ess switch, the system not only features fast and reliable service, but provides plenty of room for growth as well.

At its heart, wireless communication means mobility and access. Today's cellular user expects

CLOCKWISE FROM ABOVE:
RITA REED, DIRECTOR OF CUSTOMER SERVICE, LEADS A TEAM OF PROFESSIONALS OFFERING 24-HOUR SERVICE.

THE COMPANY CONTINUES TO EXPAND ITS RETAIL PRESENCE WITH THE ADDITION OF NEW AMERITECH CELLULAR CENTERS THROUGHOUT THE ST. LOUIS METRO AREA.

WITH AN AMERITECH CELLULAR PHONE, CELLULAR MODEM, AND LAPTOP COMPUTER, THE OPEN-AIR OFFICE IS A REALITY IN THE CONSTRUCTION INDUSTRY.

Clockwise from below:
Bill Gibson, vice president and Missouri general manager, and Connie Foster Taylor, new products manager, continue to introduce St. Louis to a host of new wireless services.

Ameritech Cellular Service keeps St. Louisans in contact with each other and with the world—even from a bike trail.

Ameritech's number is easy to remember: 444-4444.

The company serves busy St. Louisans with a quality network and the lowest airtime rates in town.

In 1994 Ameritech introduced its brand name in St. Louis by asking St. Louisans "What does it mean?"

Ameritech Cellular helps keep families in touch (bottom right).

and receives a much higher level of service than simple telephone service. Ameritech offers voice mail and custom calling features such as call forwarding, three-way conference calling, and call waiting. Ameritech is the only St. Louis cellular company to offer paging services.

Ameritech also is a leader in data services—assisting customers who use the cellular network to transmit data in addition to voice. With a laptop computer and a cellular phone modem, Ameritech's wireless data customers can download information from their mainframe computer or LAN, even from remote locations. They have the capability to send faxes, correspond by electronic mail, and transmit other data without access to a conventional landline telephone modem.

Innovations to Serve Customer Needs

New Ameritech services continuously enter the scene. Most recently, the company introduced AccessLine,™ a revolutionary feature that assigns a single phone number to each customer in place of pager, fax, cellular, home, and business numbers. This "personal" number follows users throughout the day providing greater ease of communications. International roaming services will also be introduced by Ameritech so St. Louis residents can travel with their cellular phone overseas. Voice-activated dialing is another new service Ameritech will soon debut.

But technical innovation is only a part of the demand for increasingly sophisticated service. Innovative new pricing and proprietary rate plans also distinguish Ameritech from its competitors. The Ameritech Business Concepts

plan allows business customers who use several cellular phones within an account to pool their usage for volume discounts. No other St. Louis cellular carrier offers such a plan. Businesses with cellular service in different areas can qualify for the company's National Accounts Program. The program provides integrated voice, data, and paging services, as well as invoicing and management reporting—all through a single national contact.

While the growth of cellular communications in business has been spectacular, its acceptance by individuals has been surprising. With an easy-to-remember phone number—444-4444—and innovative marketing programs, Ameritech has helped make cellular telephone service less intimidating for St.

Louis consumers.

As cellular service has evolved from strictly a business tool to a part of everyday life, it has grown more user friendly. Telephones and battery packs have become smaller and lighter. Ameritech continues to add cellular towers throughout Missouri and Illinois, expanding coverage and improving call quality. Monthly bills are easier to read and understand, and users now can charge their cellular service to major credit cards. The company's exclusive Cellular Rewards program allows users to earn points, based on cellular phone usage, which can then be redeemed for a variety of quality products and services, including free cellular airtime, car rentals, hotel stays, and airline tickets.

One of the original benefits of cellular telephones was to keep in touch while on the road. Ameritech has not forgotten this basic need of its customers. The company has affiliated with the North American Cellular Network (NACN), allowing easier communications when away from home.

Another innovative program, which teams Ameritech with the Metropolitan St. Louis Police Department, is Ameritech Cellular Patrol. Benefiting Ameritech customers and the community as a whole, this program provides cellular phones and free airtime to local Neighborhood Watch groups. "The Patrol helps close a gap in the Neighborhood Watch program," explains Gibson. "Previously, if a watcher saw something suspicious, he or she had to go back inside, find a phone, and call the police. During that time the suspect could disappear. Now, with a phone right alongside, the watcher can call authorities and keep track of the suspect."

Sometimes during periods of rapid growth, companies can get too big too fast and lose sight of what made them successful in the first place. Ameritech executives want to make sure that doesn't happen to them.

"Customers are at the center of everything we do, and at the heart of every decision we make," says Gibson. "Every business must continue to ask itself: 'How does this benefit the customer?' Our products and programs are designed around our customers. Business forecasts don't predict success. The key to success is to continue to meet our customers' needs and exceed their expectations."

Linda Wokoun (far left), vice president of marketing, demonstrates the use of a cellular modem with a notebook computer.

The latest in cellular technology is on display at Ameritech Cellular centers every day (left and below).

St. Louis Community College's Center for Business, Industry and Labor

There's an organization in St. Louis whose business is helping other businesses. Its professionals dramatically improve job effectiveness, business processes, and bottom-line productivity by forging "Performance Improvement Partnerships" with local companies. The Center for Business, Industry and Labor (CBIL, pronounced "Sybil"), an enterprise of St. Louis Community College and a nonprofit provider of training and performance improvement services, is committed to energizing and expanding the St. Louis economy. More than half a million workers and hundreds of companies in the area—from start-up businesses to Fortune 500 conglomerates—praise CBIL's customized services; "roll up your sleeves" attitude; and hands-on ideas, involvement, and implementation.

CBIL's 80 staff members and adjunct consultants work on-site in factories, stores, headquarters, and outlets of diverse industries that include manufacturing, telecommunications, chemical processing, health care services, retail, and automotive. Experienced project managers, instructional designers, quality control experts, computer system engineers, professional facilitators, and technical writers offer much more than training.

CBIL provides timely, cost-effective services for Pepsi-Cola's St. Louis operations.

CBIL helps small companies that must outsource specialized skills. "CBIL forced us to reflect on issues we might otherwise not have tackled and helped us to generate ideas that fit our culture. They enabled us to learn new techniques and to do real work in digestible chunks," says O'Brien Company's president, whose management committee learned how to become proactive and productive.

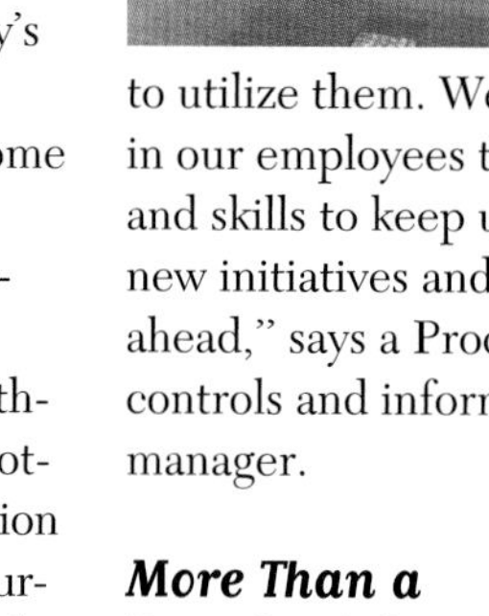

CBIL introduces and implements comprehensive systems. "We couldn't have done this without CBIL. The support we've gotten has been excellent. Their vision is top notch," says the quality assurance manager of NORDYNE. The company's plants switched to ISO 9000 standards, a complex system demanding interlocking policies, procedural documentation, and quality control.

CBIL provides start-up help to new businesses. "After consulting with us, CBIL offered far more than we had originally planned," says the human resources administrator of LRA St. Louis, whose goal was having employees operate as highperformance teams.

CBIL works with well-established businesses to introduce new systems and products. "CBIL played a critical role in the cultural transformation of the plant. Their manner and approach are holistic," says Nabisco's local plant manager. A new product demanded new production lines, technology, computer-based maintenance equipment, and sanitary changes.

CBIL shows businesses how to "grow" learning environments. "CBIL knows the capabilities of St. Louis resources and how best to utilize them. We want to invest in our employees the knowledge and skills to keep up with all the new initiatives and technology ahead," says a Procter & Gamble controls and information systems manager.

CBIL offered start-up help to LRA St. Louis, whose goal was having employees operate as high-performance teams (far right).

More Than a Decade of Service

CBIL began in 1984 when community leaders asked educational institutions to help train workforces for new industries. St. Louis Community College—already the second-largest institution of higher learning in Missouri, with more than 30,000 credit students—was a natural incubator for the initiative. Established by voters in 1962, the college's programs include college-transfer curricula and more than 100 career programs leading to the associate degree. A supplier of technical and entry-level employees for engineering, business, health, and community service organizations, St. Louis Community College provided expert resources for the project.

At first, CBIL was just a referral service between workers and target manufacturing and industrial companies. According to Rebecca Admire, who has provided vision and guidance as CBIL's director since 1984, "We defined a niche in the marketplace—instruc-

CBIL helped Nabisco transform its plant when a new product demanded new production lines, technology, computer-based maintenance equipment, and sanitary changes (far left).

tional design."

That nucleus of training programs and services grew exponentially to encompass every facet of performance improvement. "We help our clients bridge the gap between their current status and their corporate goals," explains Admire. "Our services address every element that contributes to employee performance improvement and ultimately company success."

Admire says CBIL partners with corporations to first "assess workers' skills and all the factors that contribute to performance, like the environment and feedback system, rewards, and incentives."

Next, CBIL helps to set realistic goals and create focus. For instance, a quality consultant may work on-site for as long as a year to evaluate approaches, make recommendations, and format systems documentation.

CBIL staff members document technical procedures and policies, and print them in attractive operations manuals, on-site posters, and portable job aids. CBIL's production group includes graphic artists, cutting-edge design software, and high-level production services.

Pepsi-Cola's plant manager says, "They quickly produce everything we need. It's much better and more cost-effective than any work on the outside." That's high praise from a "visual factory" ranked number one among the "Top 10 New Plants in the U.S."

CBIL provides detailed equipment operations, volume updates, and helpful tips at its graphic information centers.

CBIL's instructional designers create and facilitate customized training programs and also draw from a large library of proven materials. The organization strives to enrich current skills, develop new competencies, and integrate classroom work with on-the-job experiences.

Finally, CBIL specialists evaluate and measure quality, continuous improvement, and productivity initiatives, and continually fine-tune them. CBIL also helps corporations secure state-assisted training services under the Missouri Customized Training Program, and is the primary St. Louis provider.

"I see nothing but growth ahead," says Admire, "professional growth among workers, growth in profit for our clients, and new business growth for St. Louis."

What does this all add up to? A results-oriented, customer-focused resource for St. Louis businesses—The Center for Business, Industry and Labor.

With CBIL's help, Procter & Gamble employees have the knowledge and skills to keep up with new initiatives and technology.

Consolidated Communications Inc.

Despite his family's century-old legacy to the industry, Consolidated Communications Inc. Chairman Richard A. Lumpkin—the fourth generation of Lumpkins to lead CCI—still marvels at the advances made in telecommunications since his great-grandfather founded the company in Mattoon, Illinois, in 1894. From its roots as a local telephone company, CCI has grown into a diverse group of modern telecommunications-related companies, spanning both sides of the Mississippi in metro St. Louis. Its revenues doubled during one three-year period, beginning in 1992, and the privately held company continues this meteoric growth today.

Clockwise from top:

Consolidated is a founding member of the Independent Telecommunications Network, a 22,000-mile, worldwide fiber-optic network.

Consolidated provides complete business services, including long-distance and private lines.

The Consolidated Calling Card provides easy access to CCI long-distance service—even away from home.

Consolidated Communications Directories published more than 6 million directories in 1994 for communities in 39 states.

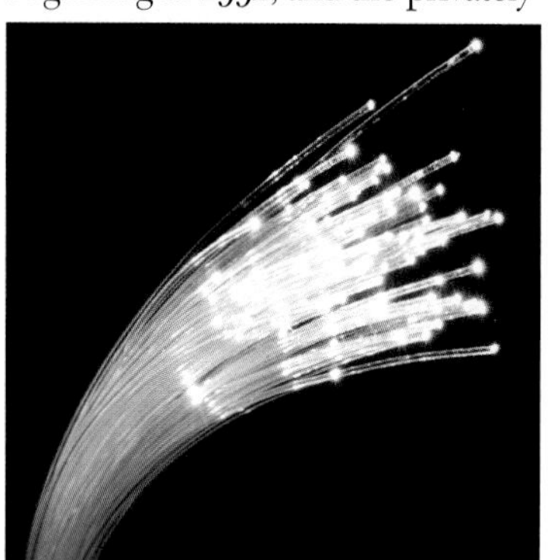

◀ BILL TILLEY

"Although my great-grandfather had a vision of telecommunications for everyone, I don't believe he would have conceived of the possibilities we have available today," says Lumpkin. "Perhaps he glimpsed its potential, but what's clear is that he saw opportunity. Our progress is an illustration of the human drive to build something of lasting value."

Deregulation Spurs Growth

Many of CCI's service opportunities grew out of the deregulation of the telecommunications industry. "We've become one of the most progressive phone companies that emerged from the deregulation era by deploying our resources to create value and provide savings for our customers," says Ken A. Harrington, vice president and general manager of CCI's St. Louis-based Telecom Services Division. For instance, CCI helped found the Independent Telecommunications Network, a 22,000-mile fiber-optic network that links CCI's own network and other independent regional fiber-optic companies to the worldwide network.

◀ SCOTT SMITH

In Illinois, CCI's original company, Illinois Consolidated Telephone Company, is the largest privately owned telephone company in the United States. It is ranked 26th overall, with more than 84,000 subscribers in east central Illinois. CCI's Telecom Services Division provides an array of telecommunications services, including long-distance service; private lines for voice, data, and video transmission; and complete business and mobile services.

◀ SCOTT SMITH

Other CCI subsidiaries are Consolidated Communications Public Services, which provides operator services for other telephone companies and public telephones; Consolidated Communications Directories, a national telephone directory publishing service that includes the former Old Heritage Advertising and Publishing Co.; and Consolidated Telemarketing of America, which provides telemarketing and other related services for the telecommunications industry.

◀ SCOTT SMITH

The Customer Comes First

CCI's corporate headquarters in Mattoon remains the pivotal point for a business that employs about 1,400 people. Although the telecommunications world has taken great strides, the company's core values of superior customer service and savings, commitment to its communities, and support for its employees have not changed.

Through its St. Louis-based operation, established in 1985, CCI has invested more than $1 million to support St. Louis-area community projects. The firm has contributed funds for the expansion and upgrade of the St. Peters (Missouri) Rec-Plex, and the Olympic track-and-field and soccer stadium at Southern Illinois University at Edwardsville. In 1994 CCI introduced the information superhighway to the public at the St. Louis V.P. Fair (now known as Fair Saint Louis) via computer workstations, and offered free long-distance calls to anywhere in the United States. Other projects involve ongoing sponsorship of a leading local television station's volunteer recruitment program for community organizations, and support of organizations such as the Make-a-Wish Foundation, Regional Commerce and Growth Association, Youth in Need, Inc., Junior League of St. Louis, Lift for Life Gym, and Girl Scout Council of Greater St. Louis.

In Illinois, CCI is a partner with the Lt. Governor's Distance Learning Foundation in bringing modern telecommunications to high schools and community colleges. The firm established interactive video and audio networks to provide "distance learning" in a system called the Prairie Learning Connection, which links 17 member schools in the Illinois communities of Charleston, Effingham, and Mattoon. CCI also initiated the innovative Earning for Learning program. Five percent of revenues from Consolidated's long-distance service generated by residential customers is given to a school district's foundation or educational fund in the communities. The moneys then fund projects or purchase equipment, a real bonus for cash-strapped school districts.

Individual employees also support education and community groups through service on local school and community college boards, parent-teacher organizations, and a variety of other organizations. CCI sponsors an annual Special Olympics Family Festival in Illinois, which is run by 5,000 volunteers representing both CCI and scores of other companies and community groups. This event is the largest of its kind in the world.

Opportunities for CCI's future growth focus on additional government deregulation and development of new technologies, says Harrington. CCI may enter new markets where the company can provide superior service to current providers, or partner with larger telecommunications firms to provide customized services. CCI decides which avenues to pursue based on market direction and customer need. "We are solution-oriented and for decades have been responding to our customers' changing needs," Harrington says. "We provide what's important to today's business decision makers—fair prices, well-coordinated services, leading technology, quality planning, and responsiveness 24 hours a day."

CCI plans to continue investing not only in new services, but in its own people through training and incentives for excellence. CCI's employees are key to a continued relationship-building strategy with customers. "We believe customers will seek telecommunications companies who can provide sound advice and counsel and who can help them make the myriad telecommunications decisions critical to the success of their businesses," Lumpkin says. "We're not here just to make a profit. We're here to make a difference with our customers and our communities."

▶ SCOTT SMITH

▶ SCOTT SMITH

▶ ZEHR PHOTOGRAPHY

▶ SCOTT SMITH

Clockwise from below:
A percentage of Consolidated's long-distance revenues is returned to the communities CCI serves. A portion of that money goes to support local school districts.

Consolidated Communications Directories is headquartered in Effingham, Illinois.

Consolidated Telemarketing of America, located in Charleston, Illinois, provides telemarketing services for a variety of industries.

Consolidated's Network Operations Center in St. Louis assures reliable, uninterrupted service for customers 24 hours a day, seven days a week.

GenCare Health Systems, Inc.

GenCare Health Systems operates several closely related managed health care products, including the largest HMO in Missouri; a point-of-service product known as Premier; a preferred provider organization (PPO); a workers' compensation PPO, GenComp; a dental HMO; and GenCare Senior for Medicare beneficiaries. ■ Formed in 1985 as a joint venture between Sanus Corporate Health Systems and McDonnell Douglas Corporation, GenCare was created in an effort to control spiraling health care costs. General American Life Insurance Company purchased GenCare in 1986 and took it public in 1991. United HealthCare Corporation, a highly regarded national leader in managed health care, purchased GenCare Health Systems in 1995.

Since 1985 GenCare has expanded dramatically into multiple counties in Missouri and Illinois. GenCare also has grown by controlling medical costs for employers and providing a high level of service to its members.

GenCare contracts directly with thousands of independent physicians who see members in their private offices. Using the company's "care coordinator" approach, health plan members choose a primary care physician who provides most routine medical services and makes specialist referrals when necessary. This approach gives members the benefit of care continuity and consistent record keeping.

Prevention Oriented

GenCare's commitment to innovation has led to the company's development of preventive health initiatives that address some of the most devastating and costly illnesses among the health plan's members. And a number of wellness programs have been created along nationally recognized guidelines and customized to the needs of specific employer groups in an effort to help individuals adopt healthy lifestyles. Among the company's most successful programs are PreNatal Plus®, designed to help identify and manage potential problem pregnancies; breast cancer awareness programs that emphasize the importance of early detection; and immunization reminders for families with children.

At GenCare, prevention programs don't stop or start with members. A panel of practicing physicians meets regularly to develop, review, and recommend guidelines for physicians' use in promoting preventive health care measures.

Over the years, GenCare has regularly surveyed its members, who consistently report high levels of satisfaction with their health plan, their physicians, and the broad range of services covered. Problem areas are addressed promptly and resolved quickly in an effort to increase member satisfaction. In addition, national organizations have reviewed GenCare, including the National Committee for Quality Assurance, which first granted the health plan provisional accreditation in August 1994, and the Utilization Review Accreditation Commission, which has accredited GenCare's Medical Department.

Thomas J. Zorumski (right), President of United HealthCare of Missouri and GenCare Health Systems, Inc.

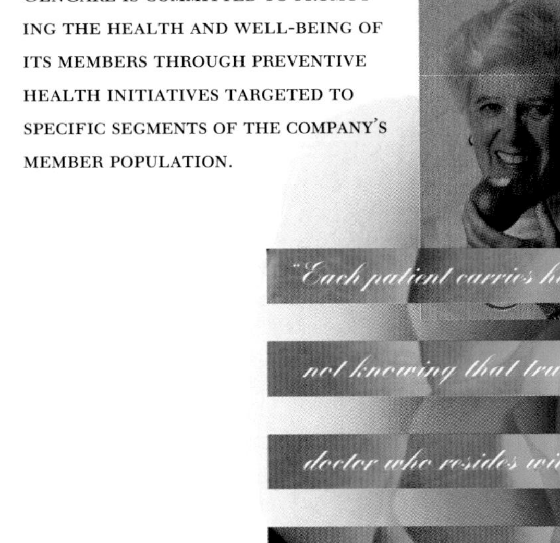

GenCare is committed to promoting the health and well-being of its members through preventive health initiatives targeted to specific segments of the company's member population.

Fair Saint Louis

IN 1981 ST. LOUIS BUSINESSMAN ROBERT R. HERMANN ORGANIZED A corps of civic leaders to create an event that would promote metropolitan St. Louis to the rest of the country. With the help of 100 community leaders and approximately 3,000 volunteers, the group presented its first three-day Fourth of July fair, held on the St. Louis riverfront. The 90-acre Jefferson National Expansion Memorial, with the majestic Gateway Arch as its centerpiece, provides the perfect setting for what has become one of the largest and most attractive Independence Day celebrations in America.

Originally called the V.P. Fair, the event followed the tradition of the Veiled Prophet Parade begun in 1878 to generate enthusiasm for the region. In those days, the parade was held at night and featured lavishly decorated, lighted floats, presided over by a mythical potentate called the Veiled Prophet. Now, the fair kicks off with a similar daytime parade through the streets of downtown St. Louis. Hundreds of thousands of people from throughout the Midwest attend the parade and fair each year.

Combining dazzling air shows, big-name entertainment, spectacular fireworks, and family-oriented activities, the fair offers food, events, and exhibits for three days of fun. All events are free to the public. Past fairs have featured entertainment ranging from the Beach Boys and Elton John to Bill Cosby and Dolly Parton, attracting an overflow crowd to the weekend gala.

The huge success of the fair is due to strong financial support from individuals, the corporate community, and in-kind business contributions, as well as the dedicated efforts of some 7,000 volunteers annually. Diverse leadership, volunteer recruitment, and activities that appeal to people of all ages assure extensive involvement of a cross-section of the community's population. Vendors operate food and bazaar booths to meet every whim of fairgoers. Although a portion of their profits goes back to the fair, community booths benefit significantly from fair proceeds. In 1994, for example, more than 30 not-for-profit organizations earned a combined $205,000, which helped to support their respective year-round programs.

Through the years, when there has been an excess of revenue, the V.P. Fair Foundation has made gifts to the community, including the Leonor K. Sullivan Boulevard overlook stage and promenade, and the lighting of the Eads Bridge. Such improvements have vastly enhanced the historic St. Louis riverfront.

In 1995 the fair became officially known as Fair Saint Louis. Its leaders feel the new name more effectively describes the event and better reflects the spirit and pride of the St. Louis metropolitan region, as well as bringing additional national focus and recognition to "The Great American Celebration." The fair also offers an opportunity for corporate sponsors to participate in the area's biggest and most prestigious civic event, providing high visibility for their products and services.

Fair officials plan to continue producing the event annually, enhancing it each year with new and attractive program features while retaining those that have proved popular with the fairgoing public.

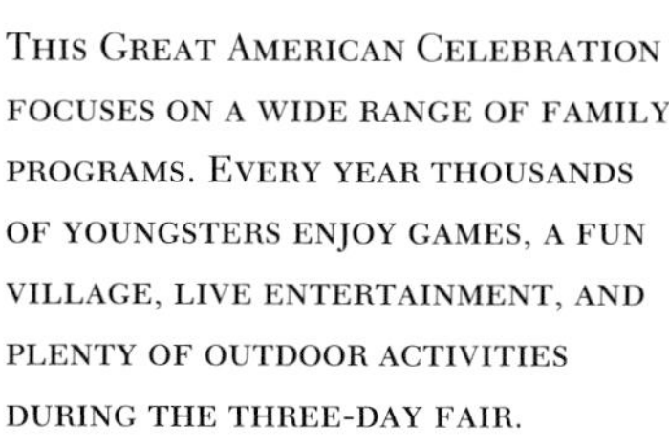

THIS GREAT AMERICAN CELEBRATION FOCUSES ON A WIDE RANGE OF FAMILY PROGRAMS. EVERY YEAR THOUSANDS OF YOUNGSTERS ENJOY GAMES, A FUN VILLAGE, LIVE ENTERTAINMENT, AND PLENTY OF OUTDOOR ACTIVITIES DURING THE THREE-DAY FAIR.

FAIR SAINT LOUIS DAZZLES ITS AUDIENCE EACH EVENING WITH A BRILLIANT, SPARKLING WORLD-CLASS FIREWORKS DISPLAY.

Mills & Partners, Inc.

Only a decade old, Mills & Partners, Inc. has become one of the nation's leading management groups. With extensive management expertise and financial resources, the company excels in the acquisition, management, and marketing of commercial and industrial technology manufacturing companies. ■ Located in St. Louis since its founding in 1985, Mills & Partners has assembled a spectrum of industry holdings that boast a combined sales revenue of more than $1.2 billion. Products manufactured by companies under the Mills & Partners umbrella are produced in plants worldwide, effectively making St. Louis the global corporate headquarters for producers of basic components and accessories covering a wide range of industrial applications.

Led by James N. Mills, Mills & Partners operates as a holding company, acquiring new companies through leveraged acquisitions, then developing and implementing strategies to assure that the businesses remain market-share leaders. Mills calls it a "buy-and-build" approach. "We're unique in that we have access to capital, and provide the senior management necessary to acquire and effectively manage and grow companies," he explains. Mills & Partners has participated in transactions having a combined listed value of more than $3.5 billion, ranging from less than $5 million to over $1.2 billion.

Mills & Partners' access to the capital needed for major acquisitions occurs through its financial partner—Hicks, Muse, Tate & Furst, Inc., of Dallas. Hicks, Muse, Tate & Furst, Inc., has a formal strategic arrangement with Mills & Partners to acquire and operate companies, and the two groups jointly screen numerous investment opportunities.

Mills, a St. Louis native, organized Mills & Partners by assembling some of the most capable senior managers in production, finance, marketing, and human resources. In addition to Mills, who is chairman of the board and chief executive officer, the corporate officers are David M. Sindelar, senior vice president and chief financial officer; Larry S. Bacon, senior vice president, human resources; and W. Thomas McGhee, general counsel.

Prior to the founding of the company, Mills had held senior executive positions for more than two decades with a variety of successful major manufacturing companies, including Thermadyne Holdings, a former component of Mills & Partners that went public in 1994. After living in 18 different cities, Mills chose to base his company in St. Louis because of his hometown roots and the city's location. "St. Louis has an ideal central geographic location from which to manage our many companies. Plus, it's a good, solid

Headquartered in St. Louis since its founding in 1985 (right), Mills & Partners has assembled a spectrum of industry holdings that boast a combined sales revenue of more than $1.2 billion.

Mills & Partners' leadership includes (from left) James N. Mills, Larry S. Bacon, W. Thomas McGhee, and David M. Sindelar.

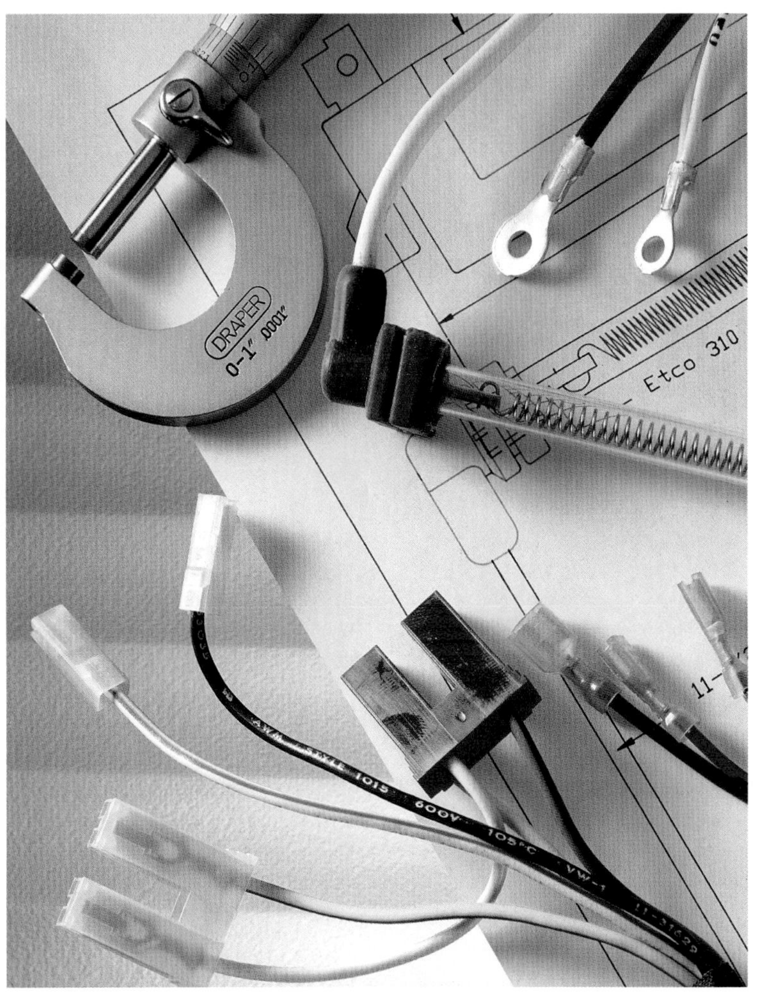

WIREKRAFT IS A MARKET LEADER IN SUPPLYING WIRE AND WIRE HARNESSES TO THE AUTOMOBILE AND APPLIANCE INDUSTRIES.

community," he says.

Companies under the firm's management include Berg Electronics, Inc., Jackson Products, Inc., and Wirekraft Industries, Inc., all three with executive offices in St. Louis.

Berg Electronics, Inc.

Acquired in 1993 from chemical giant Du Pont, Berg Electronics represents one of the largest global manufacturers and designers of electronic connectors, integrated circuit sockets, and cable assemblies. Berg also represents the largest of the Mills & Partners companies.

Berg has a long-held tradition for quality specialty electronic products. Berg's products can be found in thousands of modern factories, offices, and households. These products are used in virtually every electronic product, including computers, printers, disk drives, modems, VCRs, radios, airplanes, appliances, and automobiles. Each of the company's products is designed to meet customer-specific needs. Major customers include AT&T, IBM, Hewlett-Packard, Hitachi, Seimens, Northern Telecom, Compaq, and Seagate.

Given the successful implementation of its buy-and-build approach, combined with the rapid expansion of Berg's sales force, Mills & Partners anticipates a bright future for Berg. In fact, since the initial acquisition, Berg has advanced from the number seven position worldwide as a producer of electronic connectors to a solid number four. A significant growth step occurred with the 1994 acquisition of AT&T Microelectronic Connector Systems Business in Lee's Summit, Missouri, which supplies AT&T Corp. with connector systems. Other strategic Berg add-on acquisitions include Harbor Electronics, Socket Express, Mold-Con/Tri-Tec, and McKenzie Technology.

"We want to expand into market segments where we're not as active," says Robert N. Mills, president. His brother James, who serves as Berg's chairman, agrees, citing more acquisitions in the making. Leading that list of acquisition targets are automotive connectors, followed by fiber optics and advanced consumer

CONNECTORS MANUFACTURED BY BERG ELECTRONICS CAN BE FOUND IN THOUSANDS OF MODERN OFFICES AND HOUSEHOLDS.

BERG HAS ADVANCED FROM THE NUMBER SEVEN POSITION WORLDWIDE AS A PRODUCER OF ELECTRONIC CONNECTORS TO A SOLID NUMBER FOUR.

products such as camcorders and televisions. Berg's growth plans are international in scope, involving major supply contracts from abroad. Already, the company's sales are evenly split among North America, Europe, and Asia. The company also plans to continue its aggressive research and development into new products.

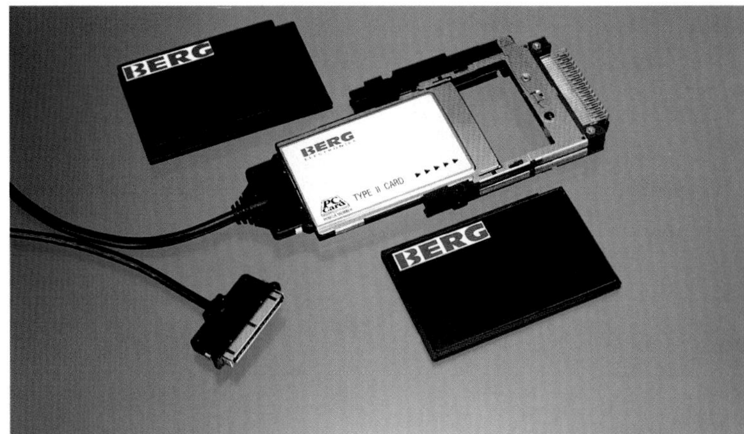

Jackson Products, Inc.

Jackson Products and its Flex-O-Lite division represent two more of the newer acquisitions in Mills & Partners' mix of commercial and industrial companies.

Jackson Products manufactures a stylish array of safety products for the cutting and welding industry. The company's products include welding helmets, hard hats, face shields, safety eyewear, respirators, and welding accessories such as electrode holders, clamps, and cable connectors. Like all Mills & Partners companies, Jackson's products are market leaders.

JACKSON'S ELECTRONIC QUICK CHANGE™ WELDING HELMET PROVIDES WELDERS PRECISION PROTECTION AGAINST EYE DAMAGE WITHOUT HAVING TO FLIP THE HELMET UP AND DOWN WHILE WORKING.

Jackson's safety products incorporate advanced technology. For example, a view filter used in one of its welding helmets, called Electronic Quick Change (EQC™), automatically darkens at a rate of less than 0.1 milliseconds—beating the light of a welding arc to the eye. This means that a welder not only has precision protection against eye damage, but no longer needs to flip the helmet up and down while working.

In addition to cutting and welding applications, Jackson's eyewear is worn by a wide range of industrial workers, health care workers, hazardous materials handlers, agricultural workers, and more. The relatively low-cost, highly effective products produced by Jackson not only protect workers from serious injury, but can save an industry from enormous financial outlays in accident-related costs. The company's marketers expect increasing sales as safety consciousness grows, noting that the United States lags behind Europe in these issues.

Robert H. Elkin took over as president of Jackson Products after the acquisition of Flex-O-Lite in 1994. Flex-O-Lite, one of the largest U.S. producers of glass beads, literally lights up the highways and movie screens. The company manufactures a reflective, glass-beaded product that is used in applications ranging from the white and yellow pavement tape applied on roadways to movie screens and reflective clothing. Other uses include reflective surfaces for airport runways, license plates, and safety barricades. Another Flex-O-Lite product line that is hard to miss includes the reflective cones, flags, and arrow boards used with highway construction.

Flex-O-Lite's products are leaders in their niche markets. The company's history spans 50 years. The stable customer base and long history of producing high-value industrial products, plus excellent growth potential, made Flex-O-Lite an excellent fit for Mills & Partners' mix of manufacturing entities.

Wirekraft Industries, Inc.

Wirekraft Industries, Inc. is a fully integrated manufacturer of wire and wire harnesses used for major products essential to modern life. These products include washing machines, dishwashers, refrigerators, microwave ovens, and automobiles. Wirekraft, composed of a wire division and a harness division, was acquired in 1992.

The wire division manufactures insulated wire—enough in

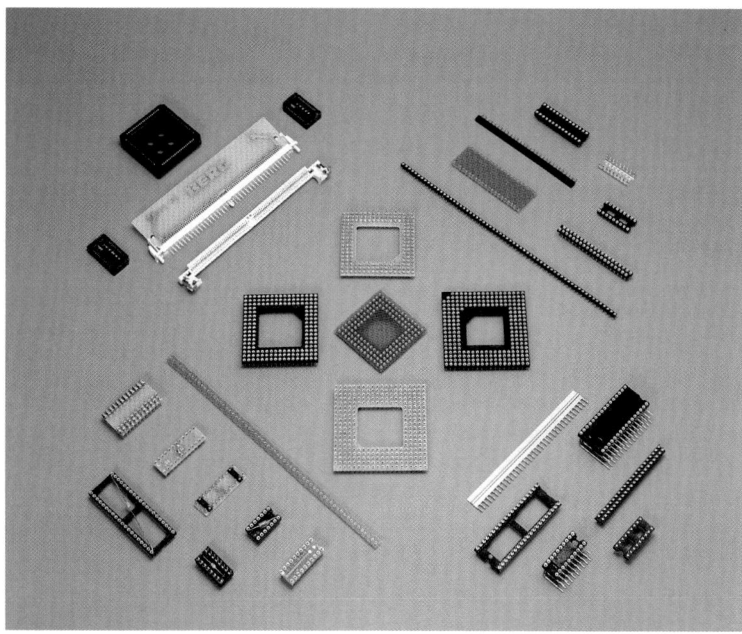

Each of Berg's connectors is designed to meet customer-specific needs, allowing it to interface with compatible devices.

its 35-year history to circle the globe several times. Its products are used in appliances, automobiles, and boats. The division's product line also includes electronic lead wire, speaker wire, and battery cable wire.

The harness division manufactures wire harnesses—the molded plugs with multiple pin connections that connect groups of wires together in virtually every appliance category (refrigerators, dishwashers, washing machines, dryers, ranges, and freezers). This division is the leading manufacturer of appliance wire harnesses in the United States. The company also makes a number of other products, including truck trailer cables, resistance heaters, and specialty wire assemblies made to customer specifications.

Revenues since 1992 have grown by more than 80 percent, largely as a result of Mills & Partners' buy-and-build strategy. In 1993 Wirekraft acquired a high-temperature wire manufacturing operation in Bremen, Indiana. In 1994 the company acquired ECM (the wire harness division of General Electric located in Mexico) and invested in the expansion of its wire mill in El Paso, Texas, as well as the purchase of a wire mill in Nogales, Mexico. Led by William J. Kriss, president, the company's future plans include pursuing computer cable assemblies, automotive assemblies, and appliance harness acquisition opportunities.

Poised for Future Growth

In 1995 Mills & Partners completed another significant acquisition. This acquisition of Omega Wire, Inc., a leading indepentent manufacturer of noninsulated bare and tin-coated copper and cable products, is considered a strategic fit with Wirekraft. Omega sells its wire and cable to the appliance, telecommunications, computer, and auto industries.

Looking forward, Mills & Partners will continue to pursue aquisitions and offer numerous products that are increasingly important to commercial and industrial customers alike. On the heels of its first decade of business success, this St. Louis company is poised for an exciting future of growth.

Wirekraft's wire products are precision processed and monitored for quality and service.

FROM THE EARLIEST DAYS BEFORE THE LOUISIANA PURCHASE, when Spanish explorers spied sparkling pieces of lead-rich galena as they traveled northward along the Mississippi River shoreline, lead has played an integral role in the development of the Gateway to the West. The Doe Run Company, with headquarters in St. Louis, is ensuring today that this important natural resource continues to be supplied in an environmentally responsible and innovative way.

Named after Doe Run Creek in the Missouri Ozarks, The Doe Run Company roots were first established in 1886 by St. Joseph Lead, a progressive lead-mining business near Bonne Terre, Missouri. With an objective of acquiring and mining 150 acres near Flat River, Missouri, Doe Run and its ancestors helped identify the great lead-bearing lands of the Flat River district. By 1889 the company had constructed and put into operation a new lead smelter in nearby Herculaneum, which after substantial reconstruction and continuing upgrade, is still among the best and largest in the world. Doe Run's current headquarters has been in St. Louis since 1986. From its modest beginning near Bonne Terre nearly 130 years ago, Doe Run has grown into a world-class mining operation with facilities located 100 miles southwest of St. Louis near Viburnum, Missouri—the heart of what has become known as the New Lead Belt. Located near Viburnum are six hard-rock underground mines; four mills; the country's newest, and one of the largest, state-of-the-art lead smelters; and a high-tech recycling facility.

Doe Run is the single largest integrated producer of lead in North America, with milling capacities of 30,000 tons of ore daily. Its 1,000 employees produce more than half of all lead mined in the United States, and generate over $175 million in annual sales. The company integrates the mining, smelting, and processing of the ore, along with recycling, into a full line of shapes and alloys of both primary and secondary lead. Doe Run leads the industry not only in production, but in environmental responsiveness and innovation as well, while maintaining unrivaled employee safety.

CLOCKWISE FROM RIGHT:
DOE RUN PROCESSES LEAD WASTE MATERIAL IN ITS STATE-OF-THE-ART, ENVIRONMENTALLY SOUND FACILITY LOCATED IN BOSS, MISSOURI.

STATE-OF-THE-ART AUTOMATION ALLOWS DOE RUN TO OPERATE FOUR MILLS, WITH AN AGGREGATE PRODUCTION CAPACITY OF 30,000 TONS OF ORE PER DAY.

MOLTEN LEAD IS TRANSFERRED TO THE DROSSING FLOOR IN 10-TON LADLES.

Educating the Consumer

"Lead is the most recycled metal in our society," explains President and CEO Jeffrey L. Zelms, "and we believe in, and are committed to, lead life-cycle management, whereby the metal—lead—is managed from the ore in the ground through its primary use, back through recycling and secondary uses as well." Doe Run's Buick Resource Recycling Facility, located in Boss, Missouri, reclaims 80,000 tons of refined lead annually. When first dedicated in 1990, the facility projected that 85 percent of the lead reclamation would be derived from automobile batteries, the largest user of lead. But in four short years, a multitude of newly recognized sources has reduced that figure to 50 percent.

The balance is derived from diverse sources of which consumers are often unaware. "Most people simply don't recognize the many ways lead is used in their

everyday lives," explains Zelms. Car batteries, television and computer screens, lead foil found around dental X-ray film, weights in golf clubs, ammunition, and the lead weight belts needed for undersea diving enthusiasts are just a few of the uses for this essential and highly recyclable metal.

One of the company's priorities is to promote its product as an essential mineral that can be managed in an environmentally responsible manner. Where high levels of lead had accumulated after 100 years of smelter operation, for example, Doe Run replaced the soil in residential yards. Water used in the smelting process is recycled many times over before being discharged. The water the plant does discharge contains less than half the amount of contaminants permitted by the Missouri Department of Natural Resources. Through the use of efficient vacuum air filters and bag houses that remove particles produced from blast furnaces, Doe Run has been able to reduce its air emissions 75 percent in the last two decades. The company has been cited by the Environmental Protection Agency as a model of how American industry, state environmental agencies, and the EPA are successfully working in partnership to reduce environmental hazards.

The New York City-based Renco Group, Inc. purchased Doe Run in April 1994, and the company's sights are set firmly on the future. Zelms believes that concern for the environment has provided the opportunity for his company to continue to help guide the St. Louis business community into the next century. "Through a better understanding of the planet, and by adapting to the needs of the 21st century, The Doe Run Company believes it is well-positioned to be responsive to the marketplace as well as being stewards of natural resources," he says. "Our concern for the environment has generated a new world of products and services, and it is this new marketplace that will provide for continued growth of the lead industry and The Doe Run Company."

Clockwise from below:
Molten lead is created from sinter by the blast furnace. The bullion then goes to the refinery for purification and alloying.

The company offers a variety of lead and lead alloy products to meet specific customer needs. Pictured is a 60-pound pig of lead which is 99.99 percent pure. It can also be cast in five-pound caulking links, 100-pound pigs, and one-ton ingots.

Mining involves drilling and blasting limestone rock 1,000 or more feet below the Earth's surface.

Physicians Health Plan of Greater St. Louis, Inc.

THE NEED TO PROVIDE ADEQUATE, AFFORDABLE HEALTH CARE to the greatest number of Americans has sparked some of the most emotional debates in recent history. These health care issues have given rise to health maintenance organizations (HMOs) as a source of medical services for people who agree to use doctors who are members of the organization. While Physicians Health Plan℠ of Greater St. Louis, Inc. (PHP) technically can be defined as an HMO, the plan differs in a significant way.

"This is true 'open access,'" says Michael F. Neidorff, president and CEO of PHP. "Our plan preserves our members' right to choose their own private practice physicians, their own hospitals, and their own specialists without a referral." PHP is the only HMO in St. Louis that does not require a member to designate a primary care physician or "gatekeeper" to coordinate health care for an individual.

PHP's network of St. Louis-area physicians share the plan's commitment to quality care access, cost containment, and, subsequently, business success.

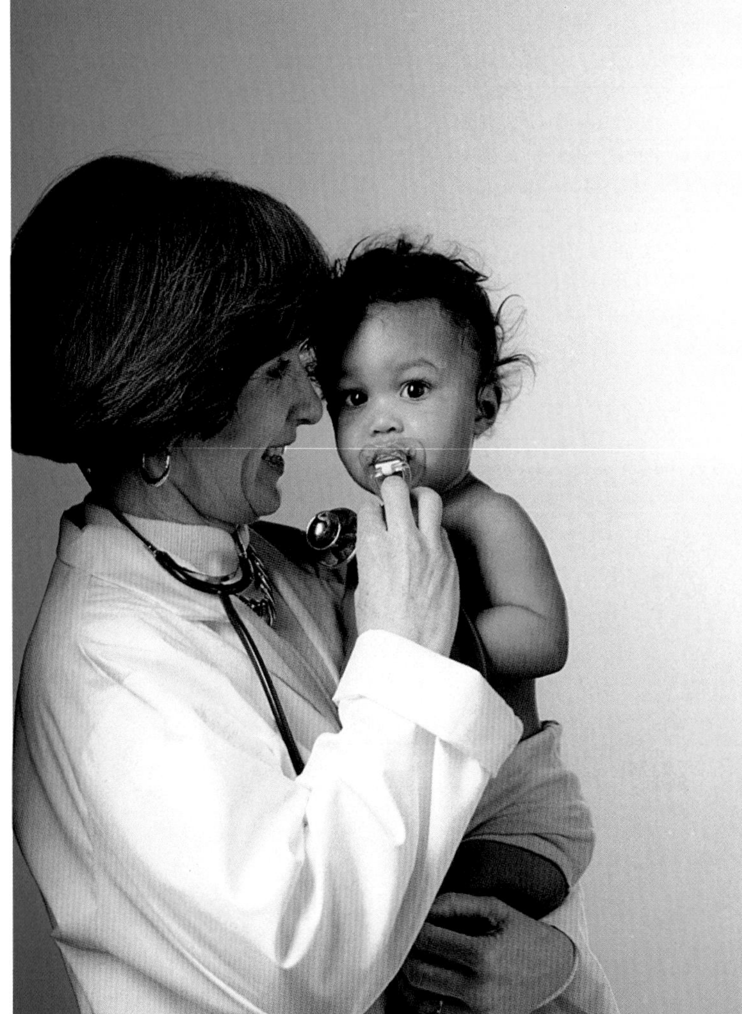

Involving the Care Providers

PHP was founded in 1985 by a group of nine physicians, and now has some 170,000 members who have access to more than 3,500 doctors, 51 hospitals, and 535 pharmacies. The company is owned by United Healthcare Corporation of Minneapolis, one of the nation's major health care organizations, with offices in 21 states. PHP's network of St. Louis-area physicians share the plan's commitment to quality care access, cost containment, and, subsequently, business success.

"Traditional indemnity insurers and other managed care plans lack this relationship with their providers," Neidorff says, "and without that fundamental relationship, they lack the means to efficiently and effectively control costs. Our policies reflect standards of community practice with strict enforcement by our local physician board members and committees."

PHP's growth has been steady; the organization has operated without a deficit since 1989. The plan's managed care philosophy is based on the integration of three strategic areas: influencing utilization of health care services so that neither too few nor too many services are delivered; influencing the cost of health care services by contractual agreements with providers; and measuring performance after services are delivered in order to continually improve the level of quality.

PHP selects its providers by considering factors such as a balance of practice specialties, geographic accessibility, and the commitment of providers to working within a managed care system. A comprehensive credentialing process guarantees that 20 mandatory requirements are met before a provider becomes a part of the network. Each physician's performance is measured, comparing him or her to other physicians in the same specialty area. Physicians receive feedback and education concerning quality, cost-effectiveness, and access.

A Choice of Plans

PHP offers three major plans: an HMO, which covers all medical services after a small copayment; CARUS, a Medicare supplement for individuals; and PHP Plus, a managed care product that allows participants to choose between participating and nonparticipating providers. The level of benefit is based on whether a participating or nonparticipating physician is selected. PHP Plus was designed to address employer concerns over rising health care costs and multiple administration problems associated with offering several levels of benefits. It offers ease of administration and the advantage of having all employees covered under one risk pool. While the PHP Plus plan is more expensive than PHP's HMO, it works especially well for companies with a large percentage of employees who reside outside the metropolitan area where most

of the plan's participating physicians are located.

PHP utilizes a variety of means for keeping costs down. The plan stresses the importance of wellness and dedicates resources to help keep its members healthy by providing coverage for preventive care, rather than restricting coverage to illness and injury. A 1992 study in the *Journal of Occupational Medicine* shows that every dollar spent on wellness saves $3.40 in medical costs. PHP also eliminates the paperwork associated with the filing of claims, as the physicians submit bills directly to PHP for payment.

In 1994 PHP introduced its comprehensive wellness program for businesses large and small. The program includes nutritionists, aerobics instructors, and other such specialists. Stress reduction and healthy lifestyles are emphasized, and a wellness directory permits members to get discounts at local gyms and health clubs. A unique part of the wellness initiative is the BabySteps program for pregnant women. Expectant mothers are offered additional benefits and attention, including a 24-hour information hot line during and after pregnancy, as well as a newsletter on a trimester basis that helps the mother follow the progress of her pregnancy. In addition, early involvement in the BabySteps program enables case managers to determine high-risk patients.

PHP employs 160 people in St. Louis. The company participates regularly in health fairs throughout the greater St. Louis community, and is a supporter of Opera Theatre of St. Louis, St. Louis Symphony Orchestra, Boy Scouts, American Parkinson's Disease Association, Student Body Steps for Life, Wife-Widow-Woman, Alzheimer's Association, and St. Louis Vipers in-line hockey team.

In early 1995, United Healthcare purchased GenCare Health Systems, a St. Louis-based PHP competitor, and joined the two, doubling the number of members served. The merged company is now the largest HMO in the state of Missouri. Although changes in the company's name, structure, and products offered will occur as a result of the merger, its goals—quality care, affordable cost, and open access—will remain unchanged.

SOME 170,000 PHP MEMBERS HAVE ACCESS TO MORE THAN 3,500 DOCTORS, 51 HOSPITALS, AND 535 PHARMACIES.

SINCE THE EARLY 1900S, THE FORERUNNERS OF NORDYNE, A pioneering company in heating and air-conditioning systems, have been carving a bold path in the future of the HVAC industry. Since 1919 a company named Miller in Holland, Michigan, and St. Louis-based Intertherm have earned the respect of their industry for their innovative products and customer service. For most of their history, these companies focused on creating products for the manufactured housing (also known as mobile home) market, and both were at the top of their industry.

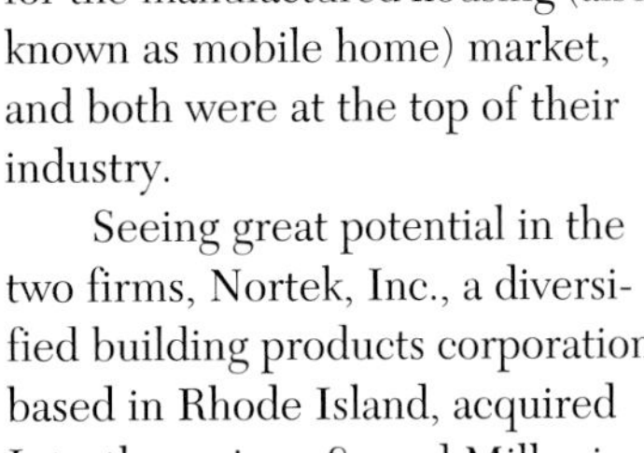

Seeing great potential in the two firms, Nortek, Inc., a diversified building products corporation based in Rhode Island, acquired Intertherm in 1985 and Miller in 1986. When merged, a new name arose from their sense of drive and purpose, and NORDYNE—"dyne" being a unit of force—was created.

Clockwise from above:
Air conditioner production at NORDYNE's facility in Boonville, Missouri.

Automatic brazing is one manufacturing technology that has been added in recent years to improve quality.

President and CEO Bob Ractliffe (center), Vice President of Marketing and Sales Dave LaGrand (left), and Vice President of Engineering Wayne Reedy have been with NORDYNE throughout its restructuring and its doubling in size.

Developing High-Efficiency Products

During the early '90s, NORDYNE faced tough, new standards brought about by the U.S. Department of Energy. New laws required higher than ever efficiency levels in heating and air-conditioning products. In order to comply, NORDYNE developed entirely new product lines within two years. Not only did the company comply, but it produced a great variety of high-efficiency products, some of them unique.

Among the most noteworthy was the Powermiser,™ an integrated hot water heat pump system used widely in residential housing. The Powermiser recaptures waste heat from an air-conditioning or heating system and uses it to heat water—resulting in substantial energy savings. With products such as the Powermiser, NORDYNE laid the groundwork for future profitability.

To further improve its processes, NORDYNE expanded its plant in the city of St. Louis, as well as doubling the size of its Boonville, Missouri, facility. A new, central warehouse was built in St. Peters, Missouri, replacing several smaller ones. From this single, large warehouse, NORDYNE's products are distributed globally. Although the bulk of its business lies within the United States, the firm also markets its products in Canada, the Caribbean, Central and South America, the Middle East, Japan, and Europe.

Nationally known NBC weathercaster Willard Scott has been the spokesman for NORDYNE's Intertherm and Miller heating and cooling products since 1989. Scott's affable, trustworthy image complements a company that prides itself on being friendly and responsive to the customer.

Settling in the Midwest

Some tough decisions were made during the early days of the merger that created today's NORDYNE. To increase growth, management decided to expand into the greater residential market. To successfully compete with heavy hitters such as Carrier, Trane, York, and Lennox, every facet of the operation had to be streamlined. By integrating the old Intertherm and Miller organizations, reducing staff size, and consolidating operations, NORDYNE managed to cut overhead by 25 percent.

In 1988 the Miller plant in Michigan was closed, and St. Louis became headquarters for the company. "The center of gravity for heating and cooling products in the United States was and is the St. Louis area," President Robert E.G. Ractliffe says, in explaining the company's choice of a home base. "St. Louis is also the center of our supplier base, and the workforce is top-notch, too." Currently, NORDYNE's top-notch workforce numbers between 1,000 and 1,500

employees, depending upon seasonal fluctuations.

Ractliffe came to NORDYNE in 1989 as president and CEO with a directive to lead the company in its new direction. Ractliffe refocused NORDYNE's objectives, establishing a set of goals for the future: to protect and increase base businesses (products for manufactured housing and electric heat); to increase residential and parts businesses; and to continuously improve products, processes, people, and profitability.

Thanks, in part, to this new focus, NORDYNE's sales volume since 1990 has climbed steadily. In 1994 the company's annual sales reached approximately $250 million—double the 1990 figure.

A Soggy Setback

It has not been all smooth sailing, however. The Great Flood of 1993 almost cost NORDYNE its life. As Ractliffe remembers, "Our plant in south St. Louis happens to be located in a dip near the River Des Peres. The Great Flood started to come up through the drain system."

Quick action saved the plant from total destruction. NORDYNE employees, volunteers, and contract construction companies protected valuable equipment by raising it three feet. They sandbagged, pumped water, and built dikes—even smashed the connection between the plant and the city's main drain system. "By isolating ourselves from the system, we limited the water level to under three feet," says Ractliffe. "Instead of losing everything, we were out of production for just six weeks. And we retained all our customers." Today the plant production and operations are back to normal, with new flood protection devices securely in place.

The future looks promising for this innovative manufacturer. NORDYNE is embarking on a new management system called DFT, or Demand Flow® Technology. DFT is a comprehensive strategy designed to permit the company to build its products based on actual customer demand, rather than a sales forecast. NORDYNE will, therefore, be even more responsive to its customers' requirements, and will do so with significantly less inventory. The new system will be in full swing within a year.

NORDYNE's management believes that the DFT system complements the company's longtime philosophy of focusing on the customer. Says Ractliffe, "We take the opposite approach from our competition. We tell the customer that we'll do things their way, and we literally do. That's why we are able to compete in a market dominated by billion-dollar companies."

With its focus on flexibility and satisfying each individual customer, NORDYNE has become the fastest-growing company in the heating and cooling industry, and its staying power seems secure.

Clockwise from above: NORDYNE's corporate headquarters is located in West Port.

Nationally known NBC weathercaster Willard Scott has been the spokesman for NORDYNE's Intertherm and Miller heating and cooling products since 1989.

Furnace production takes place at the company's Grand Avenue facility in St. Louis.

The Great Flood of 1993 curtailed NORDYNE's furnace production for six weeks—but not its spirit.

Robotic welding is another new technology that has boosted quality.

Embassy Suites

A STAY AT THE EMBASSY SUITES PRESENTS VISITORS TO ST. LOUIS WITH an exciting plate full of possibilities. Located in historic Laclede's Landing along the riverfront, Embassy Suites prides itself on not being just another hotel. Instead, it reflects the unique charm of its historic surroundings, offering its guests a promise of twice the hotel, twice the fun, and twice the value available elsewhere—a real St. Louis experience.

The combination of location, services, and entertainment value makes Embassy Suites a delightful venture, according to Bill Buck, general manager. With amenities such as an indoor pool, whirlpool, sauna, steam room, fitness center, game room, and billiards table, guests can have a wonderful time without ever leaving the hotel.

An Impressive Transformation

Hotels of Distinction—a Palm Springs, Florida, firm known for breathing new life into hotels—purchased the Embassy Suites franchise through the Promus Companies of Memphis, Tennessee, in 1991. Hotels of Distinction Chairman Alan Tremain and President Jean-Claude Mathot saw the potential the eight-year-old property held, and began an impressive transformation.

An eight-story enclosed garden atrium is the signature design feature of the hotel. The 297 two-room suites open onto the spacious atrium courtyard where a hint of New Orleans exists amid the white wrought iron railings and cool mauves and greens. Fountains and waterfalls surrounded by greenery seem to bring the outdoors inside.

Guaranteed Excellence

For prices comparable to a single room at other hotels, the Embassy Suites provides a two-room suite with wet bar, free cooked-to-order breakfast, and a manager's reception each evening with complimentary beverages. "We are the only chain that promotes a 100 percent guarantee of excellence," Buck says. "If our services don't meet the guest's expectations, we adjust the bill accordingly." Because of the well-trained staff and high performance standards, guests rarely complain.

Whether in St. Louis for business or pleasure, visitors can also

AN EIGHT-STORY ENCLOSED GARDEN ATRIUM IS THE SIGNATURE DESIGN FEATURE OF THE EMBASSY SUITES IN ST. LOUIS. THE 297 TWO-ROOM SUITES OPEN ONTO THE SPACIOUS ATRIUM COURTYARD.

find great food and entertainment in the Embassy Suites' very own karaoke lounge. Known as the Dirtwater Fox Cafe, its name is based on a colorful folk legend about a traveling New Orleans minstrel.

Guests ready to venture out for fun and sight-seeing don't have far to go. The Embassy Suites is just minutes away from riverboat gambling, the Gateway Arch, the America's Center Convention Center, and downtown shopping at St. Louis Center. Sports fans can enjoy the excitement of nearby attractions such as Busch Stadium, the new Kiel Center, and St. Louis' new domed stadium. Cultural and educational venues abound, as well. The zoo, art museum, symphony, municipal opera, and science center are all within two miles of the Embassy Suites on Laclede's Landing.

Taking Care of Business

Business travelers at the Embassy Suites can take advantage of special services created by Buck, who pays close attention to the unique needs of business guests. Embassy Suites continually strives to improve its business services by listening to its guests and responding promptly.

Currently, 8,000 square feet of flexible meeting, banquet, and ballroom space serve the various groups that visit the riverfront hotel. Upgraded meeting rooms, suites, and public spaces can accommodate groups of up to 400 people. Embassy Suites also prides itself on its state-of-the-art communications systems—voice mail, computer modem connections, and two televisions with cable are standard in each suite for added convenience and comfort.

Many special services ease the way for those conducting business at the Embassy Suites. A "Preferred Partners" plan provides corporate members with a program of preferential treatment and rates, such as bonuses for company travel planners. The hotel's Conference Services Department offers the "Meetings in a Minute" service, so that gatherings of all sizes can be arranged through just one contact person. The Embassy Suites is proud to stand behind corporate meetings with the 100 percent satisfaction guarantee.

For conventioneers staying at the Embassy Suites, transportation via the new Metrolink light-rail system is available just two blocks from the hotel. St. Louis' first-rate municipal transportation system will then take them to the America's Center Convention Center in minutes.

There seems to be no stopping the St. Louis Embassy Suites. As the rapidly growing tourist and casino trade creates an even greater demand for first-class accommodations in downtown St. Louis, the hotel is perfectly positioned to fill the bill. In an era of generic lodging establishments with lackluster service and amenities, guests are welcoming the refreshing charm of the Embassy Suites on historic Laclede's Landing.

Guests can enjoy great food and entertainment in the hotel's Dirtwater Fox Cafe, which takes its name from a colorful folk legend about a traveling New Orleans minstrel.

BJC HEALTH SYSTEM WAS ESTABLISHED JUNE 1, 1993, TO STRENGTHEN the delivery and better contain the cost of health care services throughout the greater St. Louis region. The move combined the strengths of three of St. Louis' most prestigious health care institutions—Barnes Hospital, The Jewish Hospital of St. Louis, and Christian Health Services (CHS). In 1994 the system was expanded to include Missouri Baptist Health System and St. Louis Children's Hospital.

CLOCKWISE FROM RIGHT: BJC'S SERVICES INCLUDE LEADING-EDGE SURGICAL PROCEDURES.

THE SYSTEM ALSO OFFERS NEONATAL AND PEDIATRIC CARE FOR CHILDREN WITH SPECIAL NEEDS.

IN ADDITION TO NATIONALLY ACCLAIMED PRIMARY AND SPECIALTY CARE, BJC FOCUSES ON WELLNESS, PREVENTION, AND HEALTH EDUCATION.

BJC is the first health care system in the nation to combine a regional network of community hospitals with an academic medical center affiliated with a leading national medical school—Washington University School of Medicine. As the region's only truly integrated health care system, BJC provides a full continuum of care ranging from prenatal and infant services to senior care. This spectrum of services includes acute, long-term, outpatient, and urgent care; and occupational, corporate, and home health services. BJC also provides an array of health care-related services such as ambulance and air transportation; durable medical equipment services; and managed care initiatives like HMOs, PPOs, and specialty managed care services.

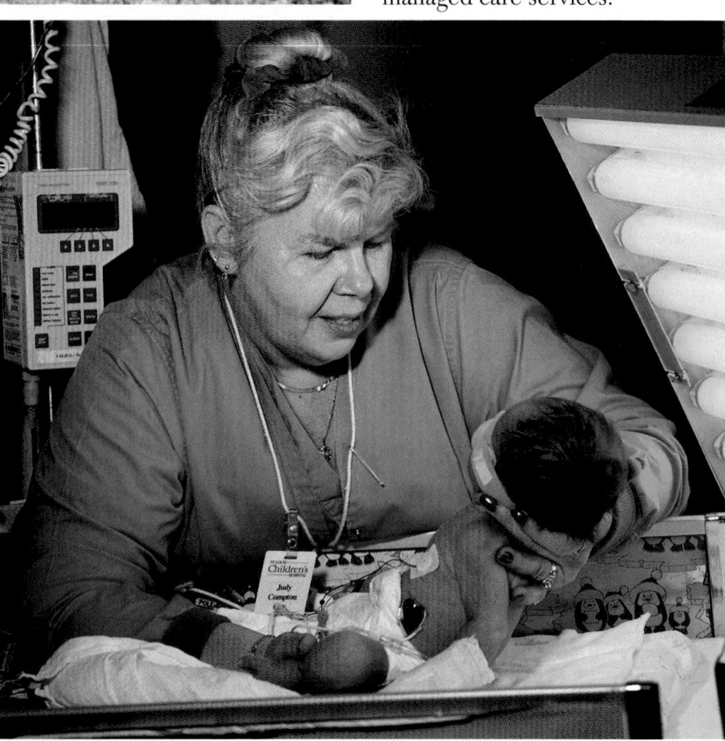

"BJC has unique strengths that will help us change the way health care is planned, delivered, measured, and financed," says Fred L. Brown, president and CEO of BJC. Those strengths are common governance, shared assets, a united management team, a single planning function, a common database, and a superior medical staff that includes private-practice physicians, as well as Washington University School of Medicine faculty.

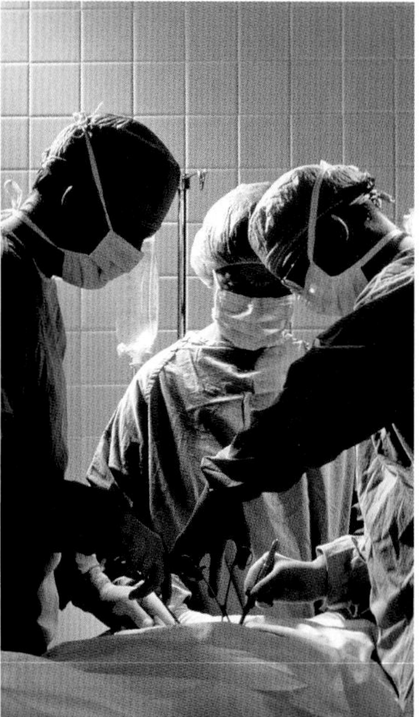

"This merger," Brown asserts, "anticipated where our nation is heading in its health care needs." Brown heads BJC's Senior Management Council, a governing body that charts strategic direction for the system. In addition to the presidents of Barnes Hospital, Jewish Hospital, Christian Hospital Northeast-Northwest, St. Louis Children's Hospital, and Missouri Baptist Medical Center, the council includes the president and senior executive officer of system affiliates, the executive vice president of finance, the executive vice president of medical affairs, and the executive vice president of administration.

By combining the capabilities of its St. Louis-based and regional members, BJC is striving to vastly improve the coordination of health care, to control costs, to increase access, and to enhance quality by matching patients' needs with the most appropriate clinical setting.

A Tradition of Quality Care

The St. Louis-based institutions of BJC have been serving the community's health care needs for more than 100 years.

Barnes Hospital opened in 1914, built through the $840,000 bequest of St. Louis businessman Robert Barnes, the owner of one of the most extensive wholesale grocery chains in the city. Starting with only 26 patients, the hospital today is a 1,208-bed nationally acclaimed hospital, which also serves as a major teaching affiliate of Washington University School of Medicine.

The hospital is recognized around the world for its expertise in organ transplants, heart surgery, diabetes services, and radiation therapies to treat cancer. In July 1994, *U.S. News & World Report* magazine again placed Barnes among "The Best of the Best"—a category that included only 15 hospitals ranked among the top 10 in at least four of the 16 specialties studied.

Barnes' St. Louis-based entities that have been integrated into BJC include two 100-bed suburban hospitals, Barnes St. Peters and Barnes West County hospitals.

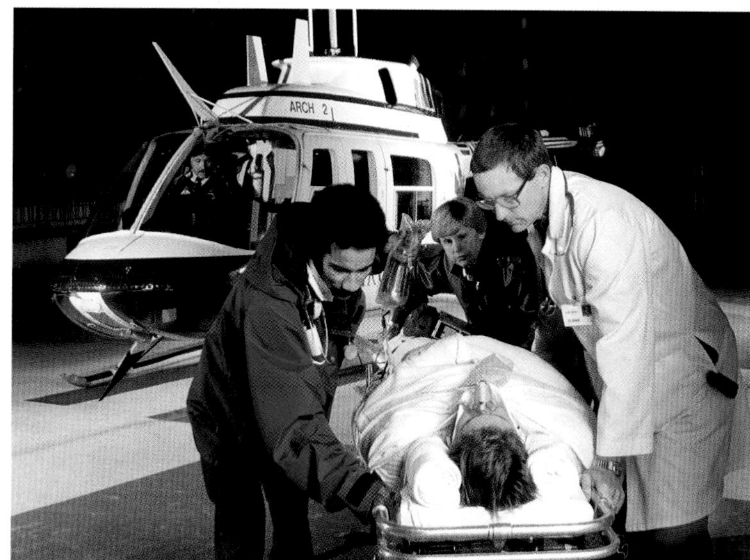

▶ JAMES VISSER

Also added were a skilled nursing facility, an occupational medicine subsidiary, and a home care services corporation.

The Jewish Hospital of St. Louis, another member of BJC, was founded in 1902 in response to the needs of Jewish immigrants and physicians who moved to the American Midwest from Europe in the 19th century. Today, Jewish Hospital is a community health care facility, as well as a 450-bed teaching hospital for Washington University School of Medicine. The affiliated Jewish Hospital College of Nursing and Allied Health offers quality health education programs in a hands-on setting.

One of the nation's leading medical research centers, Jewish Hospital is among the top 10 hospital recipients annually of funding from the National Institutes of Health. Researchers at Jewish Hospital routinely publish articles in such areas as normal and abnormal cell development, bone resorption, and chronic renal disease. The Program on Connective Tissue Disorders, one of six such centers in the United States, is based at Jewish Hospital. And the strong community support that led to the birth of Jewish Hospital still energizes the institution. Jewish and Barnes hospitals are featured individually in the recently published book *The Best Hospitals in America*.

Christian Health Services traces its beginnings to the original Christian Hospital founded in 1903 by the Christian Women's Benevolent Association. CHS brought to BJC a regional identity in Missouri and southern Illinois—with eight hospitals, five long-term care facilities, a retirement community, and diversified health service enterprises. Anchored by Christian Hospital Northeast-Northwest in St. Louis and Alton Memorial Hospital on the Illinois side of the river, Christian Health Services has garnered a reputation not only for high-quality clinical services but also for management skill and business acumen. Christian Hospital Northeast-Northwest is noted for excellence in cardiothoracic surgery, oncology, emergency medicine, neurosurgery, women's services, and its Center for Mental Health.

Missouri Baptist Medical Center was founded in 1884 when Dr. William Mayfield opened his St. Louis residence for the care of the sick. Known at that time as the Missouri Baptist Sanitarium, the facility housed and treated many of the area's ill until the need outgrew the facility. Mayfield approached the Baptist community, which helped him raise funds to purchase a large mansion at Taylor and Bell avenues. Missouri Baptist remained at that site until 1965 when it opened the doors of a new medical center on 55 acres in west St. Louis County. Today, the center is most noted for its centers of excellence that focus on cardiology, oncology, and orthopedics, and is recognized as a major regional provider of health care

Clockwise from below:
Research to combat disease and improve community health is another BJC priority.

President and CEO Fred L. Brown (left) and Chairman of the Board Charles F. Knight help chart BJC's strategic direction.

When a quick response is critical, BJC has the resources to bring help fast.

▶ ROBERT C. MORRISON

◄ JAMES VISSER

through its network of nearly 60 rural specialty care clinics in Missouri and southern Illinois. Missouri Baptist also is at the core of the Missouri Emergency Heart Network, which provides lifesaving services to rural facilities in the event of cardiac emergencies.

St. Louis Children's Hospital was founded by eight pioneering women in 1879 in a small private home in downtown St. Louis. The hospital became affiliated with Washington University School of Medicine in 1910 and has grown into one of the top 10 pediatric health care institutions in the United States. It is a recognized leader in the treatment of childhood cancer, cystic fibrosis, growth disorders, sickle cell disease, premature birth, renal disease, epilepsy, asthma, and craniofacial deformities.

The hospital is also a leader in pediatric organ transplantation. Doctors at St. Louis Children's Hospital performed the heart transplant on the youngest Missourian to successfully undergo the procedure, and replaced the liver of one of the world's youngest liver transplant patients. The hospital was also the site of the first successful pediatric cochlear implant in the region, and is home to the first designated pediatric lung transplant program in the United States. In the 1950s, the governance of the hospital changed

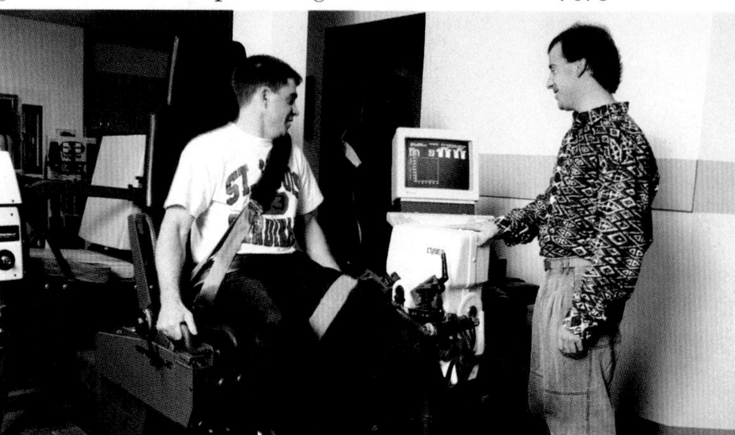

from a board of managers to a board of trustees, which remains in place today. The hospital's auxiliary, founded in 1954, and community supporters raise more than $6 million and contribute more than 71,000 hours of service annually to assist the institution in achieving its mission.

Building on the traditions of excellence of its members, BJC Health System has become the second-largest employer in St. Louis. The system now includes 5,127 licensed beds, 6,244 medical staff members, 24,975 full- and

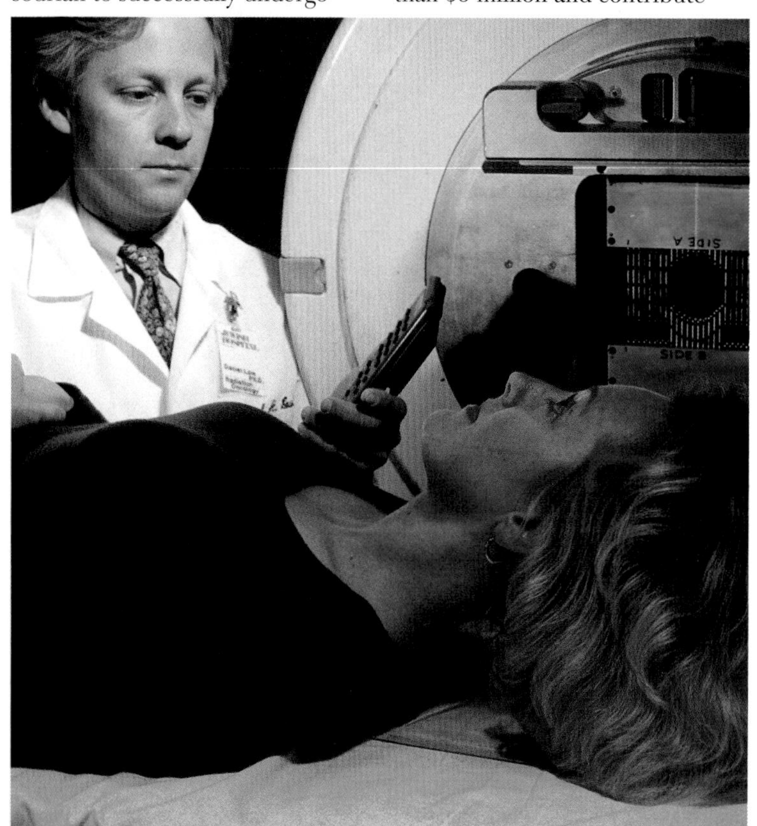

part-time employees, and 10,592 auxiliary members and volunteers.

CLOCKWISE FROM ABOVE: PHYSICIANS WITH THE TRAINING AND COMPASSION TO EXCEL IN THEIR FIELDS ARE PART OF THE BJC TEAM.

ALLIED HEALTH PROFESSIONALS ASSIST PEOPLE OF ALL AGES IN GETTING BACK IN ACTION OR RETURNING TO WORK.

A COMMITMENT TO IMPROVING COMMUNITY HEALTH IS REFLECTED IN THE SMILE OF ONE OF 10,000-PLUS VOLUNTEERS WHO GIVE THE GIFT OF TIME TO BJC.

THIS ATMOSPHERE OF COMPASSION AND CARING IS BOLSTERED BY THE LATEST IN MEDICAL TECHNOLOGY.

Renowned Expertise, Competitive Costs

The system's primary goal is to maintain the highest level of quality while controlling the cost of health care in Missouri and southern Illinois. To meet that challenge, more than 20 performance improvement teams working throughout BJC are charged with reducing the cost of care without compromising quality. The organization, for example, is containing costs by sharing equipment and reducing administrative expenses. By consolidating lab testing, BJC expects to save $200,000 to $400,000 per year in outside lab fees. Likewise, a streamlined purchasing and distribution process, known as just-in-time, is helping significantly reduce the costs of storing, sorting, and distributing supplies. Thanks to these and other streamlining processes in place throughout the system, BJC had already identified more than $25 million in savings systemwide by the end of its first year as a system.

In another effort to collaborate with community partners, BJC merged the nursing programs of Barnes Nursing College and the University of Missouri, St. Louis—thus creating the largest nursing school at a public university in Missouri. The new college, which opened in the fall of 1994, enables students to pursue advanced nursing degrees and get clinical practice at the diverse facilities throughout the BJC system.

Another benefit of the BJC system is managed care contracts that respond to the needs of area employers and other payers. For example, BJC has signed a contract to provide physical exams, wellness programs, accident prevention, and other such health care services for the St. Louis Police Department. "These benefits and many more mean better lifelong health care at competitive costs for the people of the metropolitan St. Louis area," says Charles F. Knight, chairman and CEO of Emerson Electric Company and chairman of BJC's 21-member board of directors. Knight predicts that BJC Health System will continue to look at potential partners who share its mission, as well as continue to transcend traditional hospital care—going out into the community with a focus on preventive medicine, wellness, home health care, and senior care.

"We exist, above all, to improve the health of the people and communities we serve," adds Knight. "Our combined presence in the St. Louis area and our geographic reach in Missouri and southern Illinois position us for a significant role in a managed care configuration that is, clearly, the future of American health care."

The Edison Center dining area at St. Louis Children's Hospital offers a pleasant setting for a meal or a break.

▲ CHUCK DRESNER

BJC offers a lifetime of high-quality, cost-efficient care—starting at the beginning of life and extending to senior care that includes skilled nursing, retirement center facilities, and a seniors membership program.

Regal Riverfront Hotel

A 25-YEAR-OLD ST. LOUIS LANDMARK IS HAVING THE TIME OF ITS life. Although a newcomer by name, the Regal Riverfront Hotel is a familiar silhouette on the St. Louis skyline: the pillar-shaped luxury hotel was completed in 1969 and changed hands twice before its 1991 acquisition by Regal Hotels International. The new owners gave the hotel a head-to-toe, $15 million renovation that included upgrading all of the guest rooms and transforming the Grand Lobby into a three-level atrium with a panoramic view of St. Louis' signature attraction, the Gateway Arch. Even the exterior was refurbished to complement the nearby landmarks and office buildings. The new and improved hotel opened its doors to its first guests in 1993.

The Place to Stay for Leisure and Business

Guests at the Regal Riverfront Hotel can relax right in the heart of downtown St. Louis. From the hotel, guests are treated to views of the riverboats and barges on the mighty Mississippi and, when they step out of the door, are minutes away from the Cervantes Convention Center at America's Center, Busch Stadium, Forest Park, and shopping at St. Louis Centre.

But many guests don't want to leave the comfort and style of the Regal Riverfront Hotel. Among the 800 plush guest rooms, there are accommodations to suit everyone—from families to business travelers to heads of state. Ten of the rooms are spacious VIP suites, three are executive suites, and 15 are luxurious hospitality suites. Guests can relax beside an indoor or outdoor swimming pool, or enjoy meals at one of a number of hotel restaurants. The Park Cafe and the Fourth Street Grill, for example, serve colorful, casual meals. Martini's Lounge in the Grand Lobby offers beverages and sophisticated piano music, while The Dugout bar caters to the sports-loving crowd.

And a favorite of guests and St. Louisans alike is the elegant Top of the Riverfront, a revolving restaurant that offers breathtaking views of the Mississippi River from atop the hotel. The Top of the Riverfront features innovative American cuisine in a romantic setting and is open for evening dining and Sunday brunch, serving exquisite meals complemented by panoramic views of the entire St. Louis metropolitan area.

As the local business community continues to bring guests to town, the Regal Riverfront Hotel offers a variety of amenities to

make their stays as productive as possible. Top-notch service has made the hotel a popular convention host, and the Regal Riverfront's twin tower structure allows for separate housing of large groups. Meeting and banquet facilities are tailored to the needs of each group. And with 63,000 square feet of meeting space on a single level, the largest hotel ballroom in Missouri, and a 15,000-square-foot exhibit hall, the Regal Riverfront is hard to beat.

To ensure the continuation of the hotel's high level of service, management at the Regal Riverfront strives to motivate employees through a number of recognition and awards programs. Employees are trained in the company's philosophy that every person deserves special treatment, whether guest or fellow employee. The hotel truly lives up to its slogan: "The Regal treatment is reserved. For everybody!"

Having a Regal Day

The future promises even more success for the Regal Riverfront Hotel. Its parent company, Regal International Holdings Limited, is a formidable competitor in the international lodging market and was responsible for the design and construction of several outstanding hotels in Hong Kong—the Regal Kowloon, the Regal Airport, the Regal Riverside, and the Regal Hongkong. In the 1990s, the Regal Hotel Group launched an expansion program in North America and opened new properties as far north as Anchorage and Toronto and as far south as Scottsdale and Nashville.

Regal's U.S. management subsidiary, Richfield Hospitality Services, Inc., is committed to building a quality U.S. operation, says Executive Vice President Paul Sistare. "Regal is accomplishing that not only by buying promising properties, but by offering top-notch service at each hotel."

In addition to the strength of its ownership and management, the Regal Riverfront's location bodes well for the future. St. Louis, the "Gateway to the West," is becoming an increasingly popular vacation destination and convention host that is reasonably priced and easily accessible by air and highway.

According to Director of Marketing Janice Drewry, both leisure and convention travelers have made the hotel what it is today. "And as the word continues to get out," she says, "and our name recognition grows, so will our sales figures." Already boasting an impressive occupancy increase of 12 percent, the hotel shows no signs of stopping. Friendliness and flexibility seem to be a successful formula, and the Regal Riverfront Hotel is sticking with it.

Despite the hotel's convenient location near downtown attractions, many guests don't want to leave the comfort and style of the Regal Riverfront (left).

The hotel's $15 million renovation included transforming the Grand Lobby into a three-level atrium with a panoramic view of St. Louis' signature attraction, the Gateway Arch.

St. Louis Health Care Network SM

IN 1994 SIX MEMBERS OF THE SSM HEALTH CARE SYSTEM JOINED WITH DePaul Health Center and Saint Louis University Health Sciences Center to form the Saint Louis Health Care Network,SM an integrated delivery network dedicated to improving the health of people in the St. Louis metropolitan region and surrounding Missouri and Illinois communities. ■ "By joining our organizations in one comprehensive health care delivery network, we are able to offer a full range of health care services to better serve our communities. Our collaboration also enables us to broaden geographic access to health care, eliminate duplication of services, and reduce costs, thereby making quality health care affordable and convenient," explains Stephanie McCutcheon, the network's president and CEO.

The network consists of three organizations: a physicians' organization, which aligns with physicians to develop physician integration strategies and establish guidelines for patient care management; a managed care organization that forges relationships with employers and insurance companies for managed care; and an organization that manages the network's hospitals and resources.

It is the physician leadership component that truly sets the network apart. "Physicians have played a key role in the design and management of the St. Louis Health Care NetworkSM from its inception," says Daniel J. Murphy, M.D., president and CEO of the network's physicians' organization. "Physicians are essential to the process since they are closest to the community. Because they care for people every day, they are best able to act as a patient advocate in every aspect of health care."

"This unique cooperative relationship means that the participating physicians and health centers are working together with patients, employers, third-party payers, and others to refine quality health care delivery, to provide comprehensive health care benefits, and to contain rising costs," says Kevin F. Kast, president and CEO of the network's managed care organization.

The network is geographically broad and community-based, blanketing the St. Louis area with 2,242 licensed hospital beds, 9,100 employees, and a network of more than 1,200 primary care and specialty physicians. The network's goals are to provide quality, accessible, and affordable health care; promote wellness and preventive medicine; consolidate programs for economic and programmatic strength; and establish collabora-

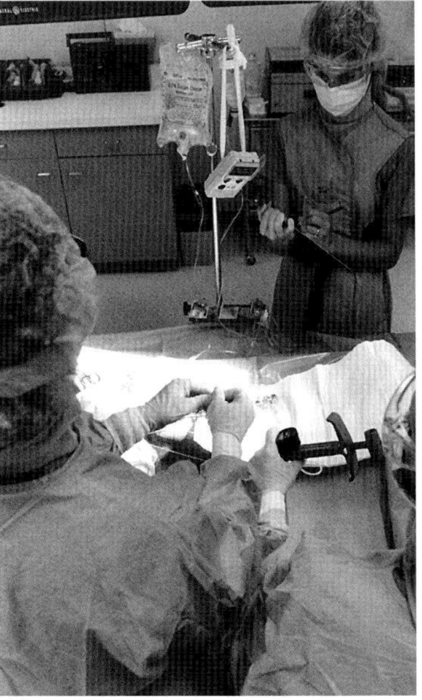

CLOCKWISE FROM TOP RIGHT:
ST. JOSEPH HEALTH CENTER, LOCATED IN THE HEART OF ST. CHARLES, IS THE MOST COMPREHENSIVE HEALTH CARE PROVIDER FOR ST. CHARLES, LINCOLN, WARREN, AND PIKE COUNTIES IN EAST CENTRAL MISSOURI.

SAINT LOUIS UNIVERSITY HEALTH SCIENCES CENTER IN MIDTOWN ST. LOUIS IS A WORLD-RENOWNED LEADER IN HEALTH SCIENCES EDUCATION, RESEARCH, AND SPECIALIZED TERTIARY/QUATERNARY CARE.

CARDINAL GLENNON CHILDREN'S HOSPITAL SERVES MORE THAN 170,000 CHILDREN AND THEIR FAMILIES FROM THROUGHOUT MISSOURI AND SOUTHERN ILLINOIS EVERY YEAR THROUGH INPATIENT AND AMBULATORY CARE PROGRAMS.

▼ LANDER-GOLDBERG

tive relationships with managed care providers.

Participants in the St. Louis Health Care Network[SM] include DePaul Health Center, serving the north county area; St. Mary's Health Center, serving midtown St. Louis; St. Joseph Hospital of Kirkwood, serving south and southwest St. Louis County; Cardinal Glennon Children's Hospital and SSM Rehabilitation Institute, which provide specialty services to all of the St. Louis area; and St. Joseph Health Center and St. Joseph Hospital West, the leading health care providers serving St. Charles, Lincoln, Warren, and Pike counties. Saint Louis University Health Sciences Center in St. Louis, which comprises high-tech medical treatment, sophisticated research, and teaching, serves as the network's academic affiliate. In addition, regionalized programs in occupational medicine and behavioral medicine provide comprehensive services throughout St. Louis.

Sponsored by the Franciscan Sisters of Mary and based in St. Louis, the SSM Health Care System has a rich tradition of serving the community since 1872. The SSMHCS owns, operates, and manages 22 entities. including 18 acute care health centers in six states.

DePaul Health Center

DePaul Health Center was founded more than 165 years ago when four courageous Daughters of Charity journeyed to the frontier village of St. Louis and established the first hospital west of the Mississippi. Today, at DePaul, that same spirit of faith and compassion continues. The 553-bed complex, with its state-of-the-art medical technology and expert staff, complements the mission of the Daughters of Charity to respond to the physical, emotional, spiritual, and social needs of each patient.

DePaul consists of an acute care facility, St. Anne's Skilled Nursing Services, and St. Vincent's Mental Health Services. Services include a comprehensive cancer treatment center, modern cardiac care facilities, complete orthopedic surgery and rehabilitation services, ambulatory surgery and outpatient diagnostic services, and a family-oriented maternity program.

St. Mary's Health Center

As a full-service, acute care, community-based teaching hospital, St. Mary's has one of the oldest and busiest cardiology programs in the St. Louis area, offering a full range of preventive, diagnostic, and therapeutic services from bypass and valve replacement surgeries to cardiac rehabilitation.

Caring for moms and babies is a St. Mary's tradition, with more than 3,000 babies born at the health center annually. Both well-baby and neonatal intensive care nurseries are staffed around-the-clock by pediatricians from Cardinal Glennon Children's Hospital. St. Mary's is the home of the Saint Louis University School of Medicine's OB/GYN department and also is designated a high-risk treatment center equipped to handle complicated pregnancies and deliveries.

Other medical and surgical services cover everything from audiology to urology, oncology to

▲ STEPHEN R. DOLAN

St. Joseph Hospital in Kirkwood (top left) provides comprehensive medical and surgical services, including the newly opened Breast Care Center.

Daniel J. Murphy, M.D. (below, left), president and CEO of the network's physicians' organization, and Stephanie McCutcheon, the network's president and CEO.

St. Louis artist and graphic designer Faith Lippert, who was born with cerebral palsy, created this artwork (top right) in 1990 for SSM Rehabilitation Institute's 90th anniversary observance.

Caring for moms and babies is a St. Mary's Health Center tradition, with more than 3,000 babies born at the health center annually.

neurosurgery. St. Mary's is proud of its state-of-the-art emergency department and its Women's Well, a comprehensive program devoted exclusively to meeting women's health needs.

St. Joseph Health Center

St. Joseph Health Center is the most comprehensive health care provider for St. Charles, Lincoln, Warren, and Pike counties in east central Missouri. Located in the heart of St. Charles, the campus consists of the 362-bed regional medical center, a physician office building, and an outpatient diagnostic complex.

Throughout its 110-year history, St. Joseph has combined a tradition of leadership, service, and quality care with a dedication to meeting each patient's physical, emotional, and spiritual needs.

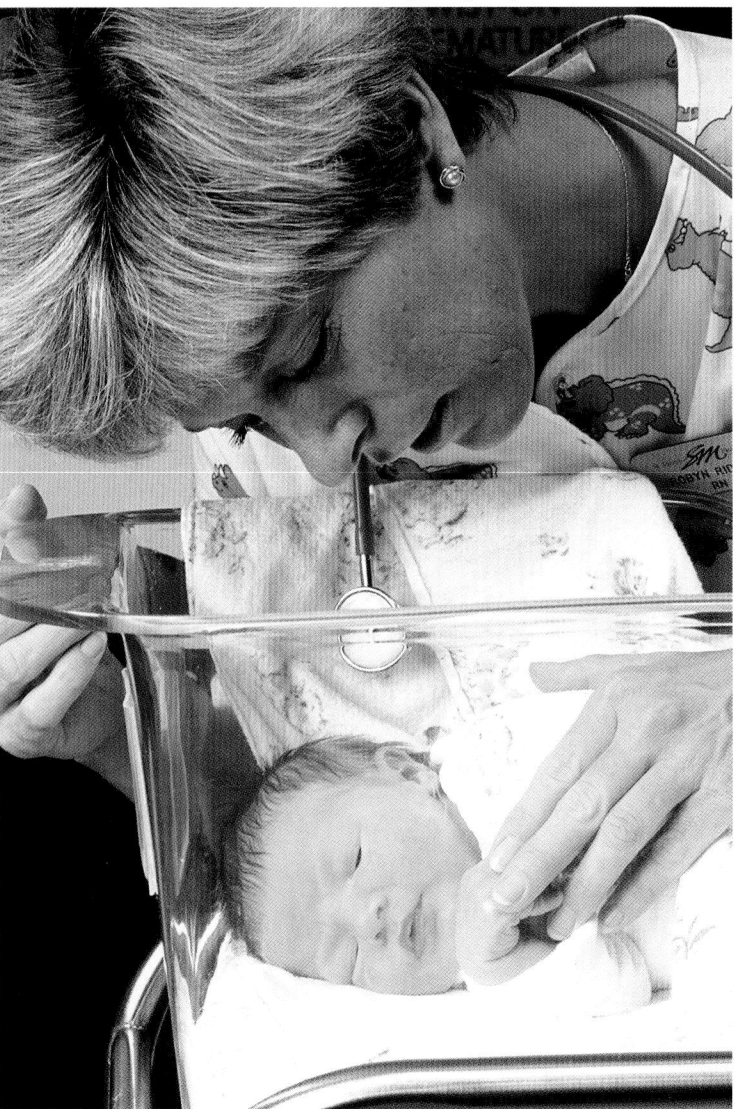

State-of-the-art services include the regional trauma center, hospice program, advanced obstetric and neonatal programs, Cardinal Glennon pediatric unit, and cardiovascular and oncology services. Specialty departments offer a full range of services in behavioral medicine, physical medicine and rehabilitation, chemical dependency, and obstetrics and neonatology.

St. Joseph Hospital West

Extending St. Joseph's healing ministry westward, this 100-bed general, acute care hospital opened in 1986. Although smaller in scope, the modern facility reflects St. Joseph's tradition of caring for the community.

Located in Lake Saint Louis, St. Joseph Hospital West offers convenience and comfort to the residents of western St. Charles, Lincoln, and Warren counties. Emergency, general surgical, and general medical services are provided at the hospital or are coordinated with St. Joseph Health Center in St. Charles.

St. Joseph Hospital

St. Joseph Hospital of Kirkwood provides comprehensive medical and surgical services to a wide area of the city of St. Louis, as well as St. Louis, Jefferson, and Franklin counties.

Sponsored by the Sisters of St. Joseph of Carondelet, the health center opened in 1954 in a 150-bed facility that was previously a federal marine hospital. It flourished with community support, and today has more than 300 beds and is part of an ongoing effort to meet the changing health care needs of its community. The hospital became a member of the SSM Health Care System in 1993.

Its facilities include a modern Emergency and Outpatient Surgery/Services Center, Imaging Center, physician office buildings, and the newly opened Breast Care Center. Comprehensive services include cardiology, physical and occupational therapy, home care, skilled nursing, and a maternity program that features mother-baby nursing.

Cardinal Glennon Children's Hospital

Cardinal Glennon Children's Hospital, a tertiary care pediatric medical facility, is a referral center for children from birth to age 18. The hospital serves more than 170,000 children and their families from throughout Missouri and southern Illinois every year through inpatient and ambulatory care programs.

Cardinal Glennon is a Level I Trauma Center, caring for more than 57,000 children each year in its emergency room. The Regional Poison Center and Pediatric Research Institute also are housed within the complex.

The hospital's extensive medical and surgical expertise includes a comprehensive pediatric organ transplant program, one of the few pediatric sleep disorders programs in the nation, and the only pediatric inpatient rehabilitation facility located within an acute care health facility in the Midwest.

Established in 1956 as a private, not-for-profit pediatric hospital, Cardinal Glennon is owned by a board of governors appointed by the Archbishop of St. Louis. It is operated by the SSM Health Care System and is a teaching hospital affiliated with the Saint Louis University Schools of Medicine and Nursing.

SSM Rehabilitation Institute

The SSM Rehabilitation Institute provides comprehensive medical rehabilitation (CMR) services throughout metropolitan St. Louis and Illinois. The institute, headquartered in Creve Coeur, is Missouri's largest freestanding provider of medical rehabilitation. The institute was founded in 1900 as Mount Saint Rose Throat and Chest Hospital in St. Louis. It currently emphasizes inpatient and outpatient services for persons recovering from a range of injuries and physical impairments.

The Rehabilitation Institute's inpatient facilities include a 60-bed CMR unit and a 20-bed skilled rehabilitation unit at St. Mary's Health Center, Richmond Heights; and a 20-bed unit at St. Joseph Health Center, St. Charles. Outpatient facilities include SSM Outpatient Rehabilitation Center, Hazelwood; and physical therapy centers in Chesterfield, Sunset Hills, and Fairview Heights, Illinois. SmartRehab, a not-for-profit division of the Institute, provides rehabilitation management and consulting services to health centers and long-term care facilities.

The Institute, accredited by the Commission on Accreditation of Rehabilitation Facilities (CARF) since 1987, provides rehabilitative medicine specialists to help patients recovering from head and spinal cord injuries, stroke, trauma, burns, amputation, orthopedic injuries, arthritis, work injury, and neurological disease achieve the highest level of independence possible. Its team of professionals, including psychologists, rehabilitation nurses, physical and occupational therapists, speech pathologists, therapeutic recreationists, social workers, and pastoral care workers, is led by board-certified physiatrists who specialize in physical medicine and rehabilitation.

Saint Louis University Health Sciences Center

Saint Louis University Health Sciences Center in midtown St. Louis is a world-renowned leader in health sciences education, research, and specialized tertiary/quaternary care.

Established from a small department of medicine created by Saint Louis University in 1836, the Health Sciences Center reflects its Jesuit heritage by fulfilling a commitment to educate tomorrow's health care professionals, conduct breakthrough research, and render compassionate care.

There are five major units: Schools of Medicine, Nursing, Allied Health, Professions, and Public Health, as well as Saint Louis University Hospital—the flagship academic regional referral center for adult patient care. With sophisticated technology, innovative teaching, and research, the schools and hospital have helped make St. Louis a preeminent medical force in America.

With ever-expanding programs and nearly 5,000 caregivers on its faculty and staff, the Health Sciences Center is a major contributor to both the economic and physical health of the St. Louis community. Patients from a large bistate region surrounding the St. Louis metropolitan area take advantage of the Health Sciences Center's high-tech diagnostic and treatment services as well as the Level I Trauma Center at Saint Louis University Hospital. From allergy to vascular surgery, from advanced imaging to one of only five vaccine centers in the United States, and from bone marrow transplantation to therapeutic technologies under investigation, the Health Sciences Center is a renowned health care leader committed to total excellence.

A St. Louis Partner

By combining the resources and clinical expertise of its member physicians and health centers, the St. Louis Health Care Network[SM] is dedicated to improving the health status of the community. The network welcomes the opportunity to partner with other physicians, health centers, and sponsors with similar values who wish to join in a shared health ministry in the St. Louis metropolitan region and surrounding Missouri and Illinois communities.

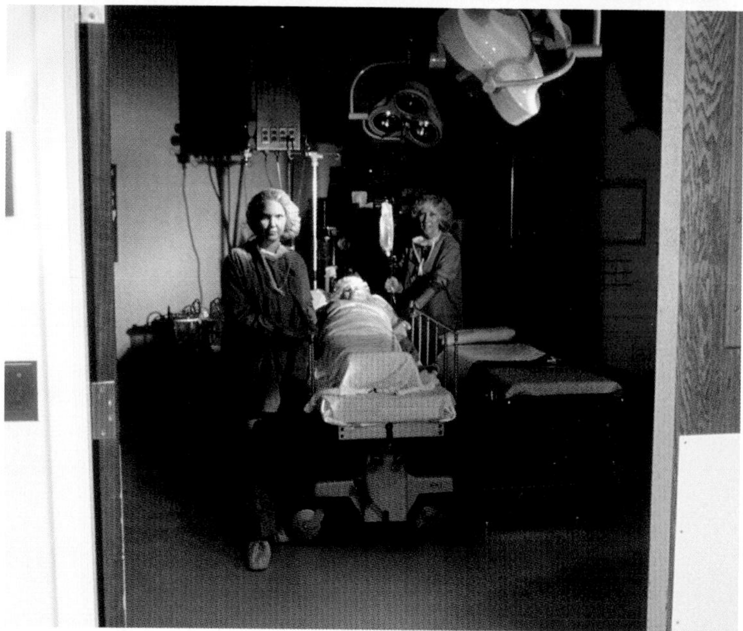

THE 553-BED DEPAUL HEALTH CENTER (TOP), WITH ITS STATE-OF-THE-ART MEDICAL TECHNOLOGY AND EXPERT STAFF, STRIVES TO RESPOND TO THE PHYSICAL, EMOTIONAL, SPIRITUAL, AND SOCIAL NEEDS OF EACH PATIENT AND TO PROMOTE COMMUNITY WELLNESS.

LOCATED IN LAKE SAINT LOUIS, ST. JOSEPH HOSPITAL WEST (BOTTOM) OFFERS EMERGENCY, GENERAL SURGICAL, AND GENERAL MEDICAL SERVICES TO RESIDENTS OF WESTERN ST. CHARLES, LINCOLN, AND WARREN COUNTIES.

HealthLine® Corporate Health Services

FROM THE GATEWAY ARCH, ONE CAN SEE SAINT LOUIS UNIVERSITY, the first higher learning institution west of the Mississippi. As part of the community since 1818, Saint Louis University traces its Catholic traditions under Jesuit patronage to 1828. The university, one of 28 Jesuit colleges and universities, is one of four Catholic medical schools in the United States. It was from here in the mid-1970s that a series of forums sponsored by the university's Health Sciences Center helped St. Louis business leaders identify their current needs and future health care concerns. As a result, the concept of health promotion and treating work-related injuries and illnesses was brought to light, leading to the birth of HealthLine® Corporate Health Services, a company offering businesses a full line of occupational health care and services.

AMONG THE SERVICES HEALTHLINE® OFFERS ARE SIX STRATEGICALLY LOCATED HEALTH CENTERS IN THE ST. LOUIS AREA (ABOVE).

HealthLine,® formed in 1983, is a not-for-profit corporation and is a wholly owned subsidiary of Saint Louis University. As a member of the Saint Louis University system, HealthLine® is strengthened by its ability to utilize specialty resources, training, and research from an education-based institution. In return, HealthLine® actively participates in the university's occupational medicine and public health programs, allowing medical students to practice medicine firsthand in an occupational health care environment. HealthLine® also supports additional health care resources through its Authorized Referral Network, which currently includes more than 1,600 physicians, 12 hospitals, 72 multispecialty service locations, and 32 rehabilitation sites.

HEALTHLINE® IS A WHOLLY OWNED SUBSIDIARY OF SAINT LOUIS UNIVERSITY (TOP RIGHT AND BELOW), WHICH TRACES ITS CATHOLIC TRADITIONS UNDER JESUIT PATRONAGE TO 1828.

Homer H. Schmitz, Ph.D., executive director of HealthLine,® oversees the responsibilities of 154 full-time employees servicing client needs in Missouri and southern Illinois. Providing all aspects of health care, qualified HealthLine® personnel aggressively, yet safely take measures to ensure quality occupational health care for approximately 2,400 corporate clients who employ nearly 300,000 workers. A variety of health care services are offered, ranging from substance abuse testing, to supplying and staffing six strategically located health centers in the St. Louis area, to 24-hour emergency care at the university hospital, to furnishing full-service on-site medical units for major national corporations.

Expanding Services

The initial thrust of HealthLine® was to promote health awareness and offer disease prevention services to local and national businesses. Today, HealthLine® offers a comprehensive line of occupational health care services, standing by its philosophy that work-related injuries are potentially preventable. By identifying and correcting the causes of injuries, employer and employee are both well served, resulting in cost-effective solutions.

As a vital partner in the welfare of the greater St. Louis community, HealthLine® offers informa-

tional programs to clients to educate employers on a variety of subjects concerning employee safety, current industry trends, and product services. HealthLine® also sponsors client- and community-based health fairs and other related events. Larger-scale activities are also significant in responding to the needs of the community. During the Great Flood of 1993, for example, HealthLine® provided emergency aid by supplying hepatitis A, immunoglobulin, and tetanus immunizations.

"As the work environment, technology, and industry become more complex and as government regulations on health care requirements and safety standards continue to change, the demand for a more sophisticated means of approaching and solving health care problems for workers will grow," says Director of Client Services Paul Shatusky. "The future of the health care industry is to provide for workers and their families at one place, for one fee. Provider networks like HealthLine® will supply all needed health care services as a single provider entity."

U.S. Title Guaranty Company, Inc.

DRIVE AND DETERMINATION COUPLED WITH A STRONG SENSE OF COMMUNITY responsibility and employee responsiveness typify the Midwestern work ethic, and no company exemplifies that better than U.S. Title Guaranty Company, Inc. Established in 1993 by CEO David M. Dolan, the company's market share doubled during its first 18 months of business, making it the third-ranked title company in the St. Louis area, with its sights firmly fixed on the number one spot.

The Clayton-based firm, underwritten by Stewart Title Guaranty Company, attributes its phenomenal success to a strong sense of integrity in fulfilling clients' needs promptly and accurately. Thirty-eight years of practicing real estate law convinced Dolan that diligence in providing accurate service is the cornerstone of a successful business. "David Dolan's philosophy is to get it done right, and on time," says Wendy Warden, vice president of marketing. It is this responsiveness to individual needs and the firm's reliability in executing its business faithfully that have earned U.S. Title a large, loyal customer base in both the residential and commercial closing markets in a short period of time.

Industry Responsiveness

Recognizing industry needs and acting on them is another key to the company's success. "If there's a better way, we'll implement it," says Warden. The company's Home Buyer's Hotline, the first of its kind in the title industry, allows potential buyers to receive immediate rate quotes or simply ask questions regarding title insurance. The firm's U.S. Express service, designed for the home equity and refinance market, has the ability to issue mortgagee commitments of title insurance in just 24 to 48 hours.

U.S. Title also employs state-of-the-art technology in serving both its residential and commercial clients. All of the company's 15 offices are electronically linked so that closings can be accessed and completed at any location. All 92 employees have been cross-trained as well, to increase efficiency and diminish delays. President W. Stewart Kenney's 42 years in the local title business, in addition to the average staff manager's 15 years in the industry, offer a wealth of experience and expertise for the client.

Employee Responsiveness

U.S. Title also has discovered that being responsive to its employees and creating a work environment in which staff members are committed to furthering the company goals engender a more productive work environment. "We constantly solicit employees' ideas for improved customer service in an attempt to make every staff member a company innovator," says Nathaniel S. Walsh, executive vice president and general counsel.

"We promote flexible work schedules for our staff in which their needs are of great importance to us," adds Warden. The firm's positively charged atmosphere and the can-do attitudes of its staff have helped foster the record sales growth the company has attained.

U.S. Title's commitment to community involvement underscores the firm's belief in giving back to the community that has made its success possible. As legal counsel to the St. Louis Board of Realtors; as a strong supporter of the Women's Council of Realtors, the Real Estate League, and the Home Builder's Association; and through its philanthropic efforts on behalf of the Kiwanis Club, the Muscular Dystrophy Association, Easter Seals, and Junior Achievement, U.S. Title exemplifies the best St. Louis has to offer in business and community involvement.

Based in Clayton since its founding in 1993, U.S. Title attributes its phenomenal success to a strong sense of integrity in fulfilling clients' needs promptly and accurately. Pictured are (from left) W. Stewart Kenney, president; Wendy R. Warden, vice president of marketing; David M. Dolan, CEO; and Nathaniel S. Walsh, executive vice president and general counsel.

Photographers

Douglas Abel worked as a registered architect for 12 years while pursuing photography from both a creative and an architectural point of view. Today, he is self-employed as the owner of Douglas Abel Photography, specializing in architectural photography. Abel's photographs have been published in *Architecture* magazine and have appeared in architectural marketing materials and catalogs. A graduate of the University of Kansas, where he received bachelor's degrees in environmental design and architecture, Abel is a lifelong St. Louis resident.

Leon D. Algee, Jr., is a freelance photojournalist who has done work for the Associated Press, *Suburban Journal*, *Post-Dispatch*, *USA Today*, *Chicago Tribune*, and Kansas City *Star* newspapers, as well as for Saint Louis University and Webster University. He enjoys news feature and sports photography. Algee is also active in volunteer and community service work, particularly with the Mathews-Dickey Boys Club. He is a St. Louis native and a graduate of Webster University, where he received a bachelor's degree in media studies.

David Altman, a St. Louis native, is a freelance photographer and owner of David Altman Photography. His areas of specialty include commercial photography and portraiture. Altman has earned degrees from Webster University in media studies and from the University of Tennessee in art and architecture. His clients include Maritz Travel Catalog and McCarthy Construction. Altman has won awards from the St. Louis Artists' Guild, Art St. Louis, and the *Post-Dispatch*. He enjoys photographing nature, forgotten buildings and places, and outdoor portraits of children.

Joan Baker, a photographer for B D Sports Photography and a paralegal for Lewis, Rice & Fingersh, is a member of the St. Louis Camera Club. She is a lifelong resident of Madison County, Illinois, and graduated from Southern Illinois University at Edwardsville, where she received a bachelor of science degree. Baker has won several photography contests, and one of her photos was accepted for the cover of the *Journal of the Missouri Bar*. Her favorite photography subjects are the eagles that winter in the Alton, Illinois, area.

Robert Bishop, president of Bishop Photography, Inc., specializes in commercial photography and portraiture. He has photographed most of the Fortune 500 CEOs or presidents in the St. Louis area and has been commissioned to photograph executives for General Dynamics, McDonnell Douglas, the May Company, A.G. Edwards, Mark Twain Banks, Interco, and TWA. Bishop's work has been published in the *Post-Dispatch*, as well as *Time*, *Newsweek*, *Sports Illustrated*, *Business Week*, and *Fortune* magazines. He was a founding member of the American Society of Media Photographers, serving as president for four years, and he started the award-winning newsletter *Focus*. Bishop is a graduate of Washington University.

Phil Brammer works as a service representative for Southwestern Bell and is a freelance photographer specializing in motivational slide shows. Brammer has done work for clients including Southwestern Bell and Maryville University. He has won photography awards from the St. Louis Camera Club and the St. Louis Artists' Guild. A native of Duluth, Minnesota, Brammer moved to the St. Louis area in 1963. He enjoys nature photography, phototravel, holiday events, weddings, and architectural photography.

Jan Broderick specializes in modernist photography and currently works for A.G. Edwards. In addition to her work with the St. Louis Art Museum and National Park Service, she produced and directed "Charles M. Russell: American Artist," a film that won the C.I.N.E. Golden Eagle Award. She has served as vice chairman of the St. Louis County Air Show Committee and the V.P. Fair (Fair Saint Louis) photography committee, and as chairman for the St. Louis First Night celebration. Broderick is a graduate of the University of Missouri-St. Louis, where she received a bachelor's degree in art history and a master's degree in American history.

Lorette Burke is the owner of Lorette Burke Freelance Photography. She is a member of the Photographic Society of America, the St. Louis Camera Club, and the Collinsville Area Camera Club. Burke has traveled to more than 100 countries on all seven continents, selling her photographs through various photo stock companies.

Elizabeth M. Crosby, a native of East Longmeadow, Massachusetts, has been a photographer since the age of 12. She specializes in portraiture, travel, and scenic photography. Crosby's photographs have been published in *America the Beautiful*, *Colorful Missouri*, and *Images of St. Louis*. She and her husband have traveled extensively around the world where she has photographed many remote and exotic areas.

Travis A. Curd II settled in the St. Louis area in 1962 after spending years in a variety of states traveling with his family and father, who was in the U.S. Marine Corps.

Ray Davis, owner of Ray Davis Photography, rediscovered photography in his fifties after expressing an interest in the field as a young man. The second time around, Davis left his 30-year career in insurance/risk management and pursued photography with a "spiritual fervor." As a professional photographer, Davis specializes in environmental and home portraits, and wedding photography. Originally from New Bedford, Massachusetts, he moved to St. Louis in 1971. As a member of the St. Louis Camera Club, Davis has been a winner in the color, nature, and photojournalism slide competitions.

Walter Deptula, a Chicago native, has photographed on a freelance basis since 1988. His photographs have been published in *Chicago: Second to None*, *Des Moines Visions*, and *Wichita: Visions from the Heartland*. Deptula now copublishes the *Chicago Scenes and Events* calendar with photographer Jeff Voelz.

Patricia Donovan is a native of St. Louis and owner of Pat Donovan Photography, where she specializes in photographing people. Donovan's work was published in *Images of St. Louis*, as well as in numerous brochures, promotional materials, newsletters, and newspapers. Her photography is exhibited locally at the Center for Photography.

Cathy Ferris is a photographer from St. Louis.

Sue Ford is the owner of Sue Ford Photography. She received a degree in photography and film production from Southern Illinois University-Carbondale. Ford's specialties are landscapes and still life photography. She is developing an increasing interest in sports photography, following her participation in a *Sports Illustrated* workshop held in St. Louis during the U.S. Olympic Festival. Her photographs have been published in *Photographers Forum* and *International Photographer*. Ford was awarded the 1992 Merit Award in the Olympus International Photo Contest.

Patti Gabriel, a native of St. Louis, is a graduate of the University of Missouri, Columbia. As the owner of Patti Gabriel Photography, she specializes in portraiture, environmental studies, and the use of alternative processes with photographs. Gabriel's clients have included Monsanto, the May Company, St. John's Mercy Medical Center, Cardinal Glennon Children's Hospital, John Deere, and Mosby Publishing.

Casey Galvin is employed by MEMC Electronics Material Inc. Galvin's photography has been published in the *Nikon World* magazine, the Nikon World Calendar 1995, and *Photographers' Forum* "Best of Photography 1993." Originally from Des Moines, Iowa, Galvin has been a St. Louis resident since 1963.

Shellee Graham is a graphic designer with Pagoda, a footwear importer for Brown Group. Since 1990 she has been getting her kicks documenting and exhibiting photographs of the famous Route 66, a photographic journey mirrored by a literal one in March of 1991, when Graham drove the highway more than 2,000 miles from Chicago to Los Angeles. Her work has appeared in *A Century on Wheels: Celebrating 100 Years of the Automobile in America*, *Mobilia Magazine*, *Old Cars Weekly*, *Mother Road Journal*, and *Slow Lane Journal*. Her solo exhibit, "Return to Route 66: Photographs from the Mother Road," has toured museums across the country. Graham has won the Art Honors Award from Art St. Louis, as well as awards from the Quincy Art Center, Red Mesa Art Center, and Atlanta College of Art.

Lee Harris, originally from Little Rock, Arkansas, owns Harris Graphic Design, where his clients include Datamax Office Systems, Fleishman Hillard, Missouri Historical Society, Price Waterhouse, and the St. Louis Convention and Visitors Commission. Harris' photographs have appeared in the *Post-Dispatch*, *Suburban Journal Newspaper*, *Passenger Transport Magazine*, *Railway Age Magazine*, *St. Louis American*, and *Discovering African-American St. Louis*. Harris has studied photography and design at Washington University, Webster University, and the University of Missouri-St. Louis.

David Hinkson specializes in air show photography. He is currently the chairman of photography of the Saint Louis County Fair and Air Show and has held that post for the St. Louis V.P. Fair and the St. Louis Blues and Heritage Festival. Hinkson, originally from Ohio, has lived in St. Louis since 1964. He earned a bachelor's degree in science from the University of Missouri-St. Louis.

Lisa Johnston, a graduate of Syracuse University, holds a bachelor of science degree in photojournalism. Johnston moved to the St. Louis area in 1994, and currently owns and operates lisa A. johnston photography, specializing in all types of photojournalism and digital imaging. Johnston has photographed a range of events from the Clinton inauguration, to the presentation of the Liberty Medal to Nelson Mandela and Frederik Willem de Klerk, to the Bosch Indy Car Grand Prix. Johnston is an active member of the St. Louis Artists' Guild, having won several awards in a number of its gallery exhibitions. She is an avid Internet surfer and is the curator of an online gallery featuring her digital imaging on the Internet's World Wide Web.

Carol Kane, a native of St. Louis, specializes in garden and landscape photography. Her favorite subject is the Shaw Arboretum, particularly the area around the serpentine wall and the cemetery dating back to Civil War times, and the original buildings and areas dating to Henry Shaw's time at the Missouri Botanical Garden. Kane's photographs have been published in *Images of St. Louis*.

Marshall Katzman, M.D., has always been interested in art, and began photographing in the early 1960s as a way of documenting his travels. Over the years, he has gotten involved in abstract color photography, shooting images of urban environments. His work has been published in *Images of St. Louis* and the *Post-Dispatch*, and is part of several collections, including the Sofitel Hotel Gallery in Lyons, France.

Ted Kiburz is a St. Louis native and an amateur photographer willing to tackle almost any subject in black-and-white or color photography. Kiburz is a retired general engineer with the Department of Defense. While his photographs have been used in an army technical manual, *St. Louis: Home on the River* is his first venture into professional photography.

Bill and Sherry Lubic operate Lubic & Lubic Photography, a stock photography company located in Defiance. They specialize in nature, wildlife, and travel images, and their work has appeared in *Living Bird*, *Pacific Discovery*, and *Wilderness*, as well as on several calendars and cards. Sherry Lubic is also a location assignment photographer, photographing everything from environmental portraits of archaeologists and zoologists to architecture and hair fashions.

Ken Luebbert, a native of St. Louis, owns and operates Photo Sensations. His areas of specialty are photo decor, special events, scenic photography, and candids. He has photographed outdoor and travel locations, and has been published in materials for the University of Missouri and in *International Photographer*. Luebbert has won awards from the St. Charles Artist Guild and the Pallotine Art Show. He enjoys photographing the Ozarks and all areas of Missouri, preferring to shoot "straight" photographic images produced via camera and darkroom without electronic image manipulation by computer.

Ray Marklin, a photographer from St. Louis, has traveled extensively for his photographs, but it was a photograph he took nearby titled "Flood Heroes" that was shown on national television by President Clinton when he signed the Flood Relief Bill. Marklin spent five months over the last two years in Eastern Europe photographing people in a variety of living conditions and situations. His other travels include a Caribbean charter boat trip during which the boat's steering broke and bad weather left the vessel perched atop a reef. A Mayday call illicited responses from about 20 local "pirates" who arrived to "rescue" Marklin and his mates. The story had a happy ending as Marklin's group was whisked from the boat by the charter company's manager who negotiated a $4,000 payment for the boat's "rescue."

Annie Marshall's photographs can be seen in *Country Woman*, *Unitarian World*, *UUA Directory*, and *Mature Years*. She has won honors in "Fathers," a local newspaper photography contest, and the black-and-white division of the St. Louis Zoo Contest. A five-time winner of the St. Louis Camera Club's "Slide of the Year" award, Marshall has exhibited in two juried shows. A Missouri native, Marshall received a bachelor's degree in education and a master's degree in English from the University of Missouri in Columbia.

Paul Marshall is a native of St. Louis whose photography subjects include landscape and children. Marshall's photographs have been published in *Images of St. Louis*, as well as in various local newspapers. Marshall has won awards in several local photography contests. He received a bachelor of arts degree in theology from Lael University and currently works for McDonnell Douglas Aerospace.

Don McLaughlin specializes in still life and landscape photography. His photographs appear in the Valcour Printing Inc. calendar and on eight postcards of St. Louis. He has won awards in the University City Photo Contest and in the *Post-Dispatch* photo contest. As the four-color pressman for Valcour Printing Inc., McLaughlin not only photographed for his company's calendar, but also ran the press that printed his photos. McLaughlin runs his own studio from his home on a part-time basis. A native of Scranton, Pennsylvania, McLaughlin moved to St. Louis in 1963.

Thomas W. Miller resides in Collinsville, Illinois. He earned his bachelor's and master's degrees from Southern Illinois University at Edwardsville, and currently works for the Illinois Environmental Protection Agency and the *Suburban Journal*. Miller specializes in landscapes, infrared photography, sports, and photojournalism. His work has been published in *Popular Photography* and *SHOTS* magazines, a St. Charles Parks and Recreation brochure, the Camp Ondessonk yearbook, the Illinois Environmental Protection Agency's *Environmental Progress* newsletter, and the Madison County Humane Society newsletter. Miller has won the Springfield Area Arts Council Award and several awards from the "On My Own Time" juried art exhibits.

Kathleen M. O'Donnell, a native of St. Louis, is the owner of Kathleen M. O'Donnell Photography, specializing in fine art photography, nature subjects, and abstracts. O'Donnell has won numerous awards from the Columbia Art League, St. Louis Artists' Guild, Greater St. Louis Artist Association, Missouri Spring Festival of the Arts, Kirkwood Historical Society Art Show, Tillis Art Show, Art World, St. Louis Camera Club, Mississippi Valley Salon of Photography, and Art St. Louis. She received her bachelor's degree from Lindenwood College in St. Charles, Missouri, and has continued her education at the College of New Rochelle in New York.

Tom Patton is a professor in the department of art and art history at the University of Missouri-St. Louis. He earned his bachelor of fine arts degree from the San Francisco Art Institute and his master of fine arts degree from the University of New Mexico. Patton has won the Visual Artist Fellowship from the National Endowment for the Arts, and his photography has been included in more than 150 museum and gallery exhibitions. His work is also in permanent collections of major museums in the United States, Japan, and Australia.

Kristen Peterson, a native of New York, has lived in St. Louis since 1964. She runs Photography by Kristen Peterson, specializing in the photography of people. Peterson's work has appeared in *Better Homes and Gardens*, *Esquire*, *Newsweek*, *Omni*, *People*, *Time*, *Art Today*, *Town & Country*, and *U.S. News & World Report* magazines, and books including *Images of St. Louis* and *Encyclopaedia Britannica*. Peterson has an extensive list of clients, including AT&T, Dillard's, Neiman-Marcus, St. Louis Art Museum, and Yves St. Laurent. She also has photographs exhibited at Washington University, the Dietrich Stone Gallery, and the National Museum of Women in the Arts. Peterson has won 70 awards in photography and journalism and was included in the 1991 edition of *Who's Who in Photography*. Peterson graduated from Hamline University in St. Paul, Minnesota, with a bachelor's degree in art and photography.

Lewis Portnoy, a native of St. Louis, has photographed practically every major sporting event in North America for his clients, including NBC Sports, Anheuser-Busch, and the Los Angeles Olympic Organizing Committee. His photographs have been published in *Life*, *Time*, *Newsweek*, *Popular Photography*, *Sports Illustrated*, and *Sporting News*. His work is included in a permanent exhibition at the International Museum of Photography. Lewis is the photographer of four books—*Saga of the St. Louis Blues*, *Stealing Is My Game*, *On Down the Road*, and *Horse Camping*.

David W. Preston, a location photographer and owner of David W. Preston Photography, has photographed in more than 100 cities and has more than 50 magazine covers to his credit. His client list includes Anheuser-Busch, Xerox, the U.S. Olympic Festival '94, and *Big Eight/Big Ten* magazine.

Brent Reed specializes in portraiture, industrial/advertising, and studio still life photography. Originally from Ontario, Canada, he moved to St. Louis in 1988. Reed graduated from McMaster University in Ontario with a degree in chemical engineering and is employed by Petrolite Corporation, for which he photographs a variety of corporate assignments. Reed enjoys nature, wildlife, and travel photography, and is a music enthusiast in his free time.

Cindy Rhoades, a lifelong St. Louis resident, is a graduate of Webster University. She is employed by Color Associates Creative Imaging Group, where she specializes in photo-realism and mixed-media. Rhoades has been published three times in *Photographer's Forum*, where she received two honorable mentions. She also enjoys international travel.

Sheri Saunier, a native of St. Louis, works for W. Schillers & Company. She received a bachelor's degree in fine arts from Webster University, and studied at the university's Vienna campus. Her clients include Southwestern Bell and Mercantile Bank. She has been a participant in the annual juried show at Webster University and has had two pieces accepted in the St. Louis Artists' Guild photography competition.

Alan Schlesinger, a native of New Hampshire, moved to St. Louis in 1993. He earned a bachelor's degree from UCLA and attended Yale University School of Medicine. Currently, Schlesinger works as a pediatric radiologist at St. Louis Children's Hospital. Schlesinger has won numerous awards from the Photographic Guild of Detroit and the St. Louis Camera Club, and enjoys photographing his children. He also enjoys landscape and travel photography.

Larry Sherron is the owner of Larry Sherron Photography, Inc. A native of Tampa, Florida, Sherron has lived in St. Louis since 1970. He attended St. Louis Community College, the University of South Florida, and St. Petersburg Junior College. Sherron specializes in general commercial photography, and his clients include Price Waterhouse, Arthur Andersen, Bryan Cave, Thompson Mitchell, MCI, Nordyne, Missouri Historical Society, Laclede Steel, Boatmen's Trust Co., and Federal Reserve Bank.

Jim Sokolik specializes in location photography, using his many travels around the world as subjects for his work. He enjoys photographing nature and architecture. Sokolik is a native of St. Louis. His work has appeared in

Gallery at Left Bank Books, Locus Gallery, Art St. Louis, St. Louis Artists' Guild, Mark Twain Bank Gallery, Componere Gallery, Nevertheless Press, Atrium Gallery, and St. Louis Artists Today. His clients include AT&T, Ralston Purina, Barnes Hospital, Smith Kline Labs, Ozarks Federal Savings & Loan, and Tockman & Wock Law Firm. Sokolik received a second-place award from *Sierra* magazine in the "color photo abstracts in nature" category and has been published in *Images of St. Louis*; in the St. Louis calendar "A Personal View of St. Louis Landmarks"; and in *Colorful Missouri*, a color photo book of Missouri.

Ernst Stadler, a native of Germany, is a freelance photographer who has written extensively on American history, especially on the American West. While still residing in Germany, Stadler worked in the newsroom of Radio Free Europe in Munich. Stadler wrote an article for the *Bulletin* of the Missouri Historical Society on Karl May, a German writer whose 40 books on the American West shaped the way Europeans viewed America, although he never saw the United States until two years before his death. Stadler's photographs can be seen in *Life*, *Lens*, *Maine Invites You*, *Images of St. Louis*, *Tucson Daily Citizen* magazine, and the Anheuser-Busch calendar. Some of Stadler's favorite subjects are cemeteries, giant figures by the roadside, and anything out of the ordinary.

Wm. Stage specializes in commercial archaeology and has published the book *Ghost Signs*, a collection of his 120 color and black-and-white photographs ranging from cities such as New York to towns like Belzoni, Mississippi. Stage's photographs have appeared in Sutton Loop Gallery, Mark Twain Bank Gallery, Albrecht Museum of Art, Locus Galley, the Forum, Saint Louis University, the Mitchell Museum, and Missouri State Museum Gallery. Originally from Grand Rapids, Michigan, Stage has lived in St. Louis since 1978. He graduated from Thomas Jefferson College with a bachelor's degree in philosophy, and currently works for the *Riverfront Times*. Stage has also been published in the *Post-Dispatch*, *St. Louis Globe-Democrat*, *Christian Science Monitor*, *National Lampoon*, and *Signs of the Times*.

Denise Sweitzer-Winchell specializes in wildlife, steeplechase racing, and architectural photography. She and her husband, Wyn, are the official photographers for the St. Louis Benefit Polo Awards. Among her numerous photography awards, Sweitzer-Winchell received first-place honors in the 1994 St. Louis Zoo Friends Association photo contest, as well as winning three earlier honorable mentions in the same contest. Her work has been in juried exhibitions at the St. Louis Artists' Guild, the Creative Art Gallery, and the Garret Gallery. Sweitzer-Winchell's favorite subjects include animals in motion and people performing.

David Swimmer is an attorney who specializes in what he calls "humanscape," a mixture of portraiture and landscape photography. A St. Louis native, he received his law degree from Saint Louis University. Swimmer works on a small scale with deliberately primitive equipment in natural light. He rolls, processes, prints, and frames his photographs from his home basement.

Gary Tetley, a graduate of the Washington University School of Architecture, is a native of St. Louis. Tetley specializes in architectural detail and abstraction, and is a registered architect involved in historic preservation. He began photographing St. Louis' historical architecture after witnessing the demolition of an architecturally significant building. Tetley's photographs have been published in *Images of St. Louis*, and in *Art Saint Louis* and *St. Louis Artist Today* exhibition catalogs.

Jeffrey L. Vaughn resides in Alton, Illinois. His photography is represented by the Locus Gallery in St. Louis, the Harris Gallery in Houston, and the Szoke Gallery in New York. He has exhibited in galleries in Alabama, California, Georgia, Illinois, Indiana, Kansas, Louisiana, Missouri, New Jersey, New York, North Dakota, Oklahoma, Texas, and Wisconsin over the last 15 years. Vaughn specializes in outdoor photography, making good use of his proximity to the Mississippi River.

Stan Waxelman is an analytical chemist at Clark Oil Refinery. Specializing in building structure as a basis for composition, Waxelman is planning an exhibition that will feature interaction between buildings and trees in large-format color photographs. Waxelman is a native of St. Louis.

Wyn Winchell is a self-taught photographer who specializes in photographing animals in their natural settings. Along with his wife, Denise, Winchell is the official photographer for the St. Louis Benefit Polo Awards. Winchell also enjoys photographing steeplechase racing, outdoor events, festivals, and architecture. He has won first- and second-place awards in two CPI photo contests, two honorable mentions in the Eckert's/Fox Photo/CPI photo contest, second place and three honorable mentions in St. Louis Zoo Friends Association photo contests, and an honorable mention in Missouri Botanical Garden's Festival of Festivals 1991 photo contest. His work has been in juried exhibitions at Creative Art Gallery, Garret Gallery, and St. Louis Artists' Guild.

Cindy Wrobel, a native of Detroit, is the owner of Cindy Wrobel, Design & Illustration. She has done work as an illustrator/designer for a range of clients from large corporations—such as Monsanto and New York Life—to small businesses. Wrobel is also an artist, working in mixed media including pastel, photography, clay, and collage. She has lived in the St. Louis area since 1980.

Tom Zant is a professor at St. Louis Community College-Forest Park. His photographs have been published in *Images of St. Louis*, the *Forest Park Review*, and *Photo Flash*. In the spring of 1992, while teaching at Christ Church College in Canterbury, England, Zant was able to photograph a significant part of the country. His areas of specialty include landscapes and travel photography.

Index to Sponsors

NEXT PAGE: A FINAL, SWEEPING photo of the Gateway Arch is a reminder that St. Louis is only as great as its people.

PAGE 416: PAUL MARSHALL